# Two Ships

## Also by David S. Reynolds

AS AUTHOR

*Abe*

*Walt Whitman's America*

*John Brown, Abolitionist*

*Waking Giant*

*Mightier Than the Sword*

*Beneath the American Renaissance*

*Faith in Fiction*

*Walt Whitman*

*George Lippard*

AS EDITOR

*Lincoln's Selected Writings*

*The Quaker City*

*Venus in Boston* (coedited with Kimberly Gladman)

*The Serpent in the Cup* (coedited with Debra J. Rosenthal)

*Uncle Tom's Cabin*

*A Historical Guide to Walt Whitman*

*George Lippard, Prophet of Protest*

# Two Ships

## *Jamestown 1619, Plymouth 1620, and the Struggle for the Soul of America*

DAVID S. REYNOLDS

Penguin Press
New York
2026

PENGUIN PRESS

An imprint of Penguin Random House LLC
1745 Broadway, New York, NY 10019
penguinrandomhouse.com



Illustration credits appear on 441–42.
*Designed by Amanda Dewey*

Names: Reynolds, David S., 1948– author
Title: Two ships : Jamestown 1619, Plymouth 1620, and
the struggle for the soul of America / David S. Reynolds.
Description: New York : Penguin Press, 2026. |
Includes bibliographical references and index.
Identifiers: LCCN 2025038111 (print) | LCCN 2025038112 (ebook) |
ISBN 9780593490235 hardcover | ISBN 9780593490242 ebook
Subjects: LCSH: Slavery—Political aspects—United States—History |
Antislavery movements—United States—History |
Puritans—New England—Influence | English—Virginia—Influence |
United States—Colonial influence | Political culture—United States—History |
United States—Politics and government
Classification: LCC E446 .R44 2026 (print) | LCC E446 (ebook) |
DDC 306.3/620973—dc23/eng/20260326
LC record available at https://lccn.loc.gov/2025038111
LC ebook record available at https://lccn.loc.gov/2025038112

Printed in the United States of America
1st Printing

The authorized representative in the EU for product safety and compliance is Penguin Random House Ireland, Morrison Chambers, 32 Nassau Street, Dublin D02 YH68, Ireland, https://eu-contact.penguin.ie.

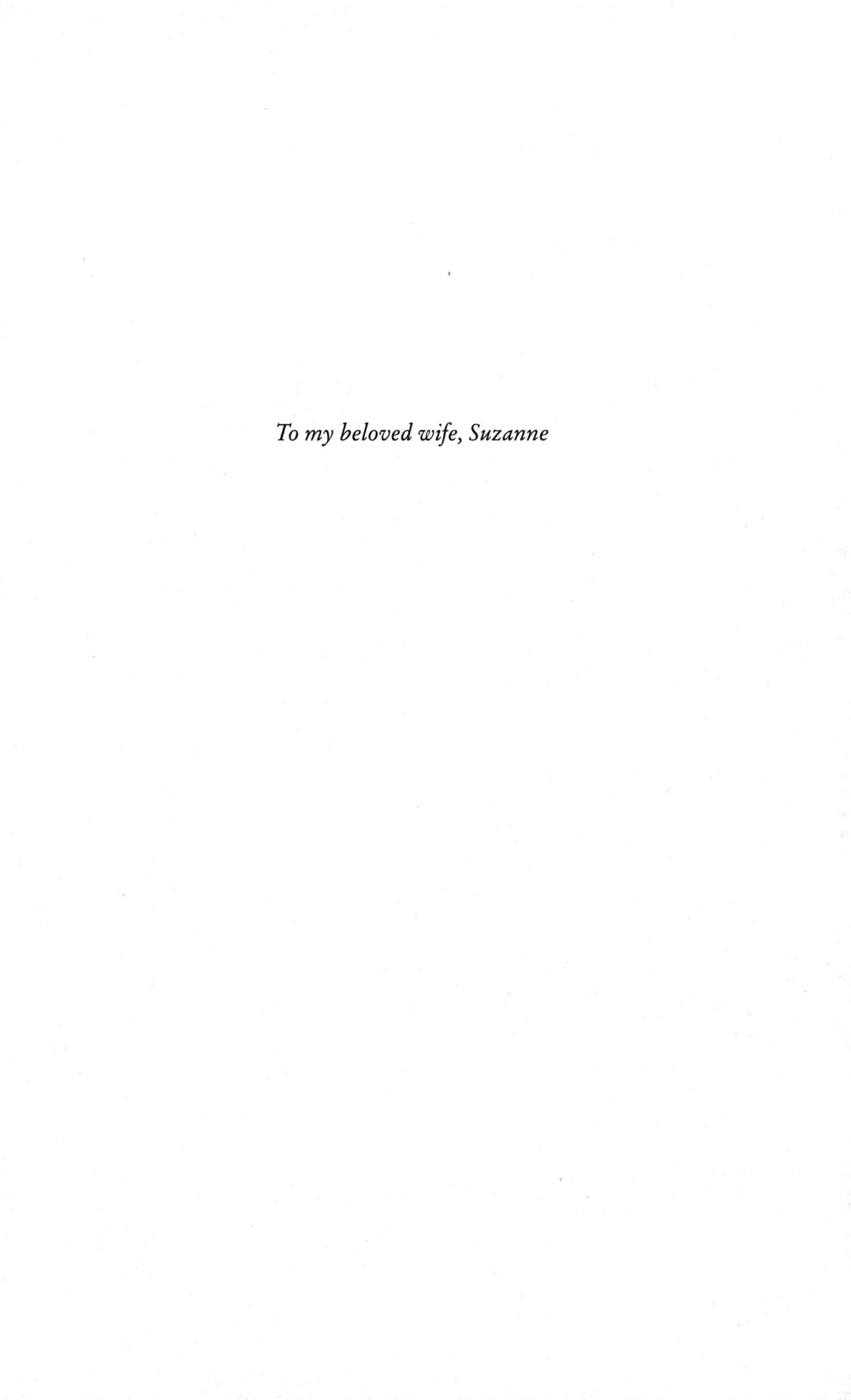

*To my beloved wife, Suzanne*

# CONTENTS

# PREFACE

During the years I worked on this book, I discovered personal connections with many people and places. I am descended from numerous *Mayflower* passengers, including William Brewster, John and Priscilla Alden, Richard Warren, Mary Chilton, and John Howland, who are discussed in the following pages. I was born in Providence, Rhode Island, which was founded by Roger Williams, who introduced the doctrine of the separation of church and state to America. I grew up in nearby Barrington in a home overlooking Narragansett Bay, named after the Native American tribe that originally inhabited the region to the west, on the other side of the bay. Our house, a converted lighthouse on Nayatt Point ("Nayatt" is Wampanoag for "at the point"), looked across the bay at the far-off Warwick, named after Robert Rich, the Second Earl of Warwick, an influential Puritan who helped establish New England and Virginia, served politically during the English Civil War, and was close to the revolutionary Puritan Oliver Cromwell. Someone I knew in Barrington lived on Governor Bradford Drive, originally named in honor of William Bradford, the longtime leader of Plymouth Colony. I attended Moses Brown School for a time, unaware that Brown, a Rhode Island Quaker, was a pioneering abolitionist. My father would drive me to school on a road called the Wampanoag Trail (Route 114), which follows an old path trodden by the Natives who were initially friendly with the Pilgrims.

But this book was not motivated by personal associations. As a cultural historian, I was very curious about the frequent references in Civil War–era speeches and periodicals to two ships that had arrived in America nearly 250 years earlier. One of them, often simply called "the slave ship," was the *White Lion*, an English vessel sailing under Dutch colors, which brought twenty to thirty Africans to Jamestown, Virginia, in 1619. The other was the *Mayflower*, which arrived at Plymouth, Massachusetts, in 1620.

I was struck that, despite the vast span between the ships' arrivals in 1619 and 1620 and the firing on Fort Sumter in 1861, many of Lincoln's contemporaries framed the Civil War as a clash between the "Jamestown ship," symbolizing the slaveholding South, and the *Mayflower*, representing the antislavery North. "In the holds of those two ships," Senator Charles Sumner declared, "were the germs of the present direful war, and the simple question now is between the Mayflower and the slave ship. Who that has not forgotten God can doubt the result? The Mayflower must prevail."[1] After Lee's surrender to Grant at Appomattox, a Northern journalist jubilantly announced, "The Mayflower and the Slave ship have met in hostile combat. The contest has been long and severe. . . . The Slave ship has foundered. The Mayflower floats in triumph."[2]

The more I looked, the more figures I found—politicians and reformers, African Americans and whites, men and women—who highlighted the two ships to make a point about slavery. References to the two ships overlapped with the legacy of the seventeenth-century conflict in England between the Puritans—the religious reformers who supported Parliament against royal absolutism—and the Cavaliers—traditional Anglicans who believed in the divine right of kings.[3] In the minds of many nineteenth-century Northerners who looked back at history, the *Mayflower* Pilgrims were trailblazing freedom seekers—

and prophets of antislavery reform—because of their connections with the Puritan resistance to the oppressive Stuart monarchs, while the slave ship was associated with the royalist Cavaliers who settled in Virginia and planted slavery there. For Confederates, in contrast, the *Mayflower* seeded a Northern culture that was fanatical and self-righteous, eventually yielding horrid isms like abolitionism, Mormonism, and spiritualism, while the Cavalier South was genial, tolerant, and orderly, with established institutions like slavery and the Anglican church.

Frederick Douglass declared the *Mayflower* to be the main source of human rights in America. He said in an 1860 speech, "The *Mayflower* came to establish the Bible, the Magna Carta, the right of habeas corpus, trial by jury, the marriage institution, equality in the eye of the law, deference for order, and all the institutions which had made Britain to flourish, and which tended to ennoble and dignify the human race."[4]

Douglass was just one of many antislavery figures who made such pronouncements about the *Mayflower*. Telescoping backward, they focused on Plymouth Colony in its first two decades. Why the emphasis on the *Mayflower* and early Plymouth? Because the later history of New England was messy. Many historians view New England's history as a tale of decline. The "city on a hill" ideal, articulated by Massachusetts governor John Winthrop in 1630, gradually succumbed to settler colonialism and exploitative trade with the West Indies, where enslaved Native Americans were exchanged for Black people, who were in turn carried to New England and enslaved there.[5] Three New England colonies—Rhode Island, Massachusetts, and Connecticut—became hubs in the international slave trade. This period also saw wars against Native tribes, the persecution of heretics, and the infamous Salem witch trials. New England can be seen as a cautionary tale about the dangers of zealotry and unleashed profit seeking.

It was precisely this eventual decline that made early Plymouth Colony stand out as a beacon of democratic experimentation and egalitarianism. By overlooking the troubling aspects of New England culture, later advocates of liberty during the Revolutionary and Civil War eras idealized Plymouth in a way that did not seem to apply to its neighbor to the north, the Massachusetts Bay Colony. Indeed, Plymouth had witnessed remarkable innovations: the Mayflower Compact, which has been compared with the Declaration of Independence and the Constitution with its proclamation of government by consent; trial by jury, which Plymouth established in 1623; lay preaching, conducted for years by William Brewster, which broke with the orthodox restriction of the pulpit to ordained ministers; the abolition of quitrents, a holdover from feudalism by which land was not owned but leased from the Crown or proprietors; and a written code of laws, which Plymouth first passed in 1636, that established a rudimentary bill of rights that anticipated later key American documents. Also, unlike Massachusetts, Plymouth did not legally enshrine slavery.

As Richard Bailey has noted, theology in colonial New England fostered racial thinking.[6] However, in time, Puritanism developed antislavery tendencies. Efforts to win over the enslaved to Christianity were made by New Englanders, notably the magistrate Samuel Sewall and the clergyman Cotton Mather, who believed that the souls of Black and white people were equal before God. They took steps—quite dramatic ones in Sewall's case—toward channeling New England Puritanism toward abolitionism.

During the eighteenth century, the First Great Awakening triggered the rise of new forms of Puritanism in the North that provoked growing calls for the gradual abolition of slavery, especially among the Calvinistic New Divinity preachers around the time of the American Revolution. Religion lay behind the decision of most Northern states to enact the gradual abolition of slavery.

It is clearly true that some Southern colonists were angry about the emancipation proclamation issued in 1775 by the British governor of Virginia, Lord Dunmore. Overall, however, the strongest motivation behind the American Revolution was not the protection of slavery but animus against British oppression—an animus, shared by Southerners and Northerners, that was deeply entrenched well before Dunmore's edict. The cultural memory of the Plymouth landing and the English Civil War energized the revolutionary spirit. Puritan impulses were especially strong among Northern Patriots like John Adams and James Otis, but they also drove leading Southerners, including Patrick Henry and Thomas Jefferson.

That Jefferson, Henry, and other Southerners were influenced by the Cromwellian revolt does not mean that there weren't profound sectional differences in America. The conflict between the "Puritan" North and the "Cavalier" South had a deep, stormy background, which this book traces. But sectional differences were largely set aside during the American Revolution due to a shared desire for independence from England.

This unity proved temporary. Statistically, the North and South were very different when it came to slavery. To use Ira Berlin's terms, the North was a society with slaves, while the South was a slave society.[7] Census records, tax rolls, and other documents show that by 1770, 2–4 percent of the population in New England and 6–8 percent in the Middle colonies were enslaved, compared with 40–45 percent in the Chesapeake colonies and 50–60 percent in the Lower South.[8] Even when considering the North's commercial involvement in slavery, there is no doubt that the North was a more natural breeding ground for abolitionism than the South. That's why the dichotomy between Plymouth and Jamestown was so powerful, especially because the parallel conflict between the Puritans and the Cavaliers infused it.

Slavery, hotly contested during the Constitutional Convention in 1787, thereafter became an ever more bitter wedge issue, especially with the arrival in 1794 of the cotton gin, which ushered in the slave-dependent King Cotton, destined to rule the South. By 1800, most of the leading Cavalier families of Virginia had scattered. Still, the Cavalier myth spread among Southerners who absorbed the Cavalier identity and its boasted values, such as honor, geniality, and devotion to institutions, especially the South's peculiar institution.

Meanwhile, admiration for the early New England settlers grew stronger in the North. The Old Colony Club, a group of *Mayflower* supporters from New England, first met in Boston in 1769. Committed to reviving the democratic ideals of early Plymouth, the club started Forefathers' Day, which was celebrated annually (except during the American Revolution) on December 22, the purported date of the *Mayflower*'s arrival at Plymouth. Forefathers' Day became a major annual event in the North and among the broader New England community across the country, lasting through the nineteenth century and culminating in the blowout *Mayflower* tercentennial celebration in 1920.[9] During that time, festivals honoring the Pilgrims took on the political tone of the era. The most influential period was between 1845 and 1865, when the Pilgrims were seen as powerful freedom fighters who inspired the abolition movement. For many antislavery reformers, not only the *Mayflower* passengers but also Cromwellian Puritanism served as key symbols in the fight for emancipation and human rights.

Abraham Lincoln recognized the vital role culture played in the downfall of slavery. "Public sentiment is everything," he declared.[10] In his time, public sentiment reflected a rift that was seen to go back to the two ships, which came to explain America's origins. For many nineteenth-century Americans, the underlying war was between the 1619 ship and the 1620 ship, between Jamestown and Plymouth, between the proslavery Southern Cavalier and the antislavery Northern Puritan.

Profound polarization can exist even in the most diverse country. The divide between North and South was not solely political; it was also deeply personal. The intense conflict between the "Puritan" North and the "Cavalier" South affected the collective psyche during the Civil War era, symbolized by the opposing ships.

These symbols reflected a deep difference between the two original epicenters of colonial America, Virginia and Massachusetts. And Virginia really was fundamentally a product of the Cavalier side of the English Civil War—Anglican, hierarchical, patriarchal—just as Massachusetts was a product of the Puritan side. The fever in the blood that boiled over into America's own much bloodier Civil War began to roil at least 250 years earlier. Perhaps needless to say, it still has not cooled.

# Two Ships

## *Chapter One*

# Launchings

The idea that the "antislavery" *Mayflower* can be pitted against the 1619 Jamestown "slave ship" has a large germ of truth. But like most things, it's complicated.

Many of the *Mayflower*'s passengers, coming from a background of persecution and tyranny, established a society in which basic human rights were affirmed. Religion as practiced in Plymouth had a democratic tendency because it put all people on the same level under God and allowed church members to choose their own magistrates and clergy.[1] When fully acted on by Roger Williams, the exile from the Massachusetts Bay Colony who fled to Plymouth before establishing Rhode Island to the south, this outlook yielded the separation of church and state, respect for Indigenous people, and antislavery legislation.

As for the *White Lion*, which brought the "twenty and odd negroes" to Jamestown in August 1619, while it did not introduce slavery to the Americas—enslaved Africans had been carried to Spanish and Portuguese colonies for more than a century, and Indigenous peoples had long held captives of war in bondage—it was the vessel that first brought Africans to an English colony destined to become part of the United States.[2]

## THE BACKGROUND OF 1619

In notes for a speech in 1855, Abraham Lincoln mentioned the Jamestown ship after discussing the earlier enslavement of Africans, which traces back to Spain and Portugal. The international slave trade began in earnest in the 1500s, when Spain and Portugal transported well over one hundred thousand Africans to the Americas to work on plantations or in mines. Spanish expeditions, which carried enslaved Black people with them, attempted short-lived settlements on the South Carolina–Georgia coast in 1526 and at Pensacola, Florida, from 1559 to 1561. St. Augustine, Florida—America's oldest continually inhabited European-founded city—was established in 1565 by Spanish colonists who owned enslaved Africans, many of whom later gained freedom through self-purchase or manumission.

As Lincoln noted, the English were transporting enslaved Africans to the Americas by 1562, when the sailor John Hawkins sold about three hundred captives in the West Indies. In 1586, Sir Francis Drake, having stolen slaves from a Spanish town in South America, arrived at the English settlement on Roanoke Island, off the coast of current-day North Carolina, with "Indians from Cartagena, . . . 200 negroews, Turks and Moors, who do menial service," in the words of a witness.[3]

Spain's aggressive colonization of the West triggered the events that led to Jamestown. The English nobleman Sir Robert Rich, the Second Earl of Warwick—known in his time as "the head of the Puritans"—was committed to defeating the international forces of "popery," especially Catholic Spain.[4] The owner of England's largest private fleet, Rich plotted to use his ships to interrupt Spain's thriving commerce in the Caribbean.

Slavery was probably not at the top of Sir Robert's mind when he embarked on his pirate mission from Jamestown. He had been scheming to make an attack on Spanish trade with Virginia's deputy governor, Samuel Argall, with whom he co-owned a ship, the *Treasurer.* Their plan carried high risks. King James I had signed a peace treaty with Spain in 1604 and had proclaimed that "all Piracies and Depredations upon the Sea . . . of his Majesties Friends and Allies" were crimes punishable by death.[5] The king was furious when the celebrated adventurer Sir Walter Raleigh attacked a Spanish colony on the coast of South America; Raleigh was subsequently beheaded for plotting treason against the king.

Small wonder that Robert Rich took extreme caution in his scheme. He secured for the *Treasurer* letters of marque (license to capture enemy ships) from Savoy, Italy, a state often in conflict with Spain. In Jamestown, Samuel Argall pretended to direct the *Treasurer* north to Cape Cod on a trading voyage. Secretly, he sent the *Treasurer* south to the West Indies in search of Spanish plunder.

In the Caribbean, the *Treasurer* had a chance meeting with another British ship, the *White Lion*, a privateer that was sailing under Dutch letters of marque. In late July 1619, the ships captured a Portuguese vessel, the *São João Batista*, in the Bay of Campeche off Yucatán. The *Batista* turned out to be a slave ship that had departed Angola two months earlier, headed for Veracruz, Mexico. The *Batista* had left Africa with 350 Black people in its hold, about 40 percent of whom died during the voyage.[6]

This extraordinary death rate suggests how horrific the journey had been. The *Batista* was overloaded; it had been licensed to carry only about hundred captives. On a lower deck of the ship, the Africans were shackled close together, lying with one's head to another's feet. In the tropical heat, temperatures soared above one hundred degrees. Air circulation in the pitch-dark hold was minimal, as was sanitation. The stench of excrement, vomit, and perspiration was overwhelming. Once a day, the enslaved were fed cassava gruel or corn and beans along with salted sardines. Periodically, the captives were brought to the main deck for exercise. The bodies of the dead—two or three a day, on average—were heaved overboard. An untold number of the enslaved jumped into the ocean, preferring death to the unrelenting misery.

The captains of the *White Lion* and the *Treasurer* selected some sixty Black people, divided them up, and headed to Virginia. The *White Lion* got there first, arriving at Point Comfort on August 20. In the words of the Virginia official John Rolfe, the ship "brought not any thing but 20 and odd Negroes, which the Governor and Cape Marchant bought for victualls."[7] The *Treasurer* came a few days later with an additional thirty or so Africans. Discovering that the mission's ringleader, Samuel Argall, had been taken to England on suspicion of illicit activities, the *Treasurer*'s captain, Daniel Elfrid, sold a few of the Africans in Virginia and then voyaged to Bermuda, where he sold the remaining people.

## WHAT HAPPENED IN JAMESTOWN?

Slavery was formally legalized by Virginia's General Assembly through a sequence of statutes, beginning with the 1662 law enforcing *partus sequitur ventrem* (the child inherits the status of the enslaved mother). This was followed by restrictions on manumission in 1691 and by the harsh codes of 1705, which defined enslaved people as property on the same level as domestic animals or inanimate things. The presence of a small but meaningful population of free Black people earlier in Virginia reflects the ad hoc decisions made about Black workers before the 1662 law.[8]

Settled in 1607, Virginia struggled through a decade of food shortages, epidemics, and economic problems before it began to find its stride with the cultivation of tobacco, soon to become the colony's staple product. Spearheading Virginia's growth was the English politician Sir Edwin Sandys, the head of the Virginia Company, the body of English investors that King James I had chartered to develop the colony of

Virginia. Determined to make Virginia a commercial competitor to Spain, whose Caribbean colonies thrived on tobacco and sugar, Sandys vigorously promoted the export trade. In 1618, the company adopted the headright system: Virginia planters who transported laborers from overseas received fifty acres for each person brought over. The newcomers typically served four to seven years as indentured servants before receiving their freedom and a modest allotment of supplies to begin life on their own.

Some of the Africans who arrived in Virginia between 1619 and 1662 became indentured servants, though most Black workers were immediately enslaved.[9] Among the few Blacks in early Virginia—about two dozen in 1623, three hundred in 1648, and two thousand by 1670—the percentage of free Black people was comparatively high on Virginia's Eastern Shore.[10] During the 1660s, the percentage of Blacks in Northampton County who were listed as free ranged between 20 and 30 percent.[11] Looking at the numbers, George M. Fredrickson remarks that free Blacks in the area comprised "a larger portion of the total Black population than they would in any subsequent time during the slave era."[12]

In seventeenth-century Virginia, there were two main paths to freedom for the enslaved: manumission and self-purchase. Some enslavers voluntarily emancipated their bondspeople, usually in their wills. In most cases, manumission reflected the fact that a high percentage of the early generations of Virginia Blacks were Christians, having been baptized by Jesuit missionaries who were part of the Spanish and Portuguese colonization of Africa. The principle that Christians must not be permanently enslaved had some acceptance in Virginia until 1667, when the General Assembly passed a law saying that "the conferring of baptisme doth not alter the condition of the person as to his bondage or ffreedome."[13]

More common than manumission was the practice of allowing enslaved people to purchase their freedom. Many landowners in early

Virginia adopted a form of slavery, harking back to ancient Rome and practiced in some of Spain's American colonies, that permitted the enslaved to hold property and earn income that could be applied to buying emancipation.

Slaves who were offered a chance for self-purchase had to work hard for their freedom.[14] An enslaved worker produced, on average, around 1,500 pounds of tobacco per year working for an owner from sunup to sundown, six days a week, with Sundays and brief holidays off.[15] To buy freedom, a slave typically had to pay at least that yearly amount—usually much more—in tobacco or other goods. Even if one spent all available off-hours farming or raising livestock, it took many years to accumulate enough to attain freedom. The situation of the people of African origin who were brought to Virginia in the seventeenth century against their will was only less oppressive relative to the harsher racial system that later emerged.

Besides meager opportunities for economic advancement, Black people in early Virginia were granted certain legal rights. Blacks and whites in Virginia received similar legal sentences, even in cases of violence and illicit sex. Working-class Black people mingled freely with working-class whites. Ira Berlin notes that in seventeenth-century Virginia, "Black and white servants ran away together, slept together, and upon occasion, stood shoulder to shoulder against . . . established authority."[16] Studies have indicated that as many as a third of children born out of wedlock in Northampton County in the mid-1660s resulted from sex between a Black man and a white woman, who was usually an indentured servant.[17] There were instances of interracial marriage, such as the ex-slave Francis Payne, who married a white woman, Amy; in his will, he left "to my lovinge wife . . . my whole Estate [movables and] unmovables, making her my . . . executrix."[18]

However, by the century's end, such possibilities would all but disappear. The overwhelming majority of Virginia's Black population was enslaved, as the colony's slave codes stiffened and the hierarchical Cavalier mentality took over among Southern whites, as we will see.

## BEHIND THE *MAYFLOWER* AND PLYMOUTH

The *Mayflower* Pilgrims believed that they were freedom seekers, escaping centuries of bondage. William Bradford, a *Mayflower* passenger who served as Plymouth's longtime governor, began his *History of Plymouth Plantation* by describing the oppression that religious intolerance had caused over the centuries. The "Heathen Emperours" of ancient Rome, Bradford wrote, initiated the kind of "bloody & barbarous persecutions" that were later inflicted on alleged heretics during the Inquisition and under English monarchs.[19] King Henry VIII's persecution of Catholics had been followed by the ruthless anti-Protestant campaign of his Catholic daughter, Mary I. Under Mary's rule, around 280 Protestants were executed—most of them by being burned at the stake.[20] Mary's crusade against Protestants was vividly captured in John Foxe's *Book of Martyrs*, an influential work among the Pilgrims. Bradford wrote of "Mr. Foxe [who] recordeth . . . those worthy martires & confessors which were burned in queene Marys days & otherwise tormented."[21]

It was the practices of Mary's Anglican successors Elizabeth and James I that most directly affected Bradford and his fellow Puritans. Elizabeth and James imposed strict Anglican conformity, penalizing Catholics as traitors and Puritan Separatists as religious dissenters. Elizabeth oversaw the execution of nearly two hundred Catholics, including her cousin Mary, Queen of Scots, whose beheading was gruesomely botched when the errant executioner sliced parts of her neck twice with his axe before finishing her off with the third blow.

Elizabeth was also harsh on Puritans (Protestants devoted to "purifying" the English church of all remnants of Catholicism, such as vestments, rituals, and church hierarchy). Prominent dissenters—Elias Thacker, Henry Barrowe, John Penry, John Copping, and others—were hanged for speaking or writing against the Anglican Church. Many others were imprisoned.[22]

James I continued the crackdown on religious nonconformists. For James, the king not only controlled the church but also had a direct link to God. James verbalized the doctrine of the divine right of kings that would inspire later Stuart monarchs. James declared, "Kings are not only God's lieutenants upon earth, and sit upon God's throne, but even by God himself they are called gods."[23] As for the Puritans, he vowed, "I will make them conform themselves or I will harry them out of this land or worse."[24]

He put his threat into action. Bradford wrote that the Puritans became "slaves" of the monarchy; they "were hunted & persecuted on every side. . . . Some were taken & clapt up in prison, others had their houses besett & watcht night and day, & hardly escaped their hands; and the most were faine to flie & leave their howses & habitations, and the mean of their livelehood."[25]

In the face of the ongoing monarchical onslaughts, some gave up the idea of purifying the church and decided to separate themselves from it. Separatism had arisen as early as the 1570s under the radical Robert Browne, whose followers were popularly known as Brownists. Separatist groups sprouted in London as well as Nottinghamshire and Lincolnshire in northeastern England.

The group that would become the Pilgrims emerged in the rural Nottinghamshire hamlet of Scrooby, about 150 miles north of London. The Separatist William Brewster, a government official, served as postmaster in the region. He lived in a large manor leased by Samuel Sandys, whose brother Edwin Sandys would prove to be important both for the Pilgrims and for the settlers of Virginia. The Scrooby manor became the clandestine site of religious services held by the Cambridge-educated clergyman John Robinson, who had broken with the Anglican Church. Attendees at the Scrooby services included, besides Brewster, many local supporters, including the young William Bradford, who lived in nearby Austerfield.

By the fall of 1607, the Nottinghamshire Separatists had grown so restive under James that they decided to leave England. The Dutch Republic was an attractive destination. An alliance of seven provinces, led by Holland, whose long war with Spain (1568–1648) was at a temporary standstill, the Dutch Republic offered religious tolerance. Robinson's group made two attempts to go there secretly by ship. The first one, in 1607, failed, resulting in the temporary imprisonment of some of the Separatists. The second, the following year, was successful. Robinson described the group's escape as a "flight in persecution," comparable to the exodus of Moses.[26]

Arriving in Holland in August 1608, the refugees lived for a year in Amsterdam, a city of one hundred thousand where several other groups of English Separatists had already moved. Dissension among the groups broke out, impelling Robinson to take his flock twenty-five miles southwest to Leiden, a manufacturing town of forty-four thousand that had a famous university.

The Puritan conflict with Catholic Spain shaped the Separatists' long stay in Leiden. The centuries-long Spanish Inquisition had led to the execution of thousands of alleged heretics, including Protestants. Mercilessly oppressed under Spanish Habsburg rule, the Calvinistic Dutch Republic had been fighting since 1568 to gain independence. In April 1609, both sides, exhausted, agreed to the Twelve Years' Truce—just as John Robinson's Separatist congregation was settling in Leiden. The Separatists found themselves in a peaceful Protestant environment. Peaceful but very challenging. As Bradford wrote, the refugees confronted "the grim & grisly face of poverty" in a country with "differente maners & custumes" and a "strange & uncouth language."[27]

Coming from different social classes and educational backgrounds in England, most of the Separatists were reduced to taking mundane jobs, about half of them in the textile industry, the mainstay of Leiden's economy.[28]

Occupations for the Separatists included wool comber, glover, twine maker, leatherworker, hatmaker, serge weaver, tailor, and silk maker. William Bradford, who arrived in Leiden when he was twenty, wove fustian, a heavy cloth. Other jobs were cabinetmaker, brewer's employee, mason, watchmaker, carpenter, mirror maker, tobacco seller, and tobacco-pipe maker. William Brewster became a tutor of English and a printer of books.

If the Separatists' jobs had an equalizing effect, so did their religious practices. The congregation made key decisions, such as admitting members or electing the pastor and the elder (the lay leader). Robinson described his church as "popular and democratical" in that it allowed "the people freely to vote in elections and judgments of the church."[29] The only monarch, Robinson wrote, was Christ. The pastor and elder had special positions in the church, but not a unique connection to God. The church's humblest member was on the same level, spiritually, as its leaders. In the fellowship of faith, Robinson wrote, "every one is made a king, priest, and prophet, not only to himself but to every other, yea to the whole."[30]

Robinson put great emphasis on "prophesying"—that is, speaking spontaneously under divine inspiration. The pastor and the elder read Bible passages in parts of the service, but they did not deliver the sermon from a written text. Instead, they prophesied. So did others who were present. In Robinson's words, everyone in the congregation was "a prophet to teach, exhort, reprove, and comfort himself and the rest." Women did not participate in church decision-making but were permitted to prophesy, which was highly unusual for that time.

After three years of meeting at the homes of members of the congregation, in 1612 the group bought a sizable property near Leiden's

Pieterskerk (St. Peter's Church) on which Robinson lived in a two-story house and others occupied smaller dwellings on the land.[31] The group gathered on Sundays for Sabbath worship either on the first floor of Robinson's house or in nearby spaces. A service lasting two to three hours, led by Pastor Robinson and Elder William Brewster, was followed by a meal and an afternoon service during which members of the congregation prophesied. The Separatists learned about toleration in Leiden, but they also got vivid reminders of intolerance. Bradford's comment that the group went to Holland because they had heard there was "freedome of Religion for all men" reflected the Dutch Republic's founding document, the 1579 Union of Utrecht treaty, which said that "every particular person shall remain free in his religion, and that no one will be pursued or investigated because of his religion."[32] This proved true up to a point. People outside of the Dutch Reformed Church were not persecuted, but they were required to worship in private and could not hold community events. The Dutch Reformed Church claimed status as the "public" church of the Netherlands—that is, the only one with government sanction and the freedom to practice openly. The English Separatists had to meet privately, despite their Calvinistic doctrines being similar to those held by the Dutch Reformed Church.

A well-known conflict over these doctrines revealed that beneath Holland's appearance of tolerance, there lay narrow-mindedness and exclusivity. In 1618, a group of ministers led by Jacobus Arminius issued a remonstrance (a public petition) requesting permission to teach that moral behavior contributed to one's salvation—an idea that departed from the Calvinist principle that humans, depraved since the fall of Adam, were entirely in the hands of an omnipotent God, who had predestined a select few to go to heaven and the rest to hell. The request for a more hopeful doctrine by Arminius and his followers, who were called the Remonstrants, met with stiff opposition from Leiden's Calvinist leaders, known as the Counter-Remonstrants.[33]

The two groups engaged in an open debate. John Robinson, the author of many books on religion, participated in the contest on the Counter-Remonstrant side. But he could not foresee the extreme actions that the controversy would lead to. The Calvinism of the Counter-Remonstrants was officially endorsed by an international synod in the South Holland town of Dordrecht (Dort in English). The Synod of Dort not only reinforced Calvinist orthodoxy but brought to power Counter-Remonstrant politicians who persecuted Arminians, most notably Johan van Oldenbarnevelt. Long revered as the heroic leader of the Dutch Republic's war against Spain, the seventy-one-year-old Oldenbarnevelt was tried by a special court, convicted of treason, and executed. Other leading Arminians, including the philosopher and jurist Hugo Grotius, were imprisoned, while many more were deposed from office or forced into exile. Robinson, though staunchly opposed to Arminian doctrine, rejected calls to suppress the Remonstrants, insisting that magistrates could not compel faith. In Leiden he encountered the Mennonite historian Pieter Twisck, whose expansive book *Religion's Freedom* assembled more than a thousand historical examples defending liberty of conscience from early Christianity onward. Often described as the earliest systematic history of arguments for toleration, Twisck's work helped shape the intellectual atmosphere in which Robinson's thinking evolved. Even without proof of a direct meeting, Robinson and his congregation moved in circles where dissenting views on liberty circulated widely, and these ongoing exchanges encouraged his gradual shift toward broader principles of toleration in the years ahead.[34]

Robinson's toleration anticipated that of Roger Williams, who would introduce the separation of church and state to America. The Leiden years had changed Robinson. A member of his group noted that he "was more rigid in his course and way at first than towards his latter end," when "there was nothing more hateful to him" than "schism and division"; by then "his study was peace and union, so far as might agree with faith and a good conscience."[35]

To be sure, Robinson maintained a Puritan distaste for practices of the Anglican Church that had no apparent biblical basis, such as reading the Book of Common Prayer, kneeling before a crucifix, or having priests wear a cap or surplice. But he thought it was wrong to impose one's views on people of different faiths. His outlook became so open that he and his group were denounced by strict Separatists in Amsterdam, who called his church "[as much] a harlot as either her mother the Church of England or her grandmother Rome."[36] Robinson responded to such criticism by declaring that "I have one and the same faith, hope, spirit, baptism and Lord which I had in the Church of England." His goal was "to preserve the unity of the spirit with all that fear God to have peace with all men." Although his theology was Calvinist, he thought that Calvin, Luther, and other Protestants had gone only so far in understanding Christianity, the meaning of which was always unfolding. God, for Robinson, was eternally unknowable. The best that humans could do was to seek God constantly. In this sense, all thoughtful people of faith were Pilgrims—they were on an unending journey toward a knowledge of God's message.

## PLANNING AND VOYAGE

By 1617, some of Robinson's followers wanted to leave Holland. The Dutch environment was pulling the group away from its English roots. It also fostered laxness about the Sabbath and drew the younger generation toward what William Bradford called "the great licentiousness of youth in that countrie."[37] Thoughts turned toward the Americas. The Dutch Republic's truce with Habsburg Spain would end in 1621. Although moving to America posed dangers, the Leiden group reasoned that "as great miseries might possibly befale them in this place [Holland], for the 12 years of truce were now out," and "the Spaniard might prove as cruell as the salvages of America."

But where would they go? Guyana in South America was a popular choice. Warm and favorable to agriculture, it was one of the few tropical places in the West that Spain had not yet colonized. On the other hand, Spain would surely become envious if England established a successful colony there. As Bradford wrote, "the jealous Spaniard would never suffer them long; but would displante or overthrow them," just as "he did the French in Florida." The Separatist group would be "too smale to resiste so potent an enemie, & so neare a neighbor."

If not Guyana, where? Northern Virginia was agreed on. At the time, Virginia extended from the current-day Cape Fear, North Carolina, all the way north to the Long Island Sound. The Separatists decided on an area near the mouth of the Hudson River.

First, they needed to get approval from King James. That came through the well-connected Sir Edwin Sandys. In the late fall of 1617, two members of Robinson's group went to London. They met with Sandys, requesting his help in securing King James's permission for the Leiden group to establish an English colony in North America. Although Sandys did not support religious separatism, he wanted to boost the population of Virginia, and he had long respected William Brewster and others in the Leiden congregation. Calling himself "your very loving friend," he wrote to Brewster and Robinson, promising that he would inquire with people he knew in the royal circle.[38] This "loving friend" had to be cautious, because he had alienated James by criticizing the doctrine of the divine right of kings in Parliament.

Edwin Sandys's backing of democracy in Virginia also infuriated the king. Sandys, who said he aimed "to make a free popular state there in which the people should have noe government putt upon them except by their owne consents," created Virginia's General Assembly, America's first body of elected representatives (which met initially in July 1619, a month before the arrival of enslaved Black people on the *White Lion*). Because he defied James's autocratic rule, Sandys was reported to be "the king's greatest enemye."[39]

To communicate the Pilgrims' request to the king, Sandys used his friend Robert Naunton, James's secretary of state, as an intermediary. Naunton carried a statement from the Pilgrims, declaring that they recognized the supreme authority of the king and the Church of England. They didn't mention that they had separated from that church. Naunton informed James of the Pilgrims' plan to establish a colony in America where they hoped to "live under his government and protection" and "enjoy freedom of conscience." James did not give open support but said he would "not molest them, provided they carried themselves peaceably."[40]

He asked what occupation the Pilgrims would pursue in the New World. When Naunton said "fishing," the king chuckled, "So God have my soul, 'tis an honest trade; 'twas the apostle's own calling." In June 1619, a patent was issued authorizing the Pilgrims to migrate to the Virginia colony.

Financial backing came from London merchants John Peirce and Thomas Weston, who regarded colonization as a promising enterprise. They assembled a syndicate of about seventy English investors, later known as the Adventurers, to support the Separatists' plans. In February 1620, the group arranged a patent through the Virginia Company that envisioned the colony in northern Virginia as a joint-stock undertaking. Under its terms, profits would be shared between settlers and investors, and after seven years the colonists could purchase the investors' shares and assume full ownership of the settlement. With the way clear for migrating, the Leiden congregation in the spring of 1620 discussed who would go on the first voyage. About a third of the congregation wanted to be among the early emigrants. Because the majority did not want to leave, it was agreed that Reverend Robinson would remain in Leiden and move to America later with others. The voyage was initially scheduled for June, but delays necessitated rescheduling for July. The plan was to travel by ship to Southampton, England, where a second ship and additional passengers would join the journey.

In late July, Robinson held a feast in his home in celebration of the Pilgrims' mission to settle in America and create a godly community there. Hymns were sung, and Robinson delivered an inspiring sermon. The next day, many in the group went to Delfshaven, a port town twenty miles south of Leiden. There, the emigrants boarded a small ship, the *Speedwell.* On July 22, as it departed, those on shore shed tears and prayed aloud. At Southampton, the *Mayflower,* which the Adventurers had funded, awaited with additional travelers, mainly people intent on moving abroad for commercial reasons. The *Mayflower* and the *Speedwell* set sail for America but had not gone far before the *Speedwell* sprang leaks. The two vessels returned to England, making port in the town of Dartmouth about August 12. Eleven days later, after the *Speedwell* was repaired, the ships left again for North America. But three hundred miles into the trip the *Speedwell* again proved unseaworthy, and the ships returned to Plymouth, England. Several would-be emigrants lost resolve and opted out of the voyage. On September 6, the *Mayflower* headed off alone across the Atlantic.[41]

According to recent estimates and historical records, the *Mayflower* carried about 135 people—102 passengers and over 30 crew members. Among the passengers were about 37 Leiden Separatists, later known as the Pilgrims, and approximately 65 others, the so-called strangers—merchants, craftsmen, laborers, and a few orphans recruited to round out the new colony. The company included 44 men and 18 women, all of them married, with 3 of the women pregnant at the start of the voyage. There were also about 40 children and youths, the youngest being one-year-old Humility Cooper. During the crossing, a son was born to Stephen and Elizabeth Hopkins, whom they fittingly named Oceanus. Even two dogs—a large English mastiff and a small spaniel—shared the cramped quarters of the ship on its storm-tossed passage across the Atlantic.[42] The Pilgrims saw everything that happened, favorable or unfavorable, as providential and biblical—God's will at work.[43] One man, a servant named William Buttten, died at sea. His death was viewed as a sign of God's just punishment of evildoers. Bradford described Butten as "a proud & very profane" man who cursed the passengers and said he looked forward to seeing half of them die so that he could throw them into the ocean and take their belongings. Midway in the journey, he contracted "a greeveous disease, of which he dyed in a desperate maner, and so was him selfe the first that was throwne overbord."[44]

The *Mayflower* had fair sailing until it reached the mid-Atlantic, where it met with turbulent weather. The ship's center beam broke and caused leaks until it was pushed back into place by a huge jackscrew that passengers had brought from Holland. The storms grew so fierce that the crew sometimes took down the sails and let the ship float freely in the mountainous waves.

The people on board lived in a dark space below the main deck that was around five feet high, twenty-four feet wide, and fifty-eight feet long. Additional space was taken up by the pole of the mainmast in the middle and the mizzenmast at the front. The windlass and the capstan, bulky machines used for hauling items from the cargo hold below, also occupied room, as did a thirty-foot shallop (a single-sail boat) that would be used for trips ashore. Seawater seeped in through the ship's crudely caulked seams. Food consisted of hard biscuits, dried fish or meat, pickled foods, cereal grains, and beer (then a common drink, even for children, because keeping water pure for an extended period was difficult). Most passengers slept on straw mattresses on the planking of their deck; some improvised hammocks or wooden pallets. Besides the two months of the voyage, many of the passengers, mainly women, would live on the ship for an additional four to six months while a settlement was being built.

On November 9, after a sixty-six-day voyage, land was sighted. Driven off course, the *Mayflower* had arrived at Cape Cod. The decision was made to sail south to the Hudson River area, the ship's original destination. That proved impossible because of rough seas. Within a day, the ship returned to Cape Cod. It dropped anchor in what is now

Provincetown Harbor on November 11. Over the following weeks, parties went ashore, explored, and found firewood and corn that the Nauset tribe had buried. The corn was a godsend for the famished passengers, but Nausets attacked the English, who scattered their assailants by musket fire. Although no one was killed in this so-called First Encounter, the settlers felt that they were confronted with what Bradford called "a hidious & desolate wildernes, full of wild beasts and willd men."[45] But they rejoiced over reaching America—a truly remarkable providence.

On December 18, 1620, the *Mayflower* anchored near a place that had already been named New Plymouth by explorer John Smith in 1614. After a small group went ashore to survey the site, the main body of passengers first came ashore on December 21 to begin building their settlement. Did they alight on what came to be known as Plymouth Rock? Contemporary records from the period don't say. But that was the recollection of the ninety-four-year-old Elder Thomas Faunce when in 1741—more than a century after the landing—he identified a boulder that he said was where the shallop from the *Mayflower* had landed. There were questions regarding the rock and the identity of the first person to step onto it. Was it John Alden, the *Mayflower*'s cooper, or Mary Chilton, the teenage daughter of James Chilton (who at sixty-four was the ship's oldest passenger)? Whoever made that leap, Plymouth Rock would become a potent cultural symbol.

Equally potent was the Mayflower Compact. Signed on November 21 by forty-one male passengers on the ship, the document established a "civil Body Politick" with the power to pass laws and select officers "most meet and convenient for the general Good of the Colony."

Tremendous importance was later assigned to this hastily prepared manuscript. For Civil War–era progressives, the Mayflower Compact embodied the spirit of freedom that lay behind the goal of emancipation. In the 1830s, the historian George Bancroft wrote, "In the cabin of the Mayflower, humanity recovered its rights," representing "the birth of popular constitutional liberty."[46] Recently, the legal scholar Julia L. Ernst has described the Mayflower Compact as "the historical precedent for future seminal documents in the formation of the American governmental system, including the Fundamental Orders of Connecticut, the U.S. Articles of Confederation, the Virginia Declaration of Rights, the Northwest Ordinance, and particularly the U.S. Constitution."[47]

How accurate were these assessments? Only somewhat, if applied to the Mayflower Compact alone. John Quincy Adams took a broader view. As an antislavery congressman, he declared in 1843, "The Plymouth Colony is remarkable for having furnished the first example in modern times of a social compact or system of government instituted by voluntary agreement, conformably to the laws of nature, by men of equal rights, about to establish their permanent habitation as a community in a new country." Adams asserted, "The change was a total one, a democratic revolution."[48]

*Chapter Two*

# Roots of American Democracy

The potential for liberty and democracy was there from the start—in the very soil, so to speak. That was how Alexis de Tocqueville, the French historian who visited the United States in the 1830s, looked back on the colonial origins of America. In his magnum opus, *Democracy in America*, Tocqueville wrote that "all the English colonies, at the time of their birth, shared a great family resemblance. . . . All, from their beginning, seemed destined to present the development [of a] democratic liberty of which the history of the world did not yet offer a complete model."[1] Many settlers of North America, Tocqueville noted, were exiled or persecuted people suddenly reduced to subsistence living in a wilderness environment. He explained, "It is hardly the happy and the powerful who go into exile, and poverty as well as misfortune are the best guarantees of equality that are known among men."

These insights apply to both Jamestown and Plymouth: wretched conditions put the colonists, from the poorest to the most privileged, on the same level. Ralph Waldo Emerson noted that the homely New

England phrase "I'm as good as you be" was "at the bottom of Plymouth Rock"; it pointed to the nature-forged democracy of the Plymouth settlers, who said, as Emerson put it, "we are a little too close to the wolf and famine that anybody should give himself airs here in the swamp."[2] He could have said the same about Jamestown.

If similar trials faced the Jamestown and Plymouth settlers, what explains the profound differences between the two colonies as they developed? Here again, Tocqueville is instructive. "In the midst of this general coloration" of liberty forged in adversity, he wrote, there were "very strong nuances" of difference between the settlements, which in time expanded into a vast divide between the North and the South.

Early differences in religion, laws, and slave systems planted seeds for societies that eventually developed into the opposing cultural identities of the Cavalier South, with its hierarchical class system and reliance on chattel slavery, and the Puritan North, which moved toward democratic government, free labor, and ultimately widespread opposition to slavery.

## SUFFERING AND SOCIAL LEVELING

Living conditions in early Jamestown were extraordinarily harsh. The settlers who arrived in Virginia between 1606 and 1612 were largely unprepared to raise and store food and were further challenged by a severe drought. Waves of famine and disease devastated the colony, forcing settlers to trade beads and copper with the Powhatans in exchange for food. During the "Starving Time" winter of 1609–10, the colonists resorted to eating dogs, rats, shoe leather, and, according to some accounts, even human remains. Disease, malnutrition, and periodic Native attacks—including the Powhatan War of 1622, which killed 347 colonists, about one third of the population—continued to decimate Jamestown. By 1624 only about one in five colonists who had settled in Virginia since 1607 was still alive.[3]

The Plymouth settlers also faced extreme challenges.

Before the *Mayflower* passengers went ashore on five had died aboard the ship—one at sea, four while it was anchored off Cape Cod. The settlers faced great suffering during the first winter. Many died from exposure, scurvy, and "other diseases which this long voiage & their inacomodate condition had brought upon them," as William Bradford reported.[4] By April 1621, about half of the original 102 passengers had died, along with many crew members.[5]

One can imagine the torment suffered by those who witnessed the deaths of family members and friends. It was one thing to believe, as many of the pious colonists did, that those who died during that terrible first winter were destined for a blissful afterlife. It was another thing to watch those loved ones suffer and die. Survivors must have felt a devastating sense of loss and isolation. Consider the eighteen-year-old Priscilla Mullins, who lost her parents and her brother Joseph during that first terrible winter. Or her friend Mary Chilton, thirteen, whose parents, Leiden Separatists participating in the Pilgrims' godly experiment, also died. Or another *Mayflower* teenager, Elizabeth Tilley, who endured the deaths of her parents and her aunt and uncle. The husband and niece of Susanna White died. That niece, Dorothy May Bradford, drowned after falling from the *Mayflower* into the frigid waters of Provincetown Harbor while her husband, William Bradford, was ashore exploring Cape Cod. William pressed on to remarry and become a leader of Plymouth Colony.

His resilience was shared by the colony as a whole, which lost its first governor, John Carver, in April 1621. William Bradford, elected to the governorship shortly after Carver's death, oversaw the colony for much of the following three decades and wrote the definitive history of the Plymouth settlement. Bradford was just one of many who moved from tragedy to renewal. The orphaned Priscilla Mullins married the *Mayflower*'s barrel maker John Alden. This union produced ten or eleven children, some seventy-eight grandchildren, and thousands of descendants, including three presidents, a vice president, and many other notables, such as the poet Henry Wadsworth Longfellow, who made his fifth great-grandparents one of history's most famous couples in his 1858 bestseller, *The Courtship of Miles Standish*, in which Priscilla coyly asks John, who has come to deliver a marriage proposal from Standish, "Why don't you speak for yourself, John?"[6] Mary Chilton, another survivor of the starving time, moved from sorrow to stability when she wed John Winslow, a rising figure in Plymouth who later carried his family to Boston; together they nurtured a bustling household of ten children and many grandchildren. Elizabeth Tilley, who had watched four dear relatives perish during the colony's darkest season, married John Howland, himself a symbol of providence after being swept into the Atlantic and miraculously hauled back by a halyard. Their marriage flourished into ten children and an extraordinary eighty-nine grandchildren, whose descendants would one day include Ralph Waldo Emerson, Franklin Delano Roosevelt, and both presidents Bush—reminders of how the fragile lives launched from the *Mayflower* unfurled into a legacy that profoundly shaped the American story for generations to come.

The death rate soon normalized in Plymouth, but settling in remained a slow, torturous process. In the first year, the settlers built seven homes and four communal structures. Using simple tools like axes, hoes, and hammers, they felled trees and erected cottages with rough-hewn boards for framing and siding. They gathered marsh reeds, bundling and tying them into the thatched roofs that marked settlement. Inside the cottages, they sealed the walls with timber planks and clay daub—a mixture of clay, sand, and dung—rather than full wattle construction, the English technique of weaving upright sticks with twigs and branches before plastering surface, a method unnecessary in timber-rich New England. To keep out the weather, windows were few

A re-creation of Pilgrim houses in early Plymouth Colony at the Plimoth Patuxet Museums in Plymouth, Massachusetts.

and typically covered with oilpaper and wooden shutters, since glass was a rarity. The home measured four hundred to six hundred square feet and consisted of a single room, the hall or chamber, with a fireplace at one end for cooking and warmth. Without brick kilns or stone tools, they built chimneys of wooden frames coated in clay, a design that, with thatched roofs, made fires a serious threat.[7]

Houses improved over time, and Plymouth Colony grew. By 1691, when the colony was absorbed into the Massachusetts Bay Colony, it included eighteen towns, from Rehoboth, thirty-three miles west of Plymouth, to Eastham, on the upper arm of Cape Cod, and, on the other axis, from Scituate, thirty miles north of Plymouth, to Little Compton, over fifty miles to the southwest. Because of shallow harbors and sandy soil, none of the towns experienced booms in shipping or agriculture. Plymouth Colony's population remained modest, reaching seven thousand in 1690.[8]

Economic arrangements in Plymouth were fluid. After a brief period of communal labor, about nineteen households were in 1621 given small plots on the slopes of Fort Hill (later Burial Hill). A land division in 1623 allotted each settler a private acre, ending the communal system and opening the way for later buying and selling of land as private property became the norm.

Landowning was fraught with uncertainty because the Plymouth settlers claimed lands that Indigenous peoples had long occupied. The relationship between the colonists and Native Americans had begun inauspiciously when the Pilgrims arrived on Cape Cod and, on December 8, 1620, found themselves attacked by the Nauset tribe. The Nausets, a coastal group within the Wampanoag Confederation, which occupied much of present-day southeastern Massachusetts and parts of Rhode Island, had harbored deep resentment toward Europeans since 1614, when the English captain Thomas Hunt kidnapped about twenty-seven Native people from the region and sold them into slavery in Spain.

Far less hostile to the Pilgrims than the Nausets were the Pokanokets, a Wampanoag tribe centered southwest of Plymouth in Sowams—today's Barrington, Warren, and Bristol, Rhode Island. The Plymouth settlers and the Pokanokets depended on each other, because both were in a weak condition. The settlers suffered from disease and malnutrition, while the Wampanoags had been recently ravaged by a plague that had decimated them and made them vulnerable to their enemies, the Narragansetts. The chief, or sachem, of all the Wampanoags, Massasoit, welcomed the Pilgrims and, with the help of the English-speaking Natives Tisquantum (aka Squanto), Samoset, and Hobomok, established a formal relationship of mutual assistance and protection. The initially friendly connection between the Pilgrims and the Pokanokets stands out as a bright anomaly in the long, dismal history of white-Native relations that was to follow.

The eventual decline of this friendship, ironically, can be attributed to the friendship itself. Massasoit exhibited his goodwill toward the British by pledging loyalty to King James. The sachem's affection toward the whites grew when, in March 1622, the Pilgrim Edward Winslow trekked to Massasoit's Sowams home and gave him food that led to the sachem's apparently miraculous recovery from a severe illness. To treat their neighbors fairly, the Plymouth court ruled that settlers could not acquire Native land without the court's approval. Massasoit traded huge tracts of territory for items like coats, hatchets, hoes, and cloth.

Tensions between the whites and Natives escalated exponentially after Massasoit died in 1661.[9] Massasoit's sons Wamsutta and Metacom, who approached the Plymouth court requesting English names, became Alexander and Philip, respectively. Wamsutta died within a year of assuming the position of sachem, leaving it to his brother. Although Metacom was initially reluctant to yield more property to the settlers, he ultimately sold them so much land that he found himself and his people stranded on their Sowams tribal seat near Mount Hope (in present-day Bristol, Rhode Island). Large portions of the territory once occupied by the Pokanokets were now in the possession of the British colonizers. Metacom and the Wampanoags joined other Algonquian tribes to reclaim land and prevent further expansion by colonists.[10] The brief, intense King Philip's War, 1675–76, proved disastrous for the Native population. Metacom was killed, beheaded, and quartered. Not only were the Algonquian warriors roundly defeated, but they lost more territory, accelerating a cycle of land takeovers, war, and removal that would continue for more than two centuries.

A similar displacement of Native tribes was occurring in Virginia, where many Indigenous groups—coastal tribes like the Powhatans, the Rappahannocks, and the Meherrins; Piedmont nations such as the

Manahoacs and the Saponis; and several mountain tribes—experienced the ravages of settler colonialism.[11] The white settlers of New England and Virginia, by and large, were Protestants competing against Roman Catholics from Spain and France for control of North America. Evangelization among the Native populations was part of this larger religious war. Virginia scored an early victory when, in 1614, the tobacco planter John Rolfe married a young Native woman, Amonute (more widely known as Pocahontas), who converted to Anglicanism under the baptismal name Rebecca and became an enduring symbol of the so-called civilized savage. In New England, Puritan missionaries like John Eliot devoted themselves to winning over Natives to Calvinistic Congregationalism, turning them into "Praying Indians" who lived in communities of their own.

## RELIGION IN VIRGINIA AND PLYMOUTH

As the Southern and Northern settlers believed they were bringing Christian light to pagan darkness, they developed two distinct forms of religion that undergirded what would become the sectional divide behind the Civil War.

The locales of religious worship in Virginia and Plymouth were initially makeshift. John Smith recalled that the earliest settlers of Virginia congregated under a sail draped over tree branches or, in bad weather, inside "a rotten tent."[12] The pastor preached from a plank fastened between trees, and the congregation sat on logs. By 1619, however, Jamestown had a large, British-style church.

In Plymouth, religious services were held in one of the colony's common houses and, when that burned down, on the bottom floor of the town's fort. Plymouth's first meetinghouse, with a bell, did not arrive until 1648.

In their simple places of worship, the Jamestown and Plymouth settlers held distinctly different kinds of services: Anglican in the former, Separatist in the latter.

In 1609, Reverend William Crashaw delivered a sermon in London, urging emigrants headed for Virginia to promote the Anglican faith to the exclusion of other faiths. He warned that neither "papists" nor "Brownists, nor factious Separatists" should be allowed to "nestle" in Virginia. "Let your lawes be strict," he advised, "especially against swearing and other prophanenesse." Atheism or blasphemy, he insisted, should be punished by death.[13] The Virginia colonists followed his advice about having strict laws. In 1612, Sir Thomas Dale, the lieutenant governor of Virginia, issued *Lawes Divine, Morall and Martiall*, mandating that the clergy must conduct Anglican services twice daily and that settlers must attend all services. The death penalty would be inflicted on anyone who was heard to "speake impiously or maliciously, against the holy and blessed Trinitie" or "do any act, which may tend to the derision, or despight of Gods holy word."[14]

Initially, Virginians were preoccupied with surviving, dealing with the Native tribes, and establishing their economic footing, which prevented them from strictly enforcing these laws, which were subsequently modified. As it turned out, people of different faiths who worshipped peacefully lived unmolested in Virginia until the crackdowns on Puritans in the 1640s and the Quakers in the 1650s. But Anglicanism remained the colony's official religion. Virginia's first comprehensive law code, passed in 1619 by the newly formed General Assembly, stipulated that members of the clergy were expected to "exercise their ministerial function according to the Ecclesiastical lawes and orders of the churche of Englande."[15] The clergy were actively involved in many aspects of daily life in Virginia, including marriages, baptisms, funerals, and other ceremonies. Church wardens were assigned to police the moral behavior of the people in their district. Any settler who did not attend church on any Sunday "without an allowable excuse" must forfeit a pound of tobacco—a price that increased to fifty pounds for anyone who failed to attend church for a month.[16] Altogether, the law stated, there should be "uniformity in our church as neere as may be to the canons of England; both in substance and circumstance, and that all persons yeild readie obedience unto them under paine of censure." A person who disparaged a minister without substantial reason was subject to a fine of fifty pounds of tobacco.

Although such penalties were not regularly imposed, the forms and rituals of the Church of England permeated Virginia society. The Book of Common Prayer—the church's liturgy—was read not only from the pulpit but at home as well. Virginia law required that "neither minister nor reader teach any other catechisme than that by the canons appointed and inserted in the booke of common prayer" and that "noe reader upon presumption of his owne abilities do attempt the expounding that or any other catechisme or the scriptures."[17] Ceremony and rote repetition were thought to instill respect for divine truths.

If churchgoing, the Book of Common Prayer, and ministerial involvement in private ceremonies made life in Virginia structured and hierarchical, religious holidays made it festive. Virginians celebrated the holy days of the Anglican calendar—Christmas, Twelfth Night, Easter, Michaelmas (September 29), and others—with feasting or fasting, according to the occasion. The Book of Common Prayer, as updated by King James I in 1604, listed roughly twenty-five holy days, many dedicated to Christian saints, such as Matthias (February 24), Bartholomew (August 24), Matthew (September 21), and Andrew (November 30). Over the seventeenth century, several saints' days came to be celebrated with eating, drinking, sports, and entertainment of all kinds. Often raucous, the revels nurtured the South's self-image as genial and hospitable.

This frame of mind—structured by ritual and hierarchy, enlivened by festivities—was worlds apart from the culture of the Separatist Puritans in Plymouth Colony. The *Mayflower* passenger Edward Winslow said of Plymouth, "We came here to avoid the hierarchy, the holy days, the Book of Common Prayer, etc."[18] As they had in Leiden, the Plymouth settlers observed the Sabbath but did not use a fixed liturgy during their services. They rejected rituals such as making the sign of the cross at baptism or requiring wedding rings. They sang biblical psalms but not hymns. Separatists, unlike Anglicans, did not use ministers at marriages and funerals, which they regarded as civil rather than religious ceremonies.

Nor did they celebrate the Anglican holy days or saints' days, including Christmas and Easter, which they considered holdovers from Roman Catholicism, unsanctioned by the Bible. Thanksgiving, commonly associated with the Pilgrims, was not initially a designated holiday. The Pilgrims gave communal thanks whenever they were especially grateful for God's favor. As stated in Plymouth's code of laws, it was "in the power of the Governor & Assistants to command solemn daies of humiliation by fasting &c. and also for thankesgiving as occasion shall be offered."[19] In the fall of 1621, to celebrate their first harvest, the Pilgrims held what is remembered as the First Thanksgiving, a three-day festival with many Wampanoags present, aimed at thanking God for the colony's survival of its first grueling year. By the 1670s, Thanksgiving was regularly observed in the fall throughout New England.

As for the involvement of ministers in everyday affairs, which was a part of life in Virginia, that was complicated in early Plymouth. The Pilgrims were very pious, but they did not have a regular minister. The layman William Brewster conducted religious services twice on the Sabbath. By all reports, Elder Brewster was caring, compassionate, intelligent, and inspiring. He was so crucial to Plymouth that he has been called "the Father of New England."[20] But because he was not an ordained minister, he lacked the credentials to perform the two main sacraments, baptism and communion.[21] The Pilgrims eagerly awaited the arrival of their leader, Reverend John Robinson, who sent them letters of guidance from Leiden. But his planned move to the New World met with unforeseen delays. Because some of the Plymouth settlers and many of the financial backers in England were Anglicans, anger flared over the lack of sacraments and the domination of Separatist religion in the colony. In 1623, Brewster wrote to Robinson requesting permission to administer sacraments, but Robinson replied that it was "Not lawfull" for a layperson to do so.[22] Disgruntled settlers protested publicly against the "Want of both the Sacraments" in the Plymouth church. Governor Bradford replied defensively, "The more is our Greiff that our Pastour is Kept from us by whom wee might Injoy them; for wee used to have the Lords supper every sabbath and Baptisme as often as there was occasion of Children to Baptise."[23] But "our Pastour" never arrived. The sixty-year-old John Robinson died on March 1, 1625.

Anglicans among the Merchant Adventurers in England sent Reverend John Lyford, hoping he would replace Brewster. An Oxford-educated divine who led a church in Armagh, Ireland, Lyford arrived in Plymouth in 1624. He pretended to sympathize with the Separatists, but they only made him a church adviser, not their pastor. Offended by his minor role, he wrote letters to England sharply criticizing the Plymouth church. Twice, Governor Bradford intercepted these letters and revealed Lyford as an enemy of the colony. Additionally, stories circulated about Lyford's history of sexual improprieties: In Ireland, he was accused of raping a woman, having a child out of wedlock, and sleeping with many of his family's maidservants—acts that Bradford chose not to detail, "for they would offend chast ears to hear them related."[24]

And so Plymouth continued with William Brewster in the pulpit. A "Mr. Rogers," who was an ordained minister, came over from England in 1628, but church members found him to be "Crased in his braine"; he was promptly shipped back to England, where, it was later learned, he "Grew quite destracted."[25] The following year, Reverend Ralph Smith arrived. He was qualified to administer the sacraments, but he was an ineffective preacher. The church records reported that during his time as pastor "[the] minnestry it was low with us, . . . for . . . Ralph Smith . . . proved but a poor healp . . . being of very weake p[a]rtes." Smith occupied the pulpit, but Brewster continued to be Plymouth's chief religious counselor. Smith served for five years and then resigned, "p[a]rtely by his own willingnes as thinking it to[o] heavy a burden and p[a]rtely att the desire and by the p[e]rswasion of others."[26]

In the decades following Smith's departure, Plymouth struggled to find a suitable clergyman, unlike other towns in the expanding Plymouth Colony that fared better. Ralph Smith's successor, John Reyner, was described as "an able and a godly man, . . . unreproveable in his life & conversation."[27] Nonetheless, he clashed with another minister, Charles Chauncy, over baptizing methods—Reyner favored sprinkling, while Chauncy insisted on bodily immersion. Reyner resigned in 1654. For fifteen years, Plymouth had no minister; a lay preacher again took the pulpit. In 1669, the Reverend John Cotton Jr., a Harvard-educated son of a well-known New England minister, arrived. An orthodox clergyman with a strong evangelical style, Cotton invigorated the declining congregation. However, controversy followed him. Before his arrival in Plymouth, he faced charges of sexual offenses and was excommunicated from a Boston church, which reinstated him only after he showed penitence. In Plymouth, he was reportedly involved in several "Notorious Breaches of the Seventh Commandment," according to diarist Samuel Sewall.[28] Stories of his adulterous conduct prompted his resignation as pastor in 1697.

Roger Williams lived in Plymouth for a time. A distinguished chaplain from London, educated at Cambridge, Williams moved in 1631 to the Massachusetts Bay Colony, which was governed by Puritans who sought to reform the Church of England without leaving it. Williams, in contrast, was a radical Separatist. He was offered the pastorship of the Boston church, but he refused the job, because, in his words, he "durst not officiate to an unseparated people."[29] He also turned down an offer from the Salem church. He shocked the magistrates of the Massachusetts Bay Colony by declaring that the colony's English charter was invalid because Native Americans were the legitimate owners of their land, which, he insisted, white colonists must purchase fairly. Also, he was a Baptist—that is, he believed that baptism should be granted only to adults, not at birth, as was commonly believed.

These dissenting views made him unwelcome in the Bay Colony. In 1632, he moved to Plymouth to live among the Separatists there. He occasionally preached and "prophesied"—speaking off the cuff about religion—with William Brewster. However, he quarreled with the Plymouth church, perhaps because he found Pastor Ralph Smith too Anglican-leaning. He returned to Salem but was soon brought to trial for heresy. In late 1635, the General Court of Massachusetts banished him to England. Before the punishment could be carried out, in the cold winter of 1636, he escaped on foot southward through the snow, finding refuge along the way offered by the Wampanoag sachem Massasoit, who sheltered him until spring. Williams struck a deal with the nearby Narragansett people, who gave him land in exchange for access to English trade goods, which they had previously obtained in Plymouth or Boston. Williams settled in a beautiful area at the headwaters of Narragansett Bay that he later named Providence. Within a few years, many of his followers and other dissidents joined him there. In 1643, he traveled to England and, through Robert Rich and other Puritans, secured a patent from Parliament for a colony that later merged with Aquidneck Island (also known as Rhode Island), Newport, and Warwick to form the State of Rhode Island and Providence Plantations (changed in 2020 to the State of Rhode Island). It's interesting to consider what could have happened if Roger Williams had remained in Plymouth instead of founding Rhode Island. Under his influence, Plymouth might have become even more progressive than it ultimately became.

Witness what occurred in Rhode Island. Williams, having faced persecution and exile, instituted freedom of religion there. His deep devotion to separatism led him to denounce the mixing of man-made politics and God-centered faith. Williams's ideas were influenced by toleration-friendly thinkers like the English Separatist John Murton and the Dutch scholar Pieter Twisck, a Mennonite who, as we saw, also shaped John Robinson's thinking.[30] Also, Williams was deeply influenced by his immersion in the cultures of the Narragansett, Wampanoag, Pequot, and other Native peoples. Although he initially hoped for their Christian conversion, he never shared the harsher European view that they were "savages," and his perspective broadened during the Pequot War (1636–38), when he acted as mediator and translator between the English and the Pequots. He traveled among Native communities, as he later wrote, "many hundreds of times," having "varieties of intercourses with them, day and night, summer and winter, by land and sea," studying "all sorts of Nations of them, from one end of the Country to another."[31] He abandoned coercive missionary efforts and insisted that belief must be voluntary. His book *A Key into the Language of America* (1643) showed that in several respects Indigenous peoples lived with greater civility and moral consistency than many English Christians. He wrote a poem that began

> Boast not proud *English,* of thy birth & blood,
> Thy brother *Indian* is by birth as Good.
> Of one blood God made Him, and Thee & All,
> As wise, as faire, as strong, as personall.[32]

In *The Bloudy Tenent of Persecution* (1644), he denounced religious wars and maintained that different faiths should be tolerated. Protestantism itself was inherently varied. Rejecting the ceremonies and rites of Roman Catholicism opened the way to personal interpretations of the Bible, which over time yielded countless denominations and sects, ranging from quasi-Catholic High Church Anglicanism to Quakerism, where services consisted of congregants' speaking under the inspiration of the inner light. Emerson remarked with half-serious hyperbole, "The Protestant has his pew, which of course is only the first step to a church for every individual citizen—a church apiece."[33] America would eventually far outdistance other nations in the variety of its faiths.

Roger Williams's Rhode Island, with its policy of toleration, pioneered this uniquely American miscellany of religions. Its founding document, known as the Providence Agreement, was, as Donald Lutz notes, "the first expression in the new world of the separation of church and state."[34] New England's loose pebbles rolled into Rhode Island. The orthodox Massachusetts minister Cotton Mather sneered that Rhode Island's religious groups were "a *colluvies* [a hodgepodge] of *Antinomians, Familists, Anabaptists, Antisabbatarians, Arminians, Socinians, Quakers, Ranters*, every thing in the World but . . . real Christians."[35] In this sense, Rhode Island was a forerunner of the pre–Civil War North, which swarmed with Protestant-bred "isms" that became demonized by Southerners, with their structured Episcopal Church.

Among the religious rebels in Rhode Island was the outspoken Anne Hutchinson, who had been exiled from Massachusetts due to her antinomianism—the idea that salvation comes through divine grace alone and that divine law supersedes unjust human laws. Hutchinson shared with Roger Williams and the Plymouth Separatists a reliance on the Geneva Bible. Produced by English Calvinists who had fled Mary Tudor's anti-Protestant persecutions, the Geneva Bible appeared in 1560 and ran through multiple editions until 1604, when King James denounced it as "very partiall, untrue, seditious, and savouring, too much, of dangerous, and traitorous conceits."[36] What bothered him were the Geneva Version's extensive marginal comments, which were critical of earthly monarchs and church ministers. The Geneva Bible's annotations argued that God alone was the king, whereas human monarchs were often tyrants; also, preachers were frequently "false prophets" whose teachings could mislead true believers, who should be permitted to voice their own religious insights.[37] King James, with his commitment to the divine right of kings and church rituals, authorized a new translation of the Bible, which, he specified, must have "no marginall notes." The King James Version appeared in 1611 and quickly gained popularity during the early decades of the seventeenth century, supplanting the Geneva Bible as the standard English translation.

But before it fell from view, the Geneva Bible had a major impact. It was the Bible of John Robinson's congregation in Leiden. William Bradford quoted from the Geneva Bible in his *History of Plymouth Plantation*, in which he described the group of English expatriates who produced the Geneva Bible as believers in the Holy Gospel alone, as opposed to the Episcopalians, with their "courts, cannons, & ceremonies," who used their "lordly & tyranous power to persecute the poore servants of God."[38] The Geneva Bible influenced William Brewster: Its anti-monarchical theme emboldened him to issue from his Leiden printing press a book that attacked the divine right of kings so sharply that he was threatened with imprisonment; its sanction of religious teaching by laypeople made possible his tenure as Plymouth's lay preacher, whose afternoon services on the Sabbath featured prophesying by congregants.

The Geneva Bible's warning against "false prophets" inspired Anne Hutchinson to stand up to Massachusetts' leading preachers and hold religious meetings in her home, which were attended mainly by women.[39] Her unconventionality resulted in her being tried by the General Court of Massachusetts, which banished her from the Bay Colony. She settled on Aquidneck Island in Narragansett Bay, soon a section of Roger Williams's colony.

## PLYMOUTH'S DEMOCRATIC EXPERIMENT

The separation of church and state, which became a fundamental principle of the United States under the Constitution, is rightly associated with Roger Williams, who pioneered it in Rhode Island. However, the contribution of Plymouth Colony to advancing this and other democratic ideas, like expanding suffrage, is not sufficiently recognized.

The democratizing instinct that had guided popular voting among John Robinson's congregation in Leiden became even more pronounced aboard the *Mayflower*, in part because the Separatists found themselves in a minority among the ship's passengers, and thus, at least at first, in the colony itself. The Pilgrims, already accustomed to popular voting under Robinson, were faced with a situation in which they had to find a common ground with non-Separatists in order to establish a workable community.

The Mayflower Compact, when compared with the founding documents of Jamestown, points to the distinct identity of Plymouth. The Mayflower Compact begins religiously—"In the name of God, Amen."—and announces the voyagers' aim "to plant the first colony in the northern parts of Virginia," a task "undertaken for the glory of God and, Advancement of the Christian Faith, and the Honour of our King and Country." Such assertions could be expected from any group of English settlers confronted with the prospect of establishing a colony in the wilderness. But other than these vague phrases, the Mayflower Compact—a clear, 197-word statement—is neither religious nor nationalistic. It does not threaten punishment for impiety, or promote the English church, or give biblical guidelines for a Christian society. Instead, it announces the *Mayflower* passengers' agreement to "covenant and combine ourselves together into a civil Body Politick . . . And by Virtue hereof [to] enact, constitute, and frame, such just and equal Laws, Ordinances, Acts, Constitutions, and Officers, from time to time, as shall be thought most meet and convenient for the general Good of the Colony."[40]

This statement carried forward the spirit of John Robinson's "popular and democratical" church in Leiden.[41] But it was not just innovative religion that lay behind the open-endedness of the Mayflower Compact. Another factor was the *Mayflower*'s unplanned landing well north of the Pilgrims' original destination. The charter and patent signed in England no longer applied, because the colonists were many miles above the forty-first parallel, which clips the edge of current-day Westchester County, New York, and was then the northern border of Virginia.

In 1621, the newly organized Council for New England, which superseded earlier Virginia Company authority, issued the first Peirce Patent to Plymouth. Obtained through John Peirce, it allowed the settlers to inhabit and trade in New England but offered no firm boundaries or full title. A second patent, secured by Peirce in 1623, again granted limited rights but proved awkward because it was issued in his name alone. The colony's seven-year term, however, derived not from these patents but from the joint-stock agreement with the Adventurers described earlier, leaving unresolved questions about long-term governance and legal ownership. [42]

The Council for New England followed through on its promise. A key member of the council, Robert Rich, the Second Earl of Warwick—who, as we saw, was behind the 1619 landing at Jamestown—became its president and issued a new patent in 1629. Called the Warwick Patent or the Bradford Patent of 1629/30, this document identified Plymouth's boundaries, finalized the colonists' takeover of the joint-stock company that had been controlled by the Merchant Adventurers, and authorized the settlers "to frame and make orders and ordinances and constitucions [sic]" provided that they were "not repugnante to the lawes of Englande."[43]

Under the patent, the Plymouth settlers gained ownership of a sizable amount of territory that included what became Plymouth County, Bristol County, a section of eastern Rhode Island, and most of Barnstable County on Cape Cod—nearly two thousand square miles in all. The patent also gave Plymouth a 195-square-mile tract of land on the Kennebec River in current-day Augusta, Maine, where there was a fur-trading post.[44]

Significantly, the Warwick Patent made no mention of a quitrent. The system remained in place until the American Revolution in most of the South but not in much of the North, following the example of Plymouth. Although Plymouth's earlier patent (1621) had specified a rent of two shillings per one hundred acres, payable after seven years, those rents were apparently never collected. Under the 1629 patent, the Puritan-led Council for New England directly granted land ownership to the Plymouth colonists. Around the same time, the council established nearby Massachusetts Bay as a colony free of quitrents. Other Northern colonies adopted similar policies. As historian Beverley Bond explains, "The Puritans were vehemently opposed to the distinction between lord and tenant and were determined to be 'supreme lords of their own lands, equal before God and the law.'" Virginia and other Southern colonies, in contrast, maintained a monetary connection to the Crown that accompanied its religious ties with the Church of England.[45]

Free from a quitrent or a charter from the Crown, Plymouth colonists were largely independent. In the words of a nineteenth-century Massachusetts congressman, they were "under no authority whatever, and without any rule of government, restrained by no charter, and acknowledging no authority but that of a distant monarch who had not deigned to tell them how he would have them governed."[46] Annual elections were held, during which a governor and a group of assistants were chosen to preside over the General Court, which initially consisted of "freemen" (male residents who were not indentured servants) who voted on laws and handled court cases. The Revolutionary War–era author Mercy Otis Warren noted, "The old Plymouth colony remained for some time a distinct government. They chose their own magistrates, independent of all foreign control."[47]

With Plymouth having led the way, other New England colonies—especially those with English charters—became quasi democracies.

Plymouth's neighbor to the north, Massachusetts Bay Colony, is a case in point. The charter that organized Massachusetts Bay in 1629 was an unusual kind of royal charter, by which the Crown left the colony largely self-governing. As in Plymouth, officials were chosen through popular elections. There was an annual election for governor, deputy governor, and other magistrates. The General Court made its own laws, while the Court of Assistants also served chiefly as an upper house and judicial body.[48] Similar charters were issued to other New England colonies. As Michael G. Hall notes, "In the formative years between the first migration and 1684, the Puritans, not only in Massachusetts but to a large degree in all the New England settlements, enjoyed virtual autonomy vis-à-vis the government of England."[49]

Unlike the Separatist Pilgrims, who had broken entirely with the Church of England, the Massachusetts Bay Colony sought to create a purified Christian community that would stand as a model. Its spirit was expressed in *A Model of Christian Charity*, the lay sermon given in 1630 aboard the *Arabella* by John Winthrop, who would become the long-serving governor of the colony. Winthrop declared that his group had a covenant (an agreement) with God to become an exemplary society based on fairness and mutual aid among its members. Winthrop famously captured this message in his statement, based on Matthew 5:14, destined to be repeated endlessly in political speeches throughout American history: "Wee must consider that wee shall be as a citty upon a hill. The eies of all people are uppon us."[50]

The image of the city on the hill has come to stand for American democracy as a shining example to the world. Over the centuries, reform-minded Americans who protested against oppression, such as the anti-monarchical Patriots of the American Revolution and nineteenth-century opponents of the Southern Slave Power, looked back on the Plymouth and early Massachusetts Bay colonies as experiments in democracy.

Those experiments were prompted by what was happening in the mother country, where King Charles I and his Anglican bishops persecuted Puritans and tried to suppress popular government. Between 1630 and 1640, approximately twenty-two thousand Puritans emigrated to the New World, fleeing royal oppression and seeking freedom in North America, primarily in New England.[51]

It was during these decades of ferment that the Plymouth and Massachusetts Bay Colonies made innovations in representative government, including the issuance of clear codes of law. Under the Tudor and early Stuart monarchs, written laws in England had been prolix, obscure, and inconsistent. Reformers called for condensed laws that would be readily understandable by the average reader. New England, with its crystal-clear law codes, spearheaded this reform.[52] The concise statement of democratic principles would in time be a hallmark of American political expression, as later exemplified by statements like "all men are created equal" and "of the people, by the people, for the people" or the Thirteenth Amendment, which abolished slavery in a forty-three-word statement. The simplicity of political rhetoric in America began with the Mayflower Compact. It took a more comprehensive form in the 1636 Plymouth Code of Law and the Laws and Liberties of the Massachusetts Bay Colony of 1641 and 1648. The codes established the two colonies as "a government of laws, and not of men."[53]

Those famous words, written by John Adams, would appear in the 1780 Massachusetts Constitution. Plymouth Colony led the way in the legal codification of principles that would underlie American democracy. Unlike Massachusetts, Plymouth did not have church membership or property holding as legal requirements for voting during its early decades. For example, Plymouth's military leader, Myles Standish, did not join a church yet was politically active, as was another settler, Peregrine White, who remained unchurched until late in his long life. The colony's reputation for broad voting privileges was so pronounced that William Bradford wrote jocularly to a friend in England that reports of women and children voting in Plymouth were untrue.[54] According to Plymouth's 1636 code, known as the Pilgrim Code of Law, white males who took an oath of loyalty to the colony and were approved by town selectmen could vote for the colony's governor, other government officials, and local constables. To accommodate towns that were distant from Plymouth, the 1636 code allowed for proxy voting.

Before the passage of the 1636 code, Plymouth had introduced to New England the idea that no one is above the law, which would become an underpinning of American democracy. Plymouth established trial by jury in 1623. The fact that two *Mayflower* passengers of different classes, the merchant Stephen Hopkins, known as a "gentleman," and his indentured servant, Edward Doty (who became a freeman), made many court appearances and were, from all indications, treated fairly in their trials shows that social standing made little difference in legal matters. In one case, the court required Hopkins to continue supporting a female indentured servant who became pregnant (though the child was not his) even after he attempted to dismiss her.[55]

A striking instance of law-related equality was the trial of Susanna Winslow Latham and her husband Robert Latham, who were tried for abusing their indentured servant John Walker, a youth who died after severe beating, neglect, and exposure. In the trial, it emerged that Walker had been mistreated, starved, and left out in the cold, where he froze to death. The Lathams were charged with cruel treatment causing his death. They escaped execution for lack of conclusive evidence, but Robert was branded on the hand and fined.[56]

Another social leader, John Alden, a highly respected member of the court, was detained in Boston on a murder accusation arising from a fatal fur-trade dispute; the charge was soon dismissed, and he was released without trial. Alden's fellow *Mayflower* passenger John Billington, in contrast, was convicted of murder because the evidence against him was solid. A signer of the Mayflower Compact, Billington, originally from London, in 1630 shot and killed an enemy, John Newcomen, who became the first settler shot by another settler in Plymouth. Billington was tried, convicted of murder, and hanged.

In short, Plymouth settlers were subject to judgment before a court, regardless of social position, age, or gender. Natives were also heard by the court, as in 1638, when three white runaway servants who had robbed and fatally wounded a Nipmuc messenger were sentenced to death; the witnesses whose testimony secured their conviction were members of the Nipmuc community.

In 1636, Plymouth became the first British colony in New England to enact a comprehensive code of laws. Building on English common-law practice, the later so-called Pilgrim Code of Law emphasized jury trials, elected magistrates, and procedural safeguards. Whereas Massachusetts Bay relied heavily on biblical models in shaping its statutes, Plymouth's legal system was notably more secular, drawing chiefly on inherited English legal principles and on additional rules created within the colony to address local needs and guide its own evolving governance and daily practice there.[57] One historian calls the Pilgrim Code "the first American constitution," and another affirms that "the 1636 code established a constitution of the type that was to become familiar in America after the Revolution."[58] The constitutional historian Donald Lutz goes so far as to say that the Pilgrim Code is "a candidate for the honor of being the first true written constitution in the modern world."[59]

The Pilgrim Code features due process, a basic bill of rights, and voting eligibility without explicit religious or property requirements. It states that laws must be made "by consent according to the free liberties of the state," exercised by freemen in yearly elections of a governor, seven assistants, and other specified officials. Taxes, the code said, "shall be laid upon the whole . . . without partiality so as the freeman be not spared for his freedome, but the levy be equall." The Pilgrim Code liberated trial by jury from the kind of religious strictures that were then being imposed in England by ecclesiastical courts. Any Plymouth freeholder "of good report" could be called for jury duty, so that "in case any man finde himselfe aggrieved, that his complaint may be heard & redressed if there be due cause."[60]

Plymouth's code of 1636 set the basis for its revised codes of 1658 and 1671, which reaffirmed individual rights under the rule of law. The 1671 code mandated that "Justice and Right be equally and impartially Administered unto all" and that "no Act, Imposition, Law or Ordinance, be made or imposed upon us at present or to come; but such as shall be made or imposed by consent of the Body of Freemen or Associates, or their Representatives legally Assembled."[61]

Plymouth also ended primogeniture, making a deceased person's estate divisible—that is, split among heirs instead of reserved for the eldest son. Eventually, all but two of the New England and Middle colonies followed Plymouth's example by abolishing primogeniture, which the more aristocratic, institutional Southern colonies kept until Thomas Jefferson aimed to make primogeniture a target in his efforts to promote democracy.[62]

## DISCIPLINE AND PUNISHMENT, NORTH AND SOUTH

While abolitionists like Frederick Douglass looked back on innovations in law and government in Puritan New England as the origins of American democracy, proslavery forces often replied that the New England settlers, far from being forward-looking democrats, were zealots whose cruel intolerance prepared the way for meddling abolitionism and Black Republicanism (a disparaging label for antislavery politics).[63] On the eve of the Civil War, *The New York Herald* published a long piece titled "The Story of Puritanism—Real Origin of Southern Secession" insisting that the Puritan-based fanaticism of the North, "where Plymouth Rock . . . is set up as an idol for public worship," had caused the South to secede. Abolitionism, said the essayist, was the odious outgrowth of early New England, with its "scourgings, fines, stocks, imprisonment, tying to carts' tales, public exposure, scarlet lettering, boring with hot irons, ear clippings, tongue splittings, branding, and hanging."[64]

In the third year of the Civil War, an article with the subhead "The Bigotry and Intolerance of To-day Borrowed from the Pilgrims" argued that "to trace a proper genealogy of the illiberal, intolerant spirit" of "Abolition bigots" one must revisit the *Mayflower* passengers and their contemporaries. The *Mayflower*, the article said, brought a few good people but many more "bad, illiberal, arrogant and intolerant ones." Among the latter, heretics were "whipped, branded, had their ears cut off, their tongues bored with hot irons, and were banished upon pain of death."[65] From this standpoint, the North's invasion of the South was the horrid culmination of the old Puritan cruelty, carried forward by what one journalist labeled "Lincoln, Seward & Co., . . . that viperous breed of the Mayflower" that must be "exterminated."[66]

Who was right? If we look objectively at New England history, we see that the proslavery side was unfairly selective in focusing on Puritanism's harshness. This is not to say that harshness did not exist. The 1636 Plymouth code assigned the death penalty to seven offenses, among them sodomy, rape, and buggery (sex with an animal). The Massachusetts Body of Liberties went further, establishing sixteen capital crimes, including blasphemy and the unjustified cursing or hitting of a parent by someone sixteen or over. It prescribed the death penalty for some sexual acts in the language of Mosaic law. Quoting passages from the Old Testament, the Massachusetts code said that "If any man LYETH WITH MAN-KINDE as he lieth with a woman, both of them have committed abomination," and "both shal surely be put to death": the same punishment would be inflicted "if any person commit ADULTERIE with a married, or espoused wife" or "if any man or woman shall LYE WITH ANY BEAST, or bruit creature, by carnall copulation," and in which case "the beast shall be slain, & buried, and not eaten."[67]

Severe words—all the more so because they supposedly came from Moses, who, Puritans believed, had talked with God. But New Englanders resorted to the death penalty sparingly in comparison with the mother country. Crimes punishable by death in England stood at 50 in the 1680s and rose to over 220 by 1815, when acts such as pickpocketing, shoplifting, and making a wrong entry on a marriage certificate could send one to the gallows.[68]

In both England and America, however, the death penalty was carried out more rarely than the laws would indicate, except in cases of violent crime. In New England, sexual crimes were punished by execution only intermittently. In September 1642, Thomas Granger, a Plymouth teenager, was tried for having copulated with "a mare, a cow, two goats, five sheep, two calves, and a turkey."[69] Convicted of buggery, Granger was hanged after he witnessed the slaughter of several animals, with which he confessed to having had intercourse. A Connecticut man named Potter, reputed to be a model Christian, was convicted of having sexual intercourse with "a *Bitch*, . . . a *Cow*, Two *Heifers*, Three *Sheep*, and Two *Sowes*." Before he was executed, Potter watched as the animals were killed.[70] In New Haven, the aptly named Thomas Hogg was found guilty in 1647 of having sex with a pig. Hogg got off relatively easily by being whipped and serving prison time.

Hogg's sentence typified the way most sex cases were adjudicated. The Plymouth court considered three buggery cases other than Granger's. Each of them resulted in a nonlethal sentence: One of the convicted men was whipped, another was set free for lack of evidence, and the third was whipped, branded in the forehead with the letter *P* (for pollution), and banished from the colony.

People found guilty of sodomy or adultery were rarely executed. In an unusual case, William Plaine of New Haven Colony was hanged in

1646 after having been convicted of engaging in two homosexual affairs and masturbating "above a hundred times" in the company of boys.[71]

A more typical sentence was handed down by a Plymouth court in 1636 for John Alexander and the servant Thomas Roberts, who were found guilty of "lude behavior and uncleane carriage one with another, by often spendinge their seede one upon another."[72] Months earlier, the Plymouth code had included sodomy among capital crimes. Still, Alexander and Roberts received nonlethal sentences: whipping, branding on the shoulder, and banishment for Alexander, and a return to indentured servitude and a prohibition against ever owning Plymouth land for Roberts.

The only recorded execution for adultery early on occurred in 1644, when Mary Latham, an eighteen-year-old woman from Plymouth who was unhappy in her marriage with an older man, took up with James Britton, who feared for his soul and openly confessed his sin. The case was tried in the Boston court, where a witness reported seeing Britton and Latham having intercourse outdoors. Although some magistrates hesitated to find the couple guilty without a second witness, the circumstantial evidence against Latham and Britton—particularly Latham's court confession that she had committed a dozen adulterous affairs—was strong enough to condemn them both to the gallows.[73]

The Britton–Latham case was the exception that proved the rule of the limited use of capital punishment for illicit sex. A historian of the early New England criminal justice system has found that "most colonial sexual crime trials were rather mundane in nature, resulting in punishments expensive or painful but not life threatening." The death penalty was "rarely applied" in cases of "rape, incest, adultery, bestiality and sodomy . . . due to the simultaneous desire to reform English custom, which resorted more frequently to the death penalty, and the scarcity of colonial labor."[74]

Nineteenth-century Southerners expressed outrage over the North's "scarlet lettering," a reference to Nathaniel Hawthorne's novel about early New England in which Hester Prynne is forced to wear the letter *A* on her clothing as punishment for having committed adultery. How common was this punishment in the colonial North? A scrutiny of the records of the Plymouth and Massachusetts Bay Colonies reveals scattered instances of it. In 1639, a Plymouth Colony housewife, Mary Mendame, whose punishment for "dallyance" and "uncleannesse" with a Native American man was to wear "a badge" (unspecified) on her left sleeve and, if she were found without it, to be "burned in the face with a hott iron." (Interestingly, the man received a lighter sentence than she, because the sexual affair, in the court's words, "arose through the allurement & inticement of the said Mary," and "hee was drawne thereunto.")[75] In 1642, Plymouth's Anne Linceford and her paramour Thomas Bray were sentenced to wear the letters *AD* for as long as they stayed in the colony.[76] In 1851, Mary Batchellor of Maine was branded with an *A* for adultery.[77] A few other cases led to the public wearing of letters appropriate to the crime, such as a man who in 1634 was forced to wear a red *D* for drunkenness for a year, or one in 1638 sentenced to affix to his shirt a *U* (uncleanness) for "attempting lewdness with divers women," or a Plymouth woman sentenced in 1657 to wear a red cloth *B* for blasphemy.[78] In 1694, Massachusetts passed a law saying that an adulterer, male or female, "shall for ever after wear a capital A, . . . cut out in cloth of a contrary colour to their cloaths"; the law was carried out against eight persons convicted of adultery in Massachusetts between 1707 and 1781.[79]

Such punishments in New England led pro-Southern commentators of the Civil War era to demonize the "Puritan" North for its history of severe moral policing. But strict regulation of behavior was not confined to Northern colonies. Punishment for crimes in many parts of colonial America involved open humiliation or physical torture that was common in all Western countries before the nineteenth century.[80] Public shaming through exposed letters or words, which had been practiced in England as far back as the twelfth century, was enforced in Southern colonies as well.[81] Every county in Maryland, for example, was ordered to have branding irons ready to burn letters on the face, hand, or shoulder: *T* for thief, *B* for burglar, *R* for rogue or vagabond, *F* for forgery, *M* for manslaughter, *I* for selling arms to Natives, and *SL* for seditious libel.[82] In 1732, Virginia adopted similar letters, which were burned on the hand as a substitute for the death penalty for certain crimes.[83]

The South punished some offenses very severely. For hog stealing, Maryland imposed ear removal for the first offense, branding with an *H* for the second, and death for the third; Virginia's punishments were whipping, ear cropping, and death.[84]

A form of punishment aimed at outspoken women was common in the Southern colonies. Women labeled as "scolds"—nagging, overtalkative, or overly emotional—were silenced by dunking them in water or clamping their tongues. In England, silencing women was long achieved with a device called a brank, a metal contraption that fitted around a woman's head and had an iron tongue with a chisel-like point to prevent speech. Instead of the brank, Americans used a piece of split wood tied to a woman's tongue.

Even more prevalent was ducking, an early form of water torture, in which a woman was repeatedly immersed in a lake or a river while tied to a very long seesaw or secured in a rolling cart or dragged behind a boat. The cultural historian Alice Morse Earle surveyed hundreds of pages of court records and found "[not] a single entry of an execution of ducking in any Puritan community; while in the 'cavalier colonies,' so called, in Virginia and the Carolinas, many duckings took place, and in law survived as long as similar punishments in England."[85]

A Virginia woman, Betsey Tucker, who had made her family and neighbors "uncomfortable" with her loud talking, was held underwater five times for thirty seconds each time; initially unflappable, Betsey finally screamed that she would "sin no more," and she trudged home in her soaked clothes.[86] Another Virginia "scolding quean," as she was called, was dunked three times in the James River from the yardarm of a ship.[87] A Northampton County woman who had slandered someone was dragged behind a boat and made to confess her sin before her minister and his congregation. Ducking was practiced in the South as late as 1819.

The pillory, a tall wooden structure with holes for the head and the hands, was a favorite instrument of punishment in the South. The person stood inside the pillory and was fastened to it, often with the ears nailed to the wood. The nailing or removal of ears was standard in England—so standard that Puritans, who frequently suffered this penalty under Charles I and Archbishop William Laud, were nicknamed "crop-ears" (their other sobriquet, "Roundheads," came from their short hairstyle). In the South, standing in the pillory was assigned to all kinds of offenses, including forgery, blasphemy, quarreling, playing dice, and wife beating.[88] In 1662, the Virginia Assembly ordered that a whipping post, a pillory, and stocks (devices in which convicted people sat publicly with their feet locked in place) be installed near every courthouse in all of the colony's counties.[89] Virginia criminalized "the high & foule offences of adultery, whoredome or fornication," as well as "swearing, prophaning God's name, and his holy Sabboths, . . . contemning his holy sacraments or any thing belonging to his service or worship."[90]

It was hypocritical of the South to charge the North with the persecution of heretics, which was present in Southern colonies from the start. In both regions, Baptists were subject to imprisonment, whipping, or exile for not attending or financially supporting established churches—Congregational in New England, Anglican in Virginia and other places in the South. In the 1640s, under the royalist governor William Berkeley, Virginia banished Puritans. Colonies that had established churches persecuted Quakers. In Massachusetts, after a 1657 law threatening Quakers with the removal of the ears and burning of the tongue failed to have an effect, a law passed the following year penalized

Quakers with banishment "upon pain of death"—a sentence inflicted on four Quaker martyrs who reentered Massachusetts after exile and were hanged between 1659 and 1661.[91] Early Virginians, like their Northern contemporaries, targeted Quakers but without inflicting the death penalty. In 1663, Virginia's General Assembly ruled that "Quakers, or any other Separatists whatsoever in this Colony" who worshipped in groups of five or more would pay a fine of two hundred pounds of tobacco per person for the first offense, five hundred pounds for the second, and be exiled from the colony thereafter.[92]

Of all the examples of Northern intolerance, the one most often pointed to by nineteenth-century Southerners was New England's execution of alleged witches. Civil War–era Southerners frequently ranted about "witch-burning" New Englanders. Although burning at the stake was one of several historical punishments for alleged witches, New England did not impose this excruciating torture. In his overview of witchcraft in Europe from AD 1300 onward, Nachman Ben-Yehuda writes, "During the 14th–17th centuries, somewhere between 200,000 and half a million people were executed (burned, beheaded, drowned, hanged or strangled) on accusations of witchcraft."[93] Eighty-five percent of those executed were women. In England, the anti-witch craze took off under Elizabeth in the 1560s, continued under James I—who, having written a book on witchcraft called *Daemonologie*, authorized many witch executions—lagged a bit under Charles I, surged under the Puritans and Cromwell, and slacked off during the Restoration.[94] In 1692, an outbreak of hysteria over supposed witches in Salem, Massachusetts, led to the execution of fourteen women and six men; all were hanged except an eighty-one-year-old man, Giles Corey, who died after two days of having stones piled on his chest.[95] Several others died in prison.

But the South had had its own cases of witchcraft—some twenty-four to thirty in all. Virginia's earliest witchcraft case, which involved depositions against a Jamestown woman, Joan Wright, accusing her of bewitching chickens and predicting people's deaths, occurred in 1626, eleven years before New England's first witch incident.[96] Eighty years later, in 1706, after periodic witch trials in the interim, Grace Sherwood of Princess Anne County, Virginia, was accused of flying around, bewitching pigs and cotton, and shape-shifting into a black cat. Sherwood underwent a timeworn ducking test: She was tied up and thrown into a river. According to this test, if a suspected witch floated, it meant that she was indeed satanically possessed, because water was thought to be too pure an element to accept wickedness. Despite being bound, Sherwood floated. This and black marks on her body, judged to be teats at which Satan suckled, convinced the Virginia court that she was a witch. She was committed to prison, but evidence suggests that she was later set free. In 2006, three hundred years after her conviction, Governor Tim Kaine cleared Sherwood's name by pardoning her. Places around the scene of her ducking still bear names like Witch Duck Point, Witch Duck Bay, Sherwood Lane, and Witchduck Road.

It's true that no witch was executed in Virginia, unless one counts Katherine Grady, who in 1654 was reportedly hanged aboard a Virginia-bound ship (she was accused of using her devilish powers to bring on a terrible storm that almost destroyed the ship).[97] But if Virginia could claim moral superiority to Massachusetts in its avoidance of executing heretics and suspected witches, its record on the central issue in early American history—slavery—told a completely different story. The ever-increasing oppression and cruelty suffered by enslaved Blacks accompanied the entrenchment of the Virginia grandees known as the Cavaliers, who brought to America the deep anti-Puritan prejudice that fueled the royalist supporters of the Stuart kings. Puritanism, meanwhile, fostered notions about individual rights, self-ownership, and hostility to the divine right of kings that, in time, contributed to abolitionism.

## Chapter Three

# PURITANISM, RACE, AND SLAVERY

The conflict between the Puritans and the Cavaliers originated in a fundamental disagreement in England over the doctrine of the divine right of kings. Championed by James I, who put the king on the level of God, the doctrine was accepted by three later Stuart monarchs—Charles I, Charles II, and James II. In the early going, divine right was challenged most forcefully by Puritans.

William Brewster, before he sailed to Plymouth on the *Mayflower*, had to hide from English agents because his press in Leiden issued a book questioning James I and the principle of divine right. A movement in the British Parliament against the doctrine began when Edwin Sandys spoke out vehemently against divine right in 1614.[1] Tensions between the Parliament and the monarchy escalated in the 1620s, until Charles I exercised his royal (and, to him, divine) authority by dissolving Parliament in 1629. During the years between then and 1640, the persecution of Puritans resulted in many ear croppings, facial disfigurings, imprisonments, and brandings in England, accelerating the emigration of Puritans to New England.[2]

In this early stage, Puritans showed little antislavery sentiment. In fact, English Puritans led the colonization of Caribbean islands that quickly became centers of sugar plantations where enslaved Black people worked under terrible conditions. Several Puritans, who would later lead the revolt against Charles I, were involved in these Caribbean ventures. After Charles was overthrown, Oliver Cromwell, during his Protectorate (1651–58), carried out his Western Design, which included the English acquisition of Jamaica, soon to become a major site of chattel slavery.

However, the Puritan Revolution also laid the groundwork for a defense of the rights of ordinary people, which ultimately contributed to the egalitarian ideal of the Founding Fathers and, later, abolitionism and the antislavery politics of Lincoln, who associated slavery with the outdated concept of divine right.

## SLAVERY AND THE LAW IN NEW ENGLAND

America's first slave code appeared as a provision in the Massachusetts Body of Liberties in 1641, eleven years before Virginia legally established slavery as a status inherited from the mother. The Massachusetts law read:

> There shall never be any bond slaverie, villinage or Captivitie amongst us unles it be lawfull Captives taken in just warres, and such strangers as willingly selle themselves or are sold to us. And these shall have all the liberties and Christian usages which the law of god established in Israell concerning such persons doeth morally require. This exempts none from servitude who shall Judged thereto by Authoritie.[3]

What begins as an antislavery statement ("There shall never be any bond slaverie . . . ") and promises "liberties and Christian usages" for bonded workers still leaves room for slavery in certain cases, such as for captives taken in "just warres," "strangers" (a vague term meaning non-Christian ethnic others), and others, as decided by "Authoritie" (probably referring to those who were officially sentenced to hard labor).

Slavery had been an issue in the region before Winthrop arrived. In 1614, the English explorer Thomas Hunt kidnapped two dozen Native Americans on Cape Cod and took them to Spain, where he sold them into slavery. One of the captives, Tisquantum, eventually made his way back to New England, where he served as an intermediary between the Plymouth settlers and the Wampanoag, Nauset, and Massachusett peoples.

The earliest enslaver in Massachusetts appears to have been the English settler Samuel Maverick, who arrived between 1623 and 1627. Maverick, an Episcopalian merchant, owned at least two Black people. According to the English visitor John Josselyn, Maverick traumatized an enslaved woman, who said she had been a queen in her country, by forcing her to couple with an enslaved man—the first known instance of slave breeding in America.[4]

Especially pertinent to Massachusetts's 1641 slave code were two interrelated historical events: England's colonization of the West Indies and the Pequot War of 1636–38.

The early English takeover of several Caribbean islands was largely the responsibility of the ubiquitous Puritan nobleman Sir Robert Rich. Always alert for opportunities to challenge Spain while expanding England's international footprint, Rich, as Douglas Bradburn notes, was "part of the leadership of every major and almost every minor colonization effort of the first half of the seventeenth century"—not just Virginia and New England but also Bermuda, Trinidad, Tobago, Barbados, and Providence Island.[5]

The fact that these and other English-occupied islands became major sites of enslaved labor did not ruffle Rich or the other Puritans involved in the Caribbean ventures, including New Englanders. One of John Winthrop's sons, Henry, ran a tobacco plantation on Barbados, settling there in 1627 when the island had, in his words, "but three score of Christians and forty slaves of negroes and Indians."[6] Another son, Samuel Winthrop, founded a plantation in Antigua that was worked by enslaved people.

Providence Island had the most direct connection to New England slavery and the English Civil War. Sir Robert Rich and several other notables in England saw Providence Island (current-day Providencia, 140 miles off the coast of Nicaragua) as a Protestant outpost against Spain and a promising place for future economic growth in the Caribbean. The 1629 founding of Providence Island corresponded with Charles I's dissolution of Parliament. While the largest group of Puritans fleeing England chose Massachusetts as the site for establishing a godly community, others saw Providence Island as a future Puritan utopia wafted by tropical breezes.

The early backers of Providence Island included figures who would become a virtual who's who in the Puritan Revolution against Charles in the 1640s: John Pym, later the parliamentary leader whose Grand Remonstrance against the king would trigger the civil war; John Hampden, the politician and soldier whose death after a battle against the king's forces would make him a Puritan martyr revered for generations; Viscount Saye and Sele, the Puritan nobleman who also helped found the New Haven Colony before becoming a funder of antiroyalist forces in England; and Robert Rich himself, who became the chief of naval operations under both Parliament and Oliver Cromwell.

The Puritan utopia collapsed. In 1641, Spain expelled the English from Providence Island. During its years under British control, the island's settlers increasingly invested in human property, buying slaves at a rate unmatched at that time in any other English colony, Puritan or otherwise, as Karen Ordahl Kupperman points out.[7] The island was "Anglo-America's first true slave society," the site of its first slave rebellion, and a place where enslaved Africans soon outnumbered white settlers.[8] The island also spread slavery. After the Pequot War, the Salem ship *Desire* carried enslaved Pequots to Providence Island and traded them for enslaved Blacks. The *Desire* returned to Massachusetts with a cargo, as John Winthrop reported, of "some cotton, and tobacco, and negroes, etc."[9]

Massachusetts now held both Native Americans and Black people in bondage. From the Bay Colony's standpoint, the enslaved Natives had been taken in a just war, and enslaved Blacks were "strangers" available for servitude. Hence, the 1641 code that established slavery in the Puritan colony. Emanuel Downing, the brother-in-law of John Winthrop, wrote in 1645 that he hoped a "Just warre" could be waged against the Narragansett tribe so that enough women and children could be seized and exchanged for more Blacks, because, Downing explained, "I doe not see how wee can thrive untill wee get into a stock of slaves sufficient to doe all our business."[10]

The Body of Liberties, which was revised slightly over the years, remained Massachusetts' law code until 1780, when the state adopted a constitution that ended slavery. Before then, slaveholding gained a foothold in Massachusetts and elsewhere in New England, but never to the extent that it did in the South. According to a census taken in 1715, out of a population of 162,150 in New England, there were approximately 4,150 Black people, roughly half of whom lived in Massachusetts.[11] By 1790, the total New England population was just over one million, 16,822 of whom (approximately 1.5 percent) were Black people, three-fourths of whom were listed as "free." These numbers contrasted sharply with Southern colonies like South Carolina, where enslaved Black people outnumbered free whites by three to two, or Virginia, where there were two Blacks for every three whites, or Georgia, North Carolina, and Maryland, where a third or more of the population was enslaved. In New York, which had more Black residents than any other Northern state, less than a tenth of the population was African American, but over three-quarters of them were enslaved.[12]

The differences between the slave systems of the South and New England ran far deeper than numbers. In New England, enslaved people generally worked as domestic servants, artisans, maritime employees, or workers on small farms. In the South, large groups of bondspeople toiled as field hands on plantations. Whereas enslaved people in the South typically lived in humble, often ramshackle cabins on plantations, those in the North generally lived in the homes of their white owners and became involved in the family's daily activities.

Another factor behind the differences in slavery between the South and New England was the concept from the Torah of Jewish "servants" and enslaved "strangers" (non-Jewish people). Adapted to New England, the difference was between Christian and non-Christian bondspeople. Black people who were already Christians or who experienced conversion were less likely to be permanently enslaved than non-Christians. Colonies outside of New England circumvented this issue through legislation that said that Black or Native people who were baptized could be permanently enslaved. Laws to that effect were passed in Virginia, Maryland, New Jersey, New York, and South Carolina—but not in New England.

Although enslaved Blacks in New England were considered taxable, movable property, they also had certain rights generally reserved for freemen. They could testify in court against white people or others; if they were killed or maltreated, their enslaver would suffer legal consequences; they could own land and other property; they could sue for their freedom, as a good number did; they could appeal to higher courts; they could make contracts with whites that the whites must honor; and their marriages were often recognized in official records.

There was, therefore, far more fluidity about slavery in New England than in the South, where slave codes became increasingly rigid and oppressive. Evidence suggests that a sizable proportion of Black people in New England were emancipated after serving for a number of years. And enslavement—usually for a short term—was also the punishment assigned to some white citizens found guilty of certain offenses. "Sold into slavery" was a common phrase applied to whites in the Massachusetts Bay courts. Here are some whites who in the 1640s were found guilty of misdemeanors or crimes and were condemned to servitude. William Andrews, convicted of assault and battery, was "censured to bee severely whipped, & delivered up as a slave to whom the Court shall appoint."[13] The same sentence was given to the convicted robbers John Haslewood and Gyles Player. John Kempe, for "filthy unclean attempts with 3 yong girles," was sentenced to three public whippings and then "committed for a slave to Leif Davenport." Evidently, such court-imposed slavery was not permanent. William Andrews, for example, was "released (upon his good Carriage) from his slavery." The housebreaker Thomas Savory was ordered "to bee sould for a slave until hee have made double restitution." The thief Elizabeth Sedgwick was "censured to bee whipt, & condemned to slavery, till shee have recompenced double for all hir thefts."

Many crimes involving Black people who, in a later period, would be lynched without a trial were adjudicated according to due process. Barney, an enslaved Black person in Middletown, Connecticut, pleaded guilty in court to castrating his enslaver's son. Due to the absence of legal precedent, the court sought advice from the colony's legislature on a suitable punishment, but the legislature was also uncertain and handed the case back to the court, which decided to carry out an "eye for an eye" sentence on Barney, who was himself castrated.[14] Nicholas, enslaved by John Roy of Charlestown, Massachusetts, was found guilty of stabbing his enslaver and threatening him with a loaded gun, for which he was punished by whipping and short prison time. For trying to kill his mistress with arsenic, Caesar, an enslaved person in Salem, was sentenced to receive ten lashes and pay the court costs.

Surveying legal cases in seventeenth-century Massachusetts, Robert C. Twombly and Robert H. Moore conclude that the colony's courts guaranteed "basic legal rights . . . including police protection, legal counsel, trial by jury, fair and considered hearings . . . without regard for skin color." Whites and Blacks "received essentially equal treatment before the law."[15]

While Massachusetts had a mixed record on race, where did Plymouth Colony stand? Plymouth, unlike Massachusetts, never legally established slavery. Its 1636 law code did not mention the institution. Even after Plymouth took a harsh turn during the governorship of Thomas Prence (1657–73), slavery was not confirmed by statute. Although the revised Plymouth code of 1671 borrowed much of the language of the Massachusetts Body of Liberties, it omitted the section condoning slavery.

Arming Black people, which was eventually banned across all the American colonies due to concerns about slave insurrections, was allowed in early Plymouth. In 1643—four years after Virginia mandated that "all persons except negroes" should be armed—Plymouth announced that those who "are of honest and good report, & freemen" could enlist in the militia.[16] This included free Blacks; the Plymouth records from that year mention an unnamed "Blackamore" among "the males that are able to bear arms from 16 years old to 60 years."[17]

The comparative fairness toward Black people in Plymouth Colony extended to court appearances. In 1653, a Black maidservant testified in court against a white woman charged with theft. An especially notable case involved Robert Trayes, a Black man in Scituate, Plymouth Colony, who fired a rifle that shattered the leg of a white man, Daniel Standlake, who died from the wound. Trayes was brought to trial, accused of having been "instigated by the diviel" to "felonuously, wilfully, and presumtrously" fire a gun, leading to Standlake's death. Despite this strongly worded charge, the jury cleared Trayes, deciding that he had killed Standlake by "misadventure." Trayes was ordered to pay the court costs and was dismissed "with admonition to lay it much to hart that one should lose his life by him, although throw misadventure."[18]

Actually, slavery was intermittently practiced in Plymouth. When Thomas Willett of Scituate died in 1674, eight Black people were listed as part of his estate. It appears, however, that at least some of them were indentured servants, because when one of them, Jethro, was assigned to Willett's heirs, the court declared that he must be freed after two years and be well cared for in the meantime.[19] (Maltreatment of servants was punishable under Plymouth law.) Thereafter, the small number of enslavers in Plymouth were typically wealthy shipowners or merchants involved in the slave trade of Newport or Boston. According to one estimate, there were fifty enslaved people in Plymouth in 1740.[20]

In New England as a whole, laws specifically targeting enslaved Black people arose during the eighteenth century. Most of the colonies imposed evening curfews on the enslaved, forbade the sale of alcohol to them, refused them the right to bear arms, and limited their social activities.

The most important restriction on Black people in New England was the denial of the vote. There appears to be no record of African Americans voting at any time in colonial New England.[21] Ironically, free Black men could vote in South Carolina until 1701, in North Carolina until 1715, in Virginia until 1723, and in Georgia until 1754.[22] In Puritan-dominated New England, emphasis on church membership and property requirements for voting created tight restrictions on suffrage. Even formerly democratic Plymouth had imposed religious and property limitations on voting by the 1660s.

Nevertheless, Black people experienced a unique form of political activity in New England: the region's tradition of so-called Negro Election Days. From 1740 to 1850, free and enslaved Blacks in several New England colonies held annual elections where local Black communities chose a "governor" or "king." Usually taking place in May or June, around the same time whites held their elections, these events were both serious and festive, ceremonial yet irreverent. Blacks were given a holiday to celebrate with parades, music, dancing, feasting, and military drills. Pageantry reigned. Many of the Black festivalgoers arrived in fancy carriages, dressed in finery borrowed from whites. During the celebration, the air filled with the sounds of African languages and music played on drums and other instruments.

Once dismissed by historians, in recent times the Negro Election Day has been called "one of the most striking examples of intense creativity" of Black people of the era, an opportunity "to create a distinctive intellectual and political culture, to have rituals, institutions, and practices of their own, . . . to achieve a measure of autonomy, and to set up a form of self-government that probably had meaningful influence on their daily life, on their status, on their interaction with each other and with whites, and on the structuring of their community."[23]

The elected Black leader and his "government" wielded power among their peers. They reached decisions on petty crimes and sometimes inflicted corporal punishment. Some Black governors contributed to the larger society at important times. The Rhode Islander Guy Watson fought bravely in the American Revolution, capturing a British general at the Battle of Newport. Another Black "governor," the enslaved Tobiah of Derby, Connecticut, won his freedom by serving in the Patriot army; his son, Eben Tobias, was also a governor; his grandson, the distinguished Ebenezer D. Bassett, worked with Frederick Douglass in recruiting African American troops during the Civil War and later served as ambassador to Haiti under President Grant, becoming the nation's first Black diplomat.[24]

## ANTISLAVERY STIRRINGS

The underlying principle of nineteenth-century abolitionism was that Black people were human beings, not things to be bought and sold as property. Frederick Douglass pointed out that "the anti-slavery movement started with one idea; . . . namely, that the slave is a *man.* No less for being a black man! No more for being a black man!"[25]

Douglass's chief advertisement for the humanity of Black people was himself—not just his powerful autobiography, in its three versions published in 1845, 1855, and 1881, but also his speeches and newspaper writings. He aroused his audiences at antislavery lectures when he spread his arms and declared with bitter sarcasm, "I am one of the *things* of the South! *Behold the thing!*"[26]

Douglass got tremendous inspiration from religious figures of the past. He argued that the rights of Black people were first promoted by Morgan Godwyn, an unconventional Anglican clergyman who served as a missionary in Virginia and Barbados between 1665 and 1680 and was so disgusted by his church's treatment of enslaved Black and Indigenous people that he penned the controversial *The Negro's and Indians Advocate* (1680). In the book, Morgan wrote that his aim was "to prove the Negro's Humanity, and to shew that neither their Complexion nor Bondage, Descent nor Country, can be any impediment thereto."[27] In an 1847 tribute to Godwyn that Douglass wrote for his paper *The North Star*, he recommended Godwyn's book to "the negro-haters of our own Christian land" and to "our own beloved and heart-broken brethren, the victims of prejudice and slavery." He added, "The book should be in all your houses, and those who can ought to purchase one and possess it."[28]

Nearly four decades later, speaking on April 16, 1883, at an anniversary celebration of emancipation in Washington, DC, Douglass held up a copy of Godwyn's book and hailed it as "the first publication in assertion and vindication of any right of the Negro, of which I have any knowledge."[29] The church's opposition to baptizing Black people, Douglass said, was "serious, determined and bitter," and Godwyn was considered "a dangerous man, a disturber of the peace of the church" for promoting the idea. Douglass noted that Godwyn advocated the

Christian conversion of enslaved people without promoting their emancipation, but he still called Goodwyn "an ethical wonder" and the "the grand pioneer" of all later antislavery spokespeople, including the Rhode Island minister Samuel Hopkins, the Black radical David Walker, the abolitionists William Lloyd Garrison and Wendell Phillips, and the Republican politicians Joshua Reed Giddings, Thaddeus Stevens, and Abraham Lincoln. Godwyn was as far in advance in his time, Douglass insisted, as the antislavery politician Charles Sumner was when he fought on behalf of African Americans in the United States Senate. Douglass declared, "What baptism and church membership were for the Negro in the days of Godwin, the ballot and civil rights were for the Negro in the days of Sumner."

Douglass may have been unaware that early Spanish and French missionaries had anticipated Godwyn's efforts to Christianize enslaved people.[30] But the intensity with which Godwyn argues for the humanity of Black people in his book justified Douglass's calling him "the starting point, the foundation" of the recognition of "the character, the manhood, and the dignity of the Negro."

It should be noted that in Godwyn's time, other important strides toward embracing people of various non-European ethnicities were taken in both England and New England. The London lawyer Henry Parker, a close adviser of Parliament and Oliver Cromwell during the English Civil War, transformed the Puritan doctrines of liberty and popular consent into an antislavery argument. Denouncing the divine right of kings and "Despoticall" slaveholders, Parker wrote in 1644, "As there is no difference of slaves and freemen before God, so neither is there in nature: Slaves are men as much as their lords; they have the same endowments of minde, the same ability of body; they are born with the same danger, and exposed to the same miseries."[31] Richard Baxter, a leading Puritan clergyman in Cromwell's time, argued that slavery was justifiable only in special situations, as in the aftermath of a just war. Baxter wrote that those who used the enslaved "as beasts, for their mere commodity, and betray, or destroy, or neglect their souls, are fitter to be called incarnate devils than Christians, though they be no Christians whom they so abuse."[32]

Roger Williams of Rhode Island demonstrated that New England Puritanism could breed interracial respect. Witnessing the cruel treatment of the Pequot people during and after the Pequot War, Williams wrote in 1637 that Native Americans were "our brethren by nature."[33] Another Rhode Islander, Samuel Gorton, was the main force behind the colony's abolition statute, the first of its kind in the Atlantic world. Gorton was a Leveller—that is, an extreme Puritan who believed that people of all races were equal under God. In the 1640s, Gorton spent time in England, where he grew close to Puritan revolutionary leaders, including Robert Rich, Second Earl of Warwick, who procured for him a patent for land near Providence; Gorton named the area Warwick. Gorton put into effect his belief that human beings, "that species or kind that God hath honored with his own image," should not be made "slaves" to one another, because God had not "made man to be a vassal to his own species or kind."[34] The law that Gorton promoted, which Rhode Island passed in 1652, mandated that "no black mankind" could be permanently enslaved; ten years was the maximum time that a bondsperson could be held to service.[35]

This groundbreaking antislavery ordinance went unheeded in its time, as did a law of 1659 that banned the importation of enslaved Africans into Rhode Island and another one of 1675 prohibiting the enslavement of Native Americans. Soon, Rhode Island was importing Africans to work on the plantations in Narragansett and the dockyards of Providence and Newport.[36] (It is unclear how many Black individuals in Rhode Island were enslaved versus indentured.) The Rhode Island ports of Bristol, Newport, and Warren, along with Boston, were active in the international slave trade. Distilleries in Rhode Island and

Massachusetts produced rum that was transported to West Africa, where it was traded for slaves, who were then shipped to the Caribbean to be exchanged for sugar or molasses, which was sent to New England to be distilled into more rum.[37]

Nonetheless, Rhode Island contributed mightily to the march toward abolition. Its 1652 law proved inspirational to nineteenth-century abolitionists. In 1831—the same year that William Lloyd Garrison published the first issue of *The Liberator*—the antislavery reformer Moses Brown of Providence reprinted the 1652 act, which appeared in newspapers with titles like "First Law Against Slavery" and "Rhode Island the First Against Slavery."[38] Moses Brown prefaced the reprint by saying that "the inhabitants of that day had a much better idea of liberty and the rights of man than too many of their descendants now have."

Moses Brown himself was one of Rhode Island's most notable contributions to the abolitionist movement. Before taking up the antislavery cause, Brown had engaged in the slave trade along with his brothers, most notably John Brown (not to be confused with the famous nineteenth-century abolitionist of the same name). One of Rhode Island's wealthiest participants in the triangle trade, the Brown family funded the institution that became Brown University. When Moses Brown awakened to his Quaker faith in 1773, he emancipated his enslaved people and went on to become a vocal opponent of the slave trade and of slavery itself.

Brown's progressive Quakerism was the product of activism that had marked the Society of Friends since its inception. The Quaker faith has been called "left-wing Puritanism."[39] Perhaps a more apt phrase is "left-wing separatism." Emerging in the 1650s during the Protectorate of Cromwell, Quakerism took to an extreme some of the most radical elements of the religious rebellion against the monarchy and the established church. Separatism's rejection of church hierarchy yielded Quakerism's replacement of church services with the meeting and of priests with ministers who led so-called waiting worship held in silence. Separatism's belief in "prophesying" by laypeople anticipated Quakerism's belief in spiritual revelations shared by individual congregants—women as well as men—who stood and spoke during worship.

The tendency among socially minded Protestants to sympathize with enslaved people reached overt antislavery expression among the Society of Friends. Lincoln took special note of early antislavery agitation among Quakers, as did Frederick Douglass, who said, "The Society of Friends had abolished slavery among themselves and had borne testimony against the evil, long before the modern Anti-slavery movement was inaugurated."[40] In the 1670s, Quakerism's founder, George Fox, and other Friends visited Barbados and Jamaica, where they were appalled by the barbarism of slavery. In 1688, Quakers in Germantown, Pennsylvania, became the first American religious body to discourage slaveholding when it issued a petition against "the buying and keeping of negroes."[41] Although the Yearly Meeting of Pennsylvania and New Jersey ignored the petition, antislavery sentiment remained a significant strain in Quakerism. In 1758, the Friends initiated a movement to abolish slavery and the slave trade throughout the British Empire. By the 1780s, Quakers internationally agreed in their Yearly Meetings that no member of the society in good standing could own a Black person. In practice, this policy went unobserved among some Quaker merchants and farmers who continued to rely on enslaved labor. But the overall drift of Quakerism was toward a moderate antislavery position—moderate because the religion believed in pacifism and gentle persuasion. The Friends took an increasingly public antislavery stance through abolitionist proselytizers like Moses Brown, Pennsylvania's John Woolman, and the French American Anthony Benezet.

## SAMUEL SEWALL, COTTON MATHER, AND THE HERITAGE OF PURITAN NEW ENGLAND

Deliberations on slavery and race also came from former persecutors of Quakers, New England Puritans. Two figures who stand out among early Massachusetts Calvinists are the Newbury magistrate Samuel Sewall and the Boston clergyman Cotton Mather.

Discussing them is complicated by the fact that both are commonly associated with the Salem witch trials, Mather as an alleged instigator through his writings, and Sewall as one of the nine judges who ordered the execution of twenty people for witchcraft in 1692. However, both men showed signs of seeing the error of their ways. Mather, despite his paranoid screeds about the supposed invasion of Massachusetts by Satan and his minions, doubted how the trials were conducted. He expressed concerns about using spectral evidence (witness testimony based on visions) against the accused; his biographer Kenneth Silverman states that Mather's "crime, morally, lay not in promoting the trials but in doing nothing to stop them."[42]

Sewall, for his part, publicly apologized for participating in the witch hysteria. Sewall's biographer maintains that his apology made him a modern man who changed the course of New England history.[43] The judge's confession of guilt was so remarkable that in 1859 the antislavery Quaker John Greenleaf Whittier penned a widely reprinted poem, "The Prophecy of Samuel Sewall," that pictured Sewall as one of "the ancient worthies," afflicted by sorrow and penitence, whose honesty set an example of virtue that was as eternal as nature:

> Green forever the memory be
> Of the Judge of the old Theocracy,
> Whom even his errors glorified. . . .

. . . . . . . . . . . . . . . . . .

Honor and praise to the Puritan
Who the halting step of his age outran,
And, seeing the infinite worth of man,
In the priceless gift the Father gave
In the Infinite love that stooped to save,
Dared not brand his brother a slave![44]

Whittier's mention here of slavery points up his awareness that Sewall was not only remorseful for his involvement in the trials but was also the first American colonist to publish an antislavery tract. Sewall's trailblazing *The Selling of Joseph* had largely disappeared from view after its publication in 1700. But Sewall retained a reputation among nineteenth-century reformers, as when Garrison's *Liberator* cited him as the prime example of "the abolitionism of old times."[45]

*The Selling of Joseph* stands as a concise distillation of antislavery arguments that would be developed in the Civil War era. The pamphlet was partly inspired by the real-life case of an enslaved Black man named Adam who went to court after his owner, John Saffin, refused to honor the indenture agreement by which Adam would be emancipated after seven years. With Samuel Sewall's help, Adam filed charges against Saffin. The Boston Superior Court ruled on Adam's behalf, declaring him to be a free man. For Sewall, the maltreatment of Adam by Saffin and the sudden rise of the slave trade in the Bay Colony exemplified the injustice of slavery.

In *The Selling of Joseph*, Sewall expressed some of the most advanced themes of antislavery Puritanism. The Puritan idea of the equality of all people under an all-powerful God produces Sewall's statement: "It is most certain that all Men, as they are the Sons of *Adam*, are Coheirs; and have equal Right unto Liberty, and all other outward Comforts of Life." God "*hath made of One Blood, all Nations of Men, for to dwell on all the face of the Earth.*"[46] Ever since the Garden of Eden, equality has transcended differences of race or nationality. In God's scheme, slavery cannot exist: "Through the Indulgence of GOD to our First Parents after the Fall, the outward Estate of all and every of their Children, remains the same, as to one another. So that Originally, and Naturally, there is no such thing as Slavery." What is practiced as slavery callously disregards the humanity of Black people: "'Tis pity there should be more Caution used in buying a Horse, or a little lifeless dust[,] than there is in purchasing Men and Women: Whereas they are the Offspring of GOD."

Next, Sewall quotes the Mosaic law against man-stealing: "*He that Stealeth a Man and Selleth him, or if he be found in his hand, he shall surely be put to Death.* Exod. 21.16." This law had long been a standard Puritan dictum: It had been included in the Massachusetts Body of Liberties and Plymouth's 1671 law code. But before Sewall, this biblical law was seen as compatible with slavery, because manstealing was interpreted as the *unjust* enslavement of people, as, for example, when one stole someone else's servant or kidnapped an African through excessive violence.

Sewall gave a fresh take on the mandate against manstealing, which in his version is a synonym of slavery itself. Sewall writes: "This Law being of Everlasting Equity, wherein Man Stealing is ranked amongst the most atrocious of Capital Crimes: What louder Cry can there be made of that Celebrated Warning, *Caveat Emptor!* [*Buyer Beware!*]"

How about the accepted principle that captives taken in a "just war" could be lawfully enslaved? Sewall's curt rebuttal was thought-provoking: "Every War is upon one side Unjust. An Unlawful War can't make lawful Captives."[47]

Sewall gives an equally pungent reply to another proslavery point—that Blacks can be enslaved because they descended from Ham, whose son Canaan received the curse of Noah in Genesis. The Ham story, which would be the underpinning of countless proslavery works, elicits Sewall's rejoinder that no one knows the intended "extent and dura-

Samuel Sewall
*Portrait by John Smibert, 1730*

tion" of Noah's curse, and, besides, "How do we know but that it is long since out of date?" And who can say for sure whether Ham is actually the ancestor of Black people?

Then there was the oft-made claim that slavery was justified because it was practiced by the patriarch Abraham, who bought hundreds of servants. Sewall poses the question: How do we know if these servants were enslaved? He writes, "Until the Circumstances of *Abraham's* purchase be recorded, no Argument can be drawn from it."

Yet another proslavery claim: It is beneficial to pagan Blacks to bring them to Christian America, where they can learn true religion. Sewall's retort: "Evil must not be done, that good may come of it."

Besides addressing several proslavery arguments, Sewall evokes the nightmare of the Middle Passage, a topic destined to become the centerpiece of many abolitionist texts. Sewall notes "how in taking Negros out of *Africa*, and Selling of them here, That which GOD has joyned together men do boldly rend asunder; Men from their Country, Husbands from their Wives, Parents from their Children. How horrible is the Uncleanness, Mortality, if not Murder, that the Ships are guilty of that bring great Crouds of these miserable Men, and Women."

Sewall's solution to the problem of slavery was simple: universal observance of the Golden Rule: "*Therefore all things whatsoever ye would that men should do to you, do ye even so to them: for this is the Law and the Prophets.* Matt. 7. 12."

Sewall ends with two passages from the early-seventeenth-century Puritan theologian William Ames. By citing Ames, Sewall anchored his antislavery arguments in one of the titans of early Puritanism, a firm critic of the divine right of kings and a Calvinist thinker known as "the spiritual father of the New England churches."[48] Ames's theory of natural law was the basis of "fundamental doctrines upon which modern democratic institutions were raised—such doctrines as the duties and inalienable rights of individual citizens, the social contract or government by consent of the people, and the right of resistance when a government exceeds the bounds of its authority." Sewall quotes Ames's statement that slavery "cannot rightly have a place, except from a grave offense . . . because Freedom from natural estimation comes closest to life itself."[49] Sewall again quotes the Golden Rule, as cited in Latin by Ames.

But did Sewall himself practice the Golden Rule? To address this question, it is helpful to recall historian Edmund Morgan's concept of "the American paradox"—the inconsistency of leaders of the American Revolution who fought for their liberty while denying it to enslaved Black people.[50] Reapplied to figures who denounced slavery or other social injustice while sometimes saying or doing things that contradicted their words, this idea can be called the reformer's paradox. Samuel Sewall was the first in a long line of antislavery spokespeople who contradicted themselves in this way. This line would include Thomas Jefferson, Theodore Parker, Walt Whitman, and many others.

The paradoxical Sewall is on display even in the forward-looking *The Selling of Joseph*. Despite his brilliant dismantling of proslavery positions and his affirmation of the humanity of Black people, he doesn't rise completely above racial stereotyping, and he doesn't see how emancipated Blacks can fit into white society. The view that African Americans can have no meaningful place in mainstream society presaged the colonization movement, which worked to remove Black people to foreign places, especially Liberia in West Africa. Among noted colonizationists were James Monroe, Andrew Jackson, Henry Clay, and, for a time, Abraham Lincoln.

*The Selling of Joseph*, by questioning the integration of Black people into American society, makes Sewall an early example of the reformer's paradox—the opposition to slavery and racism by someone who lapses at moments into a seeming acceptance of both.

Inconsistencies are also visible in Sewall's life. On the one hand, none of his Black servants appear to have been enslaved. As Zachary McLeod Hutchins notes, "There is no evidence he ever held enslaved persons for their labor, and he helped more than one win his freedom."[51] On the other hand, Hutchins has also found that Sewall, in his capacity as a merchant, advertised for sale more than two dozen Black people in at least fourteen newspaper announcements in Boston during the three decades after he wrote *The Selling of Joseph*. His participation in the slave trade is odd indeed, coming from a man who said he wrote *Selling* after "having been long and much dissatisfied with the Trade of Fetching Negros from Guinea."[52]

Sewall's fellow New Englander Cotton Mather, known as "the personification of crystallized puritanism," also leads us to recognize inconsistencies while seeing progress.[53] Mather was not an abolitionist. He owned at least three Black people. But he believed in the humanity and educability of Blacks, much like Morgan Godwyn, Frederick Douglass's choice as an important source of Black rights despite his failure to advocate emancipation. In his 1706 pamphlet, *The Negro Christianized*, Mather argued that Black people must be educated so that they could read the Bible, learn the catechism, and, ultimately, be worthy of admission to the church (an idea that appalled many whites of the time, who regarded church membership as a stepping stone to citizenship). Against those who insisted that Blacks didn't have rational faculties, Mather noted, "Their *Discourse*, will abundantly prove, that they have *Reason*. . . . The vast improvement that *Education* has made upon *some* of them, argues that there is a *Reasonable Soul* in *all* of them."[54] He included in his text a catechism, prayers, and Bible passages for Blacks to memorize in preparation for reading the scriptures. Nearly a century and a half later, Harriet Beecher Stowe, in her antislavery bestseller *Uncle Tom's Cabin*, would feature the interracial bonding between a Black man and a white girl who read the Bible together.

Although Mather did not oppose slavery, he insisted that it should be practiced with careful regard to the spiritual and physical well-being of the enslaved. Anticipating Frederick Douglass's key point about the humanity of Blacks, Mather writes, "They are *Men*, and Not *Beasts* that you have bought, and they must be used accordingly." For Mather, the Golden Rule meant loving a Black person as oneself. In his words, "Man, Thy *Negro* is thy *Neighbour*. . . . Yea, if thou dost grant, *That God hath made of one Blood, all Nations of men*, he is thy *Brother* too"—a notion that would gain powerful abolitionist meaning in the motto AM I NOT A MAN AND A BROTHER, which would encircle a pleading, chained Black figure inscribed in countless antislavery medallions and publications from the late eighteenth century onward.

Mather had huge expectations for the impact of his pamphlet. "My Design is," he wrote, "not only to lodge one of the Books, in every

Cotton Mather
*Portrait by Peter Pelham, 1728*

Family of *New England*, which has a *Negro* in it, but also to send Numbers of them into the *Indies*."[55] But not many slaveholders were interested in Mather's message of spiritual equality between the races. Even though many colonies permitted the holding of Christian Blacks and Native Americans in permanent bondage, it had long been the norm that Christians did not enslave other Christians. Many people were uncomfortable with violating this custom. New Englanders feared that church membership could lead to emancipation and, over time, possible citizenship for Blacks. In the West Indies, it was far more profitable to treat enslaved people as beasts of burden rather than as humans. (As for the South, it had become so strongly tied to slavery by 1706 that Mather didn't even mention trying to send his pamphlet there.)

*The Negro Christianized* was dead on arrival. Mather's next forward-looking project, a charity school for Black people, didn't fare much better.

Mather endorsed education on all levels, and his democratic instincts found fulfillment in his support of common schools. Black members of his congregation often visited his home, and around 1717, he opened a free school for Blacks and Indians, which held evening classes for Black and Native people, enslaved and free. He provided funds for a schoolhouse in Boston and for a teacher to offer instruction in reading.[56] Little is known about the school's operation. Nor do we know how long the school lasted, though it was still open in December 1721, when Mather wrote in his diary, "I have at my own single Expense for many years, maintained a Charity-Schole for the Instruction of Negro's in Reading and Religion."[57]

Mather's exertions to educate Blacks won little praise from whites. Some Black people were derisively nicknamed "Cotton Mather" so that, as a contemporary wrote, "if any mischief is done by them, the credit of it comes upon [Mather]."[58] A nineteenth-century historian explained, "The whites did not deem it necessary that the blacks should learn to read, and they felt no gratitude toward one who attempted to teach them."[59]

Mather even got into trouble for educating a Black man who made a landmark contribution to medicine. In 1706, Mather's congregation bought for him an enslaved African whom he named Onesimus, a biblical name signifying "useful" or "helpful." Onesimus blossomed under Mather's tutelage. The glitch in their relationship was Mather's failure to win over Onesimus to Christianity. Though Mather called Onesimus "a pretty Intelligent Fellow," he complained of his bondsman's stubborn adherence to a religion based on tribal (likely Akan) practices in Africa.[60] However, it was precisely traditional Akan practices that led to Onesimus's earning an essential place in American history. In 1716, Onesimus reported that in his region of West Africa it was customary to apply pus from a smallpox sore to an open wound, producing temporary symptoms of the illness while preventing death. He showed Mather a scar indicating where he had been inoculated.

In 1721, Boston was swept by a smallpox epidemic that killed hundreds of residents. Recalling Onesimus's account, Mather confirmed the treatment with other enslaved Africans and enlisted a Boston doctor, Zabdiel Boylston, to inoculate volunteers, using a version of the method described by Onesimus. The procedure worked. Only 2 percent of Boylston's 242 volunteers died, as opposed to 14 percent of people in the region who were not inoculated.[61]

One would think that Mather's successful inoculation experiment would have drawn strong praise, but denunciations outweighed tributes. A prominent physician, William Douglass, wrote that the fact that Mather had followed the medical testimony of a "Negroe" was a "*Rare Farce.*" He averred, "There is not a Race of Men on Earth more *False Lyars*, &c. [than Africans]. Their Accounts of what was done in their Country was never depended upon till now for Arguments sake."[62] A Boston newspaper, *The New-England Courant*, vilified Mather sharply. Someone hurled an explosive device and a disdainful note through Mather's window. Dr. Boylston reported that he faced "such a Cloud of Opposers," such "Menaces" and "Odiums" that he felt his life was in danger, and he did much of his work in secret.[63]

But Onesimus, who purchased partial freedom from Mather, gained respect over time. Experimentation with variolation continued through the eighteenth century. In 1796, the famous immunologist Edward Jenner perfected the smallpox vaccine. By 1980, smallpox, once a major killer, had been eradicated worldwide. Onesimus is remembered for "changing the course of history by spurring the first recorded inoculations in the New World, which helped pave the way for the development of the first vaccines 75 years later."[64] A 2016 magazine survey counted Onesimus as one of the "Best Bostonians of All Time."[65]

Onesimus would have disappeared from history were it not for Cotton Mather, the quintessential Puritan. Along with Sewall, Mather represented the capacity for Puritanism to affirm the humanity of Black people. Sewall and Mather accelerated the reformist energies that ran through Puritan New England and that eventually inspired the North and contributed to the downfall of slavery.

Mather in particular was a conduit of these energies. His influence ran in two directions: toward the antislavery Calvinism that gathered force during the eighteenth century and found radical expression in the New Divinity preachers around the time of the American Revolution, and toward deist reformers, some of whom became Founding Fathers.

Of the deists, Benjamin Franklin had the deepest roots in New England Puritanism. Franklin's maternal grandfather, Peter Folger of Norwich, England, was a Puritan who moved to America in 1635, during the Great Atlantic Migration, prompted by the oppression of Charles I and Archbishop William Laud. Franklin boasted that Folger was "one of the first settlers of New England, of whom honorable mention is made by Cotton Mather, in his church history of that country, entitled *Magnalia Christi Americana*, as *'a godly, learned Englishman.'*"[66] Folger devoted years to evangelizing among Massachusetts tribes.

Franklin's father, Josiah, also a Puritan, suffered persecution under Charles II. In the early 1680s, he and his growing family moved to America, "where they expected to enjoy their mode of religion with freedom," in Franklin's words. Among the works that shaped the young Ben Franklin was Cotton Mather's 1710 book, *Essays to Do Good*, which argued that good deeds, charity, and kindness to people of different ethnicities benefited both the individual and society. Mather's book, Franklin recalled, "perhaps gave me a turn of thinking that had an influence on some of the principal future events of my life." Mather had prepared the way for Franklin's daily program of moral behavior and his involvement in public projects. One can point to Franklin's antislavery pamphlets, his closeness to the Quaker abolitionist Anthony Benezet, his presidency of the Pennsylvania Society for Promoting the Abolition of Slavery, and his support of the education of Black people.[67]

Given the advances made by revolutionaries like Franklin and the Puritans who shaped them, we see why abolitionists of the Civil War era felt rooted in Puritan New England. Also understandable, given proslavery developments in Virginia, were widening differences between the North, with its Puritan background, and the South, where a powerful Cavalier identity formed. The American conflict cannot be understood without regard to the legacy of the historic war between Puritans and Cavaliers in seventeenth-century England.

*Chapter Four*

# PURITANS, CAVALIERS, AND THE ENGLISH CIVIL WAR ERA

On January 30, 1649, the day of King Charles I's beheading, London was so cold that the River Thames heaved with ice floes. The king dressed accordingly. As insulation, he donned two heavy shirts to avoid shivering, which he thought spectators might mistake for cowardly trembling. What he didn't know was that few would see him up close, because a heavy guard surrounded the scaffold to prevent onlookers from being inspired by a show of bravery or parting eloquence by the king.

The precautions proved to be justified. On the scaffold, which was outside the banqueting hall of the royal palace, Whitehall, Charles was fearless and assertive. Realizing that the thousands of spectators were beyond the reach of his voice, he told those on the scaffold—the masked headsman and about fifteen others—that he knew that few would hear his words, but he wanted to have his say. He read from prepared notes. Referring to his trial, in which a court of the House of Commons had sentenced him to death for tyranny and treason, he said that he forgave "all the world, and even those in particular that have been the chief causes of my death."[1] He prayed that the Commons's prosecutors would repent for their sins against England.

Actually, his trial had been a nontrial. The king had not entered a plea because he did not acknowledge the authority of a court that lacked representatives from the House of Lords and included only a fraction of the House of Commons, later known as the Rump Parliament. (The Commons had been recently reduced by a military operation known as Pride's Purge. The purge left behind only a remnant, or "rump," of the full Parliament.) The king could not know that the Rump would soon dissolve not only the House of Lords but the monarchy itself. In the parliamentary court, Charles had harped on the absence of popular representatives and emphasized his stature as a godly monarch who loved his "loyal subjects," the English people. "A King cannot be tried by any superior jurisdiction on earth," he had declared.[2] His words made no impression on the court, which passed the sentence: "Charles Stuart, as a Tyrant, Traitor, Murderer and a Public Enemy, shall be put to death by severing his Head from his Body."[3]

In his scaffold speech the king reiterated his godliness and his affection for his subjects. He was a "Christian king," he declared, and soon he would enjoy his heavenly reward. He proclaimed his innocence of any wrongdoing, but he was happy to be "the Martyr of the People."[4] "For the People," he said, "truly I desire their Liberty and Freedom as much as any." But, he explained, their liberty had nothing to do with "having share in the Government." Instead, it came from following the principle that "a subject and a Sovereign are clean different things," and that his authority over them created their happiness.

He wanted the execution to go smoothly. He checked the axe to confirm that it was undamaged. "Fast," he told the disguised headsman, who may have been Richard Brandon, the London executioner who had previously beheaded two people close to the king, Archbishop William Laud and the adviser Thomas Wentworth, First Earl of Strafford. "It is fast, sir," the headsman said.[5] Charles arranged his cloak and

Execution of Charles I at the Guildhall, Whitehall, London, on January 30, 1649

tucked his long dark hair under his white cap to present an open neck. Because the block for beheading was only six inches high, Charles had to lie prostrate, head on the block, instead of kneeling. He told the headsman he would extend his arms forward when he was ready. After a prayerful pause, he did so, and the axe swiftly performed its work. "When the blow was given," according to one observer, "there was a dismal Universal Groan among the people."[6] The executioner seized the king's head, held it high for all to see, and made the traditional pronouncement: "Behold the head of a Traitor." Soldiers who retrieved the corpse dipped their handkerchiefs and swords in the king's blood, cut off locks of his hair, and dug up bloodstained scaffold chips to be kept as relics or sold to curiosity seekers.[7]

Charles's execution was the culmination of the seven-year civil war that had pitted the king's royalist followers, known as Cavaliers, against forces under the Puritan generals Thomas Fairfax and Oliver Cromwell, representing the Parliament that Charles had formerly suppressed for more than a decade.

Battlefield encounters between the Cavaliers and the Puritans were paralleled by a pamphlet war that later expanded into competing intellectual arguments by apologists for the monarchy, notably Thomas Hobbes and Sir Robert Filmer, and, on the other side, Puritan-influenced authors such as John Milton, John Locke, and Algernon Sidney, who promoted popular rights and republican government.

Looking back on the beheading of Charles I, the Boston antislavery minister Theodore Parker declared in 1854, "The dreadful axe of Puritanic Oliver Cromwell shore off the divine right of kings, making a clean cut between the vicarious government of the middle ages, and the personal self-rule of modern times."[8] The beheading of Charles was, as Parker said, hugely significant, especially when put in the context of the Puritan Revolution behind it. America's Founding Fathers would find inspiration in the English Civil War, as would nineteenth-century abolitionists.

Only by discussing the seventeenth-century civil war in England can we truly understand the American Revolution, the protest against chattel slavery, and the American Civil War.

## RUMBLINGS OF PURITAN REVOLT

From the time he took the throne in 1625, Charles I had trouble dealing with Parliament. Self-important and inflexible, he accepted the doctrine of the divine right of kings, forcefully expressed by his father, James I, who had declared that kings "sit upon God's throne" and "even by God himself . . . are called gods."[9] Charles insisted that England had a "hereditary" rather than an "elective" government.[10] He was partly right. Hereditary rule applied to the monarchy and the House of Lords but not to the House of Commons. Dating from the thirteenth century, the House of Commons consisted of burgesses elected by boroughs throughout England (though voting was restricted to males who owned at least forty shillings' worth of property).[11] The people *did* have a voice in government, one that Charles chose, in large part, to ignore.

Circumventing Parliament, he single-handedly raised customs duties and taxes to fund his unpopular wars with Spain and France. Parliament protested his overuse of royal prerogative. Religious tensions simmered. The House of Commons, increasingly made up of Puritans, had serious qualms about Charles, who was married to a Roman Catholic woman from France, and about the Church of England, whose Arminian doctrines (i.e., that salvation can be achieved through "good works") ran counter to Calvinism. The Puritans were also outraged by Charles's 1626 proclamation that prohibited "publish[ing] or maintain[ing] any new inventions, or opinions concerning Religion" that were not warranted by "the Doctrine and Discipline of the Church of England."[12] The king, facing ongoing resistance, dissolved Parliament three times between 1625 and 1629, after which he did not summon Parliament again for eleven years. In his March 1629 declaration suspending Parliament, he told his "loving Subjects" that "Princes are not bound to give Account of their Actions, but to God alone."[13]

Church of England leaders bolstered the king's claim to divinity. In a sermon on Charles, Reverend Henry Valentine gushed, "A king is *Imago Dei*, the bright *Image* of God, and the most magnificent and conspicuous representation of the Divine Majesty."[14] Archbishop William Laud said that the English people should "blesse God" for having "a King that lives so, as if he were a Law himselfe. . . . A King so blessed by God for your good . . . that God hath given him a very large hea[r]t, and filled it to the brim with justice, and judgement."[15] Laud went so far as to claim divine right for himself and other bishops. He declared that "*the Calling of Bishops* is *Jure divino*, by Divine Right," a right that "takes nothing from the *King's Right or power over us*."[16] Ecclesiastical canons passed in May 1640 required all ministers, on pain of suspension, to declare in church four times a year that "the most high and sacred order of kings is of divine right, being the ordinance of God himself." Any resistance to the Crown was "treasonable against God as well as against the king," who had the power "to restrain and punish with the temporal sword all stubborn and wicked doers."[17]

From this vantage point, God, through the king and the bishops, directly controlled England and its colonies during the eleven years of Charles's so-called Personal Rule, from 1629 to 1640. It was a cruel God who had taken charge. We've seen that the 1630s were a time of democratic experimentation in New England. Plymouth Colony codified representative government. Roger Williams founded what became the religiously tolerant Rhode Island. The antinomian Anne Hutchinson and her supporters made a bold stand against orthodoxy in Massachusetts Bay Colony. But these democratic impulses were stimulated by Puritans flocking to the New World to escape the repressiveness of Charles and his bishops. Indeed, without this repressiveness, it is doubtful that movements toward human rights among Puritans in both New England and the mother country would have occurred when they did.

Before dissolving Parliament, Charles imprisoned around seventy people who refused to pay a tax known as a forced loan. In 1629, he sent the outspoken Puritan parliamentarian Sir John Eliot to the Tower of London, where he died in prison three years later. Eliot became celebrated as a martyr for the parliamentary cause.

More martyrs emerged during the king's Personal Rule, the eleven-year period when he ruled without Parliament. Puritans were persecuted by the Star Chamber (the crown's tribunal for sedition) as political dissenters and by Archbishop Laud's Court of High Commission as heretics.

Among Puritan and anti-Laudian dissenters were Alexander Leighton, John Bastwick, William Prynne, Henry Burton, and John Lilburne, who were harshly punished for publishing works critical of the Church of England. Punishments included mutilation (such as ear-cropping or branding), whipping, heavy fines, loss of profession, imprisonment, or exile, depending on the case.[18]

The Puritans defied their persecutors. They "publicized their offenses, sought their prosecutions, and welcomed their punishments," Mark Kishlansky notes.[19] The preacher Henry Burton, who lost his ears and was imprisoned for sermonizing against the Anglican church, declared that even in his squalid, frigid jail cell "my heart leaped for joy" in light of "the nobleness and pure innocency of the cause, and the uprightness and integrity of my conscience." The Puritan doctor and author John Bastwick, who suffered penalties similar to those of Burton, including the slicing off of his ears, said he was "resolved to seal the truth with my blood," adding, "if I die in that battle so much the sooner, I shall be sent in a chariot of triumph to heaven." The minister and physician Alexander Leighton, who was pilloried, starved, poisoned, and held in a rat-infested prison, proclaimed, "I am as merry as Paul and Silas were, when they were in the stocks, and in prison, who sung psalms and praises at midnight so that the prisoners heard them." While standing in the pillory, he called it "Christ's yoke," and when his ears were taken off, he said, "Blessed be God. If I had a hundred, I should lose them all for the cause."

The mutilation of the Puritan martyrs was a public spectacle that aroused strong sympathy among spectators. Remarkably, the principal Puritan martyrs survived their ordeals, and when Parliament gained power in the 1640s they were hailed as heroes.

The significance of the martyrs extended beyond their role as temporary celebrities. They openly challenged the legal actions taken against them. In doing so, they revealed flaws in the ecclesiastical courts that tried them. By refusing to take oaths before Laud's court and the Star Chamber, they conducted a strong protest against the system that denied them due process.

Critical in this regard was the stubborn resistance exhibited by John Lilburne. A Separatist who would become a prominent Leveller and then a Quaker, the cantankerous Lilburne was inflexible in resisting anything that he thought smacked of despotism. He was brought to trial several times for distributing heretical works. He persisted in refusing to take the ex officio oath, which mandated that a defendant answer all questions posed by the court. In that era, defendants had the right to challenge the charges against them, but they could not remain silent in court without being punished. Lilburne's refusal to take the oath led to his being whipped at the tail of an oxcart for two miles through the streets of London, pilloried, and sent to jail. In the pillory, with his head in a hole, he spoke so violently against the ex officio oath that he was gagged. Then he stamped his feet and tossed Puritan publications to spectators. Thereafter, he was chained to a wall in Fleet Prison. Like the other martyrs, he gloried in his punishment, which made him feel "exceedingly lifted up with spiritual consolation," in his words.[20]

In court, Lilburne famously refused to incriminate himself. He declared to his judges, "No man's conscience ought to be racked by oaths imposed, to answer to questions concerning himself in matters criminal."[21] Some argue that Lilburne's refusal to take the ex officio—first mentioned in the late-1640s Leveller tract Agreement of the People—foreshadowed the Fifth Amendment of the American Constitution, which states that "No person . . . shall be compelled in any criminal case to be a witness against himself."[22] Actually, there is no direct historical link between Lilburne and the Fifth Amendment. The right against self-incrimination would not be regularly enforced in common-law courts until the late eighteenth century. Lilburne's defiance of the oath can be best understood as a devout Puritan's updating of the medieval church doctrine *nemo tenetur seipsum prodere*—no one is bound to accuse himself. In a church setting, the doctrine meant that one could confess to a sin without reporting it to legal authorities. In a court setting, as applied by Lilburne, it meant a refusal to answer the questions of judges appointed by the church.

Around the same time that Lilburne was challenging traditional court practices, Puritans in New England were doing the same. The constitutional scholar Leonard W. Levy writes, "The maxim *nemo tenetur seipsum prodere* . . . was widely known among the Massachusetts Puritans."[23] Plymouth Colony's governor William Bradford posed the provocative question to local ministers "How farr a magistrate may extracte a confession from a delinquent, to accuse himselfe of a capitall crime, seeing *Nemo tenetur prodere seipsum*." Bradford got an interesting reply from the Plymouth Colony minister Charles Chauncy, who wrote, "I fear it is not safe, nor warented by Gods word, to extracte a confession from a delinquent by an oath in matters of life and death."[24] However, Chauncy added that magistrates might need to resort to physical punishment to extract a confession "in maters of higest consequence, such as doe conceirne the saftie or ruine of stat[e]s or countries."

Given New England's openness to innovative ideas, it is no surprise that the 1630s—a decade of persecution in England—brought a marked upsurge in Puritan emigration to the New World.[25] Charles disapproved of New England's religious diversity and democratic tendencies. Between 1635 and 1638, he issued three proclamations restricting emigration to New England. He pointed to "the Factious disposition of a great part of the People" of New England and "how unfit and unworthy they are of any support or countenance from hence, in respect of the great disorders and want of Government amongst them."[26] He didn't want religious enemies at home to escape the watchful eye of authority by fleeing to colonies where they could spread heresy. Would-be emigrants to New England could leave only if they received a license from the church.

Oliver Cromwell and his cousin John Hampden were among those who planned to relocate to New England, but Charles ordered their trip to be canceled.[27] This story brings up the ironic possibility that the king unwittingly ensured his own doom by keeping in England two of the future leaders of the war that would topple his monarchy.

John Hampden's role in this historic revolution arose in direct response to Charles's ill-considered actions and the assertiveness of the Church of England. In 1637, Charles I tried to impose the Anglican liturgy on Presbyterian Scotland, sparking riots that led to the Bishops' Wars (1639–40). To finance his campaigns, he relied on ship money, a tax traditionally for coastal defense that he extended inland without parliamentary consent. John Hampden famously challenged it in 1637–38, becoming a symbol of resistance. Needing funds, Charles summoned the Short Parliament in April 1640, but the Commons refused to grant money unless grievances were addressed, so he dissolved it after three weeks. Charles called for another parliamentary election in the fall of 1641. The English people elected a House of Commons that mostly consisted of the king's opponents, dominated by Puritans of various shades. This Long Parliament—so named because it would last from November 1640 to 1660, with brief interruptions—issued a Grand Remonstrance, written by John Pym, that listed 204 grievances against England's ruling establishment, including "Fines, Imprisonments, Stigmatizings, Mutilations, Whippings, Pillories, Gags, Confinements, Banishments."[28]

The nineteenth-century British historian Thomas Carlyle, an admirer of Oliver Cromwell and the Puritan Revolution, called the Long Parliament "the remarkablest Parliament that ever sat, the father of all Free British Parliaments, American Congresses and French Conventions, that have sat since in this world."[29] Several of America's founders would tap into the Long Parliament's revolutionary spirit.

## ROUNDHEADS VS. ROYALISTS

Within six months of the publication of the Grand Remonstrance, Parliament had sent Thomas Wentworth, the First Earl of Strafford, Charles's chief adviser, to the scaffold, which was followed two years later by the execution of Archbishop Laud. War erupted in August 1642 between Puritans, backed by Parliament, and Cavaliers, supporters of the king. Thus began the English Civil War, an umbrella term for the Wars of Three Kingdoms (1642–53), which involved England, Scotland, and Ireland. The Puritans and Cavaliers were at each other's throats on the battlefield and in popular culture.

On the military front, the Puritans John Fairfax and Oliver Cromwell led the parliamentary forces (reorganized midway as the New Model Army), which emerged victorious over the Cavalier army, commanded by Charles I's nephew, Prince Rupert. Scottish Puritans, known as Covenanters, contributed to the parliamentary cause but then soured on the alliance when Presbyterians in Parliament failed to make their religion the official state church in place of the dismantled Church of England. King Charles, defeated in battle, made a deal with Scottish royalists, who invaded England but were repulsed by Cromwell.

Ireland had long troubled English Puritans, especially after the 1641 Catholic rebellion, which saw thousands of Protestants killed. Following a 1649 uprising, Cromwell invaded Ireland, brutally attacking towns such as Drogheda and Wexford. He then moved on to Scotland, where Charles II had been proclaimed king, defeating the royalists at Dunbar. Cromwell's forces, the Ironsides, later crushed the Scottish army at Worcester—the final battle of the war. Charles II fled to Europe, awaiting his eventual return to the English throne. In 1653, Cromwell became the Lord Protector of England. He took important steps toward democracy by expanding voting rights and enforcing limited toleration. But he used military force to replace the existing

Parliament with the handpicked Barebone's Parliament, which was short-lived. He set up a military dictatorship and excluded from politics groups that included Catholics and Cavaliers, many of whom fled elsewhere, including to America. Cromwell's death in 1658 was followed by the brief rule of his son Richard and then the return of Charles II, who reestablished the Stuart monarchy in 1660.

The seesawing of power between the Puritans and the Cavaliers reflected a profound polarization in English opinions and behavior. The term "Cavalier," which derives from the same Latin root as the Italian *cavaliere* and French *chevalier* (horseman), was used by English Puritans as a term of contempt for Charles I's royalist supporters, who adopted the name as a badge of honor. The Cavaliers' devotion to the monarchy ran deep. Explaining the Cavaliers' eagerness to fight for the king, a royalist clergyman declared in 1644, "A complete Cavalier is a Child of Honour, a Gentleman well born and bred that loves his King for conscience sake, of a clearer countenance and bolder look than other men, because of a more loyal heart."[30] The Cavaliers accepted the king's claim to godliness. One of Charles I's soldiers, trying to persuade his brother to join the Cavalier army after their father had died in battle, said, "I beseech you to consider that majesty is sacred."

Honor, rooted in feudal notions of chivalry and knighthood, was a powerful motivating factor for the Cavaliers. The Earl of Derby, a nobleman convicted of treason by the parliamentary side, said just before his beheading, "I was born in honour, have lived in honour, and hope to die in honour." Honor involved not only unswerving loyalty to the king and the English church but also pride in one's lineage, reaching back many generations and bestowed as a birthright.

Along with honor went bravado and pride in sexual prowess. The Cavaliers were known for their philandering, carousing, gambling, and enjoyment of spectacles like bearbaiting and cockfighting. A Puritan pamphlet reported that the Cavalier could "out swear the French, out-drink the Dutch, and out paramour the Turk."[31] Another observer said of the Cavaliers, "When they are in their cups they swagger, roar, swear, and domineer, plundering, pillaging, and doing all other kind of wrong." A more generous assessment came from the nineteenth-century British historian Thomas Babington Macaulay, who mentioned the "profligacy" and "excesses" of the Cavaliers but added, "With many of the vices of the Round Table, they had also many of its virtues, courtesy, generosity, veracity, tenderness. . . . They had far more both of profound and of polite learning than the Puritans. Their manners were more engaging, their tempers more amiable, their tastes more elegant, and their households more cheerful."[32]

Charles I was the quintessential Cavalier of the would-be civilized type. He was an aesthete who surrounded himself with musicians, painters, playwrights, poets, scholars, architects, and landscape gardeners. He had a massive art collection that included paintings by Rembrandt, Titian, and Rubens. The Flemish artist Anthony van Dyck painted memorable portraits of the king and others in the royal circle. Charles was a superb horseman, and he enjoyed playing tennis, bowling, and attending plays. There is no evidence that he was unfaithful to Queen Henrietta Maria. His son, in contrast, was the caricature of the dissolute Cavalier. Known as the Merry Monarch, King Charles II brought to the English court the loose habits he had picked up during his European exile. He had many long-term mistresses, countless passing ones, and at least fourteen illegitimate children (but no legitimate heir by his wife, Catherine of Braganza, who had three stillbirths). His court was the scene of such raucous goings-on that the diarist Samuel Pepys lamented in 1667, "The King and Court were never in the world so bad as they are now for gaming, swearing, whoring, and drinking, and the most abominable vices that ever were in the world."[33]

Cavaliers were known for their theatrical attire. Portraits of Charles I show the king with long locks, a pointed beard, a broad lace collar,

Charles I
*Portrait by Anthony van Dyck, 1632*

Charles II
*Portrait by John Michael Wright, c. 1671–76*

turned-up lace cuffs, and a colorful padded jacket with puffy sleeves—all typical of the Cavalier style. Other elements of the style were the felt hat with a feather plume, a full coat, and boots with wide shafts. The clothing worn by Puritans was far drabber than that of the Cavaliers. The typical Puritan had close-cropped hair (thus the nickname "Roundhead") and wore a dark jacket, a plain white collar, and a broad-brimmed, conical hat known as a steeple hat or sugarloaf.

Each army claimed religious superiority over the other. The royalists fought for the Anglican Church and a king who was allegedly godlike. Their battle flags frequently promoted the divine right of kings. The banner of Charles's guards read "Dieu et mon droit" ("God and my

Stern-faced Puritans walking past carousing Cavaliers
*"Cavaliers and Puritans," in* Cassell's Illustrated History of England, *vol. 3, p. 201*

right").[34] Cavalier battle flags had legends like "Dona dei utraque regi" ("Both gifts from God are for the king") with a crown and laurel, and "Dei gratia" ("Grace of God") above a crown.

Parliament fought in defense of a Puritan religion that had been born in protest against the canons and rituals of the Church of England. Oliver Cromwell declared, "He that prays and preaches best will fight best."[35] He distributed to his troops *The Souldiers Pocket Bible* (aka the Cromwell Bible), a sixteen-page pamphlet that contained some 150 passages from the Geneva Bible favored by Puritans. Passages like "The Lord shall fight for you" (Exodus 14:14) and "For the Lord your God goeth with you, to fight for you against your enemies, and to save you" (Deuteronomy 20:4) appeared under headings such as "A Soldier must be Valiant for God's cause" and "A Soldier must Pray before he goes to fight."[36] Cromwell boasted that the Puritans did not lose a major battle after *The Souldiers Pocket Bible* was first issued in 1643.[37]

Cromwell established rules against swearing and drunkenness. His New Model Army, known as "the praying army," was a select force that felt it was on a sacred mission.[38] Many of its soldiers said prayers together, sang psalms, and read aloud from *The Souldiers Pocket Bible.* Its battle flags bore mottoes like PRAY AND FIGHT; MAY JEHOVAH HELP US, AND HELP US HE WILL; AFLAME WITH LOVE FOR SION; and WITH GOD AS OUR GUIDE, THERE IS NO NEED TO DESPAIR. Days of fasting and humiliation were held for the army to repent for its sins. Most regiments strictly observed the Sabbath.

The Puritan soldiers wreaked havoc on things associated with the Church of England. They tore down crosses, altars, stained glass windows, religious statuary, vestments, organs, and paintings of Jesus or other members of the Holy Family. They inflicted major damage on more than a dozen cathedrals, including Canterbury and Westminster Abbey. St. Paul's Cathedral suffered desecration when the army used it as a base. The royalist writer Martin Parker was brought to tears when he passed by St. Paul's in 1649. He reported, "The Church is now turned into a stable; the House of Prayer into a house of prophaneness; the place of instruction into a place of destruction; the Holy Altar is now become a Ryotous table."[39]

## THE CULTURE WAR

Parker's statement was a thrust in the culture war between the Cavaliers and the Puritans, fought through newspapers, pamphlets, ballads, and broadsides. Parker, a prolific ballad writer and occasional journalist, was a major booster of King Charles and his Cavaliers. In one ballad, he pictured "Our gracious King, our *Charles* the Great" surrounded by angels sent by "the King of Kings." Parker writes, "A Legion did present / Celestiall service to attend / King *Charles*, and him from harm defend."[40] Another of Parker's ballads, "When the King Enjoys His Own Again" (1643), became one of the most influential songs in English history. After the beheading of Charles I, the ballad's comforting assurance "A golden time is drawing near . . . When the King comes home in peace again" sustained royalists' hopes for an end of Puritan rule and the return of Charles II.[41]

This optimistic tone was uncharacteristic of the culture war, which bristled with insults. Even the godly Puritans spewed venom. In his acidic pamphlet *Anti-Cavalierisme*, John Goodwin denounced "infamous persons in all kindes, with that bloody and butcherly Generation, commonly knowne by the name of Cavaliers." Goodwin dubbed the Cavaliers a "Legion of Devils" whose aim was "to advance the tyrannicall Thrones of the Hierarchie to their former heighth, or higher, power, . . . to excommunicate and cast out all the pure and precious Ordinances of God out of his House, and to supply this defect with Antichristian, and spurious institutions."[42] William Walwyn pointed out the unfairness of "speeches only against the Puritan for plucking a [church] raile downe, or a paire of Organs, a Surplice, Crucifix, or painted window," while the facts about "daily plunderings, rapes, and murthers of the Cavaliers, women with child runne through, and many other butcheries" were ignored.[43] William Prynne decried King Charles's "Army of theevish murthering Cavaliers" who "utterly sacked and ruined" towns;

Prynne dwelt on the "*beastly crueltie* of his Majesties Cavaliers in chayning together in Ropes sundry Prisoners taken at *Brainford, Marleborough* and *Cicester* . . . like a company of *Turkish Gally-slaves.*"[44]

Cavalier authors answered in kind. "*What is a Puritan?*" asked a royalist pamphlet. "A Puritan, is one of the pestilent party, the very plague of the Church and Common-wealth . . . one that breathes nothing but sedition and calumnies . . . a phanatick spirit; with whom you may find greater ingratitude, more lies, and viler perjuries, then amongst the most infamous theeves."[45] In the 1642 broadside *The Devil's Last Legacy*, a demon hails a "Round-headed Ironmonger" as "my deare Adopted Sonne . . . my onely joy and hope"; he commands the Roundhead, "Let not a Bishop in the Land have power, neither let the Churches stand, pull down all and abolish the light, that we may live in darknesse."[46] A Cavalier poem described the parliamentary leader John Pym as a "poysonous man" and "a man whom even the Devil to fear begins. . . . A man who is now wading through the Floud / Of Reverend *Lauds* and Noble *Straffords* Bloud."[47] Cavaliers lambasted Parliament's twelve-year ban on celebrations of Christmas, Easter, Whitsunday, and other holy days, which Puritans regarded as "popish" festivals. One Cavalier ballad announced, "This Christmas time 'tis fit that we / Should feast, and sing, and merry be. . . . But such have been these times of late, / That holidays are out of date" because of Puritans, who "despise and scorn / To keep the day that Christ was born."[48]

Of all the charges that the Cavaliers made against Puritanism, the one that came closest to being true was the disintegration of a unified Puritan viewpoint. A Cavalier poem used sensational images to describe the mix of voices in England's Puritan-dominated Parliament: "Should Ravens, Bats, and the shrill Owl conspire / To twist their Notes into a General Quire," they could not produce "strains so Jarring, as do those whose throats / Warble the clamorous and untunefull Notes / . . . some whirle-wind, Sirs, has ta'en / Its Lodging up in the Fanatick brain / Of these bold sons of tumult, I dare say."[49]

The tendency of Puritanism toward fragmentation is most memorably captured by the royalist poet Samuel Butler in his influential mock-epic poem *Hudibras*, written in three parts (1663, 1664, and 1678). Butler's quixotic protagonist, Hudibras, is a self-righteous Presbyterian who rides around with a foolish squire. Among Hudibras's many flaws is his tendency to get lost in a maze of conflicting religious doctrines. An ever-changing Puritan, Hudibras acts "As if religion were intended / For nothing else but to be mended. / A sect, whose chief devotion lies / In odd perverse antipathies." Hudibras "could distinguish, and divide / A hair 'twixt south, and south-west side: / On either which he would dispute, / Confute, change hands, and still confute."[50]

Two centuries later, in 1848, a critic of abolitionism would quote these lines to denigrate various factions of the American antislavery movement that he had witnessed at a reform convention. But it was precisely the bubbling up of viewpoints within Puritanism that eventually yielded revolutionary reforms. Ralph Waldo Emerson recognized this important aspect of history. In his 1844 lecture "New England Reformers," he declared that the "fertile forms of antinomianism among the elder puritans, seemed to have their match in the plenty of the new harvest of reform."[51]

## NEW ENGLANDERS RADICALIZE THE MOTHER COUNTRY

Emerson was perceptive in recognizing antinomianism as a source of reform. The antinomian controversy of 1636–37 in the Massachusetts Bay Colony proved to be a seismic event that accelerated the disruption of English Puritanism, foreshadowing more fragmentation and experimentation to come. When the rebellious Anne Hutchinson shocked Boston magistrates by insisting that divine grace outweighed human law, she was supported by the forward-looking Puritan politician Henry

Vane Jr. Vane, having fled England to America for religious reasons, had been elected at twenty-three as governor of the Massachusetts Bay Colony. In 1636, he came into conflict with other Puritan magistrates by defending the meetings she held for women, which later resulted in her banishment from the colony for heresy. In the wake of the event, Vane wrote a pamphlet on religious toleration that became the first of the publications he produced on the separation of church and state. He made the democratic declaration that all humans "subjecting themselves to rulers and lawes" in society must remember that "*no man hath lawfulle power over another but by consent*" and "*no man can have a just interest in that which belongeth to another, without his consent*"—a passage that in 1775 would impel Reverend Jonathan Boucher, a Tory opponent of the American Revolution, to call Vane a misguided originator of the "fantastical systems of polity" discussed by Puritan dissenters during the English Civil War and developed by John Locke, with his "ill-founded and false" social compact theory.[52]

Replaced in 1637 as governor by John Winthrop, Vane returned to England and joined the parliamentary cause.[53] Over the next twelve years, he served in Parliament several times and became a leading Puritan voice in England. One of his most important moments came in 1643, when extreme tension arose between the main groups of Puritans in Parliament: Presbyterians, Independents, and a widening range of sectarians whose radical ideas—later embraced by Levellers seeking legal reform and by Diggers denouncing private property as a root of evil—laid bare the movement's deep ideological rifts.

The groups were united in their hostility toward the Anglican Church, which they sought to uproot, but disagreed about what should replace it. Presbyterians called for a hierarchical structure of synods and assemblies to control local churches. Independents (or Congregationalists) favored autonomous churches without an overarching governing council. Levellers stood opposed to any structure or even any fixed doctrine. What mattered to them was the individual's relationship with God. Churches, creeds, and, for some Levellers, even the Bible were secondary to personal belief.

Open to dissenting opinions, Henry Vane did what he could to prevent a backlash of repression by orthodox Puritans. Parliament, after early losses to royalist forces, had reached out to Scotland for military aid. Scotland agreed to supply troops in exchange for Parliament's pledge to accept the Presbyterian Solemn League and Covenant. In effect, Presbyterianism would replace Anglicanism as England's official religion. This prospect was acceptable to Parliament's Presbyterian majority but not to other Puritan MPs, who were mainly Independents or Levellers. Henry Vane, the tolerant Congregationalist from New England, protected minority religious rights by suggesting some deceptively simple words to the Presbyterian pledge. England, instead of changing its religion "according to the example of the best Reformed Churches [i.e., Presbyterianism]," would revise it, in Vane's language, "according to the Word of God, and the example of the best Reformed Churches."[54] The phrase opened the possibility for a multitude of personal interpretations of the Bible by dissenters.

Gestures toward toleration also came from two other radical Puritans: the poet and pamphleteer John Milton and the visiting New Englander Roger Williams. The two men became friends and perhaps read drafts of each other's manuscripts.[55] Milton's tract *Areopagitica* (1644) protested against a law passed by Parliament that mandated governmental licensing of books before their publication—a Presbyterian replacement of the former repressive policies of the now-disestablished Church of England. Milton, who had been censured for his writings on divorce, denounced such prepublication censorship and made an impassioned plea for freedom of speech. Although the suppression of books would not decline in England until the 1690s, Milton's *Areopagitica* had a long-term impact on debates over free speech.

Roger Williams's book *The Bloudy Tenent of Persecution*, published in London while Williams was there in 1644, argued for religious toleration so boldly that the Presbyterian Parliament had copies of it burned. Williams took Puritanism's belief in private interpretations of the Bible to the extreme of demanding a complete separation of church and state, a position that Williams shared with Henry Vane. The two men had been close to each other in New England. When Williams was exiled from Massachusetts, Vane helped him negotiate with a Narragansett sachem for the land that became Providence. When Williams went to England in the 1640s, Henry Vane worked with Sir Robert Rich to secure a charter for Rhode Island. Having helped Williams, Henry Vane became a hero among Rhode Islanders, a group of whom wrote him in 1654, "We have long drunck of the cup of as great liberties as any people we can heare of under the whole Heaven," free of "the iron yoaks of wolfish Bishops" and "the new chains of the Presbyterians tyrants," due largely to Vane. Thanking Vane for being "so noble and true a friend to an outcast and despised people," the Rhode Islanders wrote, "From the first beginning of this Providence Colonie . . . we reaped the sweete fruits of your constant loving-kindness and favour towards us."[56]

Vane also won high praise from prominent thinkers who would carry his Puritan ideas toward republican government and democracy. Vane's fellow parliamentarian Algernon Sidney, the prophet of republicanism, remarked that England "had not another man equal to [Vane] in virtue, prudence, courage, industry, reputation and godliness."[57] Milton wrote a sonnet celebrating "*Vane*, young in years, but in sage Councils old, / Than whom a better Senator ne'er held / The Helm of *Rome* . . . / on thy right hand Religion leans, / And reckons thee in chief her Eldest Son."[58] Milton appreciated Vane's openness to free discussion on religion. A uniquely creative Puritan seeker, Milton appears to have written the sonnet shortly after Vane published *Zeal Examined* (1652), a defense of freedom of conscience.

The Presbyterians, in contrast, were appalled by the growth of Puritan sects. They saw the religiously diverse New England as a source of dangerous heresies. The *Mayflower* passengers and their leader, John Robinson, were singled out for blame. Robert Baillie, an eminent Presbyterian, wrote that the Congregational churches in New England brought forth "the foulest heresies that ever yet were heard of in any Protestant Church"—all stemming originally from Plymouth Colony.[59] In Baillie's telling, early English nonconformists had fled to Leiden, where under "Master *Robinson*," they became committed to separatism. Afterward, "a part of them did carry it over to *Plymouth* in New-England" and "did perswade their neighbours who sate down with them there at *New-Plymouth*, to erect with them a Congregation after their separate way."

The hostility toward New England–nurtured nonconformity was heightened by the publication of the sensational three-part tract *Gangraena* by the Presbyterian clergyman Thomas Edwards. Strongly opposed to toleration, Edwards wrote, "Independency, and many other opinions being first broached in *New-England* have come over into *Old*."[60] He attacked Roger Williams's pro-toleration book *The Bloudy Tenent of Persecution* and blasted another visitor from New England, Samuel Gorton, for "venting strange and horrid opinions."[61]

Edwards's critique intensified the Presbyterian Parliament's concern over nonconformists. Parliament passed the infamous Heresy Ordinance, which went into effect in the spring of 1648. This law called for the suppression of "all private and separate Congregations" and imposed legal penalties on "all Anabaptists, Brownists, Hereticks, Schismaticks, Blasphemers, and all such Sectaries."[62] Anyone who spoke out against Presbyterian views on predestination, infant baptism, or heavenly reward for an elect few (the rest were destined for hell) could be imprisoned for life. For questioning the Holy Trinity or criticizing the Bible, the offender was to be branded with *B* (for blasphemy) on the left cheek; a second offense brought the death penalty.[63] The Episcopalian Star Chamber, with its cruelties, had been abolished in 1641, but a grim Presbyterian version of it had arisen.

The law's harshest penalties were rarely enforced, but some well-known dissenters were imprisoned, including the Levellers William Walwyn, Richard Overton, and John Lilburne. Walwyn promoted tolerance for all religions and argued that hell didn't exist; he claimed all believers would be saved. Overton stated that the soul died with the body and wouldn't rise until Judgment Day. Lilburne, Overton's friend and a persistent opponent of intolerance, held an unwavering opposition to religious and political oppression that led to multiple imprisonments from 1645 until his death in 1657. Nonetheless, prison did not prevent Lilburne and his fellow Levellers from producing controversial writings that reached a wide audience when published by underground presses.

The spread of Leveller ideas led to the New Model Army's historic Agreement of the People, which outlined a new English constitution. In its final version of May 1649, it called for suffrage for most adult men, religious freedom, biennial parliamentary elections, term limits for elected officials, equality before the law, clear legal codes written in English instead of Latin or Norman French, a provision against self-incrimination in court, the end of debtors' prisons, and the abolition of the death penalty for crimes other than murder.

As these proposed democratic reforms suggest, the Levellers and the Diggers were the most forward-looking of all the Puritan groups in England. Popular voting was anticipated by Lilburne's declaration that "all lawfull powers reside in the people, for whose good, welfare, and happinesse, all government and just policies were ordained."[64] Because all humans are equal in the sight of God, the Levellers argued, no one can claim control of others unless through mutual consent. Here is Lilburne again:

> Every particular and individuall man and woman, that ever breathed in the world since [Adam and Eve], are, and were, by nature all equall and alike in power, dignity, authority,

> and majesty, none of them having any authority dominion or majesteriall power, one over, or above another, . . . [except] by mutuall consent given, and agreement, for the good, benefit, and comfort [of] each other.[65]

Richard Overton wrote similarly:

> For by naturall birth, all men are equally and alike borne to like propriety, liberty and freedome, and as we are delivered of God by the hand of nature into this world, every one with a naturall, innate freedome and propriety (as it were writ in the table of every mans heart, never to be obliterated) even so are we to live, every one equally and alike to enjoy his Birthright and priviledge; even all whereof God by nature hath made him free.[66]

The historian Henry Noel Brailsford observes, "Neither slavery nor imperialism could survive where these principles were honestly professed"; also, "unmistakably they end the subjection of women"—an insight affirmed by adventurous Leveller women like Elizabeth Lilburne, who got thousands of women to sign petitions on behalf of her imprisoned husband, and Katherine Chidley, who declared that women were "equal unto men" under God and had "an equal interest with the men" in "the good laws of the land."[67]

Such radically Puritan ideas would eventually filter into the body of thought that nurtured American democracy, but they did not gain immediate traction in England. The Levellers became increasingly alienated from Oliver Cromwell, who rejected their ultrademocratic Agreement of the People, which he thought would breed anarchy with its unprecedented expansiveness on voting and religious freedom.

The situation was exacerbated by the fiery Hugh Peters (aka Peter), an unorthodox British clergyman who had spent five years in New

England before returning in 1641 to his home country, where he served as a chaplain for the Parliamentary army. Peters at first sided with both Levellers and Independents but then shifted his loyalty fully to the latter. Peters played a major role in bringing King Charles to trial before a faction of the House of Commons, an idea Lilburne, despite his dislike for the monarchy, considered a shocking breach of justice.[68] When the king was kept under house arrest at St. James's Palace, Peters was his jailer. During the trial, Peters goaded the parliamentary court by leading chants of "Justice. Justice" and "Execution. Execution" to drown out cries of "God save the king" from the gallery.[69] Days before Charles was executed, Peters gave a sermon based on Psalm 149: "I will bind their King in chains and their nobles in fetters of iron." He declared that "we will cut off the king's head. . . . Turn to your Bibles and you shall find it there: Whosoever sheds man's blood, by man shall his blood be shed."

After the king's death, a commonwealth was established that was governed by a forty-member Council of State that gagged the press, forbade soldiers from meeting, and outlawed political sermons by preachers. Levellers, their democratic dreams dashed, branded the new administration as a despotism headed by Cromwell, whom they now saw as a hypocrite. The imprisoned Lilburne told Hugh Peters, "If it were possible for me to chus, I had rather chus to live seven years under old King Charls his government . . . then one year under the present Government."[70] The Levellers attempted a military rebellion but were crushed by Cromwell. Thus ended the Leveller movement as a potent force in England.

The Rump Parliament continued until 1653, when Cromwell dissolved it through military action. (The Rump was soon replaced by the smaller Barebone's Parliament—named after one of its Puritan members, Praise-God Barebone—which in turn would be replaced by the Protectorate Parliament under Cromwell.) With regard to the Rump, Cromwell was especially bothered by Henry Vane's efforts to democ-

OLIVER CROMWELL
*Portrait by Samuel Cooper, 1856*

ratize the government by getting rid of so-called rotten boroughs, where wealth bought political representation. On April 20, Cromwell rose in Parliament and declared, "You are no parliament, I say you are no parliament; I will put an end to your sitting." At his order, a troop of soldiers entered the building and removed the MPs, including Vane and Algernon Sidney. Vane declared, "This is not honest, yea, it is against morality and common honesty." Cromwell snarled, "Sir Henry Vane, Sir Henry Vane, the Lord deliver me from Sir Henry Vane."[71]

Vane left the political arena for a time but reentered it when Cromwell issued a public call in 1656 for constructive ideas that might strengthen his government, which had witnessed military defeat in the West Indies and political failures at home. Henry Vane responded to the appeal by publishing *A Healing Question*, in which he advocated for greater religious freedom and a representative government established through a constitutional convention (a precursor to the US Constitutional Convention of 1787). Seen as an attack on Cromwell's reign, *A Healing Question* was judged to be "a seditious book" and resulted in prison time for Vane.[72] Vane, the tolerant Puritan ex–New Englander who had helped found the democratic colony of Rhode Island, was punished by Cromwell, the authoritarian English Puritan who had established military rule.

The clash between Cromwellian Puritanism and radical New England Puritanism soon became violent. Thomas Venner, a Puritan who had lived in Massachusetts for over twenty years, moved to England and devised a plot to assassinate Cromwell, whom he regarded as a tyrant. More than anyone else, Venner exemplified the historian John N. Blanton's description of Massachusetts as "a hotbed of anti-monarchist radicalism."[73] Venner had served for years in the Massachusetts militia. He took Puritanism to a militant extreme. A so-called Fifth Monarchist, he opposed slavery and earthly monarchs, anticipating the return of King Jesus. He and other former New Englanders, including John Clarke, a Rhode Island Baptist, and Wentworth Day from Massachusetts, met at Venner's home near St. Katharine Docks on the Thames in London, in an area where homeless people, vagrants, and Cromwell's political enemies were shipped to join enslaved Africans and Indigenous people working in the West Indies. Venner's group issued a manifesto mourning the shedding of "the blood of many thousands" and the loss of their "banished neighbors . . . sold for slaves to serve like beasts the will and lust of great men."[74] When Cromwell's attempted takeover of Hispaniola failed, the Fifth Monarchists declared that God had "blasted" the "wickedness" of Cromwell's "designs" to place "perfect yokes on the bodies and consciences of men."

In 1657, Venner and his comrades planned the overthrow of Cromwell. The scheme failed, and Venner was captured and imprisoned. A year after Cromwell's death in 1658, Henry Vane secured freedom for Venner and other jailed rebels. But the Restoration brought more political turmoil. Venner hatched another assassination plot, this time against the restored Stuart king, Charles II. In a tract promoting "*Civill Liberty*, and Rights of men," the Fifth Monarchists urged people to rise against the king, against "Bishops, and Hierarchy, and against these Cavaliers, whose wickedness it is not fit to name, who have already polluted the Land as venomous and unclean Creatures."[75] The tract also denounced the trade in the "*Slaves and Souls of men*," insisting that "man-stealers be punished with death" and predicting that "the true Church . . . will be brought out of the wilderness"—an allusion to the New England roots of Venner and several of his antislavery followers.

In January 1661, Venner and his band launched a bloody uprising that lasted four days and cost more than forty lives. During the rebellion, Venner and his group attacked a jail in an attempt to free prisoners who were slated to be sold away as bondslaves. Caught and brought to trial, Venner and twelve followers were sentenced to death. They were subsequently hanged, drawn, and quartered.[76] Their limbs were chopped off and displayed on city gates. Their heads were removed and stuck on poles affixed to the Tower of London or London Bridge.

Hugh Peters met the same fate as Venner and his men. Peters had won a high position in Cromwell's administration and had preached the sermon at the Lord Protector's funeral. But under Charles II, he found himself in peril. Charles was intent on punishing those who had participated in the beheading of his father. About twenty regicides had fled abroad. Among those still in England, nineteen stood trial; ten were executed, the rest imprisoned for life.[77] Hugh Peters was a special target of Charles II due to his active role in Charles I's execution. In October 1660, Peters was brought to trial, found guilty of treason, and condemned to die. In the cart that took him to the scaffold, Peters sat with a fellow regicide, John Cook, the prosecutor at the trial of Charles I, whose execution Peters was forced to watch. After castrating, disemboweling, and quartering Cook, the executioner said, "Come, how do you like this, Mr. Peters, how do you like this work?"[78] Peters replied coolly, "I am not, I thank God, terrified at it, you may do your worst." John Cook's execution, he said, was obviously intended "to terrify and discourage me," but "God hath made it an ordinance to me for my strengthening and encouragement." The executioner did his gruesome job. When he put Peters's head on a spear and raised it high, the mass of spectators exploded with cheering. The head was installed on a pole along with others on London Bridge.

Henry Vane was also executed, but under different circumstances from the regicides. Vane had been one of the few Independents in Parliament who had not participated in the sentencing of Charles I. He considered the entire spectacle unconstitutional and unjust. This attitude, along with his disagreements with Cromwell, led Charles II to initially include Vane among the Puritans who would be pardoned and exempted from punishment. But Charles changed his mind when advisers argued that Vane remained a dangerous presence because of his republican tendencies. Vane was convicted of treason and given the death penalty. He approached his death cheerfully and with Christian confidence. Emerson, who put Vane among "the democrats, as well as the saints of their times," saw Vane's heroic death as one of history's shining moments.[79] Emerson wrote, "When Sir Harry Vane was dragged up the Tower-hill, sitting on a sled, to suffer death, as the champion of the English laws, one of the multitude cried out to him, '*You never sate on so glorious a seat.*'" Vane had prepared a written speech that he hoped to read aloud on the scaffold, but he was prevented from doing so. Anticipating the interference, he had left behind a copy of the speech, in which he repeated his oft-told arguments for political liberty and religious toleration. He was awarded a relatively benign form of execution: beheading.

Others who had been more directly involved in the killing of Charles

I were treated more harshly. The corpses of Oliver Cromwell and two other regicides, John Bradshaw and Henry Ireton, were exhumed and desecrated.[80] The bodies were brought to the scaffold at Tyburn and hanged for hours before being decapitated. The trunks of their skeletons were buried at the scaffold site. The heads were sent for display on top of Westminster Hall. Cromwell's head, perched on a long wooden pole with an iron spike, remained a public spectacle for decades. Both the head and the pole reportedly became infested with worms and, in the 1680s, blew down during a storm. Its later fate is uncertain.

While such atrocities showed that the underlying Cavalier-vs.-Puritan enmity persisted, the rule of Charles II was met with widespread relief after the chaos of the war years. His father's execution day, January 30, became a holy day on the Anglican calendar: the day of "Charles, King and Martyr, 1649."[81] Statues and pictures of the martyred king proliferated. The Parliament elected under Charles II was called the Cavalier Parliament. It was now the Anglicans' turn to enforce religious rule. The Cavalier Parliament issued new laws that barred Protestant dissenters and Catholics from worshipping openly. Those who did not accept the forms and rituals of the Anglican Church were expelled. Religious conformity ruled. Toleration was anathema. Many Presbyterian ministers were ejected from their livings; meetings of Quakers, Baptists, or Fifth Monarchists were banned. Especially harsh measures were taken against Quakers, who faced trials, fines, imprisonment, or deportation.[82]

## MILTON, SIDNEY, AND LOCKE CHALLENGE DIVINE RULE

A few thoughtful observers who had been weaned by the Puritan Revolution witnessed the ongoing cultural battles and made striking advances in political and religious thought.

The English Civil War had witnessed tens of thousands of casualties and terrible acts of persecution on both sides.[83] Overall, however, the war destabilized monarchy and church hierarchy while introducing democratic principles that would contribute to the creation of the United States and, eventually, the abolition of slavery. Key to the expression of these principles were thinkers shaped in the crucible of the war, notably John Milton, Algernon Sidney, and John Locke.

Milton served as the secretary for Foreign Tongues to the Council of State under Oliver Cromwell during the Commonwealth and the Protectorate (1649–60). He translated foreign correspondence and wrote promotional material for the Cromwellian government. After 1652, when he went blind from an eye condition, he directed assistants in his work.

Politically, Milton had followed the Puritan revolutionary pattern. After publishing poetry in the 1630s, he became so frustrated and exasperated by the persecution of Puritans under Archbishop Laud that he published several antiprelacy tracts in the early 1640s. He briefly accepted Presbyterianism, but its goal of becoming England's dominant religion and its strict book licensing policy made him realize that "*New Presbyter* is but *Old Priest* writ Large."[84] His hostility to censorship informed his defense of free speech in *Areopagitica* (1644). His tolerant attitude explains his openness to the religious debates by Independents and Levellers later that decade.

Milton strongly supported the execution of King Charles, whom he viewed as a criminal tyrant. His defense of the regicide, *The Tenure of Kings and Magistrates*, appeared on February 13, 1649, two weeks after the beheading of the king. One of Milton's first writings as part of the administration of the Puritan Commonwealth was *Eikonoklastes* ("The Image Breaker"), a slashing rejoinder to *Eikon Basilike* ("The Image of a King"), the "autobiography" of Charles that had been ghostwritten by the Anglican bishop John Gauden. Milton's anti-Charles pamphlet did not enjoy the popularity of the hagiographic *Eikon*, which went through many editions and nurtured the enduring myth of Charles the Martyr. But Milton established himself as a potent foe of monarchist government.

As a government official during the Puritan interregnum, Milton wrote a sonnet praising Oliver Cromwell as "our chief of Men."[85] Although he soured on the authoritarian Cromwell, he supported the Puritan Revolution as a whole and grew alarmed when it ended after Cromwell's death and Richard Cromwell's aborted protectorship. In a 1659 tract, Milton glumly predicted the return of another Stuart monarch who "must be ador'd like a Demigod, with a dissolute and haughtie Court about him, of vast expence and luxurie, masks and revels, to the debauching of our prime gentry both male and female."[86]

When Charles II gained power, Milton miraculously evaded punishment. He went into hiding, was briefly imprisoned, and then was released. He was luckier than the Puritan author John Bunyan, who was jailed for twelve years under Charles II because he was a Baptist who held meetings in his home. Both Bunyan and Milton turned to literary expression as a way of making veiled attacks on the Stuart monarchy—Bunyan in *The Pilgrim's Progress* and Milton in his epic poems, most notably *Paradise Lost*.[87] A clarion voice against tyranny on behalf of toleration and free speech, Milton influenced America's founders, especially John Adams and Thomas Jefferson, and nineteenth-century antislavery leaders like John Quincy Adams and Charles Sumner, who cited Milton in their battles against the Southern slave power.

Another forerunner of progressive reform, Algernon Sidney, emerged from an aristocratic Puritan background and became one of history's great defenders of republicanism and popular consent. Like Milton, Sidney was shaped by the Puritan Revolution. He served in the parliamentary army, rose in the ranks, and fought heroically at Marston Moor, where he was severely wounded. In 1645, he was elected to the Long Parliament and became a major force there. Although he was on the commission that put Charles I on trial, he withdrew from it because he disagreed with its activities. He thereafter served in the Rump Parliament, but, like his friend Henry Vane, he was forcibly removed from it when Cromwell dissolved the Rump in 1653. After Cromwell's death and the short reign of Cromwell's son, Sidney joined the reconvened Rump Parliament, but that didn't last long, because General George Monck, who had served under both Charles and Cromwell, intervened and brought about the return of Charles II.

Sidney, a known participant in the Puritan Revolution, was in danger of imprisonment under the strict Anglican rules of the Cavalier Parliament. He spent seventeen years in European exile, living in Italy, France, and other countries. For family reasons, Sidney returned to England in 1677 and soon became embroiled in the Exclusion Crisis, a period marked by the prospect of Charles II's being succeeded by his Catholic brother, James Stuart, which stirred anger among Anglicans and other Protestants. Then came the publication of Robert Filmer's *Patriarcha*, a highly influential defense of the divine right of kings. Filmer had died in 1653, having published several other pro-monarchy tracts. *Patriarcha*, written around 1637, remained unpublished until its appearance in 1680, just as the question of kingly succession was a hot issue. Filmer argued that God had given Adam dominion of the world, and kings since then were descended from Adam, so that there was a string of divine kingship that stretched all the way from the Garden of Eden to modern times. This specious claim was taken seriously by defenders of the monarchy.

Sidney was infuriated by Filmer's book and by its enthusiastic reception among royalists. He had a Puritan-inspired radical side, nurtured especially by his time in the Cromwellian army, that had surfaced in his signing a guest book in Denmark with the inscription *Manus haec inimica tyrannis, ense petit placidam cum libertate quietem*; "this hand, hostile to tyrants, seeks by the sword the tranquil peace of freedom."[88] (To this day, a version of Sidney's militant statement remains the official motto of the Commonwealth of Massachusetts and the University of Massachusetts Amherst.)

In the early 1680s, Sidney wrote what became his influential two-volume book *Discourses Concerning Government*, which was published after his death. The first volume made a point-by-point refutation of Filmer's argument, which Sidney exposed as a tissue of ahistorical absurdities. The second volume presented Sidney's views of government by consent. Sidney attacked Filmer's argument that a king, as a divinely appointed patriarch, is above the law. For Sidney, law is the highest product of humanity—"It is void of desire and fear, lust and anger. It is *Mens sine affect* ["mind without passion"], written reason, retaining some measure of the divine perfection."[89] At the same time, Sidney knew that some leaders, especially ones unleashed from legislatures (such as Charles I during his Personal Rule or Charles II, who dissolved Parliament during the Exclusion Crisis), could issue self-serving, oppressive laws. Therefore, Sidney insisted on the right to rebel against unjust laws. In 1683, Sidney became implicated in the Rye House Plot, a putative conspiracy to assassinate King Charles II and his brother James. Although Sidney was only tangentially related to the supposed plot, he was brought to trial for treason. Two witnesses were required for a conviction, but in his case, there was only one witness, an alleged coconspirator. Sidney's anti-monarchical manuscript, which had been discovered in his study, was presented to the court as a second "witness" on the unusual premise of *scribere est agere* ("to write is to act"). Sidney was convicted of treason and languished in jail until his beheading on December 7, 1683. On the scaffold, he handed over a paper listing nine principles he stood for, the first four of which summarize his contribution to political thought:

> That God had left Nations unto the Liberty of setting up such Governments as best pleased themselves.

> That Magistrates were set up for the good of Nations, not Nations for the honour or glory of Magistrates.
>
> That the Right and Power of Magistrates in every Country, was that which the laws of that Country made it to be.
>
> That those Laws were to be observed, and the Oaths taken by them, having the force of a Contract between Magistrate and People, could not be Violated without danger of dissolving the whole Fabrick.[90]

After his death, Sidney was vilified by Tories, who supported the monarchy. But for the emerging Whig Party, advocates of a constitutional monarchy with strong limits on royal power, he became a martyr to liberty. James II assumed the throne in 1685, but escalating problems during his rule led to his abdication and exile to France two years later. The Glorious Revolution occurred in 1688 with the accession of James's Protestant daughter Mary II and her husband, the Dutch sovereign William of Orange—not the republican government Sidney had envisaged, but preferable to the Stuart monarchy. In 1689, Parliament posthumously reversed Sidney's conviction, which was declared to be unjust. His *Discourses* appeared in 1698. Although wordy and repetitive, the *Discourses* contained numerous forceful statements about human rights, republicanism, and the need for virtue in high places, making the book a major source of inspiration for the Founding Fathers and nineteenth-century abolitionists.

Equally influential was John Locke, who was also weaned by Puritanism. Locke had been raised in a Calvinist household. His father served as a captain in the cavalry of the Parliamentary army during the English Civil War.

Despite his Puritan background, Locke grew tired of the era's upheavals and was briefly won over by Thomas Hobbes's *Leviathan* (1651), which presented the monarchy as the only bulwark against the chaos of sects and factions unleashed by Puritanism—what Hobbes called the "many strange and many pernicious Doctrines . . . [that] distracted their Auditors into a great number of Sects, as *Brownists, Anabaptists, Independents, Fifth-Monarchy Men, Quakers*, and divers others, all commonly called by the name of *Fanaticks*."[91]

Locke at first welcomed the Restoration. During the civil war years, he recalled, the country had swung between "*tyranny* and *anarchy*," so that "human affairs are perpetually kept tumbling."[92] He explained, "Exhausted as we are by so bitter a clash of opinions and of arms, we ought to rest content with our liberty and quiet." But Charles II and the Cavalier Parliament did not bring liberty or quiet. Those outside the Church of England were under the constant threat of punishment under the harsh Clarendon Code, a series of laws that enforced Anglicanism. Fortunately, Locke came under the wing of one of England's most powerful politicians, Lord Anthony Ashley Cooper. In 1668, Locke, who had been trained as a doctor, was part of a team of surgeons who drained an infected cyst above Cooper's liver. Soon Locke lived in the lord's home as a personal physician, secretary, and confidant.

Cooper had a remarkably varied history. Having been raised among aristocratic Presbyterians, he served in the Short Parliament but was not elected for the Long Parliament. At that point, he switched sides and joined the royalist army. His sympathies, however, lay with the Puritans, and soon he won a seat in the Long Parliament. Cooper swore to the Presbyterian Solemn League and Covenant and went on to be a member of Cromwell's Council of State. After the Protectorate, he encouraged General Monck's takeover of London and the return of Charles II. The king rewarded him with a succession of appointments: Chancellor of the Exchequer, Lord Chancellor, and, in 1672, designation as the First Earl of Shaftesbury. In all his capacities, Cooper encouraged the king to extend toleration to Protestant dissenters (but not to Catholics). Due to the intransigence of the Cavalier Parliament and the High Church bishops, these efforts were largely unsuccessful. In a widely read public letter of 1675, Cooper lamented that "the High Episcopal Man, and the Old Cavalier" were "enjoying all the Power and Office of the Kingdom," producing an "*absolute* and *Arbitrary*" government that was "not to be bounded, or limited by humane Laws."[93] Thereafter, Cooper became increasingly intent on barring from power Charles's Catholic brother and heir apparent, James Stuart. Now a radical leader of the new Whig faction, Cooper headed the Parliament's unsuccessful exclusion campaign between 1679 and 1681. Imprisoned for a short time on a charge of treason, in 1682 Cooper fled to the Netherlands, where he died.

For opponents, Cooper was seen as a slippery opportunist—a "Dorsetshire-Eel," as one critic called him, or, in Samuel Butler's words in *Hudibras*, a "state-camelion" who "Could turn his word, and oath, and faith, / As many ways, as in a lathe."[94] But John Locke hailed him as "a fierce, tireless advocate of civil and religious freedom."[95] The adaptable Cooper and the topsy-turvy events he responded to helped Locke develop views on toleration, individual rights, and republican government that he would make famous in *Two Treatises of Government*, written during the Exclusion Crisis (1679–83) and published in 1689. Like Sidney, Locke was on the fringes of the Rye House Plot aimed at killing the king. Unlike Sidney, he was able to escape punishment by fleeing to Holland for six years. When he returned to England in 1689, he accompanied Mary, the new Protestant queen, who would rule England alongside her cousin and husband, William of Orange. Locke continued writing and served in several official roles in the new government. His *Two Treatises of Government*, designed, as he wrote in the preface, "to establish the Throne of our great restorer, or present King William," made him known as the Whig scribe of the Glorious Revolution.[96]

Like Sidney's *Discourses*, Locke's *Two Treatises* refuted Robert Filmer's theory of patriarchal monarchy. Locke writes of Filmer, "There was never so much glib nonsense put together in well-sounding English."[97] Given this dismissiveness, it may appear odd that Locke would devote much of the *Two Treatises* to responding to Filmer. But Locke was painfully aware that his Tory contemporaries considered Filmer's *Patriarcha* an irrefutable defense of Stuart absolutism. Locke explained that he was answering those who were "so zealous" in "crying up [Filmer's] books and espousing his doctrine." Filmer argued that Adam, who was given control over creation by God, was the first of many patriarchs and kings to come. The fatherly principle, started by Adam and passed down through generations to the first son, underpinned the divine rule of patriarchal monarchs. As Filmer writes, "As *Adam* was Lord of his Children, so his Children under him, had a Command and Power over their own Children; but still with subordination to the First Parent, who is Lord Paramount over his Childrens Children to all Generations, as *being the Grand-Father of his People*."[98] Subjection to the father, then, was history's main rule. Primogeniture was in effect. The monarch, as the father of his people, rules by divine right, just as every father controls his family members with total dominion. Humans were born in a state of slavery, not freedom. The only independence they enjoy is the freedom to follow the dictates of the divinely appointed king.

Locke challenged Filmer on every point. Humans, Locke insisted, were not initially enslaved but were free and equal in a state of nature. Adam was the parent of everyone, not just of monarchs. And what about Eve? True, the father is important in a family, but so is the mother. Locke writes, "The mother cannot be denied an equal share in begetting of the child," and "no body can deny but that the woman hath an equal share, if not the greater, [in] nourishing the child."[99] Also, Locke points out, many monarchs throughout history have proven to be terrible. More often than not, "they have denied mankind a tight to natural freedom; whereby they have not only . . . exposed all subjects to the utmost misery of tyranny and oppression" but have served "for nothing but to unsettle and destroy all the lawful governments in the world, and to establish in their room disorder, tyranny and usurpation."

The only viable alternative to patriarchal monarchy, Locke contends, is republican government based on laws created by a legislature that the people have elected. Locke writes, "The people have a right to act as supreme, and continue the legislative in themselves; or erect a new form, or under the old form place it in new hands, as they think good."[100] Government, in other words, must be formed only by the assent of those governed. Locke emphasized mixed government, which combined elements of monarchy, aristocracy, and democracy. His recommended goal was an equilibrium between these elements—what Montesquieu would later call checks and balances. Locke now differed strongly from his earlier hero, the royalist Hobbes, who claimed that humans uncontrolled by an absolute monarch would always be, by their nature, in a state of war, which could lapse into chaos at any moment.

What explains the change in Locke's views? Richard Ashcraft convincingly argues that Locke's reconsideration of the Levellers caused this change.[101] Indeed, if we put Locke's statements on the sovereignty of the people, individual rights, human equality, and government by consent next to passages by the likes of Lilburne and Walwyn we see a line running from the radical Puritans of the 1640s to Locke—a continuum of democratic thinking that becomes even more striking when we recognize that Locke had a strong influence on Jefferson, whose egalitarian language in the Declaration of Independence would yield Lincoln's identification of America with human equality in the Gettysburg Address.[102]

But how do we square Locke's ideas on equality with his apparently complicated attitudes toward chattel slavery? Some commentators are understandably discomfited by his having drafted the Fundamental Constitutions of Carolina, which stipulate that "Every *Freeman* of *Carolina* shall have absolute Power and Authority over his *Negro Slaves*, of what Opinion or Religion soever."[103] But too much can be made of this seeming contradiction in Locke. In 1669, when he wrote the Carolina constitutions, he was under the direction of the eight royal proprietors of Carolina, six of whom were staunch royalists devoted to Charles II's proslavery agenda for England's colonial empire. The basic planks of the Carolina constitutions, therefore, were already determined when Locke recorded them on paper. He wrote, as Holly Brewer observes, "as a lawyer writes a will. He was paid to revise it and to make copies, and key principles of the document preceded his involvement."[104] Also, we should note that he copied (or, possibly, originated) the remarkable statement in the Constitutions that "it shall be lawful for *Slaves* as well as others, to Enter themselves, and be of what *Church* or *Profession* any of them shall think best, and therefore be as fully *Members* as any *Freeman*."

This open passage anticipated Locke's later efforts, when he was working under William and Mary, to promote the baptism of enslaved people in Virginia—another example of the recognition of Black personhood that, as we've seen, Frederick Douglass called one of the earliest steps toward abolitionism. Another of Locke's antislavery accomplishments was advocating for the reduction of the size of massive Virginia land plots, which were on the verge of becoming plantations worked by hundreds of enslaved people, into twenty-acre parcels owned by small landowners who typically used indentured servants. Locke can be assigned to the antislavery side, especially when we consider the language of his *Two Treatises of Government*, which opens with the ringing line: "Slavery is so vile and miserable an estate of man, and so directly opposite to the generous temper and courage of our nation; that it is hardly to be conceived, that an *Englishman*, much less a gentleman, should plead for it." Locke here means political slavery to a despot, but his statement led to abolitionist declarations. In 1764, the Patriot James Otis, a catalyst of the American Revolution, quoted the statement by "Mr. Locke" that "slavery is so vile and miserable an estate of man," which Otis applied to people of different colors. In Otis's words, "The [American] Colonists are by the law of nature free born, as indeed all men are, white or black." Otis added that "enslaving those of any color" was a "shocking violation of the law of nature."[105] The same Locke quotation about the vileness of slavery appeared in abolitionist newspapers from Garrison's *The Liberator* in 1832 to the *National Antislavery Standard* in 1865.[106]

Even as these forward-looking philosophers were articulating ideas that would blossom as American democracy and abolition, their hidebound contemporaries were solidifying such institutions. The conflict between the Puritan and Cavalier, which had fueled the English Civil War, did not die out. Indeed, it took on deeper political and cultural dimensions. The Jesuit writer William Darrell noted in 1717, "We have been divided almost these Two Hundred Years into Protestant [i.e., Anglican] and Puritan, Cavalier and Round-head, Tory and Whig."[107] That division would only become deeper.

Among the institutions supported by traditionalists, chattel slavery most glaringly violated human rights. Charles II's aim to entrench slavery in England's colonies led to the creation in 1660 of the Royal African Company, which fueled the international slave trade on a massive scale. Charles's association with the colonial expansion of slavery was inscribed on a new English coin, the guinea, introduced in 1663. Named after the West African region that England raided for enslaved people and gold, the coin's images included Charles II's head encircled by the text Carolus II Dei Gratia ("Charles II by the Grace of God") as well as an elephant and a coastal castle, symbols of the slave trade.[108] The Royal African Company's seal read BY ROYAL PATRONAGE TRADE FLOURISHES; it pictured the elephant, the castle, and two Africans supporting the admiralty anchor. A 1672 proclamation stamped with the company's seal established prices for "negroes" to be sold "to all His Majesties subjects, and especially to those Inhabiting the Plantations in AMERICA."

The "Plantations in America" rapidly joined the rush to expand slavery. During the 1660s, slave codes became much stricter in several of England's colonies, including Virginia, Barbados, and Carolina. Virginia's 1662 code, which made slavery transmissible across generations, was followed by the colony's 1667 law stating that baptism did not prevent enslaving a person—a bill that anticipated the Cavalier Parliament's landmark ruling in *Butts v. Penny* (1677) that Africans, who were "the subjects of an infidel prince," could not have allegiance to a Christian king and therefore were property, just like nonhuman things.[109]

Such laws were "not just," to use Sidney's words. Did they warrant a violent response, which Sidney considered permissible for unjust laws? Yes, in the eyes of reformers—many of them influenced by Puritanism—who believed enslaved people were human beings. But absolutely not for those who accepted the Cavalier view of enslaved people as mere property.

The latter view would blossom in the American South, while the former one would find root in New England and other parts of the North. The result would be a civil war far bloodier than the one that tore apart seventeenth-century England.

## *Chapter Five*

# THE RISE AND FALL OF THE VIRGINIA CAVALIER

The English Civil War sparked political and cultural conflicts between Cavaliers and Puritans in England's colonies in the Americas, notably Barbados and Virginia.

In Barbados, English settlers with differing views coexisted peacefully during the 1640s due to the unofficial Treaty of Turkey and Roast Pig, by which anyone who uttered the word "Cavalier" or "Roundhead" had to treat those present to a home-cooked feast—a friendly way of dampening tensions that yielded spontaneous parties.[1] This genial practice ceased after the 1649 beheading of King Charles, when many Cavaliers fled to Barbados, took over the island's government, announced the exiled Charles II as king, and confiscated the estates of leading Puritans. In response, Cromwell sent a fleet of ships that blockaded the island and subdued the Cavaliers, who accepted a treaty that restored the Puritans' estates and set up a puppet Cromwellian government but otherwise left the island autonomous. The Restoration brought the Cavaliers back to power on the island, but by then, profitable sugar production trumped political or religious differences. An influx of white indentured servants and enslaved Black people, combined with an expanding planter class, made Barbados "the richest and most populous colony in English America."[2] Increasingly reliant on enslaved workers for the torturous work of making sugar, Barbados in 1661 passed a slave code that denied the enslaved even the most basic human rights: their owners could torture or kill them without reprisal. The code presaged similar ones in the Southern colonies of North America, including Virginia.

The conflict between Cavaliers and Puritans in Virginia resembled the one in Barbados, although it broke out earlier in the Old Dominion than on the island and had far greater repercussions over time. The appointment in 1642 of Sir William Berkeley, a courtier of Charles I, as the governor of Virginia marked the start of decades during which the effects of the Wars of the Three Kingdoms spread through Virginia. This included a Cavalier crackdown on Puritans, followed by almost-war with Cromwell, then renewed loyalism during the Restoration, and in the 1670s, a reprise of the English Civil War in Bacon's Rebellion. Berkeley's triumph over the insurgent Nathaniel Bacon solidified the Cavalier culture that dominated Virginia thereafter. The colony's planter elite merged patriarchy, Anglicanism, and the exploitation of enslaved labor. The Cavalier-based bloc ruled Virginia for decades until it was fractured by economic and political change. However, the Cavalier ethos persisted and eventually spread throughout the South.

## WILLIAM BERKELEY AND THE EMPOWERMENT OF CAVALIERS

The stereotype of the Southern Cavalier was rooted in reality. As David Hackett Fischer notes, "The legend of the Virginia cavalier was no mere romantic myth. In all of its major parts, it rested upon a solid foundation of historical fact."[3] Although Cavalier refugees from England and their descendants never outnumbered other social groups, they gained dominance in the colony. Royalist families began arriving in Virginia in earnest during the 1640s and 1650s, coinciding with the English Civil War and the Cromwellian interregnum. Cavalier families became owners of vast tobacco plantations worked by white indentured servants and, increasingly, by enslaved Black people. Opening the door for the Cavaliers was the royalist governor, William Berkeley.

Berkeley (pronounced *Bark*-lee) was born in 1605 in Bruton, Somersetshire, the heart of the West Country of England, the seat of most Cavaliers (Puritans, in contrast, generally hailed from the counties in East Anglia, to the northeast of London).[4] The Berkeley family reached back to ancient England and encompassed generations of aristocrats who owned hundreds of square miles. It was said that at one point the Earl of Berkeley could ride from his castle near Bath to Berkeley Square in Westminster—a trip of 112 miles—without leaving his property.[5]

The sixth of seven children of Sir Maurice Berkeley and Elizabeth Killigrew Berkeley, William (known as Will) was raised in ancestral manors. He went on to earn degrees at Oxford and then took a two-year European tour, returning to England in 1632. Through a kinsman who was in the circle of King Charles I, he secured a position as a gentleman of the king's privy chamber. He befriended the wits and authors who were part of the royal entourage, including the Cavalier poets Thomas Carew and John Suckling. Berkeley dabbled in authorship. His play *The Lost Lady: A Tragy-Comedy*—a tangled drama about love, deception, and political intrigue—was staged for the king in 1637 and published the following year. During the First and Second Bishops' Wars, which triggered the Puritan Revolution, Berkeley soldiered in Charles's campaigns against the Scots, for which he was knighted. Parliament's remonstrance against the king and the execution of the Earl of Strafford alerted him to the peril of staying in England. He considered accepting a diplomatic post in Constantinople but then decided on Virginia. Why there? A clue may lie in what historians call the younger-son syndrome.[6] Because of England's custom of primogeniture, males born after the first son received sparse inheritances, impelling many of them to seek their fortunes in the American colonies, where they established estates of their own. Whether or not Berkeley had what would have been in his case fourth-son syndrome, he persuaded the king to appoint him as governor and captain general of Virginia. March 1642 found him in Jamestown, freshly installed in the governor's seat. He had to use courtly tact and payoffs to placate the man he replaced, Sir Francis Wyatt, a popular governor who had been in office since 1639.

Berkeley served as governor from 1642 to 1676, with an eight-year hiatus during the Cromwellian interregnum. Throughout his twenty-six years in power—the longest governorship in Virginia's history—he enacted the policies of the Stuart kings. Although he saw character flaws in both Charles I and Charles II, he remained fiercely loyal to the institution of the monarchy. He was, in the words of the Virginia author Mary Johnston, "a dyed-in-the-wool Cavalier, utterly stubborn for King and Church."[7] During his first two years as governor, he tried to rid Virginia of Puritans. Under him, the Virginia Assembly passed a bill that said any minister who did not conform to the doctrines and rituals of the Church of England must leave the colony. The rule was enforced when congregations in Nansemond County, a haven for Puritans in the southeastern corner of Virginia, contacted Governor John Winthrop of Massachusetts Bay, asking him to send them pastors from New England.[8] In January 1643, three Puritan ministers arrived in Virginia only to find themselves confronted with the hostile Anglican establishment. Ordered to leave the colony, the three soon returned to New England. Expulsions of Puritans continued for several years. Some Puritan ministers and their followers moved to nearby Maryland, which offered religious toleration.

Governor Berkeley remained devoted to the monarchy. In 1649, appalled by the Puritan Parliament's beheading of Charles I, he had

WILLIAM BERKELEY
*Portrait by Peter Lely, mid-seventeenth century*

Virginia's General Assembly issue a statute saying that anyone in the colony who defended the execution of "the late most excellent and now undoubtedly sainted king" would be judged "an accessory *post factum* to the death of the aforesaid King" and be charged with "high treason." The same accusation would be made against those "denying the divine right of kings" or refusing to acknowledge Charles II as England's current ruler.[9] Berkeley dispatched his secretary of state, Richard Henry Lee, to meet with the fugitive Charles in the Netherlands. Lee exchanged Berkeley's royal commission for a new one (worthless but symbolic) and pledged Virginia's loyalty to the would-be king.

Berkeley's intractability irked Parliament, which imposed navigation restrictions on Virginia, forbidding it to deal with its favorite trading partner, the Netherlands. Infuriated, Berkeley announced to the General Assembly that Virginians had become the "slaves" of Parliament's "Tyrannicall and bloudy" regime, against which he would lead a revolution. "Do but follow me," he declared. "I will either lead you to victory, or loose a life which I cannot more gloriously sacrifice then for my loyalty [to the Stuart kings], and your security."[10] Inspired by his boldness, the House of Burgesses (the General Assembly's lower house) pledged Virginia's loyalty to Charles II. England's Council of State responded by ordering "the reducing of Virginia to the obedience of this Common-wealth."[11] Barbados, like Virginia, had flexed its Cavalier muscles by committing itself to the second Charles. England sent a flotilla of warships to the recalcitrant colonies. The ships made short work of taming Barbados, then sailed through a raging storm to the waters off Virginia. After a tense standoff, Berkeley surrendered and accepted two treaties that were not excessively harsh on the Virginians. Under them, Berkeley would step down as Virginia's governor (the House of Burgesses elected three successive governors in the 1650s). The Virginians were allowed to continue using the Book of Common Prayer for one year, during which time they must swear loyalty to the Commonwealth; if they failed to do so, they must leave the colony. William Berkeley was exempted from these requirements if he stayed out of politics.

He retreated to an agricultural life at Green Spring, his estate near Jamestown. His house, an impressive brick structure, was "arguably the largest stately mansion of its day in English North America."[12] It had a wide main building with short perpendicular wings and an arcade that overlooked a courtyard. On land that eventually included seven thousand contiguous acres, Berkeley raised livestock, produced wine, and grew tobacco, grains, fruits, and vegetables. Aiming to diversify Virginia's economy, he also developed other products, including hemp, silk, rice, flax, and wine. He became Virginia's leading planter—and the creator of the Cavalier culture that eventually spread throughout the South. Besides his strong devotion to the monarchy, Berkeley embraced the Cavalier lifestyle. He enjoyed hosting parties for his elite peers at Green Spring, which was decorated with fine artworks.

Did enslaved Black people farm Berkeley's land? We don't know. His personal involvement in slavery is a mystery. According to a Virginia clergyman, he bought three Turkish people whom he "endeavoured to Convert. . . . And to encourage them, he offered them their Freedom, and to each of them a Plantation, if they would become a Christian."[13] Two of them accepted his offer, embracing Christianity; the other one clung to Islam until he was eighty, when he also converted. Berkeley had brought many white indentured servants from England, which earned him headrights that secured him huge tracts of property. It is unclear whether he held Black people as chattel. What is clear, however, is that after he regained the governorship in 1660, slavery became legally established in Virginia. Under his watch, slavery became heritable through the mother, enslavers could go unpunished for killing disobedient slaves, and Christian baptism did not protect Blacks from being kept in permanent bondage.

Whether or not Berkeley took advantage of this opportunity to exploit Black labor, other Cavaliers did. Berkeley was mainly responsible for making Virginia what one observer called the only "refuge left in his Majesties dominions, in these times, for distressed Cavallers [*sic*] . . . to seeke [their] fortunes."[14] During Berkeley's governorship, Virginia's population rose from eight thousand in 1642 to forty thousand in 1677—an increase of 500 percent.[15] A significant proportion of the newcomers were Cavaliers who had been marginalized or persecuted under the Cromwell regime. They arrived in a colony that became especially welcoming in 1660, when Charles II came to power and William Berkeley resumed the governorship. He honored the Stuarts by announcing annual holy days in their honor. January 30, the day "King Charles the First of ever blessed and glorious memory . . . was beheaded," would "be annually solemnized with fasting and prayers that our sorrows may expiate our crime and our teares wash away our guilt" and express "our serious and hearty repentance and detestation of that barbarous act."[16] May 29, the birthday of Charles II, was to be "annually celebrated as an holy day," "in testimony of our thankfulnes and joy" for the "happy restitution" of the "late distressed majestie to the throne of his royall ancestors."

This obeisance to the monarchy was part of a larger devotion to hierarchical institutions that the Cavaliers brought with them from England. Stratification became a hallmark of Virginia culture, evident in various aspects of life, including class consciousness, religion, housing, clothing, food, and choices of entertainment.

The embedding of social hierarchy that followed the surge of Cavalier immigration provides a backdrop for Bacon's Rebellion, the 1676 eruption that Thomas Jefferson and others saw as a precursor to the American Revolution. Nathaniel Bacon had moved to Virginia from England in 1674. The cousin of a Virginia official of the same name, he briefly became part of the circle of Governor Berkeley, who appointed Bacon to his advisory council. But the two had a falling-out over policy. When Berkeley failed to respond vigorously to an attack by the Doeg tribe, Bacon rallied a diverse group of followers, including Blacks and working-class whites, to show their dissatisfaction with the governor on that matter and issues related to taxation and voting. Bacon's band invaded Jamestown and burned it. Berkeley published a statement calling Bacon a traitor who "hath none about him, but the lowest of the people." Emphasizing the wisdom of King Charles, Berkeley wrote, "His sacred Majesty will easeily distinguish betweene Mr. Bacons actions and myne, and Kinges have long Armes, either to reward or punish."[17] Bacon responded with a declaration in which he presented his rebellion as one against a cadre of complacent elitists. He charged Berkeley with governing "against the consent of the people," "for the advancement of private favorites and other sinister ends." He wrote that the "crimes of the oppressours devide and separate us who have suffered by theire oppressions."[18] Given this rhetoric of a popular revolt against the ruling class, it is unsurprising that Nathaniel Bacon was often compared with Oliver Cromwell.[19]

The rebellion ceased when Bacon died of dysentery in his military camp. After the insurrection, Berkeley took harsh measures against those who had supported Bacon. Twenty were hanged; others were whipped, imprisoned, or fined. Berkeley's merciless response to Bacon's Rebellion made him suspect even among his former royalist supporters in England, and soon he was replaced by another governor. But crushing the rebellion led to a further hardening of class boundaries in Virginia. The colony's power elite, made up mainly of Cavaliers, had defeated insurgents made up of less privileged whites and their African American cohorts. The entrenched Cavalier culture that Berkeley had envisaged was becoming a reality.

## A TANGLE OF FISHHOOKS: CAVALIER GENEALOGIES

Accelerating this solidification of Cavalierism was the inbred nature of Virginia's elite class. Most of the three hundred or so families that made up the so-called FFV (First Families of Virginia) were related to one another by blood or marriage. The historian William Cabell Bruce describes the genealogies of these leading Virginians as "a tangle of fishhooks, so closely interlocked that it is impossible to pick up one without drawing three or four after it."[20]

Significantly, the ancestor of many of these families was none other than Sir Robert Filmer, the author of *Patriarcha.* Robert Filmer was from an ancient West Country family seated in Kent County, England. He was the eldest of eighteen children. This family produced many descendants with links to Virginia. Cousins often married each other, as was the case with Sir Robert Filmer's son Samuel, who married his cousin Mary Horsmanden (who was also kin of Virginia's governor, William Berkeley). Samuel Filmer died in England, and Mary subsequently moved to Virginia, where she married William Byrd, a wealthy Virginia merchant and planter. From this union came numerous prominent Virginia families. Mary Horsmanden Filmer Byrd, whose genealogy, as David Hackett Fischer notes, "might be titled *Matriarcha*," was the mother of William Byrd II, the mother-in-law of Robert Beverley and James Duke, and the grandmother of Charles Carter, Landon Carter, John Page, and Thomas Chamberlayne—all Virginia luminaries.[21] Another family alliance that also originated in England's West Country, near the Filmer clan, included the Randolphs (ancestors of Thomas Jefferson) and the Washingtons (ancestors of George Washington). The Washingtons had at least three family connections to the Filmer–Horsmanden–Berkeley network.

This interbred social elite took control of Virginia's government as early as the 1660s and held power until the American Revolution. During that time, the governor's council, which decided land distribution and most other economic matters in the colony, consisted of a few interrelated families, many of them descended from the Filmers.

The kinship to Sir Robert Filmer did not lead to a widespread acceptance of his political ideas. For instance, his doctrine of the divine right of kings was steadily replaced by a Whig suspicion of English royalty among ruling-class Virginians, several of whom took lead roles in creating the democratic United States. What passed down through the generations was the tradition of patriarchy, which pervaded government, society, and family life. Whereas New England's family structure was relatively egalitarian, Virginia's was hierarchical. The father was the monarch of the family, and everyone else was beneath him in descending ranks, starting with his wife, followed by their children, indentured servants, and enslaved people. In this view, slavery was a benevolent institution as natural as patriarchy itself, as expressed by the Virginia politician Wyndham Robertson two centuries later, on the eve of the Civil War:

> The right to hold slaves . . . is no more open to question than the time-consecrated authority of the parent over the child, authority of the man over the woman—both decreed by nature, and justified for their wisdom and justice by the blessings they have conferred on mankind. . . . [The] patriarchal relation of master and slave . . . opens new fields for the exercise of virtues—for affectionate fidelity on the one side, and a kind and considerate guardianship on the other.[22]

The enslaved were the main victims of social stratification. Virginia's labor force was mainly made up of white indentured workers until the 1680s through the 1690s, when the availability of white workers declined and the enslavement of Black people became profitable in the plantation economy. Around 1700, enslaved Blacks constituted some 17 percent of the total Virginia population of 53,000. By 1760, when the colony had roughly 340,000 inhabitants, the enslaved made up about 40 percent of the total due to births and continuous importation of people from Africa and the West Indies.[23] By then, Virginia's slave codes had become draconian. In particular, the code of 1705 stripped enslaved Blacks of all remnants of self-ownership; the code made them mere pieces of property, to be bought, sold, separated, and punished at will by their owners. Although racism had always undergirded slavery, it became more pronounced with the expansion of race-based slavery. Cavalier ideology made the plight of enslaved people seem unalterable. The affluent Virginian Robert "King" Carter, whose property included nearly three hundred thousand acres of land and more than seven hundred bondspeople, said that the only way to control the enslaved was "to make them stand in fear" of whipping, maiming, branding, or other forms of torture.[24] In a 1727 letter to one of his property managers,

Carter described his practice of cutting off the toes of recalcitrant slaves, saying, "I have cured many a negro of running away by this means."[25] Five years earlier, Carter had received permission from a Lancaster County Court "to Cut off all his toes on one of the s[aid]d negroes feet in order to the reclaiming him & Terrifying others from the like practice."[26]

Among the many Virginia families that exemplify the human toll of Cavalierism, the family of William Byrd II provides an exceptionally vivid case history. Byrd's mother, Mary Horsmanden Filmer Byrd, was the Cavalier matriarch whose descendants, as mentioned, populated Virginia's elite class for generations. His father, William Byrd I, was a London merchant who migrated to Virginia in 1674. Taking over a sizable estate left to him by an uncle, William Byrd I became a planter, fur trader, and politician. He initially utilized white indentured servants, but as they grew scarce he turned increasingly to enslaved labor and was soon active in the Atlantic slave trade. By the 1690s, he was importing enslaved Africans through London partnerships that handled slave cargoes bound for Virginia; he sold many Black people he acquired to fellow planters.[27]

His will, written in 1700, four years before his death, shows both the dehumanization of enslaved people and the importance of primogeniture in the South. William Byrd I left "three hundred pounds Ster[ling]" to one daughter, one hundred pounds to another, fifty pounds to a grandson, and "all the rest of my Estate both reall and personall" to "to my Son Wm. Byrd for his own proper use & behoof to him & his heirs for ever."[28] This arrangement was typical in the South, where primogeniture (leaving most property to the first son or, in some cases, the first daughter) and entail (forbidding later heirs from selling or bequeathing the property) were the rule.[29] Primogeniture and entail contributed to the long-term growth of the estate of a single family line by preventing property from being spread among relatives of those who later married into the clan. The estates of individual families in the Southern colonies snowballed, whereas those in Northern colonies, most of which abolished primogeniture, were frequently dispersed over time. William Byrd I specified in his will that he was leaving to his son William his "Lands, Rents houses Plate money debts wares merchandizes househould goods Slaves Servts horses Cattell with all part or parts of shipps or vessells either in England Virg[ini]a or else where."

As the inheritor of the family estate, William Byrd II was primed to become the prototypical Cavalier, as later generations remembered him.[30] He developed the trademark Cavalier characteristics: a polished veneer, cordiality, bravado, pride in sexual prowess, a sense of personal honor, and a devotion to Anglicanism. At his plantation, Westover, on the James River, this hospitable Cavalier invited forty to fifty upper-crust guests per month for feasting, revelry, dances, cards, or billiards.[31] Some guests stayed for weeks at Westover, and he often stayed on other plantations when he was away from home. Like his fellow planters, he held patriarchal attitudes toward those on a lower rung of the social ladder than he.

Born in Virginia, William Byrd II was sent at seven to a school in Felsted, England, where he excelled at languages. He mastered Greek, Latin, French, Dutch, and Hebrew, with a reading knowledge of German and Italian.[32] At sixteen, he apprenticed with merchants in Rotterdam, visited Paris, and then returned to London, where he received legal training at the Middle Temple. Going back to Virginia in 1705, after the death of his father, he entered politics, earned a seat on the governor's council, and served as the colonial agent to England, in which capacity he was the Receiver General of Quit Rents.[33] He controlled the family plantations. Having inherited more than 56,000 acres of land, he expanded the family property to 180,000 acres, including land that became Richmond (later Virginia's capital) as well as an upper section of North Carolina.[34] He raised crops (mainly tobacco) and livestock.

His holdings were on a par with others of his class, reflecting what Robert Beverley called "the Ambition each had of being Lord of a vast . . . territory."[35] Inequality mushroomed in eighteenth-century

Virginia, marked by a huge gap between the top planters and the average landholders; by the 1760s, the wealthiest 10 percent of Virginians owned nearly half of the colony's property.[36] The proportion of Virginia land held in entail by elite families between 1720 and 1780 ran 50 percent to 62 percent in the Tidewater region and one-third colony-wide.[37] As for the Indigenous peoples of Virginia, some had been wiped out and others lived on reservations, while others had left the colony.[38]

We get an eye-opening view of Cavalier patriarchy in action from William Byrd II's diary and commonplace book. Byrd's description of his role as a father could have come straight from Sir Robert Filmer:

> I have a large family of my own. . . . Like one of the patriarchs, I have my flocks and my herds, my bond-men and bond-women. . . . I must take care to keep all my people to their duty, to set all the springs in motion and to make every one draw his equal share to carry the machine forward. But then tis an amusement in this silent country.[39]

Byrd's relationship with "my people"—the enslaved Blacks on his plantation in Westover, Virginia—included displays of kindness. He often described times when he "walked about the plantation" and "talked with my people." He distributed snacks or drinks as rewards for good work or to encourage camaraderie. "I gave my people a bowl of punch and they had a fiddle and danced."[40] To celebrate Twelfth Night, he once reported, he "talked with my people, drew twelfth cake, gave the people cake and cider."

Such benevolent gestures were not merely examples of paternalistic condescension. Byrd acknowledged that slavery was wrong. His paradoxical position as an enslaver who considered slavery evil was similar to that of other eighteenth-century slaveholders, including Thomas Jefferson. Byrd went so far as to acknowledge that all humans were equal, no matter their color. "All Nations of Men," he wrote, "have the same

William Byrd II
*Portrait attributed to Hans Hysing, c. 1724*

Natural Dignity, and we all know that very bright Talents may be lodg'd under a very dark Skin. The principal Difference between one People and another, proceeds only from the Different Opportunities of Improvement."[41]

Byrd vehemently objected to the slave trade, which England controlled. In a 1736 letter, he fulminated against "this unchristian traffick of makeing merchandize of our fellow creatures," insisting that "the farther importation of them into our colonys should be prohibited."[42] Slave traders, he noted, "import so many Negros hither, that I fear this colony will some time or other be confirmed by the name of New Guinea." He especially feared "servile war," which, he said, could "tinge our rivers as wide as they are with blood." Mentioning Jamaica's deadly Maroon Wars, in which Black fugitives in the mountains had been attacking British settlers for years, he wrote, "We have mountains in Virginia too, to which they may retire as safely, and do as much mischief as they do in Jamaica." Slavery itself was a flawed system. It worked to "ruin the industry of our white people, who seeing a rank of poor creatures below them, detest work for fear it should make them look like slaves."

Despite these antislavery arguments—all of which would later appear in the writings and speeches of abolitionists—Byrd owned hundreds of Black people and did not refrain from punishing them. For him, as for other Southerners, the plantation economy relied on the work of Black people who must be kept in line. "Another unhappy effect of many Negros," Byrd wrote, "is the necessity of being severe. Numbers make them insolent, & then foul means must do, what fair will not." His diary is full of references to enslaved people at Westover being whipped, beaten, burned, or fitted with a mouth bit.

Generally, Byrd and his wife had an overseer carry out punishment, but sometimes they did so themselves. Inhumane treatment of the enslaved was part of daily life, as normal as having a meal, reading the Bible, or practicing dance steps. Witness Byrd's diary entries about Eugene, a bed-wetting houseboy, and Jenny, a teenage maid:

> ***February 8, 1709:*** I rose at 5 o'clock this morning and read a [Bible] chapter in Hebrew and 200 verses in Homer's *Odyssey.* I ate milk for breakfast. I said my prayers. Eugene and Jenny were whipped. I danced my dance. I read law in the morning and Italian in the afternoon. . . .[43]
>
> ***June 10, 1709:*** In the evening I took a walk around the plantation. Eugene was whipped for running away and had the [bit] put on him. I said my prayers and had good health, good thoughts and good humour. . . .

> ***September 3, 1709:*** I ate roast chicken for dinner. In the afternoon I beat Jenny for throwing water on the couch. . . .
>
> ***December 16, 1709:*** Eugene was whipped for doing nothing yesterday. I danced my dance. I settled several accounts. I ate roast mutton for dinner.

Even truly repulsive punishments were listed as quotidian occurrences:

> ***December 3, 1709:*** Eugene pissed abed again for which I made him drink a pint of piss. I settled some accounts and read some news. About 12 o'clock I went to court where I found little good company.

For Byrd, controlling enslaved people was like managing one's wife. The dominant patriarch must govern both. Byrd's descriptions of how to regulate both were strikingly similar. Regarding enslaved Blacks, he wrote, "These base tempers require to be rid with a [short] rein, or they will be apt to throw their rider."[44] Regarding women: "Female passions require to be managed sometimes, to confine them within bounds and keep them, like a high-mettled horse, from running away with their owner."[45]

His view of women reflected Southern marriage customs, where the husband kept firm control over his wife, who was expected to be submissive, obedient, and meek. To maintain "Matrimonial Felicity," *The Virginia Gazette* advised, a wife must follow these rules: "Never dispute with him, whatever be the Occasion. . . . And if any Altercation or Jars happen, don't separate the Bed, whereby the Animosity will sooner cease. . . . Read often the Matrimonial Service, and overlook not the Important Word OBEY."[46]

These guidelines were hard to follow for William Byrd II's first wife. In 1706, at thirty-two, Byrd married the well-heeled nineteen-year-old Lucy Parke. Vivacious and outspoken, Lucy was given to angry outbursts. She was very different from her long-suffering mother, who had patiently put up with the sexual escapades of her husband, the slaveholder Daniel Parke II, a shameless rake who abandoned the family and left his illegitimate child with Lucy and her mother to raise while he became the governor of the Leeward Islands, where he was lynched by a mob infuriated with his corrupt behavior.[47] Unlike her mother, Lucy Parke Byrd often stood up to her husband, though she inevitably backed down. Byrd's diary describes many spousal quarrels after which she "submitted" and "was passive again."[48] A typical scene: "My wife and I quarreled about her pulling her brows. She threatened she would not go to Williamsburg if she might not pull them; I refused, however, and got the better of her, and maintained my authority."

Sometimes she retreated quickly: "My wife and I had another scold about mending my shoes, but it was soon over by her submission."[49] Even if she put up a fight, she inevitably yielded to his reprimands or his gestures of intimacy. His journal is peppered with moments of her frustration or anger being allayed by a "roger" or a "flourish": "In the afternoon my wife and I had a little quarrel which I reconciled with a flourish"; after "a terrible quarrel" at night "I lay abed till 9 o'clock this morning to bring my wife into temper again and rogered her by way of reconciliation."[50] Frequently, they had spontaneous sex in unusual places: on a billiard table, against a trestle, in his library. He was always ready to brag about his virility, reporting several times, "I rogered my wife with vigor."[51]

According to the firm double standard in the Cavalier South, a wife was expected to maintain marital fidelity, while a husband's philandering was tolerated, even expected. Typical Byrd diary entries: "Jenny, an Indian girl, had got drunk and made us good sport"; "At night I asked a negro girl to kiss me."[52]

Several times he found it necessary to simultaneously control his wife and his enslaved people, who were pawns in the hands of their quarreling owners: "My wife against my will caused little Jenny to be burned with a hot iron, for which I quarreled with her";[53] "I had a terrible quarrel with my wife concerning Jenny that I took away from her when she was beating her with the tongs"; "My wife and I had a terrible quarrel about whipping Eugene while Mr. Mumford was there but she had a mind to show her authority before company but I would not suffer it, which she took very ill."

Byrd recognized a strong difference between the moral texture of the North and the South. Although hostile to the Puritan beliefs of the "Swarm of Dissenters" who "about the year 1620" settled "a small town . . . call'd New Plymouth," Byrd praised the Pilgrims and later New Englanders for "giving no Scandal or bad Example, at least by any open and publick Vices," in stark contrast to "the Southern Colon[ists], who thought their being Members of the Establish't Church sufficient to Sanctifie very loose and Profligate Morals."[54] Byrd's words applied to himself. A devout Episcopalian and a vestryman, he regularly took communion. He had a daily routine of reading the Bible in Latin or Hebrew, and a nightly one of saying his prayers. On the other hand, he felt free to roam sexually.

After Lucy died of smallpox in 1716, his roaming increased exponentially. Fischer writes that Byrd became a "sexual predator"—a shocking statement that becomes even more so with Fischer's addendum: "The sexual activities of other planters made even William Byrd appear a model of restraint."[55] If a goal of the Cavalier was to out-roger others while remaining true to the Anglican faith, Byrd reached it in London, where he lived for four years after Lucy's death. He had sex arbitrarily with maids, prostitutes, and married or single women whom he met around town. At the same time, he continued his daily Bible reading and recited prayers (or scolded himself when he forgot to do so). Promiscuity and piety merged in the Cavalier lifestyle.

In February 1724, Byrd was married in England to the London-born Maria Taylor. Unlike the volatile Lucy, Maria was mild and conventional—not one for flourishes on billiard tables or against trestles. Within a year of their marriage, William took Maria to live in Virginia.

From his previous marriage, Byrd had three daughters, Elizabeth, Evelyn, and Wilhelmina (two sons had died in infancy). With Maria, he had four additional children: Anne, Maria, William, and Jane.

The descendants of William and Maria Byrd show the inbred nature of the Cavalier family. One of Byrd's daughters, Anne, married Charles Carter, the son of "King" Carter, the wealthiest person in Virginia. Charles Carter served many years in the House of Burgesses and owned several plantations on which he produced tobacco and wine. Byrd's second daughter, Maria, married another of King Carter's sons, Landon Carter, also a plantation owner and political powerhouse. Maria Byrd Carter died at eighteen of puerperal sepsis after giving birth to another Maria Carter, who went on to marry into another leading family, the Beverleys. Among the seventeen children of Maria and Robert Beverley were several who would marry into yet other FFV, including the Randolphs and the Corbins.

## THE FRAGMENTATION OF CAVALIER CULTURE

Surveying the family tree produced by the intertwined Byrd and Carter families, three figures show the different directions the Cavalier culture took: William Byrd III represents that culture's decadence and decline; Landon Carter demonstrates the desperate effort to sustain that culture even as it was evaporating in an age of revolution; and Robert Carter III (a nephew of Anne Byrd's husband Charles Carter) embodied its antislavery potential.

Of these figures, William Byrd III, the heir to the Byrd fortune, initially seemed the most likely to succeed. He was educated for a time in England, where, like his father, he studied law at the Middle Temple, after which he returned to Virginia, directed the Byrd plantations, and served in the Virginia government. Benefitting from primogeniture, he started out with 179,000 acres and hundreds of enslaved Black people.[56] He brought to completion his father's planned mansion at Westover, a two-and-a-half-story brick house in the Georgian style, with huge iron entrance gates, a columned front door, and an elegant entrance hall framed on one side by a parlor and living room and on the other by a library that housed one of the largest private book collections in Virginia. Outside, beyond terraced gardens, were the cabins of the enslaved.

William Byrd III fell victim to a changing economy and to Cavalier habits that he carried to an extreme. Tobacco prices fell during the eighteenth century, and Byrd's lackluster efforts to diversify his farm products failed to make up for sinking profits. Also, like other Virginians, he shunned crop rotation, manuring, and other preventatives of soil exhaustion. Demographically, Virginia shifted, as many Tidewater residents and newly arrived immigrants settled in the western sections of the colony or on the frontier beyond. Population dispersal diminished the economic status of the grandees of the eastern section of the colony.

The main reason for William Byrd III's decline was his overindulgence in Cavalier habits. Proud of their identity as hospitable pleasure-lovers (as opposed to Puritans, whom they considered moralistic prudes), Cavaliers enjoyed dancing, games, singing, and revelry. A typical evening at Byrd's Westover would find the Byrds and their guests enjoying a feast before going to one of Westover's great rooms for dancing. A small string orchestra would perform, and the impeccably dressed ladies and gentlemen would dance minuets, jigs, reels, and waltzes. While the dancing went on, some men would be in other rooms drinking, singing popular songs, playing billiards, or gambling.

The latter was Byrd III's Achilles' heel. Fueled by liquor, he gambled obsessively—at cards, dice, horse racing, whatever—for high stakes. The grand Byrd estate melted away in a sea of debt. An acquaintance remarked that Byrd "is never happy but when he has the box and Dices in hand. This Gentleman from a man of the greatest property of any in America has reduced himself to that Degree by gameing, that few or nobody will Credit him for Ever so small a sum of money."[57] He sold many of his enslaved people and was reduced to running a public lottery: A five-pound ticket bought the chance to win some acreage, farm equipment, or other property. But many people acquired tickets on credit and never paid for them.[58] The lottery was a fiasco. Byrd III found himself in the position of most other previously wealthy Cavalier families. Emory G. Evans finds that of twenty-one elite Virginia families he investigated, only four were solvent by 1775; fourteen were in serious financial trouble, and the status of the remaining three was unclear.[59]

Byrd III also had severe family problems. He fathered ten children with two wives. Cavalier families were often troubled; the domineering patriarch caused tension with the spouse and children. Byrd's first marriage ended tragically. During the 1750s, he left Westover for extended military service in the French and Indian War. In July 1760, before his return home, his wife died—almost certainly by suicide. Byrd soon remarried but became deeply conflicted over his colonial contemporaries' anger against England for a series of oppressive taxes and trade restrictions. Byrd initially sided with England, but when in November 1775 Virginia's colonial governor Lord Dunmore proclaimed freedom for enslaved people who joined the British forces, Byrd switched sides. He offered to serve the Patriots but was rejected due to suspicion over his real loyalties. On New Year's Day 1777, he shot himself. His suicide was the grim finale of an old-style Cavalier, for whom hierarchy, patriarchy, and a decadent lifestyle made a noxious mix in a changing world.

The crumbling of Cavalier patriarchy was also visible in the experience of William Byrd III's brother-in-law, Landon Carter. The son of Virginia's most powerful grandee, Robert "King" Carter, Landon Carter had all the hallmarks of the Cavalier lifestyle: education in England followed by a return to Virginia and the managing of plantations worked by hundreds of enslaved people; a grand mansion (Sabine Hall) that was the site of dancing, drinking, and gambling; government service, first as a justice of the peace and then as a member of the House of Burgesses; and a prolific family life, which in his case involved marriages to three wives who predeceased him, leaving him with eight children. Landon Carter joined the Patriot cause early, preceding even fellow Virginian Patrick Henry in protesting against the Stamp Act in 1765.[60]

But he had a serious dilemma. On the one hand, his underlying sympathies were with hierarchy and tradition. His patriarchal attitudes came out in his diary. Women he regarded as good for sex and dancing, but not much else: "Women have nothing general in view, but the breeding contests at home. It began with poor Eve and ever since then has been so much the devil in woman."[61] He also saw them as dimwitted: "A negroe and a passionate woman are equal as to truth or falsehood; for neither thinks of what they say." Of his Black workers he wrote, "Slaves are devils, and to make them otherwise than slaves will be to set devils free." He left as many as five hundred enslaved people, along with nearly fifty thousand acres of land and other property, to his sons.

He put on a public show of confidence, piety, and humaneness. He considered himself a "very kind" master. Although he always had the whip handy, he avoided excessive cruelty (in contrast to his father, with his practice of cutting off the toes of recaptured runaways). He took pride in being a generous host, providing his guests at Sabine Hall with plenty of food, wine, and entertainment. He served as an Anglican vestryman.

But the patriarchal role, which once seemed solid, was shaken to the core by the revolutionary spirit that drove his American contemporaries to war and infiltrated his domestic circle.[62] He tried to control those around him, but he faced rebellion on many fronts. His son Robert, who lived with his wife Winifred and their children upstairs in Sabine Hall, was addicted to gambling, which strained the family's finances. In his diary, Landon excoriated his "cursed" son, who was always "gaming and running about" and who became "my most vexatious tyrant and everybody seems to take a Pleasure that he is so."[63] Landon also blamed Robert and his "devilish" wife Winifred for making one of his grandsons "insufferable . . . the most outrageous scoundrel that ever appeared in human Shape." Meanwhile, his daughter Judith brazenly disobeyed him by eloping with a man he had ordered her not to see; he temporarily disowned her. Despite his show of so-called kindness to his enslaved people, he privately described them as shiftless, dishonest, and disobedient. He was furious when eight of them absconded to Lord Dunmore's forces in 1775.

Through all his failed attempts to live up to the model of Cavalier patriarchy, Landon Carter clung to tradition. Although he joined the Patriot side (mainly because he saw King George III as an inept patriarch who was "alienating the filial love of all his children," much "in the Style of Charles 1st"), he supported institutions like primogeniture and entail, which Jefferson worked to abolish (Jefferson explained that he wanted to eradicate "every fibre . . . of ancient or future aristocracy" and to lay "a foundation . . . for a government truly republican").[64] Landon Carter actually ended up leaving most of his estate to his "monster" son, Robert.[65]

Another irritant for Landon Carter was the growing presence of Baptists in Virginia. The longtime persecution or marginalization of Baptists by Virginia Anglicans helped push Jefferson and Madison to spearhead the movement toward religious toleration, which became a reality with the passage in 1786 of the Virginia Statute for Religious Freedom, a forerunner of the First Amendment. Landon Carter rejected such openness to evangelical Protestantism. When one of his enslaved people, a carpenter named Tony, embraced the Baptist faith, he wrote, "I believe it is from some inculcated doctrine of those rascals [i.e., Baptist preachers] that the slaves in this Colony are grown so much worse."[66] Outraged when an overseer received divine grace by immersion and vowed to convert enslaved people on the plantation, Carter claimed that "horrid hellish rogues and other religious villains" were creating havoc—a sentiment echoed by a Virginia newspaper that said Baptists were drawing "Slaves from the Obedience of their Masters," tearing asunder "the very Heartstrings" of plantations and leaving "all their Peace destroyed."[67]

One can only imagine Landon Carter's reaction if he had lived to see how Baptists inspired a close relative of his to perform a historic act of emancipation. Landon Carter died in December 1778, three months after his nephew Robert Carter III was baptized by immersion by Reverend Lewis Lunsford in Totuskey Creek, not far from Sabine Hall. Thirteen years later, in 1791, Robert Carter III emancipated more than 450 enslaved people—one of the largest manumissions in the United States before 1861.

The Baptist church originated in England as part of the Puritan revolt against the Anglican Church. John Smyth, one of the founders of the church, was religious refugee in Holland like John Robinson, the pastor of the Pilgrims who founded Plymouth Colony. The two pastors had led congregations in Amsterdam until Robinson took his group of Separatists to Leiden. Originally called Anabaptists ("baptized once again"), Baptists scandalized orthodox churchmen by insisting that baptism be postponed beyond infancy, until the converted embraced Jesus Christ as their savior. In America, Baptists found a home in Roger Williams's tolerant Rhode Island, where religious nonconformity created an atmosphere favorable to the colony's 1652 abolition law. The antislavery spirit reappeared in 1710 in a Baptist church in South Carolina that protested against the cruelty of that colony's infamous slave code. In the last two decades of the eighteenth century, many Baptists spoke out against slavery. By 1790, Virginia, which had become a site of religious freedom, was "one of the most 'Baptist' places in the country."[68] That year, Virginia's General Committee of Baptists condemned slavery as "a violent deprivation of the rights of nature and inconsistent with a republican government" and urged Baptists to "make use of every legal measure to extirpate this horrid evil from the land."[69]

This statement prompted no immediate political action, but the Virginia legislature had already facilitated emancipation in 1782 by legalizing manumission, which had been restricted in the colony since 1723. Manumissions proliferated for a time. Virginia's free Black population rose from less than 3,000 in 1782 to 12,866 in 1790.[70] Most acts of emancipation were small: The average emancipator owned 5 enslaved people and liberated 3 of them.[71] But several planters emancipated large numbers of people: George Washington freed 123, Samuel Gist 350 to 400, Robert Pleasants 400 to 500, Joseph Mayo 156, John Randolph 383, and Randolph's brother Richard 155.[72]

Reasons for manumission varied widely. In the case of Robert Carter III, religion and humanitarianism were the main motivating factors. When in 1791 he filed his deed of gift providing for the gradual emancipation of his enslaved people, he explained: "I have for some time past been convinced that to retain them in Slavery is contrary to the true Principles of Religion and Justice, and that therefor it was my Duty to manumit them."[73] He had steadily advanced toward this position after his baptism in 1778. During the 1780s, he banned the torture of enslaved people on his plantations. He joined African Americans in interracial worship in churches whose charters said, "Black Member to be dealt with as a White One." He held Baptist services for whites and African Americans in Nomony Hall, his mansion on the Rappahannock River, not far from the seats of Jefferson and Washington. Disappointed by the failure of a 1788 petition for general emancipation in Virginia, he declared, "I understand that the latest petition before the house of Delegates, praying for Liberation, was rejected by a great Majority. Let us then Unite in prayer to Correct this Error, for tolerating Slavery indicates great depravity of mind."[74]

Once he had liberated his enslaved people, he settled them on farms apportioned from his extensive estate, which totaled tens of thousands of acres. He moved to Baltimore, using his business agent, the Baptist minister Benjamin Dawson, to administrate the deed of gradual emancipation of the enslaved people. Carter's heirs tried but failed to have the deed canceled. Dawson saw to it that the terms of the emancipation document were carried out to the letter.

Manumissions declined notably after 1806, when the Virginia legislature required freedpeople to leave the state within one year of emancipation or face reenslavement. The Baptist church, meanwhile, backed out of politics in the South during the Second Great Awakening, the firestorm of religious revivals that swept the nation during the opening decades of the nineteenth century. In the North, evangelical religion triggered reform movements, including abolitionism, but it underwent a conservative reaction among whites in the South, where segregated worship, calls for colonization, and proslavery interpretations of the Bible prevented widespread antislavery activity. At the same time, however, all-Black Baptist churches nurtured the growth of African American Christianity, destined to be a major force for expanding civil rights.

Cavalier culture as a reality had virtually died out by the American Revolution. But as a myth, the Cavalier not only survived but grew exponentially during the eight decades after the Revolution. In the popular imagination of states below the Mason–Dixon Line, what had originally been the Virginia Cavalier became the Southern Cavalier—the embodiment of a whole civilization based on honor, independence, hospitality, and a respect for tradition that stood in stark contrast to the chaos of fanatical "isms" that was, supposedly, the Puritan North.

George Orwell famously writes in *Nineteen Eighty-Four*, "Who controls the past controls the future: who controls the present controls the past."[75] Nineteenth-century Southerners tried to control the past by retrospectively establishing a Cavalier identity for many of the Founding Fathers. If one could show that the creators of the United

States were noble Cavaliers, one could feel thoroughly patriotic in championing the South and its institutions. This Southern myth helped fuel the Civil War. Southerners liked to boast that many of the nation's founders—Washington, Jefferson, Richard Henry Lee, George Mason, and others—were Cavaliers: They were slaveholding owners of large plantations with distinguished backgrounds in Virginia's landed gentry.[76]

But it is essential to show that the founders were *not* Cavaliers in the King Carter or William Byrd sense. Whatever Cavalier tendencies they had were transformed by a fresh revolutionary vision that owed much to the early New England settlers and the seventeenth-century Puritan rebellion against King Charles I. That vision had been shaped for the founders by eighteenth-century preachers and politicians who pushed Puritanism toward democracy and human rights.

*Chapter Six*

# The American Revolution and Puritanism

How did America pull it off? How did the thirteen colonies come together to defeat the mother country in the Revolution and forge a new nation under the Constitution?

These questions, which continue to challenge historians, were thoughtfully considered by Founding Father John Adams, the second president of the United States.[1] The colonies, he noted, were marked by great differences; it was almost a miracle that they came together for a single cause. He wrote, "Thirteen clocks were made to strike together"—an achievement made possible because Southerners who transcended their Cavalier culture (Washington, Jefferson, Madison, Patrick Henry, Richard Henry Lee) joined minds with notables of Puritan New England (the two Adamses, Hancock, James Otis Jr.) and the middle colonies (Franklin, John Jay, William Livingston).[2] Concerted action became possible, Adams maintained, because these and other leaders, regardless of their geographical region, tapped into the revolutionary heritage of the Puritan settlement of New England and the Cromwellian overthrow of Charles I.

Adams regarded the New England settlers and Cromwell's rebels as key players in the historical shift from European feudalism to American republicanism. For centuries, Europe had been governed by what Adams called canon and feudal law, a system of oppression enforced by the Roman Catholic Church and feudal lords. In Adams's view, the Protestant Reformation opened possibilities for freedom but produced despotism under "the execrable race of the Stuarts," with their doctrine of "the awful and absolute sovereignty of kingship."[3] James I drove religious nonconformists out of England. Then came "King Charles's grievous and illegal Measures" and the nefarious practices of "his two oppressive Instruments Laud and Strafford."[4] These "encroachments upon liberty in the reigns of the first James and the first Charles," Adams wrote, led to a "struggle between the people" and "temporal and spiritual tyranny." The conflict became "formidable, violent, and bloody," but it had positive results.[5] It toppled a monarch, helped populate America, and inspired people who shaped American democracy—what Adams called the "Hampdens, Vanes, . . . Miltons, . . . Sidneys, Lockes," who "owed their eminence in political knowledge to the tyrannies of those reigns."

For Adams, the most significant outcome of England's religious turmoil was the settlement of New England. He explained that the "principles and feelings" behind the American Revolution must "be traced back for two hundred years, and sought in the history of the country from the first plantations in America."[6] The settlements he focused on were the Plymouth and Massachusetts Bay Colonies. Plymouth stood out to him because it represented independence from England, and Massachusetts because it fostered literacy through public schools and higher education through Harvard College, founded in 1636. The settlers of both colonies, he argued, laid the foundation for democracy because they held elections for government officials and church leaders. In his words, "After their arrival here, they began their settlement, and formed their plan, both of ecclesiastical and civil government, in direct opposition to the canon and the feudal systems. . . . Tyranny in every form, shape, and appearance was their disdain and abhorrence."[7]

Adams asked, "Who then was the author, inventor, discoverer of independence? The only true answer must be the first emigrants." As for the outstanding Patriots who later called for independence—Adams highlighted James Otis, Samuel Adams, Jonathan Mayhew, Patrick Henry, Richard Henry Lee, and Thomas Jefferson—"they were only awakeners and revivers of the original fundamental principle" of the New England settlers.[8] That principle had been established, Adams maintained, by the Forefathers' resistance to the Church of England and the monarchy. The American Revolution was an extension of that resistance.

## THE BISHOPS' WARS IN AMERICA

Adams maintained that British aggression in the eighteenth century began with overreach by the Church of England, as it had in the seventeenth century. He noted that just as James I's and Charles I's bishops had driven Puritans out of England and then tried to force Anglicanism on Scotland, so the church under the Hanover monarchs, who took power in 1714, had attempted to impose Episcopalianism on America by installing bishops there. It was "a fact as certain as any in the history of North America," Adams wrote, that "the apprehension of [i.e., anxiety over] Episcopacy, contributed . . . as much as any other cause, to arouse the attention, not only of the inquiring mind, but of the common people, and urge them to close thinking on the constitutional authority of parliament over the colonies."[9] The Bishops' Wars under Charles I had provoked resistance to the highly unpopular ship-money tax, which in turn sparked the uprising against Charles in the English Civil War. Similarly, the eighteenth-century church's attempts to fortify Episcopalianism in America led to bishops' wars that, in combination with resentment over taxes under George III, triggered the American Revolution.

Alarm in America over possible Anglican domination had been growing ever since the formation in 1701 of the Society for the Propagation of the Gospel in Foreign Parts (SPG), an international arm of the Church of England. One of the main goals of the SPG was to send missionaries to America to strengthen Anglicanism there and set in motion the appointment of a bishop based there. Due in part to the SPG's missionary work—along with colonial establishment policies and population expansion—the number of Anglican churches in the colonies grew from about 111 in 1700 to around 406 by the eve of the American Revolution.[10] The church expanded not only in the Southern colonies, where it was already established, but also in the Northern colonies, where other denominations were more prevalent.

The Anglican plan to appoint an American bishop met with fierce opposition, especially in New England. "Let all mankind know," Cotton Mather announced in 1702, "that we came into the *Wilderness*, because we would worship God without that *Episcopacy*, that *Common Prayer*, and those unwarrantable *Ceremonies*, with which the *Land of our Fore Fathers Sepulchres* has been defiled."[11] Two decades later, the formidable Harvard professor Edward Wigglesworth, whose students included several future leaders of the American Revolution, denounced the doctrines of nonresistance and passive obedience that underpinned the Church of England and the monarchy. A couple of Wigglesworth students who became Boston clergymen, Jonathan Mayhew and Charles Chauncy, laid the groundwork for other Patriots with powerful sermons that brought the anti-Anglican passions of the past to bear on the intensifying American crisis.

Like their friend John Adams, Mayhew and Chauncy were descendants of Puritans who had fled Stuart tyranny and had moved to New England. Mayhew's earliest American ancestor, Thomas Mayhew Sr., had made the crossing from England in 1631 and had settled in Martha's Vineyard, where his immediate descendants preached among the Wampanoags. Charles Chauncy's grandfather, also named Charles, had fled from Archbishop Laud in 1637 and served in Plymouth Colony pulpits for several years before being appointed as the second president of Harvard in 1654. The Calvinistic theology of the early settlers changed with time. The doctrines of predestination, original sin, and eternal damnation for all but a chosen few were rejected by Jonathan Mayhew, Charles Chauncy, and John Adams. For these men, God was benevolent, Jesus was a divinely inspired person (but not divine), and everyone could attain salvation through faith and good works. While they discarded orthodox Calvinism, they adopted what they believed was central to their Puritan ancestral heritage: devotion to independence, liberty, and government by consent. It was these political values that the three tried to revive in the face of growing signs of Episcopal power in eighteenth-century America.

Leading the way was Jonathan Mayhew, whom fellow Harvard graduate and Declaration of Independence signer Robert Treat Paine called "the Father of Civil and Religious Liberty in Massachusetts and America."[12] Mayhew's father, Experience Mayhew, had evangelized among the Wampanoag people on Martha's Vineyard for six decades. Experience Mayhew's *Massachuset Psalter* (1709), a Massachusetts translation of Bible selections, was second in importance only to John Eliot's "Indian Bible" as an early work published in an Indigenous American language. Experience Mayhew's 1727 book, *Indian Converts*, which covered four generations of the Wampanoag tribe, provides "the most extensive information we have about any Algonquian community during the early English colonial period."[13] Experience was surrounded by other Puritan-named people, including his first wife, Thankful, their daughter Reliance, and, after Thankful's death, his second wife, Remembrance, who had a sister named Patience.

Jonathan Mayhew, the fourth child of Experience and Remembrance, was raised in Martha's Vineyard, attended Harvard, and in 1747 was ordained as pastor of Boston's West Church, where he served until he died in 1766. During his nineteen years in the spotlight, he did more than any other preacher to fire up revolutionary energies. John Adams and others viewed his landmark 1750 sermon on passive resistance and disobedience as the opening volley of the American Revolution. Adams later told his friend Thomas Jefferson that Mayhew's 1750 sermon was a crucial part of "the Education of a Boy of 14 Years of age, who was destined in the future Course of his Life to dabble in so many Revolutions in America, in Holland and in France."[14] When Mayhew's sermon was published, Adams recalled, "It was read by everybody; celebrated by friends, and abused by enemies."[15] Its effect on Adams was life-changing. Adams recalled, "I read it, till the Substance of it, was incorporated into my Nature and indelibly engraved on my Memory."[16] Adams called Mayhew "a transcendent genius" and placed him among "the most conspicuous, the most ardent and influential" figures who brought about "An AWAKENING and a REVIVAL of American Principles and Feelings, with an Enthusiasm which went on increasing till in 1775 it burst out in open Violence, Hostility and Fury."[17]

Adams regarded Mayhew as the first American to respond forcefully to ominous signs of British oppression. The movement in England to establish an American episcopate gained momentum in 1741 when the Reverend Thomas Secker, the Bishop of Oxford, insisted on the installation of a bishop in America to facilitate the ordination of clergy, establish new churches, and spread the Gospel among Native Americans and enslaved Black people.

Episcopalians kept alive the memory of King Charles I. January 30, the date of Charles's beheading, had been an annual Anglican holiday since the Restoration. January 30, 1749—the centenary of the king's execution—prompted an outpouring of hagiographic sermonizing by Anglicans. Charles the Martyr Day was truly holy for Reverend Charles Brockwell, an Episcopal minister at Boston's King's Chapel who treasured a Bible that, he said, had been "given to my father by King Charles the First . . . when my father was there with the royal martyr."[18] Brockwell gave a sermon glorifying the "royal martyr" that infuriated the Congregationalist Jonathan Mayhew, who bottled his feelings until the following January, when he gave three sermons against the commemoration of King Charles. Mayhew said he would not have brought up the subject "were it not that *some men* continue to speak of it, even to this day, with a great deal of warmth and zeal."[19] His third anti-Charles sermon, preached on the Sunday after January 30, 1750, became a transatlantic bestseller when it appeared as *A Discourse Concerning Unlimited Submission and Non-Resistance to the Higher Powers: With Some Reflections on the Resistance Made to King Charles I. And on the Anniversary of His Death: In Which the Mysterious Doctrine of that Prince's Saintship and Martyrdom is Unriddled.*

In the sermon, Mayhew "unriddled" the "Saintship and Martyrdom" of Charles I by revisiting the English Civil War, which in his view resulted in the justified overthrow of a wicked king. Although he recognized that the trial of Charles I was "little better than a mere mockery of justice" and that Oliver Cromwell proved to be a flawed ruler, he argued that the execution of Charles was necessary.[20] Charles had "governed in a perfectly wild and arbitrary manner, paying no regard to the constitution and the laws of the kingdom." His "illegal and despotic measures" included imposing taxes without parliamentary approval, imprisoning enemies, reviving "several arbitrary courts, in which the most unheard-of barbarities were committed," and supporting "that more than fiend, arch-bishop *Laud* and the clergy of his stamp, in all their church-tyranny and hellish cruelties." Those who deposed Charles had made "a most righteous and glorious stand . . . in defence of the natural and legal rights of the people." They had shown that it was "warrantable and glorious" for wronged citizens "to disobey the civil powers" and "to rise unanimously even against the sovereign himself, in order to redress their grievances; to vindicate their natural and legal rights: to break the yoke of tyranny, and free themselves and posterity from inglorious servitude and ruin." The lesson of the English Civil War, Mayhew argued, was that "no civil rulers are to be obeyed when they enjoin things that are inconsistent with the commands of God: All such disobedience is lawful and glorious." These militant statements reflect the fact that Mayhew had prepared for his sermon by reading seventeenth-century antiauthoritarian classics by Algernon Sidney, John Milton, and John Locke as well as eighteenth-century works by Reverend Benjamin Hoadly, a sharp critic of the Stuarts, and John Trenchard and Thomas Gordon, the authors of the influential Whig essay collection *Cato's Letters.*

Mayhew blasted the Episcopalians for revering the memory of a king who was "*laden with iniquity*" while portraying "our [New England] ancestors . . . in the blackest colours, not only as sc[h]ismatics, but also as traitors and rebels and all that is bad."[21] Mayhew saw clear signs of an Anglican plot to take over American churches. "People have no security against being unmercifully *priest-ridden*," he declared, "but by keeping all imperious BISHOPS, and other CLERGYMEN who love to 'Lord it over God's heritage,' from getting their *foot* into the *stirrup* at all." Even a single bishop assigned to America would lead to "ecclesiastical tyranny." The same was true of political domination. "Civil tyranny," Mayhew said, "is usually small in its beginning, like the 'drop of a bucket,' till at length, like a mighty torrent, or the raging waves of the sea, it bears down all before it, and deluges whole countries and empires."

Mayhew faced a stinging Tory backlash. A correspondent to *The Boston News-Letter* lambasted Mayhew's "scandalous" pamphlet, with its "foul imputations" and "gross falsehoods . . . unjustly aspersing and traducing the pious Memories of the Royal Martyr King CHARLES the First, and the Most Reverend WILLIAM LAUD."[22] *The Boston Evening-Post*, dubbing Mayhew a "wrangling Preacher in this Town" who had just "belch'd out a Flood of Obloquy upon the pious Memory of King Charles the first," reprinted a seventeenth-century sermon eulogizing Charles.[23] But Mayhew's sermon had strong support among future Patriot leaders, who came to see it as "the first peal on the trumpet of freedom in this Western World, blown clear and loud enough to be heard over land and water far and wide."[24]

The face-off over Mayhew's sermon was part of a larger confrontation over historical interpretations of the English Civil War. On one side were conservative historians—from the royalist Lord Clarendon to the skeptical Scottish philosopher-historian David Hume to the Irish statesman Edmund Burke—who wrote histories that portrayed the Puritan foes of the Stuart monarchs as unruly fanatics who had senselessly provoked the revolution in England; in this telling, some Puritans moved away and, despite their saintly pretensions, persecuted heretics in New England. On the other side were Whig-slanted historians—notably the Independent clergyman Daniel Neal, the dissenting minister William Harris, and the author Catharine Macaulay—who depicted Charles I and his henchmen as heartless despots who were rightfully deposed by freedom-seeking Puritans.[25]

The latter view became prominent in America, in part due to the effort of the British Whig Thomas Hollis, a wealthy London-based bibliophile who wielded influence on both sides of the Atlantic. Hollis, for whom Cromwell was a hero, had spread revolutionary ideas by sending thousands of Whig writings—by Milton, Vane, Locke, Sidney, and others—to institutions and individuals in various countries. (He donated more than five thousand volumes to Harvard, where they were read by future Founding Fathers.) For Tories, Hollis was "a bigotted Whig . . . who mis-spent an ample fortune in paving the way for sedition and revolt . . . by dispersing democratical works" that "laid the first train of combustibles for the American explosion."[26] The works Hollis disseminated had a cross-fertilizing impact: He sent British writings to America and American ones to England. A fervent supporter of the American cause, he befriended Jonathan Mayhew, James Otis, John Adams, Benjamin Franklin, and other Patriots, sharing works with them and seeing to the publication of their writings abroad.

## DISCOVERING THE FOREFATHERS

Devotion to Whig principles in America strengthened the retrospective veneration of early New England, especially the Plymouth and Massachusetts Bay Colonies. The question becomes: How could Americans sympathize with ancestors, many of whom were former victims of Stuart persecution, when they themselves became persecutors in Massachusetts, expelling nonconformists and waging war against the Pequots in the 1630s; instituting chattel slavery in the 1640s; hanging four Quakers between 1659 and 1661; joining with the Mohegan and Mohawk nations in the 1670s to destroy several Wampanoag communities in King Philip's War; and executing twenty people for witchcraft in Salem in 1692?

Eighteenth-century New Englanders avoided these troubling episodes by telescoping backward to the period *before* New England persecution began and looking to the time *after* it ended. This curated collective memory emphasized the earliest phase of Plymouth—the *Mayflower* generation—and the years just after the Glorious Revolution, when Plymouth and Massachusetts Bay merged under a new charter in the 1690s.

The revival of early Plymouth history was boosted by two significant events: The designation of Plymouth Rock as the landing site of the Pilgrims; and the first communal celebration of that landing.

In 1741, when the ninety-four-year-old Thomas Faunce, a former town clerk and church elder, heard that Plymouth was planning to build a wharf over a boulder on the shoreline, he asked to be taken there. He was carried in a chair three miles from his house to the rock, which he declared was where the *Mayflower* passengers first stepped ashore. He bade a tearful farewell to the rock. Moved by his reaction, the townspeople designed the wharf so that the rock would be preserved. Faunce came to be known as "the man who saved Plymouth Rock."

Did the *Mayflower*'s shallop really land at that rock, as Faunce claimed? Early Plymouth records don't confirm this. Faunce mentioned that he first heard the story from his father, who arrived in Plymouth in 1623, two years after the Pilgrims. He might have also heard it from others. When Faunce was growing up, twenty-three *Mayflower* passengers were still alive, and a few, including John Howland and John Alden, lived into his adulthood.[27]

Whether or not the story was true, Plymouth Rock quickly became a powerful symbol. In 1774, on the eve of the American Revolution, a group of Patriots moved the rock to Plymouth's town square and deposited it at the base of a liberty pole, on which a revolutionary banner waved. The ten-ton boulder was lifted with huge screws and hauled onto a wagon pulled by twenty yoke of oxen.[28] While being lifted, the rock split in two, a fact interpreted as a sign of the imminent separation of America from England. The bottom half of the rock was left in its place on the shore while the top section was taken to the flagpole.

If Plymouth Rock became a symbol of New England's founding, so did the anniversary of the *Mayflower*'s arrival. On December 22, 1769, less than six years before the outbreak of the American Revolution, the country's first public celebration of the 1620 arrival of the Pilgrims (then called Forefathers) took place in Plymouth. The Old Colony Club, a recently formed group of young Plymouth men with ancestral roots in the *Mayflower* generation, organized the event. The day began with cannon salutes, a parade through town, and the hanging of a flag emblazoned with Old Colony 1620 on a hall built for the occasion.[29] About a dozen club members gathered there for a midday meal that re-created an early New England feast. The courses included baked Native whortleberry pudding, succotash, a dish of clams, a serving of oysters and codfish, roasted venison, seafowl, dishes of frostfish and eel, apple pie, cranberry tarts, and locally produced cheese. After the dinner, toasts were made to central figures of the early Plymouth settlement, including William Bradford, Myles Standish, William Brewster, and Massasoit, the welcoming Wampanoag sachem.

An American tradition—the observance of Forefathers' Day on December 22 (thought to be the date of the arrival of the *Mayflower*'s shallop at Plymouth Rock)—had begun.[30] Over the next century and a half, Forefathers' Day would be celebrated, initially in New England and eventually elsewhere in the nation. As time proved, Forefathers' Day held the potential for delivering conflicting messages: some conventional, others radical—even revolutionary. From a conventional perspective, early Plymouth was a society of pious people who succeeded with enterprise and conservative values. From a radical vantage point, Plymouth was a unique experiment in democracy launched by independent-minded escapees of Stuart tyranny.

Both views were voiced at the 1769 feast. Tory members of the Old Colony Club used the occasion to support America's connection with the mother country. One Tory raised a glass to "a speedy and lasting union between Great Britain and her Colonies."[31] Whig members, on the other hand, invoked Plymouth's radical heritage. One declared, "May every person be possessed of the same noble sentiments against arbitrary power that our worthy ancestors were endowed with." Another snarled, "May every enemy to civil or religious liberty meet the same or a worse fate than Archbishop Laud"—a reference to the Anglican prelate who had driven religious dissidents out of England and who was beheaded during the Cromwellian Revolution.

This radical version of Plymouth won the day, helping to fuel passions that led to the American Revolution. The Old Colony Club disbanded in 1773, due to members' political differences, but Forefathers'

Day celebrations continued to be held by the Town of Plymouth every year on December 22 through 1780. All the speakers were clergymen, including Gad Hitchcock, who urged American colonists to imitate "our renowned fore-fathers, those free born spirits" who escaped "the iron hand of oppression"; Sylvanus Conant, who praised the Puritans for resisting "their greatest enemies," Charles I and Archbishop Laud, and teaching "the general nature of that freedom, civil and religious, to which we have all an equal right"; and Samuel Baldwin, who in 1775 hailed "the progenitors of this colony" who escaped "their oppressors, persecutors, and tyrants" and, in a reference to British ships then infesting the New England coast, thanked God "that there was hemp sufficient to hang all the Tories."[32]

## AMERICANS ON THE PURITAN WARPATH

Leading politicians promoted both radical messages aired in the Forefathers' Day speeches: the one about the Plymouth forefathers planting liberty and the other about the Cromwellian Puritans overthrowing a despot. "The first planters of Plymouth," John Adams wrote, "were 'our ancestors' in the strictest sense."[33] For the first time in the record of Western civilization, Adams maintained, a body of people lived independently under their own compact and laws, untethered from an established church and only loosely tied to a monarch.

In his words, the Plymouth settlers "set up a government of their own," with "no authority from the English parliament or crown," based "on the simple principle of nature." They "never purchased any charter for government, of the crown or the king, and continued to exercise all the powers of government, legislative, executive, and judicial, upon the plain ground of an original contract among independent individuals for sixty-eight years, that is, until their incorporation with Massachusetts."

Plymouth was also special to Adams's friend and fellow Patriot Mercy Otis Warren. A descendant of the *Mayflower* passenger Edward Doty, the cantankerous servant who became a wealthy landowner, Mercy Otis was born and raised in Barnstable, which was founded in 1639 as one of the earliest towns of Plymouth Colony on Cape Cod. Connected by several generations of religious Separatists to Plymouth's settlers, Mercy inherited an independent spirit shared by her brother James Otis Jr., the firebrand whose writings and speeches helped spark the American Revolution. Mercy married her brother's Harvard classmate James Warren, a Plymouth native who also had a *Mayflower* ancestor, the merchant Richard Warren. After they were married in 1754, Mercy and James lived on a farm on the Eel River that had been passed down through the Warrens since the 1620s. After three years on the farm, Mercy and James moved into a gambrel-roofed house in the center of Plymouth, where they raised five sons. James Warren took up the revolutionary cause in the 1760s, a decade when his brother-in-law James Otis led New England in resisting the taxes that the Crown imposed on the American colonies.

Mercy Otis Warren entered the political scene in the early 1770s, when she responded, on behalf of her brother, to a letter from the British Whig historian Catharine Macaulay. In April 1769, Macaulay wrote to James Otis, praising him as "the great Guardian of American Liberty" whose views resembled "the principles on which I have written the History of the Stewart Monarchs."[34] Because Macaulay's letter arrived while James Otis Jr. was incapacitated from a brutal beating about the head by British soldiers (an injury which began his decline and ultimate adjudication as mentally ill), Mercy picked up her pen to continue her brother's political arguments, founded on the Enlightenment principles of John Locke.

Like her friend Macaulay, Mercy Warren took a Whig view of the past. Macaulay, in her six-volume history of the Stuart kings, sided strongly with the Puritan rebellion against the monarchy. Mercy Warren took a similar position in her own 1805 three-volume *History of the Rise, Progress and Termination of the American Revolution*. She began her account by describing the settlement of New England as an act of rebellion against Stuart oppression. Many New Englanders, she wrote, fled "the tyranny of the Stuart race," whose "arbitrary system of government began with the weak and bigoted reign of James the First, and continued until the excision [i.e., execution] of his son Charles."[35] James I had driven John Robinson and his Separatist followers to relocate to Holland, whence some of them crossed the Atlantic in 1620 and settled in Plymouth Colony. Mercy wrote of the colonists, "Though dispirited by innumerable discouraging circumstances, they immediately entered into engagements with each other to form themselves into a regular society, and drew up a covenant, by which they bound themselves to submit to order and subordination. . . . The old Plymouth colony remained for some time a distinct government. They chose their own magistrates, independent of all foreign control."

Continued persecution of Puritans in England, Mercy wrote, accelerated the settlement of the Massachusetts Bay Colony. Were it not for the interference by Charles I, she noted, many other Puritan rebels—among them Hampden, Pym, Warwick, even Cromwell—might have left England for Massachusetts. Given that they remained, the Puritans took on the work of overthrowing the despotic Charles and establishing the commonwealth under Cromwell and the Independents. Warren minimized Cromwell's dictatorial Protectorship, describing him as a warrior for human rights.

Warren noted that Massachusetts Bay, unlike Plymouth, had a royal charter, but it was left virtually self-regulating because its legislature was popularly elected. She conceded that the intolerance of the 1650s, when the Bay Colony Puritans executed Quakers, was inexcusable, but she thought these actions should be seen in context. They reflected "the fashion of the times, and the dangers which threatened [the settlers] from every side. . . . [Also,] they might think their conduct in some

Mercy Otis Warren
*Portrait by John Singleton Copley, c. 1764*

degree sanctioned by the example of their parent state, and the rigours exercised in other parts of the European world at that time, against all denominations which differed from the religious establishments of government."[36] In a larger sense, she wrote, there is a "strange propensity in human nature," exhibited "in almost every country," for those in power to show an "intolerant and persecuting spirit" toward nonconformists.

She pointed out that intolerance was "not confined to the New England *puritans*. . . . In Virginia, Maryland, and some other colonies, where the votaries of the church of England were the stronger party, the dissenters of every description were persecuted, with little less rigour than had been experienced by the Quakers from the Presbyterians of the Massachusetts."[37] Heretics in the South "were imprisoned, banished, and treated with every mark of severity short of death." The South's dependence on slave labor fostered "aristocratic principles" and a disregard for "the common rights of man." Also, the South did not emphasize education as strongly as did the North, where literacy rates were high due to common schools and the early establishment of Harvard College. She concluded, "Both knowledge and property were more equally divided in the colder regions of the north; consequently a spirit of more equal liberty was diffused" than in the South.

In her *History*, Mercy does not mention the Salem witch trials, a dark stain on Massachusetts. Describing the trials had created problems for previous historians. Daniel Neal, the British Whig who in the 1720s and '30s wrote histories of New England and Puritanism, had high praise for the earliest New England settlers but gave a clear-eyed rendition of the witch hysteria that broke out later on. His realism was resented by readers like Samuel Sewall, who wrote, "It grieves me to see New-England's Nakedness laid open in the business of the Quakers, Anabaptists, Witchcraft."[38] Similar resentment among readers greeted Thomas Hutchinson's *The History of the Colony of Massachusetts-Bay* (1764). Hutchinson, a Massachusetts official who was detested by the Otises and Warrens for personal reasons and for his work as a royal appointee, did himself no favor among the Patriots by publishing this book. He gave a sketchy, largely negative picture of early Plymouth, and he noted the irony of Puritans who had escaped to Massachusetts only to become oppressors there. As for his antinomian great-grandmother, Anne Hutchinson, he insisted that she never would have been banished had not Governor Henry Vane "craftily" used her to bolster his position in the Bay Colony's religious battles.[39]

Mercy Warren in her *History* emphasized that New England abandoned persecution when the Glorious Revolution occurred, and

Plymouth and Massachusetts were merged under a new charter in 1691. Fresh possibilities for democracy opened up. As a result of the Act of Toleration under William and Mary, voting was no longer restricted to church members; it was now extended to males who owned a certain amount of property. Under the 1691 charter, the twenty-eight councillors of Massachusetts were annually chosen by the General Court. The governor, appointed by the Crown, could veto individual choices but had no power to nominate them himself. The Massachusetts legislature was chosen by popular ballot, and laws and taxes were determined locally.[40] A historian of colonial Massachusetts writes, "Bay colonists recognized . . . that their charter granted them an optimal combination of autonomy and legitimacy."[41] Mercy Warren argued that the colony had achieved a "just and happy medium" between a state of nature and "those high stages of civilization and refinement, that at once corrupt the heart and sap the foundations of happiness."[42]

Suspicion of secret plans by the Crown regarding the colonies simmered beneath the surface of outward loyalty to the Hanover monarchs, who ruled England from 1714 onward. Questions arose about the Crown-appointed colonial governors, some of whom were Englishmen with reputations as corrupt foreigners who sought extravagant salaries and stole money from public funds. Benjamin Franklin noted in 1768 that colonial governors "are generally strangers to the Provinces they are sent to govern, have no estate, natural connection, or relation there, to give them an affection for the country. . . . They come only to make money as fast as they can; are sometimes men of vicious characters and broken fortunes, sent by a Minister merely to get them out of the way."[43] This was an exaggeration, as was a British observer's comment that the governors were men of "bad, if any, principles, pimps, valet de chambres, electioneering scoundrels, . . . decayed courtiers and abandoned worn-out dependants."[44] Actually, most of the governors were not venal, and fewer than half were from abroad. Nonetheless, an aura of elitist corruption surrounded them.

A case in point was the aforementioned Thomas Hutchinson, a wealthy Bostonian who served as lieutenant governor of Massachusetts from 1758 until 1769, when he became acting governor and then governor of the colony. The Otis family seems to have had a special animus against Hutchinson because he had been awarded a Boston judgeship that had initially been slated for Mercy and James's politician father, James Otis Sr. In the eyes of Mercy Otis Warren, the rise to power of Hutchinson and the accession of George III to the kingship in 1761 placed Massachusetts under a Stuart-like tyranny. The king was under the sway of his childhood mentor and first prime minister, John Stuart, the third Earl of Bute, whom Mercy described as a "nobleman of the house of Stuart" who became "the director" of "this misguided sovereign," and instilled in him "all the inflated ideas of kingly prerogative" and visions of "the acquisition of empire."[45] George III and his Parliament imposed repressive policies on the American colonies, including taxes and a large occupying force of British troops. Although Thomas Hutchinson initially disagreed with these policies, he enforced them as an official devoted to the Crown. To the Otises, Hutchinson seemed especially evil because he was a Massachusetts native who sided with the monarchy and tarnished the New England past in his *History of Massachusetts-Bay*. The American colonists, Mercy Warren wrote, were now under "a complicated system of tyranny, that threatened the new world with a yoke unknown to their fathers."

Hutchinson and other loyalist officials, including his brother-in-law Andrew Oliver, a tax agent, became targets of widespread anger after the Stamp Act was passed in 1765. A mob of Bostonians, outraged over the sweeping tax on printed materials in the colonies, ransacked Hutchinson's mansion and hung Oliver in effigy. Although the Stamp Act was repealed after popular protest, new bills brought more signs of oppression. The Declaratory Act empowered Parliament to pass binding legislation on the colonies, and the Townshend Acts introduced taxes on many imported goods. Governor Hutchinson's position became ever more precarious, mainly because of a March 1770 military incident, known as the Boston Massacre, in which British soldiers fired into a crowd, causing five fatalities, and the December 1773 Boston Tea Party, in which Patriots disguised as Native Americans dumped 342 chests of tea into Boston Harbor in protest against an import tax.

Stiff and humorless, Thomas Hutchinson had strong Tory leanings. As a child, he had wept when he read about the beheading of Charles I.[46] Although raised a Congregationalist, he often attended King's Chapel, Boston's bastion of Anglicanism. While far from being a sheepish lackey to royalty, he frowned on democracy, believing that society should be governed from above. He likened revolutionaries in Massachusetts to the wild, Puritan fanatics of early New England. He wrote in 1771, "Boston people are run mad. The frenzy was not higher when they banished my pious great-grandmother [Anne Hutchinson], when they hanged the Quakers, when they afterwards hanged the poor innocent witches."

Hutchinson thought that American Whigs were conspiring to overthrow orderly government, while his opponents viewed him as the ringleader of an oppressive Tory conspiracy. Ever since the division between Whigs and Tories had appeared in England during the reign of Charles II, each side charged the other with conducting a wicked plot. Tories accused Whigs of scheming to demolish the structure of government and church by fomenting dissension, creating factions, and destroying time-tested hierarchies. The Whigs charged the Tories with conspiring to quash the rights of the individual by using all means possible to repress dissent and interfere with freedom of speech and religion.[47]

No one was more effective in limning what the Patriots regarded as a Tory conspiracy in America than Mercy Otis Warren. In three widely read plays published in Boston newspapers between 1772 and 1775, she sharply satirized Thomas Hutchinson and his Tory associates while making heroes of Massachusetts Patriots who opposed them. Hutchinson appears in the plays as Rapatio, the pasha of Upper Servia (Boston) in the northern region of Servia (the thirteen American colonies). In her history of the American Revolution, Warren describes Hutchinson as "dark, intriguing, insinuating, haughty and ambitious, while the extreme of avarice marked each feature of his character."[48] He appears in her plays as an amalgam of Nero, Judas, and Satan.[49] Over the course of the three plays, Rapatio endorses the Boston Massacre (in *The Adulateur*), betrays the American colonies by conspiring against them with a British official (*The Defeat*), and, having returned to England, is succeeded by Tories who plot to carry out his nefarious schemes (*The Group*). (In real life, Hutchinson was replaced as governor by General Thomas Gage in 1774 and spent the rest of his days in England, where he died in 1780.)

Besides exposing alleged corruption by Hutchinson and his retinue, Mercy Warren's plays contain references to historical phenomena that motivated Patriots, including what they saw as the tyranny of the Stuarts and the heroism of the early New England settlers. In *The Group*, when the royal cause is losing ground, one of the Tory conspirators declares that their "doughty champion," Rapatio, will "prevail and terrify at last, / By bringing precedents from those blest days / When royal Stewarts, Britain's scepter sway'd, / And taught her sons the right divine of Kings."[50] Among the favorite books of Rapatio's group are a volume in praise of the Stuart kings, Thomas Hobbes's *Leviathan* (a defense of absolute monarchy), a piece by Massachusettensis (the Tory journalist Jonathan Sewall), and, naturally, Thomas Hutchinson's anti-Puritan *History of the Colony of Massachusetts-Bay*.

The opponents of Rapatio's schemers, the so-called virtuous senators with Romanized names, were Patriots in Mercy Otis Warren's circle, including Rusticus (her husband, James Warren), Brutus (her brother James Otis Jr.), and several friends, like Cassius (Samuel Adams) and Hortensius (John Adams). These characters describe how appalled their ancestors would be if they witnessed their pioneering experiment in liberty being threatened by Rapatio and his associates. *The Adulateur* starts with Cassius (Sam Adams) reminding Brutus (James Otis) of "our noble ancestors, / Who liv'd for freedom . . . / Who in this desart stock'd with beasts and men, . . . / Grasp'd at freedom, and they nobly won it; / Then smil'd and dy'd contented."[51]

Three years after Mercy Otis Warren wrote *The Adulateur*, a battle broke out between the minutemen of Lexington and Concord and invading British troops—the first skirmish in an eight-year war that would take more than twenty-five thousand American lives—about 1 percent of the population (the equivalent of 3.4 million Americans today).

In her plays, Mercy Otis Warren was precise in her selection of Massachusetts revolutionaries to portray and in highlighting their dedication to the ideals of earlier Puritan rebels. Take her brother James Otis. He sparked political turmoil against England with courtroom speeches that echoed early Puritan insurrections. Originally a rising talent as a government lawyer, Otis switched his political viewpoint from loyalty to independence, in part because of his offense at signs of royal tyranny and in part for personal grievance that his father had been passed over for the position of chief justice of the Massachusetts Superior Court, which went instead to Thomas Hutchinson. In 1761, James Otis delivered a rousing courtroom argument about the notorious writs of assistance. The event is considered a defining moment in America's revolutionary struggle.

Otis's speech revived seventeenth-century-style hostility toward the Stuarts. Writs of assistance—search warrants that gave government officials broad power to search private property without prior legal approval—dated back to the early Restoration, when King Charles II imposed them to enforce the Navigation Acts, which mandated that colonial merchants trade only with England. The untethered search warrants were intended to stop smuggling, but smuggling persisted anyway, and a new round of writs of assistance was passed between

1755 and 1760. When George III took the throne in 1760, sixty Boston merchants called on James Otis and another lawyer, Oxenbridge Thacher, to challenge the constitutionality of the writs of assistance. The merchants offered Otis a substantial fee, but he was so passionate about the issue that he served pro bono.

The court hearing took place in the stately upper chamber of Boston's Old State House. Seated at a long table were five pompous-looking justices, Thomas Hutchinson at their head, who wore immense wigs and scarlet judicial gowns. On the walls of the chamber hung large gold-framed full-length portraits of the Stuart kings Charles I and James II, looking high and mighty in their ermine and flowing robes. In this atmosphere of regal haughtiness, the thirty-six-year-old James Otis, an attorney known for his volatility, rose to his feet and lashed out against government authority. "Otis was a flame of fire!" John Adams later remarked. "Then and there was the first scene of the first Act of opposition to the Arbitrary claims of Great Britain. Then and there the Child Independence was born."[52]

In his speech, Otis criticized the open-ended search warrants as a violation of human rights. They were first issued, he declared, "in the zenith of arbitrary power, viz. In the reign of [Charles II] when Star-chamber powers were pushed in extremity by some ignorant clerk of the Exchequer."[53] One can imagine the hot-tempered Otis wagging an angry finger at the portraits of two Stuart monarchs on the wall when he described the writs of assistance as relics of "a kind of power, the exercise of which in former periods of English history, cost one King of England [Charles I] his head and another [James II] his throne."

Otis lost the case, but his argument won him instant popularity, and he was elected to the Massachusetts House of Representatives. Over the next nine years, he led a Puritan-inspired movement toward independence with his novel ideas of democracy and equality. In a 1662 speech, he compared then-governor Francis Bernard's suspension of debate over a funding bill with arbitrary power plays by the Stuarts.

Had England's rulers always exhibited such capricious intrusiveness, Otis declared, the colonies would never have escaped the "oppressions and misfortunes of the *Charles's* and *James's*" and "to this day might have been in chains."[54] John Adams regarded this speech as one of America's finest documents due to its Lockean insistence on human equality. Fourteen years before Jefferson penned the statement "all men are created equal" in the preamble to the Declaration of Independence, Otis in his speech announced, "God made all men naturally equal." No one, Otis continued, is innately superior to anyone else. As for kings and colonial governors, they were "made for the good of the people, and not the people for them."

Otis's stirring pleas went unheeded by the Crown, which imposed new taxes without giving the American colonists representation in Parliament. Whether or not he coined the phrase "taxation without representation is tyranny," as John Adams reported, he is known to have stated, "No parts of His Majesty's dominions can be taxed without their consent."[55]

Otis exhibited the fighting spirit of one of his heroes, Oliver Cromwell. In editorials that Otis wrote opposing British taxes, he adopted the pseudonym "Hampden," based on Cromwell's cousin John Hampden, who helped instigate the Puritan Revolution by refusing to pay the ship-money tax that Charles I demanded. Otis as Hampden berated the Stuarts while praising the New England settlers. Otis wrote, "The origin of the British colonies was in the cruel persecutions set on foot in church and state under the family of *Stuart*. These persecutions drove out thousands and tens of thousands, during the reigns of the three first of that arbitrary race."[56] Otis continued, "the brave tho' banished puritans, assisted only by almighty God, in a miraculous support of their piety, virtue and resolution, had surmounted all obstacles, and firmly established themselves" in colonies under charters that let them decide on local matters—a point Benjamin Franklin also made when he wrote that the Puritans, "in removing to America, a Country out of the

Realm, did not carry with them the Statutes then existing."[57] The self-rule enjoyed by New England's settlers was now threatened by British taxes and trade limitations. The "forefathers," James Otis contended, had more freedom than current-day Americans. Why, he asked, should "the next generation of men . . . not have the same right to make original compacts as their ancestors had?"[58]

Otis, however, became afflicted with a psychological disorder, which brought growing tension within his household. His wife and daughter were ardent Tories who strongly opposed his politics, further isolating him. His behavior showed signs of what might today be identified as bipolar disorder. John Adams, recording the decline of his colleague, noted in his diary that Otis had become "raving mad—raving vs. Father, Wife, Brother, Sister, Friend &c."[59] In November 1771, Otis's family brought him before a probate court, which found him to be a "Distracted or Lunatick Person" who must be remanded to custody.[60] The court was headed by his political nemesis, the Tory Thomas Hutchinson, who wrote on December 3, "Otis was carried off today in a post-chaise, bound hand and foot. He has been as good as his word, set the province in a flame and perished in the attempt."[61] For the rest of his days, Otis lived mainly in the care of family and friends. In 1783, he was struck dead by lightning as he stood watching a thunderstorm.

His mission to magnify the memory of the Plymouth settlers had been assumed by his brother-in-law, James Warren. On October 14, 1765, Warren organized a town meeting that issued resolutions declaring Plymouth's disapproval of the Stamp Act. Plymouth residents, the resolutions announced, "inhabit the spot where our ancestors founded an *asylum for liberty* . . . without the aid or assistance of any power on earth." The Plymouth group urged the Massachusetts House of Representatives to "avoid disgracing the memories of our ancestors" and issue "full and explicit assertions of our rights" through a forceful challenge to the "fatal" Stamp Act; this would show "that we never will be slaves to any power on earth."[62]

Two weeks later, on October 29, the House issued the famous Massachusetts Resolves, which stated that "all Acts made, by any Power whatever other than the General Assembly of this Province, imposing Taxes on the Inhabitants are Infringements of our *inherent* and *unalienable* Rights, as *Men* and *British Subjects:* and render void the most valuable Declarations of our *Charter*."[63] After Parliament, faced with intense protest, repealed the Stamp Act in February, the Plymouth group sent a letter congratulating Massachusetts for its bold stand against the tax. A legislative committee in Boston wrote a public reply hailing Plymouth as "the most ancient Town in New England," adding that the "fervent wish" of Boston was "that the Spirit of our venerable Forefathers, may revive and be defused [*sic*] through every Community in this Land: That Liberty Civil and Religeous, the grand Object of their View, may still be felt . . . by the present Generation, and . . . transmitted to our latest Posterity."[64]

The legislative committee that wrote the public letter was headed by Samuel Adams, a man devoted to the radical legacy of the Pilgrims. In a manifesto of 1773, Adams wrote, "May God inspire us with that ardent Zeal for the support of religious & civil Liberty which animated the Breasts of the first Settlers of the old Colony of Plymouth. . . . After the Example of those renowned Heroes, whose memory we revere, let us gloriously defend our Rights & Liberties, & resolve to transmit the fair Inheritance they purchased for us with Treasure & Blood to their latest posterity."[65]

Sam Adams, like other Massachusetts Patriots, was driven by two forces in history that he believed were intertwined: the settling of New England and the English Civil War. When Adams launched his protest against British taxation in October 1765, he drew the reasons for objection from the settler history of New England. The Stamp Act, he declared, "wholly cancels the very conditions upon which our ancestors settled this country and enlarged his Majesty's dominions, with much toil and blood, and at their sole expense."[66] Those conditions were set forth in Massachusetts' original charter. The Stamp Act was "totally subversive," Adams wrote, of the "civil government, expressed in our charter, which amply secures to the Crown our allegiance, to the nation our connection, and to ourselves the indefeasible rights of Britons." The most famous portrait of Samuel Adams, by John Singleton Copley, depicts him standing against a dark background and gazing determinedly, his left hand pointing down to the Massachusetts charter spread on a table beside him. The painting reflects Adams's belief, shared by his fellow revolutionaries, that British taxes imposed from 1765 onward were egregious violations of the longstanding charters of the colonies, which mandated adherence to English law but, except for quitrents on land in some colonies, left settlers free to decide on matters like taxes. The settlers of the Bay Colony, Adams wrote, "obtained a charter from King Charles the First, wherein his Majesty was pleased to recognize . . . the rights, liberties, privileges and immunities of his natural born subjects within the realm." Charles II, Adams wrote, arbitrarily "vacated" the charter, which was restored, in an altered form, under William and Mary.

Sam Adams was called the "Cromwell of America"—an insult when uttered by his Tory foes, but a high compliment when it came from his Whig supporters.[67] Adams, who sometimes used the pen name "A Puritan" in his newspaper writings, surely would have appreciated the comparison to the Lord Protector. In his view, Cromwell had fought for liberty. The beheading of Charles I, Adams wrote, spelled the end of "*passive obedience*, *non-resistance*, the *divine hereditary right* of kings." Under Cromwell, "the people assumed the right of free enquiry into the nature and the end of government, and the conduct of those entrusted with it"—inquiry that would lead to the idea of government by consent, an ideal illuminated by the philosopher John Locke, whom Adams frequently cited.[68] Similar Puritan-rooted impulses also motivated Samuel Adams's second cousin, John Adams. In July 1766, John Adams discovered what he called "a curious Volume" that an assistant

Samuel Adams, pointing to the original
Massachusetts charter of 1629
*Portrait by John Singleton Copley, c. 1772*

had found in a chest of drawers. Adams described the volume as "a Collection of Pamphlets, published in the memorable Year 1640, bound up together, in one Quarto Volume."[69] The pamphlets date to the earliest phase of the English Civil War. Within the treasure trove were insurrectionary speeches that indicted the monarchy and the Anglican church by John Pym and other Puritan firebrands.

Soon John Adams was using important names from seventeenth-century England and the early American colonies to voice rebellious ideas in print. Using the pseudonym Clarendon (an adviser of the Stuart monarchs who had written a history of the English Civil War),

Adams undermined Clarendon's royalist perspective in newspaper pieces. Adams has Clarendon tell the Cromwell supporter John Pym, "Since my Departure from the Earth, I have revolved these Things so often, and seen my Errors so clearly, that were I to write an History of your [Pym's] Opposition [to King Charles I] now, I should not entitle it a Rebellion; nay, I should scarcely call the Protectorate of Cromwell, an Usurpation."[70] Reacting to the vice admiralty courts that England in the 1760s used to enforce the sugar and stamp taxes, Adams as Clarendon compared protests against "the newly formed courts of admiralty in America" with the Puritans' struggles "against the star chamber, and high commission" under Archbishop Laud.[71] Likewise, he wrote, America's resistance to unrepresentative taxation in the 1760s recalled the campaign "against ship-money, and the other projects of [the] disgraceful reign" of Charles I.

In other periodical articles Adams, a descendant of the *Mayflower* passenger John Alden, took on the persona of Governor John Winthrop of the Massachusetts Bay Colony in dialogue with William Bradford, the governor of early Plymouth Colony. Trying, like his clergyman mentor Jonathan Mayhew, to arouse Americans after the repeal of the Stamp Act in 1766, Adams had Winthrop and Bradford describe their bold efforts to keep liberty alive at any cost. Winthrop writes, "True religion, my friend Bradford, was the grand motive, with you and me, to undertake our arduous and hazardous enterprise, and to plant [settlements] . . . on the plan of freedom, popular power and private judgment." Eternal vigilance, Adams's Winthrop warns, is needed to prevent "a brave and free people" from becoming "insensible to the difference, between freedom and slavery" and losing the capacity "to perceive the approaches of arbitrary power."[72]

Adams also took note of the powerful stand that Ipswich, a coastal town thirty miles north of Boston, made during the Stamp Act crisis. In October 1765 the town meeting adopted pointed instructions rejecting the tax and denying Parliament's right to impose it. Although not a violent uprising, Ipswich's defiance recalled an earlier moment in its history—Puritan minister John Wise's celebrated resistance in 1687 to Governor Edmund Andros's imposition of unlawful taxes. Wise's protest, long commemorated in local memory, later helped earn Ipswich the reputation as the "Birthplace of American Independence."[73]

John Adams discussed the rebelliousness of the current Ipswich group and highlighted the Ipswich Instructions, the group's defiant statement proclaiming that Massachusetts, according to its original charter, was not required to pay taxes to England. The instructions read: "When our Fathers Left their Native Country, they came of their Own accord and at their own Expense and took possession of a country they were obliged to Buy or Fight for and to which the [English] Nation had no more Right than the Moon."[74] This statement, Adams said, "met with such strong feelings in the Readers, that their Effect was astonishing to me, and excited some serious Reflections."[75] Forty towns in Massachusetts, he noted, quickly issued similar statements to their representatives. The Ipswich Instructions launched Adams on a train of thought that led him to conclude as he told a friend "that We were under no subjection to the British Parliament, that our Forefathers came from Leyden &c.—and . . . were considered formerly both here and at Home, as Allies rather than Subjects. The first Settlement certainly was not a national Act, i.e., . . . Neither the People of England, nor their Representatives contributed any thing towards it."[76]

If thinking about the Ipswich revolt and the early governors Bradford and Winthrop strengthened Adams's understanding of New England's original independence, the example of the Puritan warrior Oliver Cromwell motivated him to fight for America's separation from England. Adams was aware of Cromwell's flaws as a ruler but revered him anyway. "Cromwell did not establish a government as free, as he might and ought," Adams conceded, "but his government was infinitely more glorious and happy to the people than Charles's." Had

Charles gone unresisted, Adams opined, history would have reversed course. Adams wrote, "If Charles's schemes had succeeded, there is great reason to apprehend that the light of science would have been extinguished, and mankind, drawn back to a state of darkness and misery, like that which prevailed from the fourth to the fourteenth century. . . . In all human probability, liberty civil and religious, not only in England but in all Europe, would have been lost."[77]

Cromwell and his Puritans, Adams believed, had saved England from crushing tyranny; now it was the turn of Puritan-inspired American Patriots to do the same. In 1775, just as the American Revolution was beginning, Adams reported that American Patriots were prepared to meet the British with Cromwellian firmness. "If they send the sword and fire to ravage in this country," he wrote, "they will find in New-England an hundred thousand descendants of the puritans in the Charles's and James's days, who have not yet lost entirely the spirit of Englishmen under the English [Cromwellian] commonwealth."[78]

By the time John Adams made this declaration, the call for a second Cromwellian Revolution echoed throughout the colonies. The Sons of Liberty—the resistance group responsible for the Boston Tea Party, whose members included Samuel Adams, James Otis, Paul Revere, and John Hancock—venerated Oliver Cromwell. A British informer reported hearing members of the group declare "that the King was a Tyrant, a Rascal, and a Fool, and deserv'd to have his Head Cut off, as much as Charles the First," and "that Oliver Cromwell was a glorious fellow, and what a pitty it was they had not such another to espouse their Cause at the present."[79] The Sons of Liberty signed themselves as "O. C." on a 1773 notice calling for the resignation of English tax officials. The Patriot Joshua Brackett ran a Boston inn avoided by Tories called O. Cromwell's Head Tavern; outside hung a sign, which was emblazoned with an image of the Lord Protector. A Boston almanac for "1776, the year of American Independence," replaced dates honoring George III with ones commemorating Oliver Cromwell.[80] In his incendiary pamphlet *Common Sense* (1776), Thomas Paine argued that England's policies reflected the same kingly oppressiveness that had sparked the Puritan Revolution, now cleverly masked through Parliament. In Paine's words, "The fate of Charles the First hath only made kings more subtle—not more just."[81] Responding to pacifist Quakers, who claimed only God could permit violent revolution, Paine responded with sharp irony, "Oliver Cromwell thanks you," suggesting that God, who supported Cromwell, must therefore approve of overthrowing George III, "the present proud imitator" of Charles.

Founding Father Benjamin Rush, the Philadelphia doctor and politician who signed the Declaration of Independence and organized Pennsylvania's ratification of the Constitution, credited his embrace of republican thought to a conversation about Cromwell and his legacy in 1766 with the Edinburgh medical student John Bostock. Rush and Bostock discovered that each had an ancestor in Cromwell's New Model Army. The conversation led to Bostock's description of the Puritan political philosopher Algernon Sidney. Rush reported that Sidney's ideas set off an inner revolution. "Never before had I heard the authority of Kings called in question," he recollected. For the first time he realized that "no form of government can be rational but that which is derived from the Suffrages of the people. . . . This great and active truth became a ferment in my mind."[82]

By 1777, American newspapers were openly linking George III and Charles I as tyrants, a topic expanded on in a widely read article, "A Comparison between *Charles the First*, commonly called the Martyr, and *George the Third*, without the Grace of GOD, King of *Great-Britain*, &c.," that stated, "*George* the Third has perfectly imbibed the dangerous maxims of that misguided Monarch [Charles I]; he has so nearly copied him in almost every respect, that one of the *Pythagorean* opinion must certainly believe, that the soul of *Charles* is transmigrated into *George*."[83]

## CROMWELLIAN SOUTHERNERS

The fact that the article linking George III with Charles I as tyrants first appeared in a Maryland newspaper shows how far the South had come in accepting the Cromwellian view. Earlier on, the South, with its commitment to Anglicanism and its diplomatic loyalty to the monarchy, disdained the memory of Cromwell.[84] The Virginia landowner William Byrd declared in 1739 that it was "abominable to mention the name of Oliver Cromwell" in the South.[85]

The change in Southern attitudes came in the 1760s. Indeed, it was the South, not the North, that first invoked Cromwell the king killer as a metaphor for the need to overthrow George III. The Virginia orator Patrick Henry—later famous for declaring "Give me liberty or give me death"—introduced the regicide image to American political discourse. In May 1765, two months after the Stamp Act was passed, the twenty-nine-year-old Henry, a lean, blue-eyed first-year burgess from Hanover County, gave a speech in the Virginia Assembly in which he denounced British taxation and made the stunning declaration that George III should meet the fate of previous despots who had been justly killed, including Charles I. Thomas Jefferson, present when Henry spoke, later described the scene to the biographer William Wirt, whose vivid account of the speech would be memorized by generations of American schoolchildren. Wirt wrote that Henry, "while he was descanting on the tyranny of the obnoxious act . . . exclaimed, in a voice of thunder, and the look of a god, 'Caesar had his Brutus—Charles the first, his Cromwell—and George the third—[a pause, with shouts erupting from alarmed fellow legislators] *may profit by their example.*'" The shouts during Henry's pause, according to Wirt, were cries of "Treason, treason," that "echoed from every part of the house," in response to which Henry said, "If *this* be treason, make the most of it."[86]

Sympathy with the Cromwellian Revolution may have seemed treasonous in the South in 1765, but it became increasingly less so as British encroachments on America grew. In 1774, Jefferson tapped into the spirit of Puritan insurrection. Appalled by England's plan to close the port of Boston to all commerce, Jefferson thought that he could stir up revolutionary fervor in the South most effectively by reviving the militancy of the Puritan rebels of the English Civil War. He, Patrick Henry, Richard Henry Lee, and several other Virginia legislators went into the council room of the Virginia Assembly and pored over volumes of writings by John Rushworth, an English lawyer and clerk of the House of Commons during the English Civil War. Rushworth wrote scrupulous firsthand accounts of the Long Parliament, battlefield encounters between the Puritans and the Cavaliers, and the execution of Charles I. Rushworth's seven-volume *Historical Collections* contained remonstrances, petitions, declarations, and speeches produced during the English Civil War. In anger over the Boston Port Act of 1774, Jefferson and his associates perused Rushworth in search of Puritan catalysts for revolution. "We thought Oliver Cromwell would be a good guide in such a case. So we looked into Rushworth," Jefferson later recalled:

> With the help therefore of Rushworth, whom we rummaged over for the revolutionary precedents & forms of the Puritans of that day, preserved by him, we cooked up a resolution, somewhat modernizing their phrases, for appointing the 1st day of June, on which the Port bill was to commence, for a day of fasting, humiliation & prayer, to implore heaven to avert from us the evils of civil war, to inspire us with firmness in support of our rights.[87]

Applying what he found in Rushworth to Virginia, Jefferson found that the Puritan religious custom of fasting and prayer, which had proved inspirational to opponents of Charles I, had a strong impact when Virginians observed the custom on June 1, the day the British closed Boston Harbor. "Our fast produced very considerable effect," Jefferson reported; Virginians "came together in great multitudes" in support of Boston. Under the pressure of the revolutionary crisis, any cultural differences between the South and the North were momentarily put aside in the name of a unified response to England.

This spirit of colonial unity was reinforced by another practice deeply rooted in Puritan New England: the town meeting. Tocqueville affirmed, "It is incontestable that in the United States the taste and the practice of republican government were born in the towns and within the provincial assemblies."[88]

Committees of correspondence—information networks between towns, each of which held democratic meetings—were formed to coordinate resistance to England. The first longstanding committees were formed in November 1772, when Samuel Adams convened a group of Patriots in Boston after discussing the idea with James and Mercy Otis Warren in their Plymouth home. At the Boston meeting Sam Adams's group issued resolutions charging England with violating rights that had been established by New England's earliest settlers and later confirmed by the 1691 Massachusetts charter. The Boston resolutions stated, "Our Ancestors came over to this Country that they might not only enjoy their civil but their religious Rights, and particularly desired to be freed from the Prelates, who in those times cruelly persecuted all who differed in sentiment from the established Church." Later, according to the resolutions, "Our Ancestors received from King William and Queen Mary a Charter, by which it was understood by both Parties in the contract, that such a proportion or balance was fixed," that no part of the government would control other parts. This "*Equilibrium*, without which we cannot continue a free State" was now destroyed by England's overbearing actions.[89]

Within months, more than one hundred Massachusetts towns had joined the resistance network. Soon, towns in other colonies joined as well. Mercy Otis Warren wrote, "Perhaps no single step contributed so much to cement the union of the colonies, and the final acquisition of independence, as the establishment of committees of correspondence." By disseminating news of "the intrigues of *toryism* . . . and every thing else that might be thought to militate with the rights of the people," Mercy explained, the committees created "a chain of communication from New Hampshire to Georgia, that produced unanimity and energy throughout the continent."[90]

A violent incident in Rhode Island boosted the committees of correspondence, greatly strengthening intercolonial unity. On June 9, 1772, the British customs schooner HMS *Gaspee*, infamous for capturing and looting American ships suspected of smuggling, ran aground in Rhode Island's Narragansett Bay while pursuing an American packet sloop. Stuck in shallow water off a small peninsula (later named Gaspee Point), the British ship was an irresistible target for Patriots incensed at England's navigation restrictions. John Brown, a wealthy Providence merchant and a member of the Sons of Liberty, rallied a group of relatives and friends to attack the stranded vessel. Under the cover of night, the disguised Patriots rowed to the *Gaspee* in long boats, boarded the ship, engaged in a fracas in which the ship's captain was wounded, took the crew members captive, and headed for shore. As they departed, the attackers set fire to the *Gaspee*, triggering a massive explosion caused by gunpowder in the hold. The *Gaspee* burned to the waterline.

Tories were horrified. Thomas Hutchinson, governor of Massachusetts, castigated the "atrocious" violence of "our liberty people"; he suggested that the *Gaspee* arsonists should be "carried directly to England. A few punished at Execution Dock, would be the only effectual preventive of any further attempts."[91] This idea became a real possibility when a royal official, under the king's orders, appointed a commission to seek out suspects and transport them to England, where they would be tried for treason. This crime carried the death penalty. The prospect of American colonists being extradited to England violated the charters of the American colonies, which allowed for local adjudication of criminal cases. Bitter outcries, laced with anti-Stuart rhetoric, came from Whigs. John Adams compared the king's commission with the "Star Chamber Court" under Archbishop Laud.[92] Under the pseudonym Americanus, Adams wrote an article, published in many American newspapers and reprinted in London, in which he excoriated George III's "alarming star-chamber inquisition" and insisted that "an evil infinitely worse, in its consequences, than all the revenue laws which have been passed from the reign of Charles the First, to this time, now threatens this distressed, piratically plundered country."[93] In his bestselling *Oration Upon the Beauties of Liberty* the Boston preacher John Allen responded to the *Gaspee* inquest by warning, "For violating the people's rights, Charles Steward, King of England lost his Head, and if another King, who is more solemnly bound than ever Charles Steward was, should tread in the same steps, what can he expect?"[94]

As it turned out, the planned trial in England never occurred, because suspects could not be identified. But the Crown's initial reaction to the *Gaspee* affair provoked Samuel Adams to pursue the committees of correspondence with extra vigor. He wrote to Virginian Richard Henry Lee, who discussed the king's extraordinary edict with his colleagues in the General Assembly, which took decisive action. On March 12, 1773, Thomas Jefferson met with ten other assemblymen to implement committees that, in his words, "would combine all the colonies in a single aim of protesting against England," because "the most urgent of all measures was that of coming to an understanding with all the other colonies to consider the British claims as a common cause to all, & to produce an unity of action." Jefferson explained, "A comm[itt]ee of corresp[on]d[en]ce in each colony would be the best instrument for intercommunication."[95]

The committees of correspondence elicited fear and loathing among Tories. One loyalist branded the committee network as "the foulest, subtlest, and most venomous serpent ever issued from the egg of sedition."[96] Thomas Hutchinson called the committees "very dangerous."[97] A follower of Rapatio in Mercy Warren's plays declared that it had now become impossible "to break the union, and dissolve the bonds" of the Patriots, "With their Committees, working in each town / With unremitting vigilance and care, / To baffle ev'ry evil machination."[98]

In Virginia the establishment of the revolutionary committee system impelled Governor Dunmore to terminate the colony's legislative assembly in May 1774. Dunmore's dictatorial action was far more impactful on intracolonial unity than his last-ditch proclamation, eighteen months later, offering freedom to enslaved people if they joined the British side, which is sometimes featured as the main reason that a supposedly reluctant South joined the revolutionary movement. The South had enthusiastically teamed up with the North long before Dunmore's emancipation order. On May 27, 1774, the day after Dunmore dissolved the legislature, Thomas Jefferson and eighty-eight other burgesses met in the Raleigh Tavern in Williamsburg and issued a broadside expressing outrage over England's treatment of "our sister colony of Massachusetts Bay" and recommending that Virginia's "committee of correspondence . . . communicate, with their several corresponding committees, on the expediency of appointing deputies from the several colonies of British America, to meet in general congress, at such place annually as shall be thought most convenient; there to deliberate on those general measures which the united interests of America may from time to time require."[99] The broadside led to the meeting in Philadelphia of the First Continental Congress in September 1774. Representatives from all the colonies except Georgia attended the Congress—the first major political step toward separation from England.

There's evidence that the most celebrated document of separation, the Declaration of Independence, was spurred by the same Puritan-based forces that lay behind the explosive anti-British sentiment of the 1770s. Most of the American requests to the Crown before then had been petitions. Even the Massachusetts legislature, with the combative

James Otis present, when reminding England that it had traditionally allowed colonies to govern themselves, framed the point in subservient language: "It is humbly hoped that his Majesty and the Parliament, will in their wisdom be graciously pleased to continue the colonists in this happy state."[100] A declaration, in contrast to a petition, resembled a legal statement of a plaintiff against a defendant. It was made when other avenues of communication had broken down. Jefferson writes in the declaration: "In every stage of these Oppressions We have Petitioned for Redress in the most humble terms: Our repeated Petitions have been answered only by repeated injury. A Prince whose character is thus marked by every act which may define a Tyrant, is unfit to be the ruler of a free People."[101]

Declarations in English history had appeared most frequently as statements of parliamentary protest against the Stuart monarchs—especially by the Long Parliament under Charles I in the 1640s. As Stephen E. Lucas writes, "By the eighteenth century a parliamentary 'declaration' had become so associated with the battles between Parliament and the Stuart kings as to be reserved for use only in the kinds of revolutionary situations that had convulsed England in the seventeenth century—and that would divide England from her thirteen North American colonies in the 1770s."[102]

The Declaration of Independence can be seen as an updated version of a seventeenth-century anti-Stuart declaration, revised to incorporate the egalitarian vision of the Lockean Enlightenment. The opening affirmation that "all men are created equal" and are born with "unalienable Rights" harks back to two of Jefferson's favorite thinkers, Locke and Sidney, and, before them, to the Levellers of the English Civil War. The declaration's direct attacks on George III, who is referred to more than twenty times in the blistering document, expand on the anti-monarchical impulse that had been gathering force since Patrick Henry's 1765 comparison of George III to Charles I. The most detailed contemporary analysis of the Declaration of Independence, a scathing 132-page critique written in 1776 by the British Tory John Lind, compared it with protests by "the Long Parliament, whose practice, and whose principles, the Congress seems to have proposed as its model."[103]

In the late afternoon of July 4, 1776, a few hours after the Declaration of Independence was signed by delegates to the Continental Congress, a three-member committee—Jefferson, Benjamin Franklin, and John Adams—was appointed to design a Great Seal for the United States of America. Jefferson and Franklin wanted a seal that would permanently associate the new nation with biblical deliverance and resistance to oppression. When weighing language to be used on the Great Seal, the two discussed the phrase REBELLION TO TYRANTS IS OBEDIENCE TO GOD. These militant words infused the spirit of English Civil War into the American uprising against George III. The source of the phrase was a newspaper article about John Bradshaw, the judge who had presided over the trial of Charles I. The piece on Bradshaw, which had appeared in the *Philadelphia Evening Post* on December 14, 1775, reported the discovery, three years earlier, of the judge's epitaph inscribed on a cannon in Jamaica, where Bradshaw had supposedly fled as a refugee from Charles II during the Restoration. Thomas Hollis noted that Bradshaw's reputed epitaph was "often seen pasted up in the homes of North America" and contributed to the people's anger over "the asperity of the war being carried on against them."[104] In proposing the epitaph's last line, about "Rebellion to Tyrants," for the Great Seal, Franklin and Jefferson were drawing a direct line from the beheading of one despot, Charles, to the prospective overthrow of another one, George.

The epitaph, however, was false. Scholars agree that Franklin wrote the *Evening Post* article as a hoax in order to stir up revolutionary passions.[105] The facts of John Bradshaw's death were far less romantic than Franklin suggested. Although some escapees of the Restoration had made it to Jamaica, Bradshaw was not among them. He died in 1659 and was buried with great fanfare in Westminster Abbey. Two years later, under Charles II, when the corpses of Bradshaw, Oliver Cromwell, and Henry Ireton were exhumed and their decapitated heads were posted on spikes atop Westminster Hall, Bradshaw's was in the middle.

Franklin's imaginary version of Bradshaw's posthumous fate was a radical Whig fantasy meant to inspire American revolutionaries. As it turned out, Congress rejected his "Rebellion to Tyrants" phrase and, after six years of debate, settled on the now-familiar design for the Great Seal: An eagle holds in one claw thirteen arrows (the original thirteen states) and in the other an olive branch (peace). E PLURIBUS UNUM (out of many, one) is inscribed on a golden banner. On the reverse side is a pyramid (the solidity of the nation) on which is a circle containing a radiant eye (watchful Providence), with encircling Latin phrases. Franklin grumbled about the design. The eagle, he insisted, was a bird "of bad moral character"—isolated, lazy, and rapacious, always ready to kill other birds for their prey. A better choice, he said, would have been the turkey, humble yet spirited, and native to America.[106] He took satisfaction, however, that he had contributed E PLURIBUS UNUM to the seal, a phrase he may have lifted from his favorite periodical, the London *Gentleman's Magazine*, where the phrase was a running line on the cover.[107] As for Jefferson, after Congress rejected the "Rebellion to Tyrants" motto, he adopted it for his own seal—the first of countless appropriations of the phrase, which would appear, sometimes along with the rest of the Bradshaw epitaph, in periodicals and speeches throughout the nineteenth century.[108]

The fact that Jefferson, a Southern plantation owner raised Episcopalian, adopted as his favorite motto a phrase that ostensibly came from the seventeenth-century Puritan Revolution shows the degree to which a Southerner's commitment to national independence could trump his Cavalier identity. Equally surprising was George Washington, another wealthy Virginia planter who was the scion of Anglican Cavaliers. We saw that the Cavaliers of Virginia had close associations with Sir Robert

Filmer, the influential propagandist for monarchy. Washington, who had at least three ancestral ties to Filmer, rejected Filmer's legacy when he broke with Jonathan Boucher, America's most vocal proponent of Filmer. A minister and teacher who moved from England to Virginia in 1759, Boucher was hired by Washington a decade later to be the private tutor of John "Jacky" Custis, Washington's stepson. Over the next five years, Washington and Boucher struck up a cordial relationship, despite their political differences. But those differences finally drove them apart.

A committed Tory, Boucher dismissed the doctrines of human equality and democratic government as wrongheaded ideas because he associated them with seventeenth-century Puritan rebels. Henry Vane, the Massachusetts governor who had returned to England and became a leading voice against Charles I in Parliament, was, in Boucher's view, a source of later evils. Accepting the negative image of Vane in Thomas Hutchinson's history of Massachusetts, Boucher blasted Vane's notion of government by consent.[109] Boucher insisted that Vane had plenty of bad company when he joined the Long Parliament. Boucher declared that Locke's "ill-founded and false" theory that "the whole human race is born equal" originated with the Independents and Levellers of that Parliament. Boucher wrote, "There is hardly a principle or project of any moment in Mr. Locke's Treatise, of which the rudiments may not be traced in some of the many political pieces which were then produced." The inferiority of some people and the superiority of others, Boucher argued, were ordained by God. Filmer understood this essential truth and defended it doggedly. "The leading idea, or principle, of Sir Robert Filmer's Patriarcha," Boucher intoned, "is, that government is not of human, but divine origin. . . . And this principle, notwithstanding Mr. Locke's answer, is still . . . unrefuted, and still true." God was the eternal Father, and patriarchy must structure government and society. "The first father was the first king," Boucher wrote. "It was thus that all government originated; and monarchy is its most ancient form." Filmer taught "the great duty of *honouring and obeying the king, and all that are put in authority under him*." Following Filmer, Boucher said that true liberty involved "authority, settled subordinations, subjection, and obedience."

Given such a dichotomy of views, it is no wonder that Boucher and Washington had an unfriendly parting of the ways. During their years of friendship, they discussed politics "so long and so fruitlessly," in Boucher's words, that they ended up in direct opposition to each other.[110] Washington, appalled by ever-increasing British intrusions on the American colonies, became an ardent Whig, while Boucher clung to High Toryism. The relationship came to an end in 1774. Boucher wrote a bitter letter telling Washington, "You are no longer worthy of my friendship: a man of honour can no longer without dishonour be connected with you." Soon, Boucher returned to England.

Washington was completely devoted to the revolutionary cause. England, he wrote, had established "the most despotick System of Tyranny that ever was practiced in a free Government."[111] He was inspired by the example of early settlers who had established representative governing bodies in both the Southern and Northern colonies. He wrote, "As the Descendants of Freemen & Heirs with us of the same glorious Inheritance we flatter ourselves that tho. divided by our Situation we are firmly united in Sentiment. . . . We equally detest & lament . . . the Violence & Rapacity" of England, "which have led to the Effusion of so much human Blood & left us no Alternative but a Civil War or a base Submission."[112]

Cromwell could have spoken the words. And Washington could have followed Cromwell by using his appeal as a charismatic general to become a dictator. But Washington, a republican, hated the idea of power held by a single person. He made a big impact in 1783 when he voluntarily gave up his military command and in 1796 when he announced he would not run for a third term as president. Washington even hesitated to attend the constitutional convention in Philadelphia in 1787 for fear he would appear power-hungry. Pressed by trusted associates and aware of the need for a firmer national structure, he agreed to attend and was unanimously chosen to preside. Under his calm, unobtrusive guidance, the convention produced a constitutional system that balanced executive, legislative, and judicial power—the lasting hallmark of the US Constitution.

Because we view the Bill of Rights through the lens of later amendments, we tend to think of its creators as modern thinkers who sought to extend rights to marginalized groups. Not so. Progress on civil rights has been incremental, with a step forward often followed by one or two steps back, then a leap ahead. The Bill of Rights was certainly a leap, but not a jump to abolition or racial equality. Those behind the bill had mixed records on questions of race and slavery. One of the bill's gurus, Richard Henry Lee, came out strongly against the slave trade but held many enslaved Black people on his Virginia plantation. The same was true of other Southern promoters of the bill, including Thomas Jefferson, James Madison, George Mason, Patrick Henry, and Benjamin Harrison.

Neither Jefferson nor any of the other founders explicitly associated the principle of human equality with African Americans. Among the leading Patriots, the one who came closest to doing so was James Otis. He declared in 1762, "The Colonists are by the law of nature free born, as indeed all men are, white or black," and asked, "Does it follow that tis right to enslave a man because he is black?"—statements that would lead Charles Sumner, when arguing in the Senate for the Fourteenth Amendment, to praise Otis as a pioneer of rights "common to all, without distinction of color."[113]

Focused on challenging England, Otis did not pursue his idea of racial equality. But many eighteenth-century Americans outside of the political realm did. Most of them were the spiritual heirs of Puritans who had preached the equality of all humans before God.

*Chapter Seven*

# Ships, Slavery, and Sentimental Power

Ships—thousands of ships that carried enslaved Africans across the Atlantic on the Middle Passage. That's what came to mind for many eighteenth-century Americans when they thought about slavery. From 1701 to 1800, an estimated six million kidnapped Africans were transported in the holds of ships and sold in the Western hemisphere.[1] Most of the vessels embarked from Europe, with England the most active human carrier, followed by Portugal and France. American-based ships, mainly from New England, carried approximately 3.5 percent of the total. The overwhelming majority of the Africans were brought to the West Indies or South America; only about 5 percent were carried to North America.

Sharply divided opinions over the use of ships reflected ever-deepening differences over slavery. For profit-seeking merchants, enslaved people were things—goods to be bought, shipped, and sold like other items. The callousness of this viewpoint outraged a growing number of reformers who objected to the slave trade on religious or ethical grounds. Just as the Puritan heritage motivated Patriots of the

American Revolution, it helped energize the antislavery forces that would later produce abolitionism. Offshoots or affiliates of Puritanism—Quakerism, the New Divinity movement, the Baptist and Methodist churches—became vehicles for antislavery passion in eighteenth-century America. This passion was especially forceful just before and just after the American Revolution. The combination of religious fervor and revolutionary politics made the period between 1765 and 1800 a lively moment in antislavery activity. Scores of antislavery sermons, speeches, and pamphlets appeared. Northern states passed antislavery laws or included provisions for gradual emancipation in their state constitutions. Abolition societies lobbied for an end to the slave trade, and, in some cases, to slavery itself.

## RHODE ISLAND AND THE SLAVE TRADE

Rhode Island is a historical petri dish that helps us understand the growing tension over the transatlantic slave trade.

The tension is crystallized in two names that were prominent in Rhode Island: Brown and Hopkins. The wealthy Providence merchant John Brown and Esek Hopkins, the captain of one of the Brown family's slave ships, represented the commercial mentality that bolstered slavery by utterly disregarding the humanity of Black people. John's brother, Moses Brown, illustrated the rejection of proslavery thought by a conscience-stricken man who became a Quaker, emancipated his slaves, and developed into an outspoken critic of the slave trade. Joining Moses Brown was the New Divinity clergyman Samuel Hopkins (no relation to Esek), who wrote influential antislavery tracts during his pastorship at a Congregational church in Newport, the epicenter of the American slave trade.

The Brown family's ancestry dates back to Chad Brown, a Baptist who emigrated from England during the Great Puritan migration.

Chad Brown arrived in Boston in July 1638 and soon moved south to Rhode Island, where he became a close associate of Roger Williams. A signer of the document that established majority rule and the separation of church and state in Rhode Island, Brown served in local government and eventually succeeded Williams as pastor of Providence's First Baptist Church. Although nothing is known of Brown's personal views on slavery, it is notable that he defended the radical Puritan Samuel Gorton—one of the advocates behind Rhode Island's 1652 statute that limited slavery.[2]

Flash forward eight decades. The commercial spirit had seized Rhode Island. One of Chad Brown's descendants, the Baptist Elder James Brown, was appalled by the change. He delivered a sermon in 1731 declaring that "the man of God" was fading before the "the merchant man," who was interested mainly in "seeing his shop full of customers."[3]

James Brown was unwittingly describing four of his grandsons—John, Nicholas, Joseph, and Moses Brown. In various businesses, the brothers produced spermaceti candles, cloth, dairy products, vegetables, pig iron, and other goods. They carried on a steady business supplying slave societies in the Southern colonies and the West Indies with necessities.[4] Another of the Browns' products, rum, was Rhode Island's main export, exchanged for captives in the international traffic in enslaved Africans.

Despite its small landmass (just over 1,000 square miles) Rhode Island, with its 400 miles of coastline and deepwater ports, dominated the American-based slave trade. Nearly three-quarters of the American-based slave trade happened in Rhode Island vessels, which transported an estimated 106,544 Africans between 1709 and 1807.[5] Although this number paled in comparison with England, which transported approximately 2.5 million Africans during the same period, Rhode Island led America in the triangular trade.[6] By the 1760s, Rhode Island had thirty distilleries, divided between Providence and the port towns of Newport and Bristol. Rhode Islanders shipped nearly 11 million gallons of cheap, high-proof rum (known as Guinea rum) to Africa in exchange for Black people, who were transported on the Middle Passage for sale in the Caribbean or the Americas.[7] The Brown brothers of Providence were directly involved in the trafficking of enslaved Africans. Their father, James Brown Jr. (son of the elder James Brown who had lamented the rise of the "merchant man"), organized a 1736 slaving voyage of the sloop *Mary* to Africa. There, captives were purchased, transported to the West Indies, and sold, with several brought back to Rhode Island for the family's own use. Enslaved laborers helped construct the first buildings of the college that the Browns founded—later known as Brown University.

Among the voyages sponsored by the Browns was that of the *Sally* (1764–65), an expedition that starkly illustrates the horrors of the slave trade. The ship's cargo included 17,274 gallons of rum, along with tobacco, dried beef, rice, bread, flour, and 1,800 bunches of onions, all intended to purchase captives on the African coast.[8] (Onions, aside from being trading items, were thought to ward off scurvy and were used as a salve for wounds.) To defend against pirates and suppress slave uprisings, the ship was equipped with seven swivel guns, many small firearms, and thirteen cutlasses. Chains and handcuffs were aboard for securing the human cargo. To captain the *Sally*, the Browns chose their friend Esek Hopkins, who was from a prominent Rhode Island family of businessmen and politicians (his brother, Stephen Hopkins, was the sometime governor of Rhode Island and a signer of the Declaration of Independence). Esek Hopkins had commanded privateers commissioned by the Browns during the French and Indian War, and he would go on to become the commander in chief of the Continental Navy during the opening years of the American Revolution.

The *Sally* sailed from Newport on September 11, 1764, and reached Africa's Windward Coast in November. Instructed by the Browns to "dispose of your cargo for slaves," Esek Hopkins exchanged rum and other goods in Senegambia for enslaved Africans.[9] His logbook shows how the commercial mentality put Black people on the same level as inanimate things. On a typical day Hopkins exchanged rum, sugar, and onions for "1 man & 1 man boy slave," "1 woman," and "2 garles & 1 boy." The next day, "195 galons Rum" fetched a "garle" and a boy.[10] After seven months Hopkins had bought 196 men, women, and children. Twenty of the people died while he was still on the coast maneuvering to get them aboard the *Sally*. The deaths began on April 1, 1765, when Hopkins wrote that "a boye Slave died." Hopkins made a grim entry on June 8: a "woman slave hanged her Self between Decks." He sold 21 captives to other traders and set sail for the West on August 21, 1765, with 155 Africans in his hold. Enslaved men were forced to lie flat, shackled together in the suffocating darkness of the lower deck, where the ceiling allowed barely three feet of clearance. The women were confined separately, in a partitioned space.

Seven days after leaving Africa, some of the captives aboard the *Sally* broke free from their chains and staged a rebellion. Hopkins quickly resorted to armed force. On August 28, 1765, he recorded in his journal that the "Slaves Rose on us," and he was "obliged to fire on them," killing eight and badly wounding several more.[11] In addition to the eight who were killed during the revolt, two of the wounded later died. Hopkins reported that the remaining captives were "so disperited" after the failed uprising that "some drowned themselves, some starved and others sickened and died." By the time the *Sally* reached Antigua in October, only eighty-eight enslaved people were alive. They were in such poor condition that the ones who found buyers sold for one-tenth of the normal price.[12]

The voyage had been a financial failure. It was that—not the suffering of the Africans—that concerned the Browns, who were glad that Hopkins had survived but complained about "the Heavy Loss of our Int[erest]s."[13] One of the Antigua traders expressed regret for "the bad Voyage" but assured the Browns that they would succeed next time. "Had the Negroes been Young and Healthy," he wrote, "I should have been able to sell them pritty well. I make no doubt if you was to try this Markett again with Good Slaves I Should be able to give you Satisfaction."[14]

One of the Brown brothers, Moses, decided never to "try this Markett again." Moses Brown withdrew from the family business and devoted the rest of his ninety-eight-year life to the public good. Outliving three wives, all three of his children, and three of his four stepchildren, he made landmark contributions to education, public health, prison reform, manufacturing, agriculture, urban renewal, and, most notably, the antislavery cause.[15] In the aftermath of the *Sally* tragedy, Moses Brown engaged in deep soul-searching and freed his ten enslaved people. In his deed of emancipation, he declared: "The buying and selling of men . . . as slaves is contrary to the Divine mind, manifest in the consciences of all men [and] has a great tendency to encourage the iniquitous traffick and practice of importing them from their native country."[16] In 1774, Moses Brown joined the Society of Friends, embracing its dedication to the abolition of slavery.

Quakerism had become increasingly committed to antislavery principles during the century after 1671, when its founder, George Fox, witnessed the inhumanity of slavery while on a visit to Barbados. As mentioned in chapter 3, the Quaker faith has been described as left-wing Puritanism. The Puritan belief in the fundamental equality of all humans before God evolved into the Quaker emphasis on social and spiritual equality. The Puritans' tolerance for lay religious expression paved the way for Quakers to speak spontaneously against social injustice. Similarly, the Puritan impulse to challenge established institutions fostered the Quaker protest against the cruelest institution of all: chattel slavery. Although Quakers were pacifists and preferred moral persuasion over force, they could be stubborn and persistent in their campaign for abolition.

Take Benjamin Lay. Just over four feet tall, hunchbacked, with a billowing white beard and unusually long arms, Little Benjamin—as he called himself—opposed slavery in every aspect of his life. A British-born Quaker, Lay spent eighteen years in Barbados before moving to Pennsylvania. He regarded slavery as evil both morally and spiritually. He authored several reform tracts, most notably *All Slave-Keepers That Keep the Innocent in Bondage*, published in 1737 with the assistance of his friend Benjamin Franklin. Lay condemned hypocritical Christians who participated in the slave trade, calling it "the foulest of Sins."[17] He asked, "Is there any eviler Fruit in the World than Slave-keeping? any thing more devilish? it is of the very Nature of Hell itself, and is the Belly of Hell." The quintessential democrat, he wrote, "It is most certain that all Men, as they are the Sons of *Adam*, are Coheirs; and have equal Right unto Liberty, and all other outward Comforts of Life." Lay's antislavery convictions guided every aspect of his daily life. After settling in Pennsylvania, he avoided all products made by enslaved labor or derived from the killing of animals. He spun his own cloth from flax, subsisted on fruits and vegetables that he grew himself, and refused all tropical commodities, including coffee, that were tied to the slave trade.[18]

Anthony Benezet and John Woolman, two Philadelphia-area Quakers influenced by Benjamin Lay, were, like him, vegetarians who avoided purchasing products made with exploited labor. Both became prominent figures on the international antislavery scene and had a direct impact on Moses Brown. Benezet, raised among Calvinist Huguenots in France, fled persecution there and eventually settled first in London, where he became a Quaker, and then in America, where he wrote prolifically against slavery. Although Moses Brown and Benezet never met in person, they corresponded and shared mutual friends. Brown read several of Benezet's antislavery works, including *Some Historical Account of Guinea* (1771), in which Benezet presented a graphic history of the slave trade. He detailed the brutality of slavery, offering an eyewitness account in which he described "bodies all in a gore of blood, the skin torn off their backs with the cruel whip; beaten pepper and salt rubbed in the wounds, and a large stick of [hot] sealing wax dropped leisurely upon them."[19] Moses Brown took this explicit approach in the 1770s, when, in an effort to speed antislavery legislation in Rhode Island, he publicly described tortures inflicted on enslaved people, such as castration, chopping off toes, and rubbing salt and pepper on open wounds.[20]

Moses Brown was also aware of the Quaker abolitionist John Woolman of Mount Holly, New Jersey. Woolman visited Rhode Island during his tour of New England in 1760, meeting with merchants in Providence and Newport, where he denounced the slave trade, leaving a deep impression. Brown later read Woolman's *Journal*, published posthumously in 1774—the same year Brown joined the Society of Friends, just after the New England Quakers had abolished slaveholding among their members. In his *Journal*, Woolman wrote that enslaved Black people "are human creatures, whose souls are as precious as ours," a conviction that resonated with Brown's evolving conscience.[21] In answer to an opponent who said that Africans "were so wretched in their own Country, that many of them lived better here than there," Woolman declared that "Liberty was the natural Right of all Men equally."

Moses Brown's commitment to abolitionism emerged at a pivotal moment in the transatlantic antislavery movement. Two years before he joined the Society of Friends, Lord Mansfield had ruled in *Somerset v. Stewart* (1772) that slavery was unsupported by English law. Brown was convinced by the natural-rights arguments of Granville Sharp, the London barrister who represented the fugitive slave James Somerset. In one of his many antislavery tracts, Sharp famously declared, "Toleration of slavery is, in effect, a toleration of inhumanity."[22] Moses Brown took special note of Sharp's admonition "The toleration of domestick slavery in the colonies greatly weakens the claim of natural rights of our American brethren to liberty."[23] The Methodist leader John Wesley, whose pamphlet *Thoughts Upon Slavery* also stimulated Moses Brown, wrote, "Liberty is the right of every human creature, as soon

[as] he breathes the vital air. And no human law can deprive him of that right, which he derives from the law of nature."[24]

The combined influences of religion and natural rights philosophy that inspired Moses Brown caused an antislavery surge elsewhere in the colonies, including the South. A historian of Southern slavery notes, "The Chesapeake colonies made a determined effort to end the African slave trade in the decade 1765–1775 and individual Marylanders and Virginians carried the debate a step further and called for an end to slavery itself."[25] Quakers—most notably Anthony Benezet—helped spread antislavery sentiment by printing and distributing pamphlets throughout the colonies, including the South. As hostility to England ramped up, ideas on human liberty derived from Locke and Sidney reinforced this egalitarian impulse.

Although few Southerners followed Thomas Jefferson's call in 1774 for "the abolition of domestic slavery . . . in those colonies," many did heed his advice to exclude all further importations from Africa."[26] The barbarity of the slave trade had been searingly exposed in antislavery literature and was witnessed firsthand by some slaveholders. The Continental Congress's resolution in October 1774 to "wholly discontinue the Slave Trade" took effect during the American Revolution.[27]

But the congressional ban proved difficult to enforce, especially once international trade revived after the war. Rhode Island merchants resumed human trafficking more vigorously than ever.[28] The issue divided the Brown family, generating one of the most heated disputes over slavery in eighteenth-century America. In pseudonymous newspaper articles, Moses Brown attacked the slave trade, and his brother John defended it.[29]

Moses Brown endorsed a bill in 1775 calling for emancipation in Rhode Island. It was rejected, but he soon became the driving force behind Rhode Island's 1784 gradual abolition law, its 1787 slave-trade ban, and the creation of the Providence abolition society—efforts his brother John Brown resisted at every turn. The slave trade, John wrote, did Black people a favor by removing them from "savage," war-torn Africa and providing them with white protection in the New World. Enslaved people, he wrote, were the "lawful property" of their owners, and abolitionists were "dangerous to the community."[30] Noting that the Quakers were "the first founders of the abolition scheme here," John said that they wanted "to encourage and promote a civil war," aiming for "the total destruction of those who will not yield to their abolition plan."[31]

Push came to shove for the Brown family when in 1794 the US Congress passed a law restricting the American slave trade. John Brown became the first American to be tried under the law. In 1797, John was prosecuted for funding a voyage of a ship that resulted in the sale of 198 Africans in Cuba.[32] The outcry against John Brown was led by his brother Moses. A federal district court forced John to forfeit the ship involved in his 1797 venture. In a separate Rhode Island case over the same voyage, however, John was acquitted—a sign of how reluctant local juries were to convict prominent merchants. Afterward, John boasted that he had triumphed over the "Wicked and Abominable Combination I mean the Abolition Society," directly mocking Moses's efforts.[33] John went on to serve in the US House of Representatives for two years. He died in 1803, four years before Congress passed the Act Prohibiting Importation of Slaves, which went into effect on January 1, 1808.

The difference between John and Moses Brown epitomized the contrasting attitudes toward Black people that would reverberate in the nineteenth century and culminate in the Civil War. John Brown regarded enslaved Blacks as property to be used and traded; Moses Brown saw them as fellow humans who must be allowed to live freely and productively in society. Moses's openness was manifested by his treatment of Black people around him. He gave six of those he emancipated an acre of land apiece on which they could live independently as farmers, and he helped the other four get started in trades. He was always ready to assist his former bondspeople or other free Black people. Here he differed from the many white Rhode Islanders who displayed the racial prejudice that was prevalent in the North, even in states that abolished slavery and the slave trade.[34] As a historian of Rhode Island notes, Black people in the state, "their progress blocked by almost impassable barriers of ignorance and prejudice, would never know a friend more zealous for their cause than the Quaker Moses Brown," who was famous for his readiness to assist beleaguered African Americans who reached out to him.[35] He was active on the Underground Railroad, welcoming freedom seekers, who were imperiled because of the Constitution's rule about fugitives from labor, strengthened by the Fugitive Slave Act of 1793. One Newport Black man, John Quamine, wrote a note to Moses thanking him for his "boundless benevolence . . . with regard to the unforfeited rights of the poor unhappy Africans of this province."

Brown never wavered in his commitment to the abolition of slavery. In 1832, when he was ninety-five, he was visited in Providence by William Lloyd Garrison, who had founded *The Liberator* the previous year. Garrison called Brown "an extraordinary man" whose "interest in all the great philanthropic movements of the age rather increases than suffers diminution—especially in the abolition cause."[36] When Moses Brown died in 1836, Garrison's newspaper carried an obituary that stated: "The friends of the slave will not forget that he was the Black man's benefactor—a practical and consistent Abolitionist; having emancipated his own slaves, and paid them for their services previous as well as subsequent to their emancipation."[37]

## THE NEW DIVINITY MOVEMENT AND THE CALVINIST FIGHT AGAINST SLAVERY

If Quakerism had opened the way to abolitionism in the case of Moses Brown, another offshoot of Puritanism, the New Divinity movement, had a similar effect on Brown's friend and fellow Rhode Islander Samuel Hopkins. The New Divinity movement was eighteenth-century America's version of New England Puritanism, reinvigorating the old Calvinistic doctrines with rational argument and powerful feeling. This approach stimulated deep religious emotions and benevolent action, driven by God's absolute power. Emerging in the 1740s in the sermons and the theological writings of the western Massachusetts minister Jonathan Edwards, the New Divinity movement took on social purpose when it mingled with Scottish philosophy (which emphasized following the conscience) and republicanism, with its principle of natural rights. Samuel Hopkins expanded the Calvinist belief in human sinfulness to include what he called the national sin: slavery. A key sign of spiritual regeneration, he argued, was the expression of benevolence to enslaved people. Hopkins and his New Divinity colleagues provided a bridge between bygone Puritanism and nineteenth-century antislavery reform. They also planted the antislavery movement in the North, where most of them were educated and had been installed in pastorships.

Hopkins, born in Waterbury, Connecticut, in 1721, took pride in his Puritan roots. He wrote in his memoir, "I and my ancestors descended from those called *Puritans*, in the days of Queen Elizabeth, above two hundred years ago, and have continued to bear that denomination since, and were the first settlers of New England."[38] Hopkins attended Yale, then studied privately with the New Divinity leader Jonathan Edwards. In 1743, Hopkins assumed the pastorship of a church in Sheffield, in southwestern Massachusetts, where he served for twenty-five years before moving to Newport, Rhode Island. He preached at Newport's First Congregational Church from 1770 until his death in 1803.

A former slaveholder, Hopkins became an ardent abolitionist in Newport, which had the highest concentration of enslaved Black people among New England cities. In 1847, the antislavery author John Greenleaf Whittier retrospectively described Hopkins in Newport, "the great slave mart of the North," hearing "the seamen engaged in the African trade tell of the horrible scenes of fire and blood which they had witnessed" and seeing "the half-suffocated wretches brought up from their noisome and narrow prison, their squalid countenances and skeleton forms bearing fearful evidence of the suffering attendant upon their transportation from their native homes." Whittier wrote that "the angels of God," surveying the universe, would find no "nobler spectacle than that of the minister of Newport, rising up before his slaveholding congregation, and demanding, in the name of the Highest, the 'deliverance of the captive, and the opening of prison doors to them that were bound.'"[39] Another nineteenth-century observer recalled Samuel Hopkins as "the first person who in this country publicly denounced slavery and set himself zealously to work to repair the injuries inflicted upon the African race."[40] Yet another nineteenth-century eulogist called Hopkins "a great and good man—a friend of the oppressed, and a fearless rebuker of popular sin—whose name will be revered and honored by the good in all future time."[41]

The latter prediction proved wrong. Instead of being long revered, Samuel Hopkins is not widely remembered. To overlook Hopkins, however, is to ignore someone who tried to plant the United States on an antislavery foundation. In the spring of 1776, Hopkins published his tract *A Dialogue Concerning the Slavery of the Africans, Shewing It to Be the Duty and Interest of the American Colonies to Emancipate All Their African Slaves*, prefaced by a dedication to the members of the Continental Congress.

Hopkins used the widespread hostility to the slave trade as a wedge to open up the possibility of universal emancipation. In *A Dialogue* he follows in detail the cycle of the nefarious trade: the exchange of rum for captives in Africa, the nightmarish transatlantic crossing to the tropics, the sale of enslaved people for sugar and molasses, the return to New England, where more rum was produced for shipment. The slave ship, Hopkins writes, is a "scene of inhumanity, oppression and cruelty, exceeding every thing of the kind that has ever been perpetrated by the sons of men."[42] Moreover, Hopkins continues, one cannot lament conditions aboard the slave ship without denouncing slavery as well. In his words, "If the slave-trade be unjustifiable and wrong; then our holding the Africans and their children in bondage, is unjustifiable and wrong." He goes on to call for the emancipation of America's enslaved people, who then numbered over five hundred thousand.

Hopkins's progression from condemning the slave trade to calling for emancipation was unusual for that era. Just as remarkable was the rhetoric he used to attack slaveholders. Like his Puritan predecessor Samuel Sewall, he weaponized the Golden Rule against slavery. But he pushed the Golden Rule to a subversive extreme. In his tract, he imagines a complete reversal of racial roles. He asks his white readers how they would feel if Black people or Turks held them in bondage. Building on this theme, he demonstrates how his doctrine of benevolence underpins his profound belief in the equality of all humans. He also decimates proslavery readings of the Bible, arguing, for example, that the slaveholding Old Testament patriarchs or the curse on Ham had nothing to do with American slavery. As for the canard that Africans brought to America have the benefit of being Christianized, he says that Blacks were more apt to reject Christianity than to embrace it when they saw the cruelty and amorality of slaveholding Christians. An especially daring moment comes when he envisages reparations being paid to Black people after they are emancipated. He tells slaveowners, "You ought to let [your bondspeople] go out free; and not send them away empty; but furnish them liberally out of your store . . . they having a much better right to part of your estate, than your children, and, it may be, much more likely to make a good improvement of it."[43]

The American Revolution, Hopkins insisted, was God's harsh test of America for its national sin: slavery. He found it grossly inconsistent that many white Americans fought for their own liberty but not for that of the enslaved people in their midst. A successful result of the Revolution, he maintained, would be freedom for both white and Black Americans. Once emancipated, Black people should be able "to share equally with us, in that civil and religious Liberty, with which an indulgent providence has blessed these States, and to which these our brethren are, by nature, as much entitled to as ourselves."[44]

But in his view, the war brought only partial success. In a second edition of *A Dialogue*, published in 1785, he gratefully noted the antislavery impact of the Revolution: Bills for at least gradual emancipation had passed in Pennsylvania, Massachusetts, New Hampshire, Rhode Island, and Connecticut, while Virginia had terminated its long-term ban on voluntary manumission by enslavers. However, Hopkins noted, slavery persisted without a foreseeable end in the South, and the slave trade was resuming in New England, with Rhode Island once again taking the lead among American states in transporting enslaved Africans on the Middle Passage.

Hopkins did what he could to bring about the emancipation of enslaved people. He worked closely with Moses Brown to forge Rhode Island's gradual emancipation act, its ban on participation in the slave trade, and the formation of an abolition society that networked with societies in other states. In 1787, Hopkins, under the pseudonym Crito, published a series of antislavery essays that were collected in a pamphlet and sent to prominent politicians.[45] In the essays, Hopkins pointed out the hypocrisy of whites who had fought against enslavement to England without abolishing the far worse enslavement of Black people. He again called for a permanent cessation of the slave trade and the manumission of all enslaved people.

After the Constitution was ratified, Hopkins expressed overall satisfaction with it, but he was disappointed by its concessions on slavery, especially its postponement until 1808 of the prohibition of the importation of enslaved Black people. He continued his attacks on Rhode

Island merchants engaged in the slave trade, including Moses Brown's brother John.

Hopkins was hardly alone among New Divinity ministers who advanced antislavery views. The Connecticut minister Levi Hart, who studied under Hopkins after graduating from Yale, also did so. Reaching back to the early Puritans, Hart insisted that Americans must revive "the cause of Liberty" for which "our venerable Ancestors fought . . . at no small expense of their treasure and blood."[46] Just as the Patriots fought for liberty against England, "The Negro Slaves . . . have as good a right to liberty as their masters: & it is as direct a violation of the law of God to hold them in Servitude as it would be to reduce their masters to the Same State."[47] Like other abolitionists of his time, Hart targeted "the cruel and barbarous Slave Trade," in which captured Africans are "driven like cattle to the slaughter, to the sea shore, and sold to our Guinea traders, often for a small quantity of that soul and body destroying liquor, *rum*," then "bound and thrust into the filthy holds of the ships—men, women, fathers, daughters, mothers, sons, without distinction; where they are obliged to *rot together* thro' a long sea passage. . . . When they are arrived at the West-Indies they are again *exposed* in the markets, and sold like beasts of burden to the inhuman planters, by whose cruelty many more of them perish."[48] Hart called for the education of emancipated people, who, he said, were fully capable of becoming productive American citizens.

Another New Divinity abolitionist, Jonathan Edwards Jr., had special ties to early New England Puritans. One of his ancestors was Thomas Hooker, an escapee of William Laud's persecution who settled in Massachusetts in 1633 and preached there briefly before moving southwest because he disagreed with the Bay Colony's rule that only church members could vote. One of the founders of Connecticut, Hooker has been called the Father of American Democracy because of his advanced position on suffrage.[49]

Of unique importance was Jonathan Edwards Jr.'s father. The senior Jonathan Edwards, who is recognized as a major Protestant theologian, applied concepts of Enlightenment thinkers such as Locke and Newton to New England Puritanism, which became, in his hands, intellectually rich and emotionally resonant. On the question of slavery, however, he was not forward-looking. A slaveholder, he purchased a teenage African woman on a visit to Newport, Rhode Island, in 1731; he and his wife thereafter bought several more bondspeople.[50]

Jonathan Edwards Jr., diverging from his father on enslavement, pointed Calvinism in a more radical direction. The younger Edwards began arguing against slavery before the American Revolution and fully developed his arguments in his landmark sermon *The Injustice and Impolicy of the Slave Trade, and of the Slavery of the Africans* (1791). He brought a militant edge to New Divinity abolitionism. Not only did he expose proslavery arguments as fraudulent, but he insisted that slavery made no sense at all. He anticipated Lincoln by saying that if slavery were based on skin color, then people would be justified in enslaving anyone—whether European, Native American, African, or another group—who had darker pigmentation than they did.[51] Edwards Jr. compared slavery with highway robbery, as Lincoln would famously do in the Cooper Union Address.

Edwards dwelled on the inhumanity of the slave trade, describing how it tore Africans from their homes, then crowded them "so closely into the holds . . . of vessels" that they had "scarcely room to lie down" and "sometimes not room to sit up in an erect posture."[52] Many died on the Middle Passage from "the most dangerous and fatal diseases." The destiny of those who survived the voyage, Edwards pointed out, was "to drag out a miserable life in absolute slavery." They were underfed, overworked, unpaid, and subjected to tortures such as whipping, the gouging out of eyes, and the chopping off of toes, fingers, or ears. Also, Edwards noted, "lewdness" was common among slaveholders. "A planter with his hundred wenches about him," he wrote, was "like the Sultan in his seraglio."

Several of Edwards's contemporaries had previously compared enslaved people with Patriots who had sought freedom from the mother country. But Edwards insisted that the enslavement of Black people was infinitely worse than England's oppression of its American colonies. "We all dread political slavery, or subjection to the arbitrary power of a king," he wrote. "Yet such a state is inconceivably preferable to the slavery of the Negroes."[53] He called for the "total abolition" of slavery and monetary reparations for the emancipated. Former slaveholders must provide "compensation to the Negroes for the injury which they have done them," even to the extent of "leaving to them all their real estates."

Edwards's impassioned declarations were often quoted by nineteenth-century antislavery figures, from William Lloyd Garrison to William Henry Seward. Among his oft-cited statements were: "To hold any man in Slavery is to be every day guilty of robbing him of his liberty, or of man-stealing"; "Great-Britain in her late attempt to enslave America, committed a very small crime indeed, in comparison with the crime of those who enslave the Africans"; and "Every slave is naturally an enemy to the state which he is holden in slavery, and wants nothing but an opportunity to assist in its overthrow."[54]

Such citations of Edwards in the nineteenth century lend credence to David Brion Davis's contention that Jonathan Edwards Jr. and other New Divinity Calvinists were mainly responsible for ushering Puritanism toward abolitionism.[55] However, one of Edwards's ideas—that enslaved Blacks were justified in rising up against their owners—went too far for most reformers. The eighteenth century had witnessed momentous slave rebellions, including the New York Slave Revolt of 1712, the 1739 Stono Rebellion in South Carolina, and many uprisings on slave ships. Later rebellions would be fanned by the overthrow of European colonizers by Black rebels in the Haitian Revolution (1791–1804), a catalyst for slave revolts in nineteenth-century America led by Denmark Vesey, Nat Turner, and others. Insurrections, which testified to the explosive rage of enslaved people, stoked fear among mainstream Americans and even made antislavery reformers uneasy.

Jonathan Edwards Jr. was on precarious ground, then, when he justified slave rebellion. William Lloyd Garrison, a pacifist despite his vehement rhetoric, said that while he admired Edwards in general, he disagreed with the preacher's statement that "A slave may justifiably kill his kidnapper and every other oppressor, if he can obtain his freedom by no other means." In a footnote, Garrison said, "This sentiment is Dr. Edwards'. It is not held by the editor of the Liberator."[56]

One nineteenth-century figure *did* agree with Jonathan Edwards Jr. on this point: the radical abolitionist John Brown. The only person who consistently took up arms against slavery before the Civil War, John Brown was commonly called a Puritan—an epithet that is accurate if we mean the specifically antislavery Puritanism of the New Divinity movement. Brown's father, Owen Brown, had lived for a time as a teenager with the New Divinity clergyman Jeremiah Hallock in West Simsbury, Connecticut. Owen recalled that his commitment to abolitionism began in 1790, when Hallock was visited by the Newport minister Samuel Hopkins. Owen Brown overheard a conversation between the two ministers on the evils of slavery. Also, Hallock had in his home a copy of Jonathan Edwards Jr.'s sermon *The Injustice and Impolicy of the Slave Trade*. Owen Brown recalled, "I read it, and it denounced slavery as a great sin. From this time, I was antislavery, as much as I be now."[57]

After his marriage in 1793 to Ruth Mills, the daughter and granddaughter of New Divinity clergymen, Owen Brown passed his abolitionist views on to his children, including John, born in 1800. At sixteen, John Brown decided to train for the ministry and studied briefly with the New Divinity preacher Moses Hallock, the brother of Jeremiah. Family obligations dashed John Brown's plans for the ministry, but he applied Calvinist fervor to fight against slavery. As a youngster, he witnessed the brutal beating of an enslaved boy, and his family was continually active on the Underground Railroad. Fired with the passionate purpose of New Divinity Calvinism, John Brown came to believe that God had appointed him to wipe out slavery. In the 1850s, with the mushrooming of federally supported slavery, he resorted to violence in Kansas and then at Harpers Ferry, Virginia, where he made a failed attempt to trigger a slave rebellion that, he hoped, would lead to the toppling of slavery throughout the South. Instead, he was captured at Harpers Ferry, tried on three counts, and executed as a felon. A polarizing figure, he came to be viewed as an antislavery martyr in the North and as a devilish fanatic in the South.[58]

John Brown reveals both the perils and the promise of antislavery Puritanism, as it had developed over generations and culminated in his thinking. On the one hand, there had long been a strain within Puritanism that prioritized divine law over human law. The idea that an unjust human law need not be followed by inspired individuals, rooted in seventeenth-century Puritanism and carried forward through the New Divinity movement to John Brown, yielded what came to be known as the higher law, by which one looked beyond human statutes and received instructions from God or from one's conscience.

Although the higher law, rooted in Puritanism, was unpredictable, it had the positive effect of strengthening human rights when applied to the marginalized or oppressed. John Brown is notorious for his lawbreaking violence, but he devoted most of his life to trying to help Black people get ahead, and his goal was a society where minority groups had citizenship and the opportunity to pursue their dreams. Among his supporters were a number of African Americans who, like him, struggled for the cause of social equality, including Frederick Douglass, Harriet Tubman, and the clergyman and businessman James Newton Gloucester.

This drive for self-help and social advance among African Americans had been galvanized in eighteenth-century America. The case histories of the New Divinity preacher Lemuel Haynes and the poet Phillis Wheatley reveal the possibilities that Puritan-based religion opened up for some forms of African American success in a racist society.

## BLACK PURITANS CHALLENGE RACISM

It is telling that the Declaration of Independence's nation-defining statement "all men are created equal," which Lincoln would cite in the opening line of the Gettysburg Address, had been applied early on to enslaved people by an African American. The Black New Divinity clergyman Lemuel Haynes prefaced his 1776 essay "Liberty Further Extended: Or Free Thoughts on the Illegality of Slave-Keeping" with the inscription "We hold these truths to be Self-Evident, that all men are created Equal, that they are endowed by their Creator with certain unalienable rights, that among these are Life, Liberty, and the pursuit of happiness.—*Congress.*"[59] In his essay, Haynes infused the Declaration's affirmation of natural rights with New Divinity passion to produce a searing critique of slavery and a clarion call for equality.

The fact that this prophetic essay remained unpublished until 1983 helps explain why Lemuel Haynes was later forgotten by most Americans—even by the Black Theology preachers of the 1960s who merged civil rights with Christianity. We don't know why Lemuel Haynes's essay did not appear in print in 1776, but it may well be that, as a Black person, he was unable to find a publisher. At any rate, Haynes devoted himself most strongly to Black empowerment outside of writing about abolition. From 1785, when he was ordained as a Congregational minister, until his death at eighty in 1833, he served as a pastor and revivalist in New England. John Saillant speculates that later Black activists minimized Haynes because he preached to mainly white congregations instead of all-Black ones.[60] But it was precisely Haynes's ability to gain prominence while retaining his devotion to equal rights that distinguished him.

To his contemporaries, Lemuel Haynes was the quintessential American success story—"the thorough-going self-made man," in the words of a journalist.[61] His parents had abandoned him. Born in 1753 in West Hartford, Connecticut, Haynes was the illegitimate son of a man "of unmingled African extraction" and a white woman who worked for a farmer, John Haynes.[62] The woman turned over her unwanted infant to the farmer, who subsequently indentured the child to David Rose, a church deacon in Granville, Massachusetts. Although Lemuel Haynes was a bonded servant until he turned twenty-one, he was treated as a family member by the Roses, with whom he lived for thirty-two years. During the American Revolution Haynes served as a minuteman in Massachusetts and as a soldier under Ethan Allen at Fort Ticonderoga. After the Revolution, the pious Haynes studied with the New Divinity minister Daniel Farrand, a disciple of Jonathan Edwards.

Haynes experienced a conversion and was ordained as a Congregational minister. He married a white schoolteacher, Elizabeth Babbitt; the couple had ten children. Over the course of five decades, Lemuel Haynes held pastorships in Connecticut, Massachusetts, and Vermont. Although he did not escape racial prejudice (one church dismissed him because he was Black), he was widely accepted by white congregations. A masterful pulpit performer who sprinkled his sermons with humor, he was in constant demand as a revivalist. His Calvinistic sermon *Universal Salvation*, a satirical blast at Hosea Ballou's liberal religion, went through an astonishing seventy editions, fifty-four of them in Haynes's lifetime.[63]

His success among whites reflected his bedrock belief in the God-ordained equality of all humans. This conviction came through in his antislavery essay "Liberty Further Extended," in which he writes, "It hath pleased God to *make of one Blood all nations of men. . . .* Liberty is Equally as precious to a *Black man*, as it is to a *white one.*"[64] While indebted to previous antislavery writings, especially those by Anthony Benezet and Samuel Hopkins, Haynes's piece has a special poignancy because it was written by an African American in the year that America proclaimed independence. Haynes wrote, "We live in a day wherein *Liberty & freedom* is the subject of many millions' concern." But Black people, he insisted, were subjected to a "much greater oppression" than whites because of the "vile and atrocious" practice of slaveholding.

Arguments commonly made to support slavery were spurious, Haynes pointed out. Are Black people condemned to slavery because of the curse of Ham in the Bible? No, Haynes says: Africans in the eighteenth century probably did not descend from Ham, and besides, Christ had liberated mankind from all curses through his redeeming power. Are slaveholders doing Africans a favor by enslaving them, shipping them west, and exposing them to Christianity? Haynes's answer: The religious uplift of bondspeople is the last thing on the minds of enslavers. "Slave-merchants that trade upon the coasts of Africa," he writes, "do not aim at the Spiritual good of their Slaves," and "Slaves in these Colonies are generally kept under the greatest ignorance, and . . . are scarcely ever told by their white masters whether there is a Supreme Being that governs the universe; or whether there is any reward, or punishments beyond the grave."[65]

At one moment in his essay, Haynes strikes an apocalyptic tone by excoriating slaveholders with Calvinistic intensity:

> O ye that have made yourselves drunk with human blood! Although you may go with impunity here in this life, yet God will hear the cries of that innocent blood, which cries from the sea, and from the ground against you . . . *vengeance! vengeance!* What will you do in that day when God shall make inquisition for Blood? He will make you drink the phials of his indignation which like a potable stream shall be poured out without the least mixture of mercy; Believe it, Sirs, there shall not a drop of blood, which you have spilt unjustly, be lost in forgetfulness.[66]

This angry, blood-soaked passage anticipates militant abolitionists like David Walker (with his declaration "Americans!!! . . . Do you think that our blood is hidden from the Lord?") or John Brown ("the crimes of this *guilty, land*: will never be purged *away*, but with Blood") or the enslaved Nat Turner (whose doomsday vision of blood drops on corn led to his violent uprising, in which some fifty-five whites were slaughtered).[67]

But Haynes did not espouse violence. He revered his country and wanted Black people to have the same rights as others. He expressed his expansive view in his 1801 sermon *The Nature and Importance of True Republicanism*, in which he praised the nation but raised alarms about its fragility. Factions and parties already tore apart the young United States. Like Lincoln after him, Haynes emphasized the need for national unity by quoting the Bible's warning, "A kingdom divided against itself cannot stand."[68] The American Revolution, Haynes declared, was a victory over "oppression, tyranny and domination." But such revolutions had happened before without producing a lasting republic. Haynes brought attention to Cromwell's overthrow of King Charles and the establishment of a republic that became a dictatorship and was supplanted by the restored Stuart monarchy. Haynes said, "What took place in the interregnum of eleven years and four months in England, between the reigns of Charles First and Second, may show that 'tis more than possible that such a precious diamond may lose its lustre, and undergo a total extinction." This was a perceptive point, as was Haynes's insight that America was threatened by its own form of oppression: chattel slavery. Referring to "the poor Africans, among us," he asks, "What has reduced them to their present pitiful, abject state?" His clear-eyed answer: "Being subjected to slavery, by the cruel hands of oppressors, they have been taught to view themselves as a rank of beings far below others, which has suppressed, in a degree, every principle of manhood, and so they become despised, ignorant. . . . This shews the effects of despotism, and should fill us with the utmost detestation against every attack on the rights of men." Americans, he declared, must remember that "all men are born equally free and independent & have certain inherent and unalienable rights" and that the aim of a republican government is "to defend and secure the natural rights of men."

This was a strong antislavery message. But Haynes was not principally an antislavery orator. His mission was to reach the hearts and stir the consciences of his mainly white congregants, while not letting them forget the wrongs suffered by people of his race. His special contribution was to resist the racism that prevailed in the United States, North and South. His success in this regard was so signal he was hailed after his death as "the only man of known African descent, who has ever succeeded in overpowering the system of American *caste*."[69]

But to isolate him like this was misleading. He was *not* the only Black person who fought caste successfully. Haynes's most recent biographer dubs him a "Black Puritan" and places him among several other pious eighteenth-century people of color who made their mark on the cultural scene, including Phillis Wheatley, the first Black American to publish a book of poetry.[70] Like Haynes, Wheatley shows how Calvinism opened the way for Black self-assertion and acceptance among whites.

Phillis Wheatley had close ties to ships. She was named after the *Phillis*, the slave ship that transported her from western Africa to Boston in 1761, when she was about seven or eight years old. Her first published poem was about a ship. In her early teens, after working for six years as the enslaved servant of the family of the Boston merchant John Wheatley, she overheard two dinner guests, Nantucket sea captains named Hussey and Coffin, talking about a near-shipwreck off Cape Cod they had recently survived. Phillis, a budding author who had been tutored by members of the Wheatley family, wrote a poem about the event. The text, which appeared in Newport and Boston newspapers, described the Quaker captains on their storm-tossed whaling ship. Perhaps recalling emotions she experienced on the Middle Passage,

Phillis asks the captains rhetorical questions about their fright during the storm:

> *Did Fear and Danger so perplex your Mind,*
> *As made you fearful of the Whistling Wind?*
> *Was it not Boreas knit his angry Brow*
> *Against you? . . .*
> . . . . . . . . . . . . . . . . . . .
> *Did haughty Eolus with Contempt look down*
> *With Aspect windy, and a study'd Frown?*

She then wonders where Hussey and Coffin would have gone had they died in the storm—to heaven or to "the Shades below, / Where neither Pleasure nor Content can flow"? She imagines "their Souls with eager Raptures" soaring to heaven and being greeted by "the Great Supreme, the Wise."[71]

Today, the poem might seem stilted. But it is remarkable that an enslaved teen who had been brought from Africa only six or so years earlier wrote it. The gifted Wheatley had learned English sufficiently to absorb the neoclassical techniques then popular: heroic couplets, the iambic rhythm, balanced phrasing, and Homeric imagery.[72] The poem, while religious, makes no explicit reference to Christianity. It mentions ancient gods of the wind, Boreas and Aeolus, and refers to hell as "the Shades below." Wheatley had a cosmopolitan vision derived from Enlightenment authors, including one of her literary models, Alexander Pope. She and Pope had different church affiliations; he was a Catholic while she was a member of the Congregationalist Old South Church, one of the few Boston churches that clung to Calvinism and resisted the city's drift toward Unitarianism. But her poetry followed the example of Pope and other Enlightenment figures who promoted a panreligious view intended to reach people of different faiths.

When she arrived in Boston in the 1760s, the city's Congregational

Phillis Wheatley
*Frontispiece (probably by the Black artist Scipio Moorhead) of Wheatley's* Poems on Various Subjects, Religious and Moral *(1773)*

churches had already spread the Puritan idea of spiritual equality among Black converts. Scores of Black people had been baptized ever since Cotton Mather initiated the practice in the late seventeenth century.[73] Spiritual equality mingled with the Lockean idea of human quality that circulated among Boston Whigs, most of whom were Congregationalists.

Both political and religious equality found powerful expression in the Old South Church, which Phillis Wheatley joined after being baptized there in 1771. The largest building in Boston, the Old South was a meeting place for the Sons of Liberty and other Patriots. In December 1773, five to six thousand Bostonians, led by Old South Church member Samuel Adams, rallied there in preparation for the Boston Tea Party. The British Calvinist George Whitefield gave sermons in the Old South at least five times before tremendous crowds.[74] Whitefield was a friend and occasional houseguest of the Wheatley family. After his death in September 1770, young Phillis penned a poetic eulogy that praised him as a voice for equality who had offered "that Saviour" as a gift to all, including Black people. Wheatley imagines Whitefield saying:

> "Take him, ye *Africans*, he longs for you,
> "*Impartial Saviour* is his title due;
> "Washed in the fountain of redeeming blood,
> "You shall be sons, and kings, and priests to
> God."[75]

Puritan-based religion had taught Phillis Wheatley that Africans could be "kings, and priests to God," but as an enslaved woman, she could only go so far in openly advocating human equality.[76] She succeeded in delivering her opinions on race and slavery so carefully that people of opposing views admired her. Consider the circumstances surrounding the publication of her poetry volume *Poems on Various Subjects, Religious and Moral.* Doubts had been raised about the authorship of Wheatley's poems, which to many seemed too sophisticated for her to have written. In 1772, eighteen prominent Bostonians signed an attestation that appeared in her book. This heterogeneous group included Tories (such as Thomas Hutchinson and Andrew Oliver), Patriots (John Hancock, James Bowdoin, and others), and moderates like the preachers Samuel Cooper and Andrew Eliot. The majority of the group's members were slaveholders. On the other hand, some, like the merchant Harrison Gray and Reverend Charles Chauncy, held strong antislavery views.

The diversity of this group, which endorsed Wheatley after examining her, attests to the expansiveness of her vision. She wrote poems about a wide range of people: clergymen of varied opinions, a deceased infant, a five-year-old girl, an African painter, the British colonial official Lord Dartmouth, the military leader George Washington, and

King George III. Other topics included Harvard students, times of the day (morning and evening), and ancient figures like the Roman patron Maecenas and the biblical hero David. Wheatley's openness to history and contemporary experience was appreciated on both sides of the Atlantic. In 1773, she went to England to arrange publication of her poems, which Boston publishers had been unwilling to finance. She won the favor of the influential Selina Hastings, the Countess of Huntingdon, an antislavery Calvinist who sponsored Wheatley's poetry volume, which a London firm published that fall. *Poems on Various Subjects* was generally well received, and Phillis was emancipated by her owners, John and Susanna Wheatley, who both died within five years of the book's publication.

While Phillis did not promote abolitionism vehemently, she voiced complaints about slavery in her poems and in a public letter to the Native American preacher Samson Occom. In a poem dedicated to Lord Dartmouth, England's Secretary of State to the American Department from 1772 to 1775, she expressed her Whig desire for American liberty, anchoring it in her experience of enslavement. In the poem, Wheatley writes that Americans hoped Dartmouth would restore freedom despite signs that England's "wanton *Tyranny*" might "enslave the land." She then tells Dartmouth that if he wonders "from whence my love of *Freedom* sprung," she points to her experience of being kidnapped from Africa as a child:

> I, young in life, by seeming cruel fate
> Was snatch'd from *Afric's* fancy'd happy seat:
> What pangs excruciating must molest,
> What sorrows labour in my parent's breast?
> Steel'd was that soul and by no misery mov'd
> That from a father seiz'd his babe belov'd
> Such, such my case. And can I then but pray
> Others may never feel tyrannic sway?[77]

Here the "pangs excruciating" inflicted on African families by "steel'd" slave traders are compared with the misery that "others"—that is, American Patriots—would feel if they fell under the "tyrannic sway" of England. Given Lord Dartmouth's reputation as a moderate, it is understandable that Wheatley anticipated the secretary gaining "praise immortal" for dampening tensions; she could not know that Dartmouth would soon condone the use of military force against the American colonies or that his chief claim to fame would be helping to fund the "Indian Charity School" in Connecticut, run by the Calvinist minister Eleazur Wheelock that later moved to Hanover, New Hampshire, and became Dartmouth College.

Mohegan cleric Samson Occom, who was involved in promoting the charity school, played a key role in Phillis Wheatley's life. Occom had converted to Christianity in his teens, was ordained as a Presbyterian minister in 1759, and went on to preach and teach among the Montauk and Shinnecock peoples on eastern Long Island. An example for Phillis Wheatley, he became internationally famous when he traveled to England on a fund-raising tour for Wheelock's school. In a 1774 letter to Wheatley, Occom advocated the rights of Black people. In a reply that appeared in eleven newspapers, Wheatley wrote, "[I] am greatly satisfied with your Reasons respecting the Negroes, and think highly reasonable what you offer in Vindication of their natural Rights." Noting the hypocrisy of whites fighting for their own freedom while ignoring that of enslaved people, she called attention to the "strange Absurdity of their Conduct whose Words and Actions are so diametrically opposite." She universalized the human instinct for liberty: "In every human Breast, God has implanted a Principle, which we call Love of Freedom; it is impatient of Oppression, and pants for Deliverance; and . . . I will assert, that the same Principle lives in us." She added, "God grant Deliverance in his own Way and Time."[78]

There was a specifically Puritan element to Wheatley's call for liberty. Not only was she a born-again New Divinity Calvinist, but she also joined her Whig contemporaries in citing the revolutionary example of the English Civil War. Her 1775 poem "Thoughts on Tyranny" follows the lead of John Adams and others who connected ongoing British oppression to that under Charles I, of whom Wheatley writes:

> May his black deeds with all their hideous form
> Impress the wise, and treach [*sic*] the fool to learn.
> Declare abroad, that freedom don't appear
> Under the cloak of monarchy and fear.[79]

She was writing about liberty at a moment when Massachusetts was swept up in antislavery fever. In 1773, Blacks in Massachusetts issued three boldly worded petitions demanding the end of slavery. One petitioner, Felix Holbrook, lamented that enslaved Blacks had "no Property! We have no Wives! No Children! We have no City! No Country!"[80] The following year, the Massachusetts General Court passed a bill against the slave trade, though the incorrigible governor Thomas Hutchinson vetoed it. In 1777, African Americans in Boston led by the Congregationalist Prince Hall submitted to the Massachusetts legislature a "petition of A Great Number of Blackes detained in a State of slavery" demanding emancipation because "they have in Common with all other men a Natural and Unalienable Right to that freedom which the Great Parent of the Unavers hath Bestowed equalley on all menkind."[81] These and similar petitions in the 1770s went nowhere, but a later lawsuit by a Black man had a lasting impact. In 1780, Massachusetts adopted a new constitution announcing that "All men are born free and equal, and have certain natural, essential, and unalienable rights."[82] But slavery was not mentioned. That issue became central when, in 1782, the enslaved Quock Walker sued for his freedom from his abusive owner. In 1783, the state's Supreme Judicial Court ruled in

Quock's favor, saying that slavery did not have legal standing under the new constitution.

Phillis Wheatley's forward-looking views were shaped by a New England religious culture that fostered progress on the issue of slavery. She won support from two ardently antislavery Congregational clergymen: Boston's Charles Chauncy and Newport's Samuel Hopkins. Chauncy, one of the fourteen signers of the attestation of Wheatley's poetry, devoted most of his energy to challenging the installation of an Anglican bishop in America, but also fired salvos against slavery. In a widely read pamphlet, he urged readers to consider "the poor Negroes." He fumed, "It is most horribly shameful, that so many of the human species, as good by nature as their masters, and that have as good a right to the FREEDOM OF MEN, should be bought and sold as though they were cattle; and dealt with as though they were an inferior order to dogs!"[83]

Samuel Hopkins, who, as we've seen, was the chief New Divinity voice against slavery, came to know Phillis Wheatley when she went to Newport and heard him preach. The two corresponded and sought each other's help. Wheatley wanted the eminent clergyman to distribute and publicize her poetry volume. Hopkins, in turn, asked Phillis to participate in one of his pet projects: establishing a mission in Africa to spread the Gospel there. He had already enlisted two Black members of his Newport congregation, the formerly enslaved John Quamine and another individual. He also had the endorsement of Samson Occom. Hopkins and Occom pressured Phillis Wheatley to become a missionary, but she backed away. In doing so, she anticipated nineteenth-century abolitionists who rejected the transporting of American Blacks to Liberia or elsewhere.

Resisting pleas to return to Africa, Phillis Wheatley stayed in America and challenged racism through her life and writings. She married John Peters, a free Black grocer and supplier. The couple reportedly had three children who died in infancy. Faced with personal losses and economic uncertainty, Phillis was not able to get a second poetry volume into print, but she continued to write and took satisfaction in the success of the Patriot cause. Her last published work, a pamphlet titled *Liberty and Peace, A Poem*, which appeared a few months before her death, described the American Revolution as a traumatic yet glorious victory of liberty over tyranny. Phillis ended as she had begun: with a ship. She had been carried to America on a slave ship, had written her first published poem about a storm-tossed whaling ship, and had gained fame in a voyage to England. In her last poem, she pictured her nation, a symbol of freedom, as a ship sailing under fair skies:

> Auspicious Heaven shall fill with fav'ring Gales,
> Where e'er *Columbia* spreads her swelling Sails:
> To every Realm shall *Peace* her Charms display,
> And Heavenly *Freedom* spread her golden Ray.[84]

By the time the thirty-one-year-old Phillis Wheatley died (evidently in childbirth) in December 1784, her fame had declined. Within a month of her death, Thomas Jefferson archly criticized her in *Notes on the State of Virginia*. Alleging a lack of literary imagination in Black people, he wrote, "Religion indeed has produced a Phyllis Whately [*sic*]; but it could not produce a poet."[85] On one point, Jefferson was right. Religion *did* produce Phillis Wheatley—a specific Calvinistic form of religion derived from New England Puritanism. But Jefferson's comment that her poems were "below the dignity of criticism" was hamhanded. If Wheatley's poetry did not measure up to that of some of the authors Jefferson admired—Shakespeare, Milton, Pope, and others—few people's ever have. In fact, her record was extraordinary. As an enslaved nonnative speaker, she rapidly mastered English (and some Latin), read complex literary classics, and ably used neoclassical techniques in poems that covered a range of topics. She sometimes addressed racial issues with surprising progressiveness.

It was these achievements that made Wheatley an icon among nineteenth-century reformers who brought attention to the capabilities of Black people. The Quaker abolitionist and women's rights activist Abigail Mott featured Wheatley in her 1826 volume *Biographical Sketches and Interesting Anecdotes of Persons of Colour* along with other Blacks, including the mathematician and astronomer Benjamin Banneker, the Haitian revolutionary Toussaint L'Ouverture, and the cosmopolitan entrepreneur Olaudah Equiano. Wheatley became a valuable asset to the abolitionist movement. In 1827, a contributor to *Freedom's Journal*, a Black abolitionist newspaper, said that Wheatley in her poetry left "a rich legacy to our race" and put to shame "the illiberal expressions of the advocates of slavery in all parts of the globe."[86] Five years later Wheatley's work began to appear regularly in William Lloyd Garrison's *Liberator.* Garrison established a column called Literary Department in which a poem by Wheatley appeared in many successive issues. Few of the poems chosen for publication dealt directly with slavery. That didn't matter. It was Wheatley's success as an enslaved woman in publishing noteworthy poetry that made her an unprecedented example of Black accomplishment.

This is how she was presented in the 1834 *Memoir and Poems of Phillis Wheatley, a Native African and a Slave*, which greatly enhanced Wheatley's visibility. Framed as an antislavery publication, the book was prefaced by a paean to Phillis as one who rose "to the notice and approbation of the wise and good" despite her background in "the lowest condition of humanity," having been "sold and bought like a beast in the market . . . in the same land where, shortly after, the people rose in their indignation against oppression, and asserted, in the face of a frowning world, that 'All men are born free and equal.'"[87] *Memoir and Poems* was regularly listed among antislavery works in *The Liberator* and other abolitionist periodicals. Wheatley got another boost during the Civil War when the abolitionist author William Wells Brown included her in his biographical anthology *The Black Man: His Antecedents, His Genius, and His Achievements* along with Frederick Douglass, Nat Turner, Martin R. Delany, and other notables.

## REACHING THE POPULAR HEART

Although Wheatley wrote about being painfully separated from her Senegambian family, she never detailed what was likely a nightmarish experience aboard the ship that brought her to America. Emotional depictions of slave ships appeared in narratives by Olaudah Equiano and other enslaved people, as well as in sentimental poems by white women. In fact, a powerful and often overlooked genre of antislavery literature is women's poetry. Between 1790 and 1830, two poems by white women in particular stand out: Sarah Wentworth Morton's "The African Chief" and Lydia Huntley Sigourney's "To the First Slave Ship."

Morton's "The African Chief" (1792) was reprinted in schoolbooks and became so well known that the critic Rufus Wilmot Griswold could remark, a half century after the poem's publication, that it was "as familiar as our nursery rhymes."[88] The poem gained even greater visibility when the antislavery author John Greenleaf Whittier quoted passages from it in his bestselling book-length poem *Snow-Bound* (1866).

Sarah Morton was not an obvious candidate to compose one of early America's most striking antislavery poems. Born into a wealthy Boston merchant family tied to the slave trade, she moved in elite circles and counted John Adams and James Bowdoin among her acquaintances. Writing under the pseudonym Philenia, Morton published verse in Boston newspapers. Her works included the narrative poem *Ouâbi, or, The Virtues of Nature* (1790), a sympathetic tale of Native American characters, and the unfinished epic *Beacon Hill*, about the Revolution.

Like Phillis Wheatley, she also wrote numerous elegies for friends and public figures. Morton's characteristic sentimentalism gained sharper political resonance when applied to the fate of an enslaved man in her "The African Chief." The poem opens with a grim depiction of a slave ship:

> See how the black ship cleaves the main,
> High bounding o'er the dark blue wave,
> Remurmuring with the groans of pain,
> Deep freighted with the princely slave![89]

The poem follows one of the ship's passengers, a tribal chief in Gambia. A kindly family man, the chief lives peacefully in his "palmy grove" until it is invaded by "white tyrants of the deep," who seize him and put him in chains. His sobbing children cling to him as he looks with "phrenzied mind" and "stedfast eye" while his wife is subjected to "nameless wrongs" and killed before his eyes. The chief is transported to Haiti, where the island's French colonizers enslave him. "Resolved to burst the crushing chain" of slavery, he leads a rebellion, "Till by his red avenging hand, / Full many a despot stained the ground." But the chief is captured, tortured, and killed.

In this poem, Morton astonishingly indicts white oppressors at a time when most Americans recoiled from the Haitian Revolution, which had begun in 1791 and would ultimately expel European powers from the island. Morton conveys her revolutionary critique through imagery that portrays whites as "despots" and "tyrants," while describing them as "the hard race of *pallid hue* / Unpracticed in the power to feel," highlighting their moral insensitivity to the suffering of enslaved Africans.

The radical impact of women's poetry is particularly striking in the case of Lydia Sigourney's "To the First Slave Ship." Originally published in 1825 in the Black-edited newspaper *The African Repository*, the poem was widely reprinted throughout the North, not only in abolitionist sheets like *The Liberator* but in local papers read by average readers.[90] Although "To the First Slave Ship" does not endorse slave insurrection, as did "The African Chief," Sigourney outdid Morton in applying sentimental power to the slavery issue.

Lydia Huntley Sigourney, celebrated in her era as the "Sweet Singer of Hartford," produced over sixty books and numerous magazine pieces, including poems, prose sketches, and advice columns. Like Morton and Wheatley, she composed poetic elegies, commemorating friends, public figures, and social tragedies. Her belief in the equality of all humans before God, nurtured by what her biographer calls the "uncompromising New England Calvinism" of her childhood, inspired a deep sympathy for the marginalized and oppressed.[91]

Born in Norwich, Connecticut, in 1791, Lydia Huntley received a strong education from tutors and local schools. She became a teacher in her early twenties. She gave classes for children overlooked by institutions of the day, one of them made up wholly of African Americans—highly unusual for that time. She then opened a school for girls. She also pioneered education for deaf students.[92] Although she quit teaching after her marriage in 1819 to the businessman Charles Sigourney, she did not lose sight of those on the margins. In her epic poem *Traits of the Aborigines of America* (1824), she challenged the negative stereotypes and legal injustices that Indigenous people were subjected to. Along with her fellow Connecticut educator Catharine Beecher, she spearheaded a national campaign among women who flooded Congress with petitions in protest against Native American removal.[93]

Sigourney's Christian sympathy extended to Black people. In *Sketch of Connecticut, Forty Years Since* (1824), she gave moving portrayals of Blacks, including one who had been kidnapped at ten from his African home and taken west on the Middle Passage. Sigourney gives a horrific description of the ship that carried him and his fellow captives: the suffocating lower deck on which the enslaved lay shackled on boards; the constant cries of "we die! we die!" and "Africa! dear Africa!"; the periodic forced dancing and singing on the main deck, goaded on by whips and hot pokers; the wretched food; the rampant sickness, which left the living chained to "the diseased, the dying, and the dead"; corpses thrown into the ocean "with no more concern than if beasts were consigned to its depths."[94]

This prose account set the stage for Sigourney's "To the First Slave Ship," where she again depicted suffering Africans in their dark hold:

> The fetter'd chieftain's burning tear,—
> The parted lover's, mute despair,—
> The childless mother's pang severe,—
> The orphan's misery are there.[95]

The ship's sails, she says, "are spread / With ceaseless sighs from broken hearts." She asks readers, "Hear'st thou *their* moans whom hope hath fled?— / Wild cries, in agonizing starts?" She reminds us that these people are destined for lives of "Stripes,—tortures,—unrelenting hate, / And death-gasps drown'd in slavery's tears." She asks:

> Oh Afric!—what has been thy crime?
> That thus like Eden's fratricide,
> A mark is set upon thy clime,
> And every brother shuns thy side.—

As for the "pale tyrant" of "our guilty land" who holds Blacks in bondage, he "should shrink to hear . . . / The sacred truth that heaven is just,—" and should recall that Christ came as the "Saviour of the opprest."

Powerful lines. But the poem's uniqueness lay in the epigraph Sigourney placed just below the title "To the First Slave Ship":

> In August, 1620, a Dutch man of war landed twenty negroes for sale, at Jamestown; the *first slaves* ever brought into the Country. —*Beverley's history of Virginia*

The idea that the Jamestown ship represented the introduction of slavery to America had appeared in scattered history books since 1705, when Robert Beverley's *History and Present State of Virginia* was published. Beverley reported that in August 1620 (a misdating that many would repeat) "a Dutch Man of War landed Twenty Negroes for Sale; which were the First of that kind that were carried into the Country."[96] Notice how Lydia Sigourney changes Beverley's wording. His euphemistic "First of that kind" becomes her pointed "the *first slaves*" (her italics). Her poem "To the First Slave Ship" was the first widely read sentimental work by a Northerner that identified the Jamestown landing as the origin of enslavement in America.

It is telling that Sigourney's poem appeared in the 1820s, just when sectional tensions over slavery had intensified greatly. The Missouri Compromise of 1820 divided the North and the South geographically by prohibiting slavery above the 36°30′ latitude line in western territories destined to become states. Suddenly, murmurings about a forthcoming civil war were heard. The aging Thomas Jefferson wrote that the Missouri Compromise, "like a fire bell in the night, awakened and filled me with terror. I considered it at once as the knell of the Union."[97]

For a sensitive observer like Lydia Sigourney, the South—specifically that first landing at Jamestown—was to blame for the calamity of slavery. The 1820 census showed that the nation had become startlingly lopsided: In the South, enslaved Blacks made up more than a third of the population of 4,422,493, while in the North, steady progress toward abolition had reduced the number of enslaved people to just 0.3 percent of the total population of 5,643,522.[98] The dehumanization of Southern slavery outraged antislavery Northerners. The Bostonian

David Walker, in his 1829 *Appeal* [. . .] *to the Coloured Citizens of the World*, noted that slaves were treated like "horses, bulls, or hogs" on plantations; he asked passionately, "Are we MEN!!—I ask you, O my brethren! are we MEN?"[99] This was the core question antislavery figures had been asking from the beginning, and Sigourney captured it in her poem, where African captives were portrayed primarily as humans—mothers, lovers, orphans—shedding tears and crying out "wild cries, in agonizing starts." For her subject matter, Sigourney could have chosen any of the thousands of slave ships that had crossed the Atlantic before the abolition of the slave trade in January 1808, or those that illegally traded afterward. But she directly pointed her finger at the Jamestown ship, becoming the first of many Northerners to describe that ship powerfully as the origin of slavery.

Not only was Sigourney the first to associate the Jamestown ship with slavery in a widely read sentimental work, but she also portrayed the *Mayflower* as a freedom ship. Within a year of "To the First Slave Ship," her poem on the Plymouth landing, "The Pilgrims," appeared in many newspapers, including *The Liberator*.[100] Sigourney traces the voyage of the *Mayflower*, a "tiny vessel" that "leaps madly, by the tempest lashed," like "a toiling atom . . . from wave to wave." The ship reaches an "ice-bound coast," where the passengers come forth "From their long prison,—hardy forms, that brave / The world's unkindness." Faced with "bleak Nature's desolation . . . / Eternal forests, and unyielding earth," the Pilgrims could have given way to "bitter loneliness" or "sickness of the heart." Instead, "Up in each girded breast / There sprang a rooted and mysterious strength,— / A loftiness" as they recalled their original mission "to strip the pomp from sceptres" and live freely. "From *their* planting," Sigourney writes, a "bold vine spread forth," producing a country of "giant strength." She warns readers who "boast / In your free veins the blood of sires like these" not to succumb to "Mammon" or "bloated luxury." Her closing advice: "Turn ye to

Plymouth's beach,—and on that rock / Kneel in *their* foot-prints, and renew the vow / They breathed to God."

The poem gained broad circulation, as did another Sigourney poem, "Plymouth Rock," which appeared in newspapers a decade later. In the latter poem, the *Mayflower* is pictured as a ship at anchor in the wintry Plymouth Harbor with freezing passengers ready to face unthinkable hardships to ignite "True Freedom's beacon fires" that would in time make America "the Mecca" of humanity.[101]

Sigourney had succeeded in bringing to popular awareness a key symbol of enslavement, the Jamestown ship, and a key symbol of freedom, the *Mayflower*. It was left to others to summon the two ships to the very heart of the slavery debate in America.

## *Chapter Eight*

# Then There Were Two

Now everyone was talking about the two ships—the *Mayflower* and the Jamestown ship—which were said to represent antagonistic societies: the "Puritan" North and the "Cavalier" South. That's how it often seemed in the years leading up to the Civil War. Frederick Douglass referred to the two ships in several speeches, as did others, notably Senator Charles Sumner. African Americans, in particular, radicalized the two ships, which gave historical depth to the campaign against slavery. The North and the South, the story went, had sprung from diametrically opposite sources, symbolized by the ships.

As we've seen, contrasting sectional identities had been building for more than two centuries. In the North, the *Mayflower* passengers introduced political liberties in Plymouth that were developed by Calvinists like Roger Williams, Cotton Mather, and Samuel Sewall, as well as by later groups affiliated with Puritanism, particularly the New Divinity movement. In the South, the 1619 Jamestown vessel had come to be remembered as the first slave ship by the early eighteenth century, when the Cavalier values of hierarchy and subordination had helped make slavery a fixed institution.

The American Revolution brought together the North and the South in the fight for national independence, but differing views reemerged after the war. By the mid-nineteenth century, many antislavery Northerners saw American history as driven by the two ships, with the *Mayflower* symbolizing freedom and the Jamestown ship representing slavery. Southerners, on the other hand, claimed that the Jamestown ship had established slavery as a natural part of the American experiment, while the *Mayflower* was the source of abolitionism, a horrible force that threatened to tear apart the nation.

How did the two-ship dualism become so firmly imprinted that many in the North and the South felt like they were different people? The previously conflicting sectional identities, which had been buried for decades, resurfaced around 1820, sparking renewed tensions. Some, like the Massachusetts politician Daniel Webster, tried to prevent a national conflagration by patching over the sectional differences. But others harped on these differences, often using the two ships metaphor as their rhetorical weapon. The sparks between the two ships flared sporadically for three decades, and in 1861, they broke out as a raging civil war.

## REDISCOVERING THE *MAYFLOWER*

Bone-chilling temperatures gripped Plymouth, Massachusetts, on December 22, 1820. A winter storm threatened. But the atmosphere was warm with excitement over the celebration of the two hundredth anniversary of the landing of the *Mayflower.* Forefathers' Day had been observed annually in Plymouth since 1769, with a pause during the American Revolution, but none of the celebrations was like this. The day featured military salutes, a parade, a prayer service, a public dinner, and a grand ball in the evening.[1]

The most captivating part was the keynote speaker, thirty-eight-year-old lawyer and politician Daniel Webster. A source of pride for Massachusetts, Webster later served in the House of Representatives, the Senate, and as secretary of state under three presidents. A commanding figure in American politics, Webster was known as Godlike Daniel or Black Dan—referring to his dark complexion, jet-black hair, and dark, deep-set eyes that shone like smoldering coals beneath thick eyebrows. He had unmatched skill as a public speaker. Emerson called him "the great cannon, loaded to the lips." Webster's voice swung between a deep, grave bass and a sharp, clarion shrillness. He emphasized his points with expressive gestures.

He made a huge impact on those who gathered in Plymouth's First Parish Church to hear his talk "The First Settlement of New England," which came to be known as the Plymouth Oration. Generations of schoolchildren would memorize passages from the speech. One attendee, the Harvard professor George Ticknor, was so stunned that he reported, "Three or four times I thought my temples would burst with the gush of blood. . . . I was beside myself, and am so still."[2] The eighty-five-year-old John Adams did not attend the speech, but when he read it the next day, he sent Webster a congratulatory note saying, "This oration will be read five hundred years hence, with as much rapture as it was heard. It ought to be read at the end of every century, and indeed at the end of every year, for ever and ever."[3]

Doubtless Adams, who had written about Plymouth Colony as a source of the American Revolution, was moved by Webster's words about the Pilgrims:

> Their influence has essentially affected our whole history, through the two centuries which have elapsed; and as they have become intimately connected with government, laws, and property, as well as with our opinions on the subjects of religion and civil liberty, that influence is likely to continue to be felt through the centuries which shall succeed.[4]

Webster presented Plymouth Colony as a symbol of America's democratic ideals. However, he warned, those ideals were violated by an ongoing sinful practice: the slave trade.

Descended from a Puritan who arrived in New England around 1637, Webster was well informed about the *Mayflower* and its history. In his speech, he outlined key events from the sixteenth century onward, including the persecution of Puritans under Queen Elizabeth and King James I, the relocation to Holland by John Robinson and his group, their eleven-year stay there, the voyage across the Atlantic on the *Mayflower*, and the establishment of Plymouth. Webster emphasized that the Pilgrims were escaping "causeless oppression" in England.[5] He noted that religious nonconformists under "the arbitrary rule of the Stuarts" had the choice of either staying in England and fighting the monarchy or fleeing elsewhere and establishing their own society. By choosing the latter alternative, the Plymouth settlers went a long way to creating an independent colony with innovative laws and a democratic government. The Pilgrims, Webster said, formed "a government of their own . . . framed by consent, founded on choice and preference." Plymouth's abolition of primogeniture made estates "divisible among sons and daughters," so that "the property was all freehold." Webster traced the aftermath of the Plymouth settlement: England's imposition of strict navigation laws; the overthrow in the 1680s of the Massachusetts colonial governor Edmund Andros, followed by the Glorious Revolution and the Hanoverian regime, which brought more oppressive trade laws that aroused the ire of James Otis, John Hancock, and others. Plymouth and Massachusetts Bay, with their democratic institutions, religious spirit, and emphasis on public education had paved the way for American growth. "Ere long," Webster predicted, "the sons of the Pilgrims will be on the shores of the Pacific."

But he had a caveat. Inspired by the Pilgrims' stance on freedom, he generalized: "If any practices exist contrary to the principles of justice and humanity within the reach of our laws or our influence, we are inexcusable if we do not exert ourselves to restrain and abolish them."[6] The liberties Plymouth Colony had introduced were endangered in 1820 by the slave trade, which continued illegally despite having been banned in 1808. Describing this "odious and abominable trade . . . at which every feeling of humanity must for ever revolt," Webster summoned up a dramatic scene: "I hear the sound of the hammer. I see the smoke of the furnaces where manacles and fetters are still forged for human limbs. I see the visages of those who by stealth and at midnight labor in this work of hell, foul and dark, as may become the artificers of such instruments of misery and torture." He thundered, "Let us pledge ourselves here, upon the rock of Plymouth, to extirpate and destroy [the slave trade]. It is not fit that the land of the Pilgrims should bear the shame longer."

These statements, often quoted in abolitionist publications, made Webster seem like an antislavery pioneer, fired by Puritan passion. However, though he thereafter vaguely called slavery "a great moral, social, and political evil," he backed off from discussing it at length.[7] Alarmed by the rising sectional hostilities, he became a leading spokesman for national unity, second only to his Senate colleague Henry Clay, who was known as the Great Compromiser. In the two decades after the Plymouth Oration, Webster spoke at several more Forefathers' Day celebrations in different parts of the country. He didn't mention slavery, focusing instead on national togetherness. He carefully placed *both* Plymouth and Jamestown at the origins of English-speaking America. In his 1843 speech to the New England Society of New York, he referred to the *Mayflower* passengers as "a hundred saints, blessed of God and ever honored of men, landed on the shores of Plymouth . . . united, as I have said already more than once, in the process of time, with the settlement of Jamestown."[8] He noted that "the people of Virginia . . . were allowed to constitute and establish the first popular representative assembly whichever convened on this continent, the Virginia House of Burgesses."

He emphasized commonalities between Virginia and New England. While touring Southern states in 1847, he called Jamestown "the Plymouth Rock of the South," making no mention of the arrival there of the 1619 slave ship.[9] Whatever differences existed between the North and the South, he said, they were obviated by close commercial ties. At a Forefathers' Day dinner, he announced, "There is no commerce of New York, no commerce of Massachusetts, none of Georgia, none of Alabama or Louisiana."[10] There was only "the commerce of the United States," and "there is nothing more cementing, nothing that makes us more cohesive, nothing that repels all tendencies to separation and dismemberment, than this great, this common, I may say this overwhelming interest of one commerce." He showed no concern that this commerce was fueled in part by the international slave trade, which he had formerly denounced, and by the ever-expanding internal slave trade in the Southern states.

Not only did Webster put aside his criticism of slavery, but he also curried favor among Southerners. In an 1847 talk before the New England Society of Charleston, South Carolina, he supported his argument for "cordial relations" between the sections by pointing out that "sons of the Pilgrims" from Massachusetts had fought alongside Carolinians during the American Revolution.[11] Webster no longer viewed the Constitution as the pinnacle of Plymouth-based human rights but rather as a shield for slavery-protecting states' rights. Its purpose "through all time to come," he declared, was "to bind together all parts of our country in one great and glorious republic, each State governing its own internal affairs," including slavery.

This genuflecting to the South put Webster in a precarious position when he joined the 1850 debate over slavery in recently acquired western territories. Everyone watched closely when he delivered his speech in the Senate on March 7 in response to Henry Clay's compromise proposals, which included a harsh new fugitive slave law that put federal muscle behind the capture and retrieval of enslaved Blacks who fled to the North. In his speech, Webster defended the proposed law because it enforced the Constitution's clause about returning fugitives from labor. He claimed that Northerners had incited the slavery controversy. Of "the abolition societies" he said, "I do not think them useful. I think their operation for the last twenty years have produced nothing good or valuable."[12]

Within a month of Webster's speech, prominent abolitionists, including William Lloyd Garrison and Wendell Phillips, gathered at a meeting of Plymouth's Old Colony Anti-Slavery Society, where they expressed their "unfeigned surprise, deep regret, and strong disapprobation" of Webster. A resolution was passed urging the senator to reconsider his position "by all the hallowed memories which cluster around Plymouth Rock—by all that is abhorrent in slavery, and glorious in freedom."[13]

Webster did *not* reconsider his position. When Congress passed the Fugitive Slave Act in September, he was widely regarded as its father. For Southern-leaning Northerners known as doughfaces, that made him a heroic savior of the nation. On December 22, New York City, which was financially close to the South and would later support secession, hosted him at a Forefathers' Day dinner at the luxurious Astor House Hotel. Speaking as "the chief defender" of "the Constitution and the Union," Webster talked about the early settlement of Plymouth, but far differently than he had in 1820.[14] "What our ancestors saw and felt," he said, "we shall not see nor feel. What they achieved; it is denied to us even to attempt." They faced "the severer duties of life" that demanded "unbending virtues" and "austere qualities." Americans had since learned to be less insistent on absolute moral distinctions. Although Webster mentioned recent "contentions" and "angry controversies" caused by "State prejudices, local ideas," he gushed, "Over all, submerging all, *drowning* all, is that great sentiment, that always . . . *we are all Americans*." As Webster delivered these words, he pointed to a confectionery ship on the dinner table and said, "There is an imitation on a small scale, but a correct one, of the Mayflower. Sons of New England! . . . That Mayflower was a flower destined to be of perpetual bloom! . . . It will defy all climate, and all time, and will continue to spread its petals to the world, and to exhale an ever-living odor and fragrance, to the last syllable of recorded time."

The words were as sugary as the faux *Mayflower* on the table. Having abandoned his moral outrage over slavery, Webster stood for conciliation. Southerners praised him. *The Richmond Whig* announced, "We have feared the vast intellect in Mr. Webster. . . . But our distrust has been removed, and our apprehensions allayed."[15] The *Charleston Mercury* chimed in, "Mr. Webster is pervaded by a spirit of moderation, fairness and good faith on the subject of slavery."

For antislavery Northerners, in contrast, Webster was Benedict Arnold, Judas Iscariot, or Lucifer. The Quaker poet Whittier described him as "So fallen! so lost! the light withdrawn / Which once he wore! / The glory from his gray hairs gone / Forevermore!"[16] William Loyd Garrison declared, "He has reached the lowest depths of moral depravity. . . . His strides from Plymouth Rock to Carolina lead as surely to perdition."[17] When Webster died in 1852, Plymouth's Old Colony Anti-Slavery Society celebrated his passing as a wonderful event. The society's members agreed that "they had never assembled before under as favorable circumstance. Daniel Webster was no more—his great influence for evil was now at an end." Abolitionists, in the words of a speaker, were left "to exclaim only, as one in olden time, 'Good were it for that man if he had never been born.'"[18]

## TOWARD AN ANTISLAVERY *MAYFLOWER*

Ironically, the Old Colony Anti-Slavery Society was one of the abolitionist groups that had formed in the 1830s, partly inspired by Webster's 1820 Plymouth Oration, with its attack on the slave trade. Of one of the society's early events, on July 4, 1837, it was reported, "Never has there been such a meeting in Plymouth County, since Daniel Webster delivered his celebrated oration, on the 200th anniversary of the 'Landing of the Pilgrims in 1620,' in which he so admirably portrayed the *horrors of slavery*."[19] Actually, by the time this was written, Webster, with his eye on unifying the North and the South, had stopped judging slavery's horrors against the backdrop of the Pilgrims. Others, however, were so anxious over the growing sectional division that they were talking openly about two ships and two civilizations.

Tensions over slavery spiked in the 1830s. Two events of 1831—Nat Turner's insurrection and the founding of William Lloyd Garrison's *The Liberator*—had major repercussions. Although Nat Turner's slaughter of between fifty-five and sixty-five whites prompted brief antislavery discussion in the South, its long-term effect was a doubling down on the discipline of enslaved people. At the same time, the South's economy, dominated by slavery-dependent cotton, provoked a defense of enslavement on moral grounds. In 1837, the fire-eating senator John C. Calhoun declared that slavery was not an evil but rather "a positive good"—good for whites, because it supplied much-needed labor, and good for Blacks, who were materially provided for and exposed to the benefits of Western civilization.[20] Preachers found justification for slavery in the Bible, where it was practiced by the Old Testament patriarchs and allegedly justified by Noah's curse of Ham and his descendants. (Proslavery Christianity would soon cause the Southern branches of the Baptist, Presbyterian, and Methodist churches to split off from the Northern ones.)

Just as slavery was becoming ever more embedded in the South, resistance was deepening in the North. The Boston reformer William Lloyd Garrison and his followers demanded immediate emancipation—or, if that didn't come, then the peaceful separation of the North and the South. Viewing the Constitution, the American government, and the churches as corruptly proslavery, the Garrisonians were called come-outers because they abandoned voting and traditional religious worship. Garrison, a balding, benign-faced man who wore round wire-framed glasses, looked more like a scholar than an activist, but he was adamant in calling for emancipation. He established an uncompromising tone in the first issue of *The Liberator*, published on January 1, 1831: "I am in earnest—I will not equivocate—I will not excuse—I will not retreat a single inch—AND I WILL BE HEARD."[21] Although Garrisonianism would remain a fringe movement, it raised the moral bar on slavery among Northerners, who formed other antislavery reform groups and, in time, antislavery political movements, including the Liberty Party, the Free Soil Party, and the Republican Party.

Pendulum swings of action and reaction between proslavery and antislavery forces brought a startling rise in violence. Scores of riots, often targeting Black people or abolitionists, erupted—so many that Abraham Lincoln feared that a "mobocratic spirit" was overtaking the nation.[22] In 1835 alone, there were 141 recorded riots, including one in Boston in which a mob dragged William Lloyd Garrison by a rope through the streets.[23] The Illinois antislavery editor Elijah Lovejoy was murdered by a racist mob, and around the same time, Francis McIntosh, a Black man in St. Louis, was chained to a tree by whites and burned to death.

Violence against enslaved people escalated. A litany of slave tortures appeared in *American Slavery as It Is* (1839), edited by Theodore Dwight Weld and others. The book reproduced the newspaper ads of slaveowners seeking runaways, who were identified by scars, missing ears or toes, whip marks, charred flesh, and other signs of violent punishment. This was firsthand proof that, in the words of the book's introduction, enslaved people "have red pepper rubbed into their lacerated flesh, and hot brine, spirits of turpentine, &c., poured over the gashes to increase the torture"; "they are often stripped naked, their backs and limbs cut with knives, bruised and mangled by scores and hundreds of blows with the paddle, and terribly torn by the claws of cats, drawn over them by their tormentors"; "they are maimed, mutilated and burned to death over slow fires"; and so on for more than two hundred pages.[24]

Abolitionist publications were suppressed in the South. In July 1836, a mob in Charleston, South Carolina, broke into a post office, seized undelivered abolitionist mail, took it outside, and destroyed it in a bonfire. Although a federal postal law that year mandated the delivery of mail to the intended recipient, the law was largely ignored in much of the South, as many postmasters stopped delivering antislavery materials. Suppression of another kind came in Congress, where Southern legislators tabled hundreds of antislavery petitions. John Quincy Adams and other antislavery congressmen fiercely fought the gag rules. Another inflammatory subject was the proposed annexation of Texas, which many Northerners saw as a Southern plot to extend slavery westward.

The sectional difference around enslavement produced the momentous juxtaposition of the two ships in antislavery speeches and writings. The ships had floated separately into the American consciousness, starting in 1819 with the controversy over slavery in Missouri. The New York Senator Rufus King, using the misdating of Jamestown found in popular histories of Virginia, announced that the troubles over slavery had begun in "1620 . . . the same year in which the first settlement was made in the old Colony of Plymouth, [when] a cargo of negroes was brought into and sold as slaves in Virginia by a foreign ship."[25] When Nat Turner's rebellion in Virginia in 1831 prompted the state legislature to discuss abolishing slavery, the planter-politician Thomas Marshall blamed the slavery crisis on the Jamestown ship: "We can almost see the hateful form of the slaver as with her cargo of crime and misery, 'rigged with curses,' she bursts into the silent Chesapeake. . . . Fatal, fatal ship!"[26]

Meanwhile, the *Mayflower* and Plymouth Rock were achieving

iconic status. The ship and the rock were now sacred. As Tocqueville wrote in 1835:

> This rock has become an object of veneration in the United States. I saw fragments of it carefully preserved in several cities of the Union. Doesn't this show quite clearly that the power and greatness of man is entirely in his soul? Here is a rock touched for a moment by the feet of a few wretched individuals, and this rock becomes famous; it attracts the attention of a great people; the remains are venerated; far away, tiny pieces are shared.[27]

Indeed, the rock had become a mecca for relic gatherers. The top half of Plymouth Rock had been publicly accessible ever since 1774, when it broke off from the bottom half while being transported from Plymouth's shoreline to a flagpole in its town square, where it was "exposed to indignities at the hand of almost every sojourner stout enough to wield a sledge hammer," according to a journalist.[28] On July 4, 1834, the top half, weighing over three tons, was moved from the square to a safer location, just in front of Plymouth's Pilgrim Hall, in a ceremonial procession in which six boys pulled a miniature *Mayflower* in a cart decorated with flowers.[29]

By that time, the ship had become a symbol of liberty. The year the rock was moved saw the publication of the first volume of George Bancroft's bestselling *History of the United States*. Bancroft wrote, "In the cabin of the Mayflower humanity recovered its rights, and instituted government on the basis of 'equal laws' for the 'general good.' . . . This was the birth of popular constitutional liberty."[30]

The potential for an antislavery interpretation of the *Mayflower* had been sensed ever since the first Forefathers' Day fête in 1769, when a song composed for the occasion praised the Pilgrims for coming "through *oceans* to *deserts* for *freedom*" to show that humans could live "not as SLAVES, but as FREEMEN."[31] Another song, introduced at the 1798 celebration in Boston, said that the *Mayflower*'s arrival "Proclaim'd that SLAVERY'S FLOOD was o'er; / That pilgrim man, so long oppress'd, / Had found his promis'd *place of rest*."[32] Soon, attacks on chattel slavery arose, as at Plymouth's 1821 Pilgrim event, where one of the celebrants toasted early Plymouth Colony as "*The Land of Codfish and Potatoes*—Cultivated without the stripes, and harvested without the groans of slavery."[33] Lydia Sigourney, as we saw, influenced abolitionists with her poems about the *Mayflower* and the Jamestown ship.

But it was not until December 1839 that the two ships were combined in a single work that garnered national attention. That work was a Forefathers' Day speech given by the thirty-year-old Massachusetts legislator Robert C. Winthrop at the New England Society of New York in Manhattan's Broadway Tabernacle. This Presbyterian church was an antislavery hub. Winthrop's speech was reprinted in many newspapers, with nearly all the excerpts containing his account of the two ships.

Winthrop was an unlikely person to introduce to the American scene a striking antislavery image based on the Plymouth settlers. Although he was descended from two Puritan governors, John Winthrop of Massachusetts Bay Colony and John Winthrop Jr. of the Colony of Connecticut, he was an Episcopalian who wrote, "I was born a Conservative."[34] Winthrop explained that despite his deep devotion to Anglicanism, he believed that the Pilgrims were right to reject the church under the Stuarts, which, he said, was characterized by "corruptions" and "tyrannies." He declared:

> As that church and its prelates then were, let us thank God that such Separatists were found! . . . I yet rejoice as heartily as any Congregationalist who listens to me, that our Pilgrim Fathers were Separatists. I rejoice, too, that our Puritan

> Fathers of Massachusetts, who followed them to these shores ten years afterward . . . were, if not technically and professedly, yet to all intents and purposes, Separatists also.

As a member of the Massachusetts state legislature, Winthrop joined the coalition against Andrew Jackson that became the Whig Party in the 1830s. Elected to Congress in 1840, he served in the House of Representatives until 1850, including a term as Speaker (1847–49). In 1850, he was appointed to the Senate to fill the seat vacated by his mentor Daniel Webster, who had joined President Millard Fillmore's cabinet. Like the Illinois politician Abraham Lincoln, Winthrop was a northern Whig who opposed slavery.

In his 1839 Forefathers' Day speech Winthrop covered the Pilgrims' historical background—the persecution by Queen Elizabeth and the Stuart monarchs, the expatriate years with John Robinson in Holland, the perilous voyage on the *Mayflower*, the first frozen months in Plymouth, the perseverance through illness and the loss of loved ones, the establishment of democracy and common schools—all very different, in Winthrop's telling, from Virginia, where slavery was introduced early on, education was suppressed, and people lived in ignorance and decadence, though Winthrop recognized that the Southerners bravely joined up with New Englanders in the American Revolution. Winthrop hit many popular notes. He pictured Mary Chilton leaping "gently but fearlessly on Plymouth Rock," which "was a pledge that there would be no retreating."[35] He credited the "feeble, devoted band" of Pilgrims not only with planting New England and molding America but also with shaping "the whole Hemisphere"—indeed, "the whole world." He proclaimed, "The seeds of the Mayflower, wafted by the winds of Heaven, or borne in the Eagle's beak, have been scattered far and wide over the Old World as well as over the New." Familiar with George Bancroft's *History of the United States*, he contrasted the two ships, though he discarded Bancroft's accurate 1619 dating of the Jamestown ship in favor of the popular fiction of the *Mayflower* and the slave ship headed to their destinations at the same time in 1620. Winthrop asserted:

> I see those two fate-freighted vessels, laboring under the divided destinies of the same Nation, and striving against the billows of the same sea, like the principles of good and evil advancing side by side on the same great ocean of human life. I hear from the one the sighs of wretchedness, the groans of despair, the curses and clankings of struggling captivity, sounding and swelling on the same gale, which bears only from the other the pleasant voices of prayer and praise, the cheerful melody of contentment and happiness, the glad, the glorious "anthem of the free." . . . They have both reached in safety the place of the destination. Freedom and Slavery, in one and the same year, have landed on these American shores.

Winthrop went on to say that slavery in the South had expanded exponentially since Jamestown, but he confessed that he didn't know what to do about it. Like Lincoln at the time, he opposed Garrisonian abolitionism, which called for disunion and a rejection of the Constitution. Also like Lincoln, he argued in Congress against the westward expansion of slavery. But he proved to be a man of Webster-like timidity, not Lincolnesque moral courage. In speaking of the two ships, Winthrop vaguely said he wished that "some angel arm" had "interposed to arrest, avert, dash down, and overwhelm" the Jamestown ship; but that had not happened, and so "American liberty" was "doomed . . . to endure the presence of a fettered captive as a companion in her Car of Triumph."[36]

Winthrop later showed the same hesitancy during the debate over Henry Clay's compromise measures in 1850. He said that as he looked back at the day "when the forefathers of New England were planting their little colony upon that rock-bound shore" while the slave ship "made its way to Jamestown, with a cargo of human beings in bondage," he thought of "how much our fathers would have exulted, could they have arrested the progress of that ill-starred vessel, and of all others of kindred employment."[37] Whereas Lincoln continued to progress in his public statements on slavery, Winthrop backtracked. He voted against Lincoln in the election of 1860 for fear of a civil war and again in 1864, when he supported the Democrat, George McClellan, who he thought would end the war sooner than would Old Abe.

Winthrop had popularized the two-ships image, but he retreated from its radical implications. It was left to African American reformers to recognize the power of the two ships in the attack on slavery and racism.

## THE TWO SHIPS AND BLACK RADICALISM

In May 1840, just six months after Robert Winthrop's Forefathers' Day talk, the Black preacher and reformer Henry Highland Garnet extolled the *Mayflower* in a speech before a meeting of the American Anti-Slavery Society. Hailing "the moral *sublimity* of the spirit of the *pilgrims*," Garnet said that "their very sails were swelled by the breath of liberty. As pure in motive and as resistless in spirit as the waves that bore them thither, they laid the broad foundation of republican institutions."[38]

It may seem surprising that Henry Highland Garnet featured an icon of white culture, the *Mayflower*, in a discussion of slavery. Garnet had many experiences in his own background to draw from to make his antislavery point without invoking white history. His grandfather had been a Mandinka chief who was kidnapped by slave traders, brought on the Middle Passage to Virginia, and sold into slavery in

Maryland, where Garnet was born in 1815. Garnet said that his "earliest recollections" were seeing his "Christian mother enslaved by professed Christians" and hearing "the cracking of the whip, and the clanking of chains."[39] When he was ten, his family escaped to New York. As runaways, they were pursued by slave catchers and were once nearly caught. Henry attended schools in New York City and then upstate New York. He was subjected to discrimination and violence. In 1835, an interracial village school he was attending was torn down and burned by a white mob. Garnet was chased, and he fired at his pursuers from a house with a shotgun. Against all odds, he pushed forward with his education. He studied diligently, learned foreign languages, and set his sights on becoming a minister. Guided by Reverend Theodore S. Wright, an African American abolitionist and pastor of New York's First Colored Presbyterian Church (aka Shiloh Church), Garnet started religious studies and was ordained in 1842. After Wright's death, Garnet replaced him as Shiloh's minister.

Reform-minded African Americans accentuated the slave voyages in order to expose America's appalling betrayal of its founding ideals. Nowhere is this subversive strategy more visible than in one of the works that influenced Garnet: David Walker's 1829 *Appeal* [. . .] *to the Coloured Citizens of the World.* Walker, born in 1786 in North Carolina to an enslaved father and a free Black mother, later moved to Philadelphia and then Boston, where he became a clothing merchant. He was haunted by the scenes of enslavement he had witnessed while growing up as a free Black in the South. A devout Methodist, he attacked slavery with religious fervor. His *Appeal* was a Black jeremiad—an abolitionist version of the Puritan sermon, which predicted God's retributive punishment of an erring nation. The *Appeal* was smuggled to the South, where it caused such alarm that a $1,000 reward was offered for Walker's head and $10,000 for his capture and delivery to Georgia.[40] In the *Appeal*, Walker castigated America as a professedly

Christian nation that hypocritically supported the satanic institution of slavery. Whites talked of human equality while treating Black people as though they were beasts. Throughout the *Appeal* Walker quotes from the Bible and Founding Fathers like Thomas Jefferson to highlight the distance between America's noble principles and its nefarious practices. He points to the Jamestown ship as a source of America's wickedness. After tracing the transatlantic slave trade back to sixteenth-century Europe, Walker noted that it had been 209 years since "1620—when twenty of our fathers were brought into Jamestown, Virginia, by a Dutch man of war, and sold off like brutes to the highest bidders; and there is not a doubt in my mind, but that tyrants are in hope to perpetuate our miseries under them and their children until the final consummation of all things."[41]

If Walker brought the Jamestown ship into African American discourse, one of his friends, the Black abolitionist feminist Maria W. Stewart, along with Garnet, sang praise to the *Mayflower*. Born Maria Miller in Hartford, Connecticut, in 1803, Stewart was orphaned at five and bound as a domestic servant to a clergyman's family until she was fifteen, after which she educated herself in religion. In 1826, she married James W. Stewart, a prosperous Black shipping agent and veteran of the War of 1812. His death three years later left her widowed and financially vulnerable, but she found consolation in her faith. Moving to Boston, she came into contact with David Walker and William Lloyd Garrison. After Walker's death in 1830, she published *Religion and the Pure Principles of Morality: The Sure Foundation on Which We Must Build* (1831), issued as a pamphlet and excerpted in Garrison's *Liberator*. Stewart soon began delivering lectures that made her one of the first African American women to speak publicly on both abolition and women's rights before racially and sexually mixed audiences. While warning that God would punish America for the sins of slavery and racial discrimination, she urged people of color to make every effort to improve themselves. In an 1832 lecture, she pointed to the *Mayflower* passengers as examples for Black Americans to follow. She asked,

> Did the pilgrims, when they first landed on these shores, quietly compose themselves, and say, "The Britons have all the money and all the power, and we must continue their servants forever"? Did they sluggishly sigh and say, "Our lot is hard"? . . . No—they first made powerful efforts to raise themselves, and then God raised up those illustrious patriots, Washington and Lafayette, to assist and defend them. And, my brethren, have you made a powerful effort? Have you prayed the Legislature for mercy's sake to grant you all the rights and privileges of free citizens, that your daughters may rise to that degree of respectability which true merit deserves, and your sons above the servile situations which most of them fill?[42]

Both Maria Stewart and David Walker shaped Henry Highland Garnet. He met with Stewart in Boston in the 1830s, and in the next decade he reprinted, with his own money, Walker's *Appeal*, writing in the preface, "This little book produced more commotion among slaveholders than any volume of its size that was ever issued from an American press."[43] Garnet could sound like the incendiary Walker, as when he called on America's enslaved millions to revolt. In an 1843 speech in Buffalo, Garnet declared, "Brethren, arise, arise! Strike for your lives and liberties. Now is the day and the hour. Let every slave throughout the land do this, and the days of slavery are numbered. . . . Let your motto be resistance! *resistance*! RESISTANCE!"[44] Garnet followed Walker in regarding the Jamestown ship as a fountainhead of slavery, and he shared Maria Stewart's view of the *Mayflower* as a harbinger of liberty and an inspiration for Blacks in their struggle for rights. In a stirring address in Troy, New York, in 1848, Garnet contrasted the two ships:

> In 1620, the very same year in which the Pilgrims landed on the cold and rocky shores of New England, a Dutch ship freighted with souls touched the banks of James river, where the wretched people were employed as slaves in the cultivation of that hateful weed, tobacco. Wonderful coincidence! The angel of liberty hovered over New England, and the Demon of slavery unfurled his black flag over the fields of the "sunny south."[45]

Although Garnet imagined "the angel of liberty" hovering over the *Mayflower*, he bitterly said of white Americans, "Their fathers crossed the ocean in search of the freedom now denied to us."[46] The Pilgrims had laid "the broad foundation of republican institutions." Now Black people, he insisted, "claim the right of American citizenship. We claim it, but shall we ever enjoy it?"

That was the painful question African Americans faced in the 1850s, a decade of proslavery laws, a proslavery government, and the Supreme Court's Dred Scott decision, which said that Blacks had no rights that whites had to respect. With citizenship out of the question and slavery cemented in place, some Black leaders believed that the only option was emigration to Africa, Haiti, or elsewhere to establish an independent society. The *Mayflower* became a symbol of how to escape oppression by moving *out* of America. The militant Black nationalist Martin Delany described how in 1620, "Puritans made the harbor of Cape Cod, and after solemn vows and organization previous to setting foot on shore, they landed safely on 'Plymouth Rock'" while "negro slaves began to be imported to Virginia: a Dutch ship bringing twenty of them for sale."[47] Delany argued that Black people had contributed to the development of America by utilizing skills acquired in Africa and performing essential labor. Later, they fought in the American Revolution and the War of 1812. But now millions were held in slavery, and free Blacks faced "almost insurmountable obstacles." Black people, Delany wrote, could learn from "the ever memorable emigration of the Puritans, in 1620, from Great Britain, the land of their birth, to the wilderness of the New World." The Pilgrims showed "the advantages to be derived from emigration, to us as a people, in preference to any other policy we may adopt." For Delany, the desired future home for Black emigrants was western Africa. For James Theodore Holly, the first Black bishop in the Protestant Episcopal Church, it was Haiti. In 1861, Holly issued an appeal to "Citizens of New Haven! Sons of the Pilgrims!," urging them "to rally to the hearty support of this *Mayflower* expedition of sable pioneers in the cause of civil and religious liberty, which it falls to your lot to Hayti in the name of New England."[48] The same year, *The Anglo-African* magazine reported that two vessels had recently departed for Haiti "with as many colonists in all as the Mayflower brought to Plymouth."[49]

Although emigration was widely discussed, most African Americans wanted to stay in the land of their birth to challenge slavery and racism. For them, the *Mayflower* remained a motivation for activism at home. William Wells Brown is a prime example. Born around 1814 into slavery in Kentucky, he was the son of an enslaved woman and a white man who was descended from the *Mayflower* passenger Stephen Hopkins. At nineteen, Brown escaped to the North, settled in Boston, and became a novelist, playwright, and abolitionist orator. In his 1853 novel, *Clotel*, widely recognized as the first published novel written by an African American author, Brown described the *Mayflower* as "the good genius of America," which carried "the embryo elements of all that is useful, great, and grand in Northern institutions," in contrast to the "low rakish" Jamestown ship, "freighted with the elements of unmixed evil," including "idleness, lynch-law, ignorance, unpaid labour, poverty, and duelling, despotism, the ceaseless swing of the whip."[50] Brown noted that "the settlers of Jamestown, and indeed, all Virginia at that time, were mainly cavaliers, gentlemen-adventurers, aspiring to live by their wits and other men's labor." In contrast to the "law-abiding" and "constitution-making" Plymouth colonists, who did their own work, the Jamestown settlers had little liking for "persistent muscular exertion," which they forced on enslaved Blacks. Brown noted that Americans later joined together during the American Revolution, but subsequently "the people, North and South, began to look at their interests connected with each section of the country."[51] Hence, the deep divide over slavery.

No Black reformer found more significance in the Plymouth and Jamestown ships than Frederick Douglass, the ex-slave who became a world-renowned author, newspaper editor, and abolitionist speaker. Douglass's life story is so compelling that, understandably, it has dominated discussion of him. His 1845 *Narrative* is full of unforgettable scenes: the bloody whipping of Frederick's Aunt Hester; the shooting of Demby for refusing to come out of the pond; the slaves' extemporaneous sorrow songs; Sophia Auld's turn from kindness to cruelty; the succession of callous overseers and Frederick's astonishing fistfight with one of them; his struggle for self-education and his escape to the North. The later versions of Douglass's autobiography (1855 and 1881) describe his ongoing trials and triumphs from the 1850s through Reconstruction and beyond.

Douglass's biting use of 1776 in his lecture "What to the Slave Is the Fourth of July?" is well known; his interest in Plymouth and Jamestown much less so. The two ships were vitally important to his antislavery argument. They represented the fact that different destinies—freedom or slavery—had been there from the country's beginning. Over the centuries, the North had embraced the former while the South had solidified the latter. Between 1855 and 1876, he mentioned the *Mayflower* in five major speeches: two before the Civil War, two during the war, and one after it. In four of those speeches, he contrasted the *Mayflower* with the Jamestown ship.

He first mentioned the two ships in an antislavery speech he delivered in Philadelphia in the spring of 1855. Speaking when tensions had ratcheted up in the wake of the Kansas-Nebraska Act, which opened up the western territories to slavery, Douglass outlined the history of American slavery, which began when "a Dutch Galliot, plowing the sea, made port, and landed its cargo of twenty slaves on James' River, which were afterwards sold at auction."[52] He continued, "From the twenty, we number now over three millions of slaves, and 700,000 but partially free." Black people had done much of the work needed to develop America "and yet today our humanity is denied." The antislavery movement "started with one idea. . . . Namely, that the slave is *a man*." That idea was seeded when "the *May Flower* touched the rocky shore of New England."

The key role of the *Mayflower* became the central theme of Douglass's next address on the two ships, which he gave in Glasgow in February 1860. Douglass asked:

> Why this present conflict?—who were the parties to it?—where should they find the germ? The *Mayflower* and the Dutch galliot was the answer. These two elements were diametrically opposed to each other as much as were light and darkness, Christ and Belial; and these two elements were now struggling for the ascendancy.[53]

Douglass declared that the *Mayflower*, with "her liberty-loving passengers," established human rights in America while the Jamestown ship, with its "cargo of slaves," brought "the whip and the chain." In the North, you now saw "the institutions peculiar to the Mayflower," including "freedom of speech and the liberty of the press," as well as "education, industry, enterprise." In the South you saw "the whipping post instead of the school-house, and the slave prison"—everything that could make a region "gloomy, barren, and desolate."

Douglass and his fellow Black reformers had brought radical intensity to the two-ships image. They used the ships as a way of showing that a potential conflict over slavery had been a threat at the very founding of English-speaking America. That threat had since gathered strength and had become truly menacing in the nineteenth century, when slavery exploded in the South and diminished in the North.

## THE TWO SHIPS: RECOIL AND AMPLIFICATION

Reactions to this radical message about the two ships varied. Some wanted to soften the message to maintain national togetherness; others wanted to twist it for their own purposes; still others exaggerated it to fan the moral conflict over slavery.

Conservatives tried to dampen sectional conflict by presenting Plymouth and Jamestown as benign cocreators of American democracy. If one squinted at the past and overlooked the nation's darker side, American history could be said to have followed a steady pattern of progress from two humble, quasi-democratic colonies. Citing "civilization, improvement, and our republican institutions of government," Edward Everett intoned, "the torch of enlightened liberty, originally kindled at the altars of Jamestown and Plymouth, and long ago transmitted across the mountains, is travelling onward, through the wide west."[54] A New York journalist in 1837 outlined America's "great principles," including "humanity, philanthropy . . . industry and worth," writing, "From the first settlement of Plymouth and Jamestown, up to 1837, embracing a period of more than two centuries, these principles have been in constant action." The rosy conclusion: "From a few wanderers at Plymouth, Massachusetts, and Jamestown, we have become a mighty and a powerful nation."[55]

Coupling Plymouth and Jamestown in this way justified the spirit of Manifest Destiny that fueled the Mexican-American War, which would win more than five hundred thousand square miles of western territory for the United States. The expansionist president John Tyler in 1843 invited Americans to look back "some two hundred years ago and remember that the seed of civilization planted at Jamestown afterward sprung to vigor at Plymouth Rock. See it stretching forth its roots from the Pacific to the Atlantic, overshadowing a continent."[56] A New Orleans newspaper editorialized: "The people of the little colonies of Jamestown and Plymouth have gone on from one degree of greatness to another; their rapid strides to power have no parallel in history." America was now poised to fulfill "its true destiny of constant improvement" by supplanting the "idle" inhabitants of "imbecile Mexico" with "higher forms of humanity"—that is, industrious, democratic Caucasians.[57]

As this statement indicates, conjoining Plymouth and Jamestown was useful to those who prioritized expansion or preserving the Union. More typically, however, antebellum Americans sharply distinguished between the two ships. Southerners cited the Jamestown ship to justify slavery and secession. In 1842, South Carolina Democrat John Campbell referred to the ship to argue that "African slavery is coeval in this country with the settlement of civilized and Christian men."[58] Slavery, Campbell said, was not only a part of America from Jamestown onward but was also supported by the Constitution, with its proslavery implications.

In 1850, the South Carolina author William Henry Trescot maintained that the original differences between the two early settlements had since escalated to such a degree that the South should now separate from the North. Trescot wrote, "The antithesis of Plymouth and Jamestown did not end with their settlement. The growth of the two great sections radiated from different centres, diverged in distant directions, were developed from differing principles, and perfected through dissimilar experiences."[59] Currently, "the North and the South are irreconceivably hostile." Therefore, "It is time for the South to act firmly, promptly, and for ever. But one safe path is open to her honour, and that is, Secession and the formation of an Independent Confederacy."

Northerners agreed that the hostility between the sections stemmed from their dissimilar origins, but they viewed this hostility from an antislavery perspective. The abolitionist Boston minister Robert Cassie Waterston, who called the Pilgrims "the honored champions of civil and religious liberty," asserted that the contrast between the two ships meant civil war.[60] In an 1847 address that appeared in Garrison's *The Liberator* and Frederick Douglass's *The North Star*, Waterston declared: "Those two vessels coming to this country in the same year, brought with them the conflicting principles which never have been, and never can be, reconciled together. They are principles which are now in conflict; and the conflict waxes warmer, and it never will cease until the one or the other is exterminated."

The Ohio politician Joshua Reed Giddings, who served in the House of Representatives for over two decades, also highlighted the two ships. Before a cheering crowd at an antislavery convention in Buffalo on August 9, 1848, Giddings, according to a report, "alluded to the landing of the Mayflower on Plymouth Rock, and the Dutch ship, in the same year, landing in Jamestown, loaded with the sighs and groans of humanity, and were sold; and from that hour the two antagonistic principles have gone on, shooting their roots downward, and bearing fruit upward, till we found ourselves surrounded by an overshadowing [slave] power—moulding our laws, guiding our armies, and absorbing the North into her Maelstrom of rain and death."[61] Giddings was prophetic. Within a decade of his speech, there came major enactments—the Fugitive Slave Act, the Kansas-Nebraska Act, and the Dred Scott decision—and three presidents, Millard Fillmore, Franklin Pierce, and

James Buchanan, who aligned the US government behind slavery. Southerners eyed not only the western territories but also Cuba and Latin America as desirable regions to seize in order to spread slavery.

Another Ohio politician, Salmon Chase, brought the two ships to the floor of the US Senate during the debate in 1850 over Henry Clay's compromise measures. Chase, who would serve as secretary of the treasury under Lincoln and the chief justice of the Supreme Court under three presidents, brought up the two ships to counter the argument by a proslavery senator that the slavery issue had arisen only in 1820 during the discussion of slavery in Missouri. Chase insisted that the rift over slavery had begun long before, when "a Dutch ship ascended the James river, bringing the first slaves into Virginia," and "the Mayflower brought the Pilgrim founders of New England to Plymouth Rock." Chase declared, "Slavery was introduced into Virginia. Freedom was planted in New England. The contest between the despotic principle—the element and guaranty of slavery—and the democratic principle—the element and guaranty of liberty—commenced."[62]

Charles Sumner stands out for his interest in the two ships in the battle against slavery. A senator from Massachusetts for twenty-three years (1851–74), Sumner was a fervent advocate of civil rights who found special resonance in the two ships. Sumner's ancestors included the *Mayflower* passengers William Bradford, Richard Warren, and John and Priscilla Alden. His brother, George Sumner, was a noted antiquary whose field was the history of the Pilgrims, especially their background in Leiden.

As tall as Lincoln and powerfully built, Charles Sumner was a magnetic presence on the lecture platform. "Sumner stands like a cannoneer, and gesticulates as if were ramming down cartridges," Henry Wadsworth Longfellow noted.[63] At an 1847 lecture before the Boston Mercantile Association Sumner declared, "It was in the year 1620,—dear to all the descendants of the Pilgrims of Plymouth Rock as an epoch of freedom . . . that African slaves were first introduced into the

Charles Sumner
*Photograph by Mathew B. Brady*
*(between 1861 and 1874)*

English colonies of North America, thus beginning that dreadful system whose long catalogue of humiliation and woes is not yet complete."[64] Furious at fellow politicians who temporized over slavery, in 1853 Sumner said of the Pilgrims, "All must confess the true grandeur of their example, while, in vindication of a cherished principle, they stood alone, against the madness of men, against the law of the land, against their king. Better the despised Pilgrim, a fugitive for freedom, than the halting politician, forgetful of principle, 'with a Senate at his heels.'"[65]

In September 1860, only weeks before the election that would bring

Abraham Lincoln to the White House, Sumner spoke before eight thousand people at a mass Republican meeting at Myricks, Massachusetts. Titled "Example of Massachusetts Against Slavery," the speech focused on the role of the Bay State in the history of rebellions against oppression. Sumner pointed to the state's pivotal role in both the American Revolution and the antislavery movement. His comment that "the Massachusetts leaven" was "now stirring the whole country" over slavery had justification, given the state's influential antislavery spokespeople, including David Walker, Maria Stewart, William Lloyd Garrison, and Sumner himself.[66]

And considering the historical forces that had seeded the slavery debate, Sumner was warranted in going back to Jamestown and Plymouth. "Two mighty influences," he asserted, had shaped America: "the Mayflower, filled with men, intelligent, conscientious, prayerful—all braced to hardy industry—who before landing united in a written compact, by which they constituted themselves a 'civil body politic,' bound 'to frame just and equal laws,'" and, on the other hand, the Jamestown "Slave-Ship, with its fetters, its chains, its bludgeons, and its whips—with its wretched victims, forerunners of the long agony of the Slave-Trade, and with its wretched tyrants, rude, ignorant, profane." Sumner said, "Never in history was greater contrast." The two ships, he announced, "have met at last in final grapple, and we are partakers in the holy conflict." Americans had a clear choice: "The question is simply between the Mayflower and the Slave-Ship,—which of the two to choose?"

Northerners' choice of the *Mayflower* would be evidenced by the number of times the ship was mentioned during the Civil War. Southerners made the opposite choice. For them, the *Mayflower* was the source of abolitionism, the destructive force that could ruin the nation. A British visitor in South Carolina was astounded to hear cries "from all quarters" about the "cruel, persecuting" settlers of the North who had first come over on the *Mayflower.* One of the Carolinians told the journalist, "If that confounded ship had sunk with those Pilgrim

Fathers on board, we never should have been driven to these extremities!"[67] To the South, the North, reaching back to the *Mayflower*, was "tainted beyond cure by the venom of 'Puritanism,'" which over time had yielded the evil forces of abolitionism and Black Republicanism.

It didn't matter to the South that the Pilgrims were Separatists, as opposed to the Puritans of Massachusetts Bay, or that by the mid-nineteenth century, the North had become a kaleidoscope of religious denominations, sects, and cults, few of which resembled the faith of the Plymouth colonists. Distortion is intrinsic to cultural memory, especially when amplified by sectional or political bias. For Southerners, the *Mayflower* had brought Puritanism, which had yielded fanatical movements like abolitionism, now a dire threat to the Union.

## Chapter Nine

# Northern Puritans vs. Southern Cavaliers

It was the English Civil War all over again, American-style.

In 1809, the Virginia Congressman Daniel Sheffey declared that partisan enmities had "the same bitterness which formerly characterized the whigs and tories of England." However, Sheffey was relieved that America had avoided "bloody contentions" like the one between "the Cavaliers and Roundheads" of the English Civil War.[1]

Sheffey spoke too soon, of course. Such a cultural division developed in tandem with the debate over slavery. In 1834, the touring French statesman Michel Chevalier noted a huge gap between "the Yankee and the Virginian," who, he wrote, "are very unlike each other; they have no great love for each other, and are often at variance. They are the same men who cut each other's throats in England, under the name of Roundheads and Cavaliers."[2] The Southerner, he wrote, was typically a slaveholder who was chivalrous, hospitable, lazy, and bibulous, in contrast to the New Englander, who was moralistic, reform minded, hardworking, and individualistic.

The regional mindsets deepened over the antebellum decades. The

South romanticized the Cavaliers of colonial times, while the North revived the Cromwellian rebellion against monarchy (updated as the fight against the slave power) and the Puritan notion of a higher law. Sometimes the fight between two sides turned bloody, as in 1838, when the Kentuckian William J. Graves killed a New Englander in a duel, or 1856, when *Mayflower* descendant Charles Sumner was bludgeoned in the Senate by the South Carolina representative Preston Brooks, or 1859, when the abolitionist John Brown, hailed in the North as a Cromwellian Puritan, faced off against Cavalier slaveholders in his failed effort to topple slavery by attacking Harpers Ferry, Virginia.

## REVIVING THE CAVALIER

In March 1814, the forty-year-old John Randolph of Roanoke returned to his birthplace, the Mattoax plantation, overlooking the Appomattox River south of Richmond, Virginia.

Randolph was a vigorous defender of Southern rights during his nearly thirty years in Congress. A thin, beardless man with a high, shrill voice—symptoms of a genetic disorder or perhaps an adolescent illness that disrupted puberty—the eccentric Randolph would stride into Congress trailed by hunting dogs that curled up under his desk while he delivered long speeches, accentuated by wild gestures, which were by turns brilliant and sarcastic.

On that March day at his birthplace, he was overwhelmed by emotion. The ancestral manor was now vacant. "All was sad and desolate," he reported. "The fires of ancient hospitality were long since extinguished, and the hearth-stone cold. Here was my mother given in marriage, and here was I born; once the seat of plenty and cheerfulness, associated with my earliest and tenderest recollections, now mute and deserted. . . . Nothing, however, can be more melancholy than the aspect of the whole country on Tidewater—dismantled country seats, ruinous churches, fields forsaken and grown up with mournful evergreens, cedar and pine."[3]

Randolph's gloom was shared by many Virginians. The original Cavalier patriarchs, with their tremendous holdings in land and slaves, had reached their peak in the 1750s and declined thereafter. Unwise agricultural techniques caused land exhaustion. Tobacco prices plummeted. Excessive gambling and extravagant lifestyles killed off estates. Many plantations were destroyed during the American Revolution. The termination of primogeniture in Virginia in 1786 dispersed properties among heirs and relatives. With the rise of the cotton industry, the dominance of Southern agriculture shifted to states in the Deep South, leaving Virginia less competitive than it had been before. Financially straitened Tidewater families migrated westward, where a new breed of yeoman farmers, many of them Scots-Irish or German immigrants, had arisen. Virginians who looked at the diminished present were plagued by "nostalgia, pessimism, and malaise," as a historian of the state puts it.[4] When the Cavalier spirit was in full flush, it had provided a sturdy bulwark to a slave society based on hierarchy and subordination. Many Southerners wanted that spirit to be reinvigorated.

Reinvigorated it was. The nineteenth-century Cavalier myth was built on the ruins of the eighteenth-century Cavalier reality.

Mark Twain attributed the Southern outlook to "the Sir Walter disease"—the craze for chivalry, honor, and high-sounding titles that he said was fostered in the South by Walter Scott, the popular Scottish author whose novels and poetry permeated Southern culture in the decades preceding the Civil War.[5] Scott's romantic re-creations of the medieval and seventeenth-century past produced an affection for what Twain disparaged as the "sham chivalries of a brainless and worthless long-vanished society." Twain wrote, "It was Sir Walter that made every gentleman in the South a Major or a Colonel, or a General or a Judge, before the war; it was he, also, that made these gentlemen value these bogus decorations." Scott, in Twain's words, "did measureless harm; more real and lasting harm, perhaps, than any other individual that ever wrote. . . . For it was he that created rank and caste down there, and also reverence for rank and caste, and pride and pleasure in them." Twain noted that Scott fueled a nostalgia among Southerners for a bygone aristocratic, stratified society that was supportive of slaveholding. A similar point was made by Gideon Welles, Lincoln's secretary of the Navy, who blamed the Civil War on Southerners who "studied Scott's novels, and fancied themselves cavaliers, imbued with chivalry." They "came ultimately to believe themselves of a superior and better race, knights of blood and spirit." They looked down on those who "did not own slaves, and who labored with their own hands," and "they disdained and despised the pious, peddling, plodding, persevering Yankee, who would not drink, and swear, and fight duels."[6]

Walter Scott, of course, did not *create* chivalry and caste in the South, which had begun much earlier, when the Cavaliers first settled there in the seventeenth century. But Scott helped to *revive* the Cavalier spirit. In his many historical novels, which appeared between 1814 and his death in 1832, he highlighted medieval knights, feudal lords, and Cavalier loyalists under the Stuarts. In depicting the ancient battles between the Normans and the Saxons for the control of England, most famously portrayed in his bestselling novel *Ivanhoe*, Scott favored the victors, the Normans, who were thought to be more refined and courtlier than the Saxons—a preference shared by Southern slaveholders, who fancied themselves as Norman aristocrats, superior to the allegedly crude Saxon Puritans of the Northern states. Scott's aristocratic leanings were universally recognized. A proud Tory, Scott once argued with a Puritan friend who stood to his political left. Scott wrote, "I, with a head on fire for chivalry, was a Cavalier; my friend was a Roundhead; I was a Tory, and he was a Whig. . . . I took up my politics at that period, as King Charles II did his religion, from an idea that the Cavalier creed was the more gentlemanlike persuasion of the two."[7]

For Southern novelists influenced by Scott, the Cavalier was not just a gentlemanlike persuasion; it was a key building block of regional identity. Several prominent Southern authors—Nathaniel Beverley Tucker, William Alexander Caruthers, William Gilmore Simms, and John Esten Cooke—used the novel to promote the Cavalier, justify slavery, and throw barbs at the North and Puritanism.

Nathaniel Beverley Tucker set the pattern for the others. In his 1836 novel, *George Balcombe*, he wrote that there was no greater honor "than to be sprung from a race of men without fear and without reproach—the ancient cavaliers of Virginia."[8] The novel's aristocratic hero, Balcombe, helps a young man regain his ancestral Tidewater estate, the deed to which had been stolen.

Fueling Tucker's pro-Virginia passion was a belief in states' rights and a deep suspicion of the North. In *The Partisan Leader* he took the dramatic step of proposing the secession of the Southern states, more than two decades before the South seceded. A bleak imagining of the future, the novel pictures America in 1849. Martin Van Buren is up for reelection to his fourth term as president. Portraying Van Buren as a dictator whose economic policies threaten to crush the South, Tucker describes a guerrilla force in Virginia, led by a charismatic Cavalier-like hero, combating federal troops and leading Virginia in its attempt to join the other Southern states, which have already left the Union.

Tucker promoted the Virginia Cavalier while defending slavery and criticizing Puritanism. He admitted that "the northern pilgrims" carried "the theory of democracy . . . into practice to an extent known nowhere else."[9] However, the "rigid rule of puritanism" bred laws that restricted "the domestic habits, the deportment, and even the dress of individuals." The Virginia Cavalier, in contrast, combined loyalty to royal authority with a free spirit ready to cast aside that authority when necessary. Tucker wrote, "The spirit of *personal* freedom was perhaps never stronger than in the high-minded cavalier." Virginians showed that "*personal freedom and the ACTUAL ENJOYMENT of freedom can exist and flourish in defiance of the forms of government.*"

Northerners, he argued, did not understand enslaved people for the same reason that their Puritan ancestors misunderstood the Cavaliers: They were self-centered moralists. "They know no more of the feelings of our slaves," Tucker wrote, "than their fathers could comprehend of the loyalty of the gallant cavaliers from whom we spring; and for the same reason. The generous and self-renouncing must ever be a riddle to the selfish."[10] With Cavalier-like generosity, slaveholders provided sustenance and instruction to people of "the inferior race," who lovingly served their masters.[11] In this arrangement, white enslavers and their Black chattel were a big, warm family. Enslaved people learned Christian "humility" and "subordination of the heart" when placed "in direct subjection and immediate communication with a master race of unquestionable superiority,—a superiority clearly admitted and manifested in all the affairs of life."

Reconciliation between the sections was initially on the mind of another Southern novelist, William Alexander Caruthers. Called by his biographer the "chronicler of the Cavaliers," Caruthers revered eighteenth-century Virginia planters but was not too critical of Northerners.[12] Born and raised in Virginia's Shenandoah Valley, Caruthers earned a medical degree at the University of Pennsylvania. In 1823, he married the daughter of a Georgia cotton planter, who, Caruthers boasted, came from "a class of men as much like our real old-fashioned Virginia gentlemen as can well be imagined." His wife's dowry comprised a third of her late father's substantial estate, including thirty-nine enslaved people, most of whom continued to labor on Georgia plantations while the Caruthers family settled in Lexington, Virginia. There Caruthers opened a medical practice, but chronic financial difficulties soon drove him deeply into debt. A descendant reported, "His wife was reared in luxury, and together they seem to have spent—not in 'riotous living,' but in unlimited hospitality—her fortune and his own." As debts mounted, he was forced to auction off his Virginia properties—and, soon thereafter, his bondspeople. He moved his growing family north to New York. He set up an apothecary shop, befriended authors, wrote for periodicals, and in 1834 published his first novel, *The Kentuckian in New-York*. Focusing on two couples, one in New York and the other in South Carolina, the novel affirmed the intersectional amity that Caruthers thought could be gained if the various parts of America got to know each other better.

The next year brought his second novel, *Cavaliers of Virginia; Or, the Recluse of Jamestown*. This time, he followed his favorite author, Walter Scott, by writing a complicated historical novel—with love affairs, battles, imprisonment, and the like—that finally sided with conservatism. Caruthers reimagines Nathaniel Bacon's 1676 rebellion in Virginia as a triple war: against Virginia's governor William Berkeley, against warlike Native Americans, and against Puritans, called Roundheads in the novel. Caruthers presents the Roundheads as self-righteous fanatics while praising "the Cavaliers who fled hither after the decapitation of their royal master" as "the first founders of the aristocracy which prevails in Virginia to this day; these were the immediate ancestors of that generous, fox-hunting, wine-drinking, dueling and reckless race of men, which gives so distinct a character to Virginians wherever they may be found."[13]

In his final novel, *Knights of the Golden Horse-Shoe* (1845), Caruthers dramatized a key moment in the Cavalier past: the 1716 expedition across the Blue Ridge Mountains into the Shenandoah Valley led by Virginia's Lieutenant Governor Alexander Spotswood. He was accompanied by explorers from prominent Cavalier families, including the Randolphs, the Byrds, the Lees, and the Washingtons. For Caruthers, these Cavaliers pioneered a westward migration by white Southerners that would someday "transcend the Rio del Norte [the Rio Grande]," "traverse the utmost boundaries of Mexico," and, in time, appropriate "a large portion of the globe to themselves" in order "to disseminate their laws, their language, and their religion, over such countless millions."[14] Caruthers didn't directly mention spreading slavery as the South's goal, but we infer that from his portrayal of enslaved people, who happily accompany their owners on the transmontane trek. Written during the decade when the phrase "Manifest Destiny" was coined to describe America's providential mission to expand westward, *Knights of the Golden Horse-Shoe* seems to anticipate the Knights of the Golden Circle, the Southern organization formed in 1854, that aimed to create a new slave country consisting of the Southern states, the Caribbean islands, the Mexican territories, Central America, and northern parts of South America.

## THE CAVALIER: CORRECTING FLAWS, AMPLIFYING VIRTUES

The expansion of slavery became the declared goal of another Southern author, William Gilmore Simms of South Carolina. If slavery were prevented from spreading, Simms wrote in 1859, the South would be in the position of "'the scorpion girt by fire'; the Slave States will die, inch by inch, upward, like the tail of a snake!"[15] Simms explained, "It is evident that we shall require new territory to supply the place of the old. All Mexico would be civilized by negro slavery naturally, in the course of the next hundred years, were it suffered to take the natural course of things."

William Gilmore Simms was born in Charleston, South Carolina, in 1806. His mother died when he was two, and his bankrupt father abandoned him to the care of his maternal grandmother, who regaled him with stories of the American Revolution. Largely self-taught, Simms read widely, studied law briefly, and published poetry in his early twenties. In 1826, he married Anna Malcolm Giles, who died in 1832. Four years later, he wed Chevillette Eliza Roach, the daughter of a wealthy planter. The couple settled at her family's six-thousand-acre plantation, Woodlands, in Barnwell District, where Simms made his home for the rest of his life. Before the Civil War, some seventy enslaved people lived and labored at Woodlands. Simms was a prominent advocate of the South's traditional plantation culture. Exceptionally productive, he published thirty-five novels from 1834 to 1866, along with biographies, history books, and numerous shorter pieces. He also edited *The Southern Quarterly Review*, served in the South Carolina state legislature, and almost won elections for the state's governorship and a seat in the US Senate.

A defender of slavery and states' rights, Simms put the blame for the South's problems on antislavery Northerners, whom he associated with Puritanism. He pointed out the hypocrisy of abolitionists who contrasted the *Mayflower* with the Jamestown slave ship without mentioning the North's role in the international slave trade. In 1849, he reviewed William Tappan's poem "The Two Ships," which described the Jamestown ship as a "pirate" vessel that introduced the "poison" of slavery to America, as opposed to the *Mayflower*, on which, Tappan writes, "men of the pure old stock" came to "build upon the rock / . . . a Home for Man, / Where Truth and Light / Shall sway a nation by the rule of Right."[16] Simms, dismissing the two-ships theme as "one of the favorite topics of New England self-satisfaction," remarked that Tappan would have been more truthful had he written about "the history of the thousand ships launched by the Pilgrims, sons and sires—the children of the Mayflower—to beat the drowsy Dutch entirely out of the Slave Trade markets."[17]

Simms argued that tensions over slavery originated in the North, with its history of "aggressive" and "insolent" Puritanism. New Englanders, he wrote, are "the most intolerant people in the world, and have been so from the days of Cotton Mather. . . . The old malignant leaven of puritanism, which made them loathsome in England; made them the persecutors of old women & quakers . . . still pervades their society" and makes them the assailants of "Institutions which are wholly Southern."[18]

In contrast to the malevolent Northern Puritan stood the dignified Southern Cavalier. One of Simms's main goals as a novelist was to highlight the virtues of the Cavaliers of yesteryear. In his historical fiction, patterned after Walter Scott, he wove narratives of South Carolina history, particularly the era of the American Revolution. He expanded the notion of the Cavalier beyond Virginia, where many of the original Cavaliers had settled, to other Southern states. In a typical novel, he praises the "stately cavaliers in train from Virginia, Maryland, and Delaware" as well as South Carolina's "[Francis] Marion, [Thomas] Sumter, [Hezekiah] Maham, and the many other brilliant cavaliers" who contributed bravely to the American cause.[19]

In his works, Simms conveyed his vision of the ideal plantation, led by a gentleman of distinguished ancestry. Simone Vauthier notes that his heroes usually come from "old wealthy families long associated with a domain which they love. The protagonists are often represented as the keepers of a tradition of leadership, social responsibility, and *noblesse oblige*; indeed, they are sometimes shown as the inheritors of the European feudal nobility."[20] Simms envisages the well-regulated plantation as an organic unit in which everyone is interdependent. Below the plantation owner are his wife and children, then the overseer, and, at the bottom, enslaved Black people. Poor whites living in the area are assisted by the plantation owner, who acts like a feudal lord.

Simms recognized that reviving Cavalier culture presented significant challenges, many of which he captured in what is commonly regarded as his finest novel, *Woodcraft*, published in 1852. The novel's lead character, Porgy, is a good-natured but imperfect aristocrat. A waggish man whose corpulence comes from overeating and heavy drinking, Porgy has a checkered past of thriftlessness and agricultural ineptitude, which have driven him into bankruptcy. In the novel, we see Porgy slowly rebuilding his life under the guidance of a utilitarian war veteran who helps him learn to be practical and entrepreneurial. By the end, an improved Porgy is on his way to reestablishing his plantation.

*Woodcraft* is typical of Southern fiction in its treatment of enslaved people. The novel is thought to have been written in response to Harriet Beecher Stowe's 1852 bestseller, *Uncle Tom's Cabin*, which exposed the horror and injustice of slavery. Simms said that his novel was "probably as good an answer to Mrs. Stowe as has been published."[21] As editor of *The Southern Quarterly Review* he printed a scathing review of *Uncle Tom's Cabin* by Louisa C. McCord, who branded Stowe's novel as an example of "the foul load of slander and villainous aspersion so often hurled against us," now placed under "the veil of christian charity."[22] In *Woodcraft*, Porgy's cook, Tom, supports plantation life because Porgy treats him well—so well, in fact, that, when offered freedom, Tom refuses it. He tells his master, "I's well off whar' I is, I tell you; and I much rudder b'long to good maussa, wha' I lub, dan be my own maussa and quarrel wid mese'f ebbery day."[23] And so, Simms carried forward the trope of the happy slave, which had been established in previous Southern fiction and would dominate the some twenty-nine proslavery novels that appeared in the 1850s answering Stowe's *Uncle Tom's Cabin*.

Simms's main successor in the Cavalier revival, John Esten Cooke, also featured the happy slave while promoting the Cavalier figure so strongly in his widely read writings that he helped fuse it with the South's identity. From 1854 until he died in 1886 he wrote thirty books, most of them Virginia-centered historical novels with Cavalier protagonists. One of the most popular Southern authors before 1870, he was the main bridge between the Civil War-era glorification of the Cavalier and the postwar mythology of the Lost Cause.

Cooke railed at Puritans. In his history of Virginia, he castigated "the Puritan people" who in early times tried to get a foothold in the South by "intruding themselves on the good old cavaliers of the good old cavalier colony of Virginia."[24] Governor William Berkeley, "a Cavalier of cavaliers," was justified, Cooke argued, in criminalizing the practice of Puritan religion in the 1640s. Cooke conceded that the early

Puritans had "strong character" and "a certain sort of preserving courage," but they wanted chiefly "to meddle and peddle"—that is, they were grasping, intrusive moralists.[25] They were to blame for the American Civil War, because they were "the stock from which has sprung the controlling element of the horde which today invades the South." A character in one of Cooke's novels calls the Civil War a conflict of "the crop-eared Puritan against the Cavalier." He cries: "Curse the Pilgrim Fathers, and the whole canting breed of 'em! The South had been fighting them for fifty years in Congress and was ready now to meet them on the battlefield!"

Surveying American history since its origins, Cooke saw a fundamental divide:

> From the first settlement of this country two elements have been apparent—the Cavalier element and the Puritan element. The arena of the former was the South—of the latter, the North. Oil and water will not mingle; nor could the two races. Between them the Almighty had placed a barrier which the most cunning contrivance of man could not overturn;—in the blood of the two races was an element of bitter antagonism which no legislation, political legerdemain or social union could obliterate.[26]

This statement, typical of that polarized era, simplified a complex reality. In fact, throughout the South, Cavaliers of the old type—that is, aristocratic planters who owned thousands of acres and hundreds of enslaved people—were rare in the nineteenth century. In 1860, fewer than one-quarter of the South's 8 million white residents held any of the region's 3.9 million enslaved people. Among slaveholders, only a tiny fraction owned one hundred or more individuals, a somewhat larger but still small minority held between ten and ninety-nine, and the great majority owned between one and nine.[27]

Regarding the North, Puritanism underwent significant alterations and merged with various other faiths. The founders' separation of church and state had a profound effect on the region, where new denominations, sects, cults, and self-proclaimed prophets multiplied, alongside a variety of reform movements known as "isms." Furthermore, the Catholic Church went from being a minor presence in 1790 to becoming the largest single denomination in America by 1850, primarily due to a wave of immigrants from Ireland and Europe. Jewish immigrants also started to establish a notable presence in the two decades before the Civil War.

In short, diversity and variety were the norm. But as we know, two starkly opposing identities can exist even in the most diverse nation. That's what happened in the Civil War era. Southerners of all types came to see themselves as proud, honorable Cavaliers. Northerners of varied beliefs assumed the mantle of Puritanism.

## THE NEW PURITANISM

The fountainhead of what came to be called the New Puritanism was the late-eighteenth-century New Divinity movement, whose most prominent leader, Samuel Hopkins, was, as we saw earlier, a bridge between orthodox Calvinism and later antislavery reform.[28] The main figure to carry a version of Hopkinsian moral earnestness into the nineteenth century was the Presbyterian revivalist Lyman Beecher. A leader of the so-called New Puritanism, Beecher reshaped Calvinism by downplaying strict doctrines of predestination and total depravity and instead highlighting human free will, moral responsibility, and the need for active Christian reform. This theology inspired powerful reform movements.[29]

Beecher, described by his son Henry as "a Puritan of the Puritans," traced his ancestry to a group of religious refugees who came to New

England in the 1630s and founded what became New Haven Colony.[30] Raised on a Connecticut farm, Lyman Beecher entered Yale College in the 1790s, where he studied theology under Timothy Dwight, the New Divinity president who trained a generation of revivalist ministers. Beecher was especially drawn to the teachings of Samuel Hopkins, who stressed that even under an all-powerful God, human beings bore responsibility to exercise disinterested benevolence and help transform society through moral action.[31] After his ordination in 1799, Beecher rose to prominence as one of the foremost leaders of the so-called Benevolent Empire—a nationwide network of evangelical voluntary societies devoted to temperance, Bible distribution, Sabbath observance, religious education, and related causes.

Beecher believed that such moral action resurrected the mission of early New Englanders. In an 1827 Forefathers' Day speech in Plymouth, he declared that moral rules that had been enforced by Puritan colonial governments, ridiculed ever since, represented the kind of behavioral regulation that must be revived for America to survive. Calling attention to the prevalence of drunkenness, Sabbath breaking, dueling, and other vices, Beecher declared that America was on the verge of becoming "one vast reservoir of putrefaction, . . . desolation and death."[32] While he knew that reinstalling New England theocracy was impossible, he called for a massive religious effort to create voluntary organizations, which he called "providential substitutes for those legal provisions of our Fathers." He advised, "In these the nation must enroll itself spontaneously, and the spirit of the Puritans be revived, for the preservation of their institutions."

Beecher opposed slavery but believed it was a deeply entrenched institution that could not be eradicated without endangering the nation. The issue came to a head in 1830 when the twenty-five-year-old William Lloyd Garrison, attending Beecher's Hanover Street church in Boston, urged him to take up the cause of immediate emancipation.

Although Beecher acknowledged slavery's sinfulness, he demurred, claiming he had "too many irons in the fire already." Garrison reportedly replied, "You had better let all your irons burn than to neglect your duty to the slave," signaling the rising impatience of radical abolitionists with moderate reformers.[33] Seeking allies for his abolitionist efforts, Garrison found support in the lawyer Samuel Sewall, a descendant of the Puritan abolitionist of the same name. In January 1832, Garrison, Sewall, and others founded the New England Anti-Slavery Society, which convened its first meeting at Boston's African Meeting House, marking the beginning of a regional movement dedicated to the immediate emancipation of enslaved people.

Another reformer who took Beecher's religious activism in a new radical direction was the Boston lawyer Wendell Phillips. He was descended from a Puritan clergyman who had come to America with John Winthrop on the *Arabella* in 1630. Attracted by Lyman Beecher's fame in the pulpit, Wendell Phillips went to a service at Beecher's church and experienced a religious awakening.[34] Applying Beecher's religious activism to slavery, Phillips became a leading abolitionist. He witnessed the mob attack on William Lloyd Garrison in 1835, which "stirred [Phillips's] Puritanic blood to the very finger-tips."[35] Two years later, he was appalled by the murder in Alton, Illinois, of the antislavery newspaper editor Elijah Lovejoy. At a meeting in Boston's Faneuil Hall, Phillips blasted a proslavery speaker who had defended Lovejoy's killers. Phillips said of the speaker, "For the sentiments he has uttered, on soil consecrated by the prayers of Puritans and the blood of patriots, the earth should have yawned, and swallowed him up."

Phillips linked Puritanism with the crusade for immediate emancipation. Among his great heroes were the *Mayflower* Pilgrims and the Puritan revolutionaries Vane, Pym, Hampden, and Cromwell, as well as the Puritan-influenced patriots James Otis Jr. and John Adams.[36] In a speech at Plymouth, Phillips said, "What the Puritans gave to the world was not thought, but ACTION. . . . The Puritans, with native pluck, launched out into the deep sea. . . . The Pilgrims launched boldly out into the Atlantic, and trusted God."[37] Puritans, he insisted, believed in humans first, not institutions. He asserted, "The Puritans believed that institutions were made for man. Europe established a civilization, which, like that of Greece, made the state everything, the man nothing. . . . The Puritans said, 'No, let us go out and . . . make institutions for men!' That is the radical principle, it seems to me, which runs through all their history." Besides abolition, Phillips promoted women's rights and spoke out against segregated railroad cars and the forced removal of Native Americans from their land. Shedding the racism of his era, he insisted that Black people must not be barred from public events.

The subject of race takes us back to Lyman Beecher. Beecher himself was a moderate who backed colonization—the popular, though largely unsuccessful, movement to transport Black Americans to Africa or elsewhere. Among Beecher's thirteen children, several took a more progressive stance on race and slavery than he did. Standouts were his son Henry Ward Beecher and his daughter Harriet Beecher Stowe, both of whom promoted a democratic gospel that embraced people of color.

Henry Ward Beecher became "the most famous man in America," in Debby Applegate's words, because of his powerful preaching and his antislavery activities.[38] His Plymouth church in Brooklyn was a stop on the Underground Railroad, which funneled escaped slaves northward to freedom; Beecher created a sensation when in 1848 he raised enough money from his congregation to purchase freedom for the enslaved sisters Emily and Mary Edmonson of Maryland. In 1856, to support antislavery fighters in Kansas, Beecher sent rifles in boxes labeled "Bibles" or "Books." Beecher anchored his antislavery radicalism in Puritanism. "The Puritan was a man thoroughly alive to liberty," he

Harriet Beecher Stowe, Lyman Beecher,
and Henry Ward Beecher
*Photographer unknown; c. 1861*

declared. "It was the Puritan that gave liberty to old England, and it was the Puritan that brought liberty to New England and laid the foundations of the institutions on which we stand."[39] He generalized, "I love every drop of Puritan blood that the world ever saw, because it seems to me that Puritan blood means blood touched with Christ's blood."[40]

Henry's sister, the novelist Harriet Beecher Stowe, had a unique impact on American history as the author of *Uncle Tom's Cabin* (1852), the wildly popular—and highly controversial—antislavery novel that was a catalyst for the Civil War. Stowe took the step from Samuel Hopkins's

New Divinity ideas to vigorous antislavery action that her father had failed to take. She communicated her mixed views of Samuel Hopkins in her novel *The Minister's Wooing*, which takes readers back to eighteenth-century Newport, where, she writes, "there was not . . . a more thriving and reputable business at that time than the slave trade."[41] On the one hand, she praises Hopkins's selfless devotion to Black people, noting that "his hours of leisure from study were often spent in lowliest visitations among them, hearing their stories, consoling their sorrows, advising and directing their plans, teaching them reading and writing, and he often drew on his slender salary to assist them in their emergencies and distresses." But she had a serious problem with Hopkins's Calvinistic theology. She complained in the novel that Hopkins, with his notions of predestination and total depravity, had torn away the ladder between humans and God. Stowe tried to rebuild that ladder. She envisaged God as loving and all-embracing. In a religious vision that she had in the 1840s, she saw Jesus, "simple as a little child—yet majestic as a God," welcoming all believers, including "illiterate poor slaves,—the despised—the forsaken— . . . those who the world has cast out and the church rejects— . . . none are cast out."[42] She enacts this loving religion in *Uncle Tom's Cabin*, where white and Black characters meet on the common ground of Christian love.

Stowe's Puritan background had given her the courage to take the highly unconventional step of writing a novel whose popularity in the North was matched by vicious denunciation in the South. She explained, "The heroic element was strong in me, having come down by ordinary generation from a long line of Puritan ancestry, and just now it made me long to do something, I knew not what: to fight for my country, or to make some declaration on my own account."[43] She needed strength, because her novel was written in protest against the recently passed Fugitive Slave Act of 1850. Readers of her novel witnessed the harshness of the law as they followed the story of the fugitives Eliza Harris; her husband, George Harris; and their child, Harry, in their desperate efforts to evade slave catchers as they fled north. *Uncle Tom's Cabin* made Stowe a leading popularizer of the higher law—held by those who looked beyond proslavery passages in the Constitution to the law of natural justice, supported by God and morality, which its advocates considered more sacred than any human statute. Frederick Douglass wrote, "We doubt if abler arguments have ever been presented in favor of the '*Higher Law*' theory, than may be found here [in] Mrs. Stowe's truly great work."[44] Another reviewer described "the tears which [*Uncle Tom's Cabin*] has drawn from millions of eyes, the sense of a 'higher law,' which it has stamped upon a million hearts."[45]

## THE HIGHER LAW, THE CROMWELLIAN REVIVAL, AND RADICAL ABOLITIONISM

Stowe's clergymen brothers shared her commitment to the higher law. Henry Ward Beecher announced that he would never refuse to help runaway slaves. He said, "If asked, what then becomes of the Constitution" when he aided fugitives, "I reply by asking, what becomes of God's Constitution of Humanity, if you give back a slave to the remorseless maw of servitude?" He declared that he would always "put Constitution against Constitution—God's against man's."[46]

Even more assertive on the topic was another brother, Charles Beecher, whose sermon *The Duty of Disobedience to Wicked Laws* made a stir when it was published as a pamphlet in 1850. The sermon was an updated Puritan jeremiad. Charles Beecher insisted that there is a fundamental distinction between right and wrong, established by God and inscribed in the human conscience. In Beecher's words, the "principles of right are eternal, not made. They are the foundation of law, not its product."[47] Beecher returned to the basics of natural law and divine law. Slavery was wrong. So was any proslavery bill. "The slave is a man," Beecher wrote. "He has a right to be free. It is wrong to deliver him up when he has made himself free. And that clause of the Constitution which says, Deliver him up, is wrong. It is unrighteous, and God will so declare it and treat it in the day of judgment." His advice regarding the Fugitive Slave Act was blunt: "Disobey this law. If you have ever dreamed of obeying it, repent before God, and ask his forgiveness."

Charles Beecher's combative sermon had echoes of the Cromwellian Revolution, which had gained primacy among antislavery Northerners who associated slaveholding with the monarchical doctrine of the divine right of kings. The Pennsylvania Congressman Thaddeus Stevens, a pioneer of civil rights, said of slavery: "The same spirit which induced [royalists] to defend tyranny in the time of the Charleses, and the Jameses; to maintain the divine right of Kings; to inculcate the duty of passive obedience and non-resistance; and to anathematize those who resisted the tyranny of the 'Lord's anointeds'—prompts [slaveholders] now to take the side of the oppressor against the oppressed."[48]

The Massachusetts statesman John Quincy Adams drew some of the clearest links between the English Civil War and the antislavery cause. Although personally opposed to slavery, he avoided the issue during his presidency (1825–29), aware of the deep cultural rift between North and South. Reflecting on his defeat in the contentious 1828 election by the Tennessee slaveholder Andrew Jackson, Adams argued that "the bone-bred dislikes of the cavalier race for the stock of the Pilgrim Puritans [that] were summoned to the array against him" had been exploited to "ruin the reputation and paralyze the power of a President of the United States" by deceiving those "predisposed to receive falsehood for truth."[49] In 1832, when John Quincy Adams dined with the visiting French aristocrat Alexis de Tocqueville, he observed that the United States was divided between the Puritan North and the slaveholding South, highlighting the deep cultural and moral fault lines shaping the nation.[50] He expressed the view, reminiscent of his father John Adams, that American democracy began with the Puritans of Plymouth. Tocqueville made a similar point in *Democracy in America*

(1835), where he wrote of the Pilgrims, "I seem to see the whole destiny of America contained in the first Puritan who reached its shores, like the whole human race in the first man."[51]

John Quincy Adams had the opportunity to express his antislavery passion as the representative of Plymouth County in the US House of Representatives from 1830 until his death in 1848. Known as Old Man Eloquent, he spoke out against aggressive proslavery actions in Congress, such as gags on discussions of slavery or abolition. In 1842, during the debate over the gag rules, he delivered a landmark speech on the English Civil War and its connection to American slavery. An ex-Harvard professor, the well-read, multilingual Adams was deeply versed in European and American history. In his speech, he went to the core issue of the Cromwellian Revolution: the conflict between the divine right of kings and human rights. Divine right, he explained, was defended by the royalist thinkers Thomas Hobbes and Robert Filmer, who were then challenged by Algernon Sidney and John Locke, Whigs shaped by the Puritan rebellion. Hobbes, he pointed out, argued that a monarch's power must be defended by force. This viewpoint, Adams wrote, "extinguishes all the rights of man, and makes force the corner stone of all human government. It is the only theory upon which slavery can be justified as conformable to the law of nature."[52] As for Sir Robert Filmer, his specious argument about the biblical underpinnings of divine right, Adams showed, had unwittingly sown the seeds of democracy. Adams noted that Filmer wrote *Patriarcha* as early as the 1640s, during the English Civil War, and left it unpublished at his death. It appeared in 1680 at a crisis moment in the Stuart monarchy, when the dissolute Charles II and his brother, the Catholic James I, faced popular discontent. It was at this point that Algernon Sidney demolished Filmer's patriarchal theory in *Discourses Concerning Government*, the manuscript of which led to Sidney's trial and execution by beheading. Sidney, who has been called "*Puritanism's* greatest political philosopher," opened the way to the higher law by writing, "That which is not just, is not Law; and that which is not Law, ought not to be obeyed."[53] After discussing Sidney, Adams went on to another product of the English Civil War, John Locke, who carried forward the anti-Filmer argument by spelling out the natural rights philosophy that would inspire America's founders and, later, the nineteenth-century abolitionists.

Adams had deftly summarized the Puritan background of the antislavery movement. It was left to another political advocate of emancipation, William Henry Seward, to point Puritan ideas toward radical action. A lawyer from central New York, Seward was elected governor of New York in 1838 and later served as US senator and secretary of state under Abraham Lincoln and Andrew Johnson. Before the Civil War, he gained fame for two statements: his 1858 prediction of an "irrepressible conflict" between free and slave states, and his 1850 declaration, in response to the Fugitive Slave Act, that a higher moral law than the Constitution demanded opposition to slavery.[54] Harriet Beecher Stowe and her brothers were hardly the only ones who promoted the higher law idea that Seward had introduced on the national scene. A blizzard of pamphlets, articles, and speeches trumpeted the higher law, which became associated with antislavery activism.

In 1855, Seward gave a Forefathers' Day speech in Plymouth on what he called "the Puritan principle." He called for a renewal of the ideals of the Pilgrims, especially what he saw as their devotion to freedom and the higher law. He reviewed Puritan history:

> Outcasts from the established church, the Puritans bore unflinchingly their unwavering testimony against compromise, before magistrates and councils, in the pillory, under stripes, in marches, in camps, in prison, in flight, in exile . . . on the broad and then unexplored ocean, when the mariners lost their reckoning, and the ship's supplies became scanty and her seams open to the waves; on unknown coasts, homeless, houseless, famishing and dying.[55]

WILLIAM H. SEWARD
*Photograph by Mathew B. Brady, c. 1860–62*

The Plymouth settlers, Seward said, ignored "statutes of the realm" and severed "the imaginary contract between the sovereign and the subject." Instead, "they resorted directly to a law broader, older and more stable than all these—a law universal in its application and in its obligation, established by the Creator and Judge of all men, and therefore paramount to all human constitutions." Seward cited many later spokespeople for spiritual or natural law: Milton, Sidney, Jonathan Edwards, Vattel, Montesquieu, James Mansfield (the antislavery lawyer in the Somerset case), and Jefferson as the author of the Declaration of Independence. The fact that Seward could place such a wide range of people, from the orthodox Calvinist Edwards to the skeptical deists Montesquieu and Jefferson, under the umbrella of the Puritan principle shows just how powerfully Puritanism spoke to antislavery figures of Seward's time. Seward ended his speech by quoting William Bradford as telling his fellow settlers that they had broken the ice for others "to the world's end." Seward's perceptions of the Pilgrims so struck Wendell Phillips that he said Seward lied when he said that he had no Puritan blood. Phillips declared, "He says he is not a descendant of the Pilgrims. That is a mistake. There is a pedigree of the body and a pedigree of the mind. He knows as much about the Mayflower, that, as they say in the West, I know he was '*thar.*'"[56]

The Puritan-based higher law caught on among many others. The Transcendentalists were immediately receptive—predictably so, given the idealistic bases of the movement.[57] Most of them began as nonresistants who later condoned violence as their anger grew over proslavery legislation. Ralph Waldo Emerson, their leader, set the pattern. In the 1830s, Emerson was a member of a peace society. The Fugitive Slave Act of 1850 aroused a new militancy in him. He lashed out against the doughface Daniel Webster and declared that "neither constitutions, nor laws, nor covenants, nor churches, nor bibles, are of any use in themselves. The Devil nestles comfortably into them all."[58] In 1859, he became an outspoken defender of the violent John Brown, whom he compared with Jesus Christ. His protégé Henry David Thoreau made a similar change. Thoreau was initially the apostle of nonviolence—anticipating Tolstoy, Gandhi, and Martin Luther King—by going to jail in protest against slavery and writing about it in his 1849 essay "Civil Disobedience." But by 1854, the capture and return to slavery of the fugitive Anthony Burns prompted him to write, "My thoughts are murder to the State, and involuntarily go plotting against her."[59] Along with Emerson, he became the most eloquent defender of John Brown, whom he characterized as a modern-day Puritan who had justifiably taken up arms against unjust laws.

The turn to violence was shared by Emerson's friend Theodore Parker, Boston's foremost Unitarian preacher. Parker said of the Fugitive Slave Act, "Never obey the law. Keep the law of God."[60] Parker helped runaways flee north. He initially disapproved of violence, but by the mid-1850s, he kept a pistol and a sword near him to fight slave catchers.[61] Parker and other Transcendentalists, such as Bronson Alcott, goaded on a mob that tried to liberate Anthony Burns from a Boston jail after he had been caught and was on the verge of being sent back to slavery in the South.[62] When the effort to free Burns failed, he was marched in chains through the streets of Boston in front of protesting crowds and buildings draped in black. Believing now that only "violence and blood" would rid America of slavery, Parker became a member of the Secret Six that backed John Brown.[63]

Looking at America's origins, Parker pointed to the two ships: "The same year which brought the Puritan Pilgrims to New England bore quite a different freight to Virginia." The Jamestown ship introduced the "loathly plague-spot" of slavery. Parker conceded that the New England settlers were sometimes intolerant but argued that, all told, they nourished "the instinct for progressive development," with "a feeling of the equality of all men" that later flowered as democracy and abolitionism.[64]

Parker had unqualified enthusiasm for the Puritan Revolution and its leader, Oliver Cromwell. Not only did Parker declare that "the dreadful axe of Puritanic Oliver Cromwell shore off the divine right of kings" and bred "the personal self-rule of modern time," but he saw Cromwell as an exemplary ruler.[65] Parker wrote, "Cromwell is the greatest Anglo-Saxon who was ever a Ruler on a large scale. . . . We think better of mankind because he lived, adorning the earth with the life so noble."[66]

When Parker said this, Oliver Cromwell was experiencing a massive resuscitation in the North. The Cromwell revival was initiated by the Scottish historian Thomas Carlyle, whose *On Heroes, Hero-Worship and the Heroic in History* (1841) and his four-volume *Oliver Cromwell's Letters and Speeches: With Elucidations* (1845) sold well in America. Minimizing Cromwell's dictatorial tendencies and the brutal behavior of his religiously inspired New Model Army, Carlyle presented the Lord Protector as one of history's great heroes. Carlyle excused as a stern necessity the excesses of Cromwell's military campaigns in Ireland, where priests and citizens at Drogheda, Wexford, and elsewhere were slaughtered. Overall, Carlyle wrote, Cromwell was "the soul of the Puritan Revolt, without whom it had never been a revolt transcendentally memorable and an Epoch in the World's History."[67] Hypochondriac, moody, and gruff, Cromwell, in Carlyle's words, was nonetheless guided by a "ray as of pure starlight and fire!" He fought "to see God's own Law . . . made good in this world."[68] He was the no-nonsense commoner who challenged "smooth-shaven Respectabilities." Carlyle wrote, "He stood bare, not cased in euphemistic coat-of-mail; he grappled like a giant, face to face, heart to heart, with the naked truth of things!" There was a parallel, in Carlyle's view, between Cromwell and the *Mayflower* Pilgrims. Both were humble rebels against hierarchy and aristocracy. Carlyle described "the poor little ship Mayflower, of Delft-Haven: poor common-looking ship, hired by common charterparty for coined dollars; caulked with mere oakum and tar; provisioned with vulgarest biscuit and bacon . . . thou little Mayflower hadst in thee a veritable Promethean spark; the life-spark of the largest Nation on our Earth."[69]

Carlyle's sanctification of Cromwell excited American antislavery figures who connected the Puritan rebellion with resistance to the slave power. The most notable Cromwellian figure was John Brown, who claimed to be descended from the *Mayflower* passenger Peter Browne.[70] Brown's antislavery religion came straight from the New Divinity clergymen Samuel Hopkins and Jonathan Edwards Jr. via his father, Owen Brown, whose views were shaped by these two abolitionist Puritans. John Brown put antislavery Calvinism into action. A farmer and tanner who lived barely above the poverty level in various Northern states, he served for many years on the Underground Railroad. The Puritan belief in the equality of all humans under God merged in his mind with the egalitarian message of the Declaration of Independence. John Brown helped Black people in any way he could. He settled in upstate New York among African Americans, many of whom were fugitives, whom he assisted with surveying and farming. Seeing slavery as a war against a whole race, he violated proslavery laws at will. The Fugitive Slave Act impelled him to form the League of Gileadites, a secret organization whose Black members were supplied with weapons to be used against slave catchers. In 1855, he went to Kansas Territory with others to fight the proslavery forces that were pushing for the territory's admission to the Union as a slave state.[71] His battles against proslavery troops included, infamously, his direction of the nighttime murder of five proslavery settlers at Pottawatomie Creek. Three years later, after the Supreme Court had stripped Black people of rights in its Dred Scott decision, John Brown conducted the antislavery raid on Harpers Ferry, Virginia, that led to his capture, trial, and hanging.

Brown patterned himself after the Puritan warrior Cromwell, one of his heroes. When Brown fought proslavery forces in Kansas, he adopted Cromwell's dictum "Trust in God and keep your [gun]powder dry." Also like Cromwell, Brown called for prayers, Bible reading, and moral behavior in his military camps. His self-proclaimed holy war against slavery in Kansas and Harpers Ferry led many to compare him with Cromwell. For the antislavery journalist Franklin Benjamin Sanborn, Brown was "a Puritan soldier, such as were common enough in Cromwell's day, but have not often been seen since"; to the philanthropist-reformer George L. Stearns, he was "a Cromwellian Ironside introduced in the nineteenth century for a special purpose"; to Stearns's wife Mary, "some old Cromwellian hero suddenly dropped down"; to Wendell Phillips, "a regular Cromwellian, dug up from two centuries"; to the journalist Richard J. Hinton, "a puritan brought back from the days of

John Brown, holding a flag initialed SPW (Subterranean Pass Way, his counterpart of the Underground Railroad)
*By the African American photographer Augustus Washington, 1846–47*

Cromwell"; and so on.[72] Although some of Brown's admirers knew about his murderous actions in Kansas, and others questioned his violent tactics at Harpers Ferry, in general they cared as little about his excesses as they did about Cromwell's involvement in regicide or his bloodletting in Ireland. The formerly pacifist Thoreau said that Brown would deserve respect "even though he were of late the vilest murderer."[73] Thoreau put his own rhetorical signature on the common association of Brown with Cromwell. "He died lately in the time of

Cromwell," Thoreau declared, "but he reappeared here. Why should he not? Some of the Puritan stock are said to have come over and settled in New England." Brown's soldiers, Thoreau added, were "a perfect Cromwellian troop," and his powerful words in defense of enslaved people were "like the speeches of Cromwell compared with those of an ordinary king." For Thoreau, Brown was the ultimate enforcer of the higher law—"a transcendentalist above all, a man of ideas and principles."

## LINCOLN REDIRECTS THE PURITAN PRINCIPLE

The higher law may have inspired those who saw no other choice but lawbreaking to oppose the oppressive slave system, but it held little appeal for Abraham Lincoln, a lawyer and rising politician in Illinois during the 1850s, when the higher law was gaining influence in the North. Lincoln admitted in 1854 that if he had all the power in the world, he wouldn't know how to eliminate slavery in America. However, he was clear about what he would not do—he would not act impulsively based on the higher law. He wrote, "I agree with Seward in his 'Irrepressible Conflict,' but I do not endorse his 'Higher Law' doctrine."[74] He understood that the higher law, once invoked, could be directed in any way, as he observed among Southerners who claimed that God ordained slavery. He despised the Fugitive Slave Act but said it had to be obeyed because it was enacted by Congress and enforced the constitutional clause requiring the return of fugitives. "We are under legal obligations," he lamented, "to catch and return their runaway slaves to them—a sort of dirty, disagreeable job."

Lincoln admired John Brown's antislavery goals but denounced his lawlessness. After Harpers Ferry, Lincoln remarked that Brown "agreed with us in thinking slavery wrong" and displayed "great courage, rare unselfishness." "But," he cautioned, "no man, North or South, can approve of violence or crime."[75] Distancing himself and his fellow Republicans from Harpers Ferry, he ran for president in 1860 on an anti–John Brown message. In his landmark Cooper Union Address, he emphasized that the Republican Party had nothing to do with Brown, who was like any "enthusiast" who "broods over the oppression of a people till he fancies himself commissioned by Heaven to liberate them. He ventures the attempt, which ends in little else than his own execution." Social change in democratic America, Lincoln said, must come through "the peaceful channel of the ballot-box," not through vigilante violence like Brown's.

The ballot box, as it turned out, did *not* dislodge slavery: It took a long, bloody civil war to do that. But Lincoln tried hard to prevent war by adhering to the Constitution. In 1858, he said that the answer to the nation's crisis was "not war."[76] He predicted that it might take many decades for slavery to be abolished through the normal political process.

Carefully avoiding mention of the Puritan-vs.-Cavalier dichotomy in his public discourse, Lincoln instead spoke about his country as a single unit—a house—that was divided but was destined eventually to become either one thing or the other, with or without slavery. Not only did the house divided image start and end with the single unit of the house, but it also pointed to a higher power. In using the image, Lincoln borrowed from Jesus's warning "A house divided against itself cannot stand."[77]

Lincoln memorably used this religious image in his debates in 1858 with the proslavery Senator Stephen A. Douglas. When Douglas argued that the nation had long been split over slavery yet had endured, therefore showing that the house divided could survive, Lincoln replied, "Does the Judge say it *can* stand? [Laughter.] . . . If he does, then there is a question of veracity, not between him and me, but between the Judge and an authority of a somewhat higher character. [Laughter and applause.]"[78] By bringing the Bible into the picture, Lincoln was saying, in effect, that the antislavery cause had divine sanction. If Lincoln sounded here like a Puritan-based abolitionist, he sounded even more so in his seventh and final debate with Douglas, on October 15 in Alton, Illinois. Antislavery figures influenced by the Puritan heritage made a rock-solid moral distinction: Slavery was wrong, freedom for the enslaved was right. Lincoln made the same distinction at the Alton debate and even invoked the common antislavery trope of the divine right of kings:

> That is the real issue. . . . It is the eternal struggle between these two principles—right and wrong—throughout the world. They are the two principles that have stood face to face from the beginning of time; and will ever continue to struggle. The one is the common right of humanity and the other the divine right of kings. It is the same principle in whatever shape it develops itself . . . whether from the mouth of a king who seeks to bestride the people of his own nation and live by the fruit of their labor, or from one race of men as an apology for enslaving another race, it is the same tyrannical principle.

Lincoln's higher law was based not only on moral principle but, more important, on the spirit of '76. In December 1856, he attended a Forefathers' Day function in his hometown, Springfield, Illinois, where toasts were raised to the landing "at the rock of Plymouth, 230 years ago this day" and to New England, "the birthplace of political and religious liberty."[79] We don't know about Lincoln's response to the event, but such section-specific rhetoric held little appeal for him. Surely, he found more stirring another toast: "In the establishment of our national independence, the Puritan and Cavalier marched shoulder to shoulder. May their successors never forget that 'all men are created free and equal.'"

This last phrase, from the preamble of the Declaration of Independence, was Lincoln's true higher law. In his 1858 debates with Stephen Douglas, Lincoln insisted that African Americans were entitled to the life, liberty, and pursuit of happiness promised by the Declaration. Personally, he maintained close ties with African Americans in his Springfield neighborhood, where more than twenty Black residents lived. Although he initially supported colonization as a solution to racial tensions, by the second year of his presidency Lincoln shifted his focus to military emancipation, ultimately convinced that slavery had to be abolished regardless of the cost in blood. He gained immense respect for the Union's nearly two hundred thousand African American soldiers and naval personnel, without whom, he wrote, prospects for victory were dim. He became the first president to call openly for voting rights for Blacks, who, he wrote, would help "to keep the jewel of liberty within the family of freedom."[80] Blacks who knew Lincoln, including Frederick Douglass, Sojourner Truth, and Martin Delany, recognized his lack of prejudice. Douglass remarked, "In all my interviews with Mr. Lincoln I was impressed with his entire freedom from popular prejudice against the colored race. He . . . in no single instance reminded me of the difference between himself and myself, of the difference of color, and I thought that all the more remarkable because he came from a State where there were black laws."[81]

Lincoln gave the Declaration's affirmation of human equality unprecedented cultural currency by featuring it in the opening sentence of the Gettysburg Address in 1863. But he had supported the ideal of equality long before that. And he made it clear that equality included Black people. In his 1854 speech at Peoria, Illinois, he declared, "If the negro is a *man*, why then my ancient faith teaches me that 'all men are created equal' and that there can be no moral right in connection with one man's making a slave of another."[82] Speaking at Philadelphia's Independence Hall in February 1861, while on his train trip from Illinois to

Washington, he said he would rather be assassinated on the spot than surrender his belief in equality.

A noble ideal. But it was shared by very few in his time. In the four-way presidential race of 1860, Lincoln won with just 39.8 percent of the popular vote—the lowest share ever for a successful candidate—underscoring a deeper truth: the nation was no longer merely a house divided. It saw itself as two separate peoples.

## HATRED IN THE BONE

The Puritan-vs.-Cavalier conflict had been generated not only by Southern novelists, Northern ministers, and politicians. It was, in John Quincy Adams's words, "bone-bred."[83] It smoldered beneath violence in Congress. Joanne B. Freeman has found that more than seventy fights between congressmen erupted from 1830 to 1860.[84] One of them, in 1838, resulted in a duel in which the Kentucky Congressman William J. Graves killed Representative Jonathan Cilley of Maine. The duel took on larger implications when the Virginia politician Henry A. Wise, Graves's second in the duel, responded to charges that he had participated in a murder. Wise mocked his Northern opponents for calling an affair of honor a crime. He spouted sectional rhetoric: "Let Puritans shudder as they may—I here proclaim that I belong to the class of the Cavaliers, not to the Roundheads!"[85]

Similar language framed the brutal assault in May 1856 by the South Carolina Representative Preston S. Brooks on Senator Charles Sumner of Massachusetts. Brooks's cousin, Senator Andrew Butler, had often spoken out against antislavery Northerners. A fellow politician recalled that the round-faced, silver-haired Butler "was apt to flare up fiercely, to assume the haughty air of the representative of a higher class, and in fluent and high-sounding phrase, to make the Northern man feel the superiority of the Cavalier over the Roundhead."[86] Butler's harangues prompted "The Crime against Kansas," the May 19 speech in which Charles Sumner derided Butler for his infatuation with slavery. Sumner declared, "The Senator from South Carolina has read many books of chivalry, and believes himself a chivalrous knight, with sentiments of honor and courage," impelling him to protect his "mistress [who,] though ugly to others, is always lovely to him, though polluted in the sight of the world, is chaste in his sight: I mean the harlot Slavery."[87]

The speech raised the Cavalier hackles of Butler and his cousin Brooks. On May 22, Brooks entered the Senate after its adjournment, when Sumner was sitting alone at his desk. Brooks walked with a cane because of an old leg injury from a duel. He went up to Sumner and said, "You have libeled my State and slandered a relative who is aged and absent and I am come to punish you for it."[88] He proceeded to pummel Sumner with his gold-headed cane. Sumner, trapped behind his desk, which was fixed to the floor, lurched and bellowed, ripping the desk from its bolts before falling, temporarily blinded and bleeding profusely. Brooks boasted that he "gave him about 30 first rate stripes. . . . Every lick went where I intended." It was three years before Sumner returned to the Senate, where his place had been left open for him. He never fully recovered from his wounds.

This attack on a *Mayflower* descendant by a Cavalier bully created a national sensation. A Massachusetts journalist called Brooks "the honorable cavalier who did the deed of shame! . . . What a spectacle of southern chivalry!"[89] Another Northern commentator remarked, "Talk of chivalry, when this brute, Brooks, who belongs to the 'chivalric' horde of tyrants, has only the courage to assault a defenceless Senator while in his seat, attending to his official duties!"[90] An Albany paper noted "the steady recession to complete barbarism by the old Cavalier Slave-holding stock of Carolina."[91] Meanwhile, Brooks became a hero in the South. At a meeting of "prominent cavaliers" in Columbia, South

*SOUTHERN CHIVALRY—ARGUMENT VERSUS CLUB'S*;
PRESTON BROOKS ATTACKING CHARLES SUMNER
*Political cartoon by John L. Magee, 1856*

Carolina, his attack was hailed for being "applied at the right time, in the right place, on the right individual, by the right man, and with the right instrument."[92]

Then the two ships came into play. Massachusetts Congressman Anson Burlingame gave a speech in June, stating that Brooks represented a vicious society that had begun at Jamestown, one that was wholly different from the one established at Plymouth. "Freedom and Slavery started together in the great race on this continent," Burlingame declared. "In the very year the Pilgrim Fathers landed on Plymouth Rock, slaves landed in Virginia. Freedom has gone on, trampling down barbarism" and spreading liberty, faith, and education. The South had disseminated only "desolation, ignorance, and death," signaled by "the groans of its victims, and the clank of its chains," and was now eagerly looking "toward the setting sun" for more slave territory.[93] Burlingame lambasted Brooks's assault on Sumner as cowardly and unchivalrous. Evidently Burlingame was scheming for a duel challenge from Brooks, who took the bait. As the challenged party, Burlingame chose rifles as weapons (he was an excellent marksman) and the Canadian side of Niagara Falls as the dueling spot. He suspected that Brooks would back down, and he was right. Brooks said he would be waylaid and murdered if he traveled through the North to reach Canada. The duel was off. Ridiculed throughout the North but still glorified in the South, Brooks died of natural causes early the next year.

If the Sumner–Brooks affair widened the divide between Southern Puritans and Northern Cavaliers, so did *Mayflower* celebrations in New England, which took a radical abolitionist turn. Especially noteworthy was the celebration in 1849 in Plymouth of the 229th anniversary of the *Mayflower*'s landing. Speaking before an overflow crowd at Plymouth's church were many of the abolitionist firebrands of the time, including Garrison, Douglass, Phillips, Charles L. Remond, and Lucy Stone. A special guest appearance was made by the celebrated British abolitionist George Thompson. Several antislavery statements were made by the speakers. Wendell Phillips read antislavery resolutions, including one that hailed the Puritan as "emphatically the radical reformer of his day . . . and we proclaim the Anti-Slavery enterprise his lineal and only representative." Another resolution announced, "What is needed for the speedy abolition of slavery in this country is a spirit of determination, enterprise, self-sacrifice, courage, and absolute reliance on God for success, such as was sublimely exhibited to the world by the Pilgrims of Plymouth Rock—the adventurous exiles of the Mayflower."[94]

Phillips attributed even larger significance to Plymouth Rock and the Pilgrims when he spoke at the Forefathers' Day celebration six years later in Plymouth. He declared, "Men look back upon the Carvers and Bradfords of 1620, and seem to think, if they existed in 1855," they would look and act the way they did back then.[95] Phillips asked, "Do you suppose that, if [William] Brewster could come up from his grave to-day, he would be contented with the Congregational Church and the five points of Calvin? No, Sir." He affirmed, "The Pilgrims of 1620 would be, in 1855, not in Plymouth, but in Kansas" fighting the proslavery forces there with "the thousand Sharpe's rifles [sent by Henry Ward Beecher] addressed 'Kansas,' and labelled 'Books.'" Or they would be impugning slavery like Beecher in Brooklyn's Plymouth church or Theodore Parker in Boston's Music Hall. As for Plymouth Rock, Phillips generalized, "The rock underlies all America. . . . It has cropped out a great many times in our history. . . . Jefferson had it for a writing-desk when he drafted the Declaration of Independence and the 'Statute of Religious Freedom' for Virginia. Lovejoy rested his musket upon it when they would not let him print at Alton, and he said, 'Death or free speech!' I recognized the clink of it to-day when the apostle of the 'Higher Law' [Seward] came to lay his garland of everlasting—none a better right than he—upon the monument of the Pilgrims. [Enthusiastic cheering.]"

Such pronouncements about the antislavery *Mayflower* and Plymouth Rock angered Southerners, who countered by trying to establish Jamestown as the real source of America. In 1854, a group of Southerners formed the Jamestown Society, which proposed annual celebrations of the landing at Jamestown of three British ships on May 14, 1607—the correct date, it claimed, of "the first permanent Anglo-Saxon settlement" in America, "long before the New England colonists landed at Plymouth Rock."[96]

The group aimed to be "a society which would have its associate societies in the different States, similar to the Pilgrim associations which have done so much to keep alive the memory of the Plymouth colonists." A Richmond journalist reported that the society would "commemorate the landing of the Cavaliers at Jamestown" in 1607.[97] (A misleading statement: English Cavaliers did not migrate in numbers to

Virginia until the 1650s.) Noting the countless Americans who celebrated Forefathers' Day, the journalist wrote, "They have talked, written, sung, and orated about Plymouth Rock until they have persuaded themselves" that "every man, woman, and child in the U. States, born and to be born, are lineal, unmistakable descendants" of those "who kneeled on that little rock. . . . Plymouth Rock, in their eyes, was the Nidus [breeding ground] of all the population, arts, enterprise and glory of the United States." In the process, Southerners "have been grossly misrepresented, and their characters have been most infamously assailed."[98] The main speaker at the society's 1854 meeting said, "The Norman and chivalrous element was felt in Virginia. . . . Cavaliers led the way, some of whom were fond of romantic adventure."[99] In this telling, Virginia introduced representative democracy with the convening of its General Assembly in 1619, and later it was home to founders such as Washington, Jefferson, and Madison. Thus, the "first germ of a nation which now numbers twenty-five millions, and boasts of a free government . . . was first planted on the soil of Virginia."[100] The speaker said nothing about slavery.

The Jamestown Society hoped to match the reach and impact of Forefathers' Day celebrations, but the society stumbled from the start. Squabbles arose over where the society should be headquartered: in Washington, Richmond, or Jamestown? After a huge celebration in 1857, in which thousands flocked to Jamestown to hear an oration by the former US President John Tyler, the society petered out. It couldn't compete with Forefathers' Day, which had a long history and had spread nationwide in areas where New Englanders had moved. Recognition of Plymouth among widely dispersed New Englanders overwhelmed the Jamestown advocates, with their doctored history and their evasiveness on slavery. In fact, Plymouth promoters used the Jamestown Society's lie that Cavaliers dominated Virginia's original settlement by pinning responsibility for the 1619 ship on Cavaliers. The abolitionist Massachusetts minister Daniel Foster declared in 1857:

"While the Mayflower was depositing her freight of men and women who came to form an empire of education and free labor, the Cavaliers were recruiting their colony at Jamestown, and landing cargoes of negroes, stolen from Africa, to found an empire on human bondage." Extending the conflict forward to slavery battles in Kansas, Foster described "the old antagonistic parties—the Puritans and the Cavaliers—the one striving with tireless energy to plant the Rock of Plymouth on Kansas soil, and the other . . . [creating] a vile oppression."[101]

Meanwhile, plans were being laid in Plymouth for a monument that would stand as a lasting tribute to the Pilgrims. The celebrated artist and sculptor Hammatt Billings was hired to design it.[102] Billings created what would become, on its completion in 1888, the National Monument to the Forefathers, said to be "the largest solid granite monument in the world."[103] Perched on a hill overlooking Plymouth and its harbor, the eighty-one-foot-tall monument has an octagonal base that supports a tall figure of Faith, her left hand reaching to heaven and her right hand at her side holding a Bible. Seated below her are smaller figures representing Liberty, Morality, Education, and Law, along with friezes showing scenes of the Pilgrims and the *Mayflower*.

The ceremony for the laying of the cornerstone of the Forefathers Monument was held in Plymouth on August 2, 1859, to commemorate the embarkation of the Pilgrims on the *Mayflower* and *Speedwell* from Southampton, England, in August 1620. Spectators came from far and wide to witness the daylong festivities. Many politicians attended the event; others sent congratulatory letters.

Out in Springfield, Illinois, Abraham Lincoln avoided overt association with the Plymouth ceremony. Having lost the 1858 Senate race to Stephen Douglas, he continued in his law practice. Privately, he supported the Monument to the Forefathers. In his papers is a certificate recording his contribution of ten dollars toward the construction of the monument. For his contribution, he was awarded lifelong membership in the Pilgrim Society. But he did not publicly mention the donation or the membership. He continued to avoid sectional partisanship, a stance suggested by the Plymouth monument. Right up through to his inauguration in March 1861, he would try to prevent civil war by emphasizing unity. "We are not enemies, but friends," he assured the South in the inaugural address.[104] He urged all Americans to heed "the better angels" of their nature and to be moved by the "mystic chords of memory" stretching from "every battle-field, and patriot grave, to every living heart and hearthstone, all over this broad land"—a reference to the American Revolution, when the North and the South had come together in a single cause.

But it was too late. By the time he spoke these words, seven Southern states had seceded from the Union, and four more would soon follow. In the view of Southerners, Lincoln, despite his efforts to foster harmony, was a wicked "Black Republican." A Southern journalist commented that Lincoln was merely a "low and vulgar partisan of John Brown."[105] Another called him the leader of the "viperous breed of the Mayflower" in the North, showing that "the old imported English Puritan stock has not degenerated, but rather become intensified in all its perverseness," and must be "stopped or exterminated."[106] He was, in this view, a Constitution-busting radical intent on ending slavery, which the South called an institution "of divine origin, . . . permitted, recognized and commanded" in the Bible.[107] The North may have laid its cornerstone in Plymouth, but the Southern politician Alexander H. Stephens, the vice president of the Confederate States of America, declared that slavery, ordained by God and supported by ethnographic "science," was the "corner-stone" of the South.[108]

Months before his inauguration, Lincoln had written Stephens, a former congressional colleague, saying that the difference between the sections was that "you think slavery is *right* and ought to be extended; while we think it is *wrong* and ought to be restricted."[109]

That was true. But for many Americans on both sides, the conflict ran far deeper than that. As *The New York Herald*, the nation's most popular newspaper, said, "The people of the North and those of the South are distinct and separate; they think differently; they spring from a different stock; they are different every way; they cannot coalesce; the Puritan and the Cavalier . . . will always fight when they meet. There is nothing in common between them but hate."[110]

Charles Sumner put it reductively: The choice was between the *Mayflower* and the slave ship.[111] The collision of the two ships set off an explosion that would reverberate through history.

## *Chapter Ten*

# THE CULTURE WAR BEHIND THE CIVIL WAR

January 1862. The first eight months of the Civil War had gone badly for the North. Early visions of a quick victory had been shattered by Union losses at Bull Run, Wilson's Creek, Lexington, and Ball's Bluff. The initial rush of war fever, captured in Walt Whitman's exuberant poem "Beat! Beat! Drums!," had flagged. The winter in the North was frigid and snowy. General in Chief George McClellan was grounded with typhus. President Lincoln was restless over the inaction of his armies. Everything seemed stuck.

Frederick Douglass wanted to jolt the North out of its lethargy. Six feet tall, with broad shoulders and a mane of graying hair that framed a dark-goateed face, Douglass gave a resounding speech on January 16 before a packed house at Philadelphia's National Hall. He fired up the crowd with his favorite historical image: the two ships. The causes of the Civil War, he declared, reached back to "the dawn of civilization on this continent":

> In the same year that the *Mayflower* landed her liberty-seeking passengers on the bleak New England shore, a Dutch

Frederick Douglass in 1862
*Photograph taken by John White Hurn*

> galliot landed a company of African slaves on the banks of the James river, Virginia. The *Mayflower* planted liberty at the North, and the Dutch galliot slavery at the South. There is the fire, and there is the gunpowder. Contact has produced the explosion. What has followed might have been easily predicted. Great men saw it from the beginning, but no great men were found great enough to prevent it.[1]

In the same month that Douglass gave the North's version of history, the Mississippi political commentator J. Quitman Moore presented the South's. In the January issue of *De Bow's Review*, Moore traced the origins of Southern society to early England.[2] Moore claimed that the Normans, who uprooted the Saxons, established a structured society based on aristocracy and subordination. This stable social arrangement was thereafter threatened by the unruly Saxon element, which bubbled with individualism, subversive politics, and religious extremism. Open conflict between two sides arrived under the Tudor monarchs and worsened under the Stuarts, when Puritans challenged the Church of England. King Charles I and Archbishop William Laud tried to stem the Puritan upheaval through the courts, but the Puritans proved to be "grand architects of ruin," notable for "their crimes and folly," including killing the king and undermining the church. The typical Puritan, Moore wrote, was "a religious fanatic and a political agitator," "violent," "austere," dictatorial in the effort to control others, driven by "cupidity and ambition" and marked by "craft and duplicity." In stark contrast stood "the Cavalier—the builder, the social architect, the institutionalist . . . the advocate of rational liberty and the supporter of authority." Moore described the Cavalier as "chivalrous," "magnanimous," "courtly in his manners and splendid in his tastes. . . . Honor was the touchstone to his character." Transplanted to the New World, the rival groups produced "the two nationalities that now divide the empire of the American continent." The North descended into "licentious liberty" even as the South settled into "an enlightened conservatism," retaining "all the elements of an aristocracy," including "domestic servitude," while advocating "an absolute democracy" in politics—a combination exemplified by Virginian planters like Jefferson, Washington, and Madison. In another *De Bow's* article Quitman explained, "Cavalier and Roundhead no longer designate parties, but *nations*, whose separate foundations were laid on Plymouth Rock and the banks of the James River."[3]

This Cavalier version of history, with its emphasis on social stability, gave a sheen of respectability to a society that held four million Black people in bondage. For its proponents, it helped validate the formation of the Confederate States of America, which had its own constitution and its own tripartite government. The Confederacy's president, Jefferson Davis, who enslaved more than a hundred people on his Mississippi plantation, was known as "the model Cavalier."[4] Tall and lean, with hollow cheeks, a pointed chin, and a high forehead, he represented, "in face and form, the Norman type with singular fidelity," according to a fellow Confederate.[5] Davis said that those who didn't recognize that Southerners and Northerners were utterly different peoples were ignorant. "Our enemies," he said of the North, "are a traditionless and a homeless race; from the time of Cromwell to the present moment they have been disturbers of the peace of the world. Gathered together by Cromwell from the bogs and fens . . . they persecuted Catholics in England, and they hung Quakers and witches in America."[6]

Davis's counterpart, Abraham Lincoln, never accepted the two-nations idea. His goal was to restore the Union, whatever the military cost—a goal that was increasingly linked with his aim to abolish slavery. Although Lincoln did not openly support the Puritan version of history, he learned from it and acted on it in ways that he hoped would create national unity, with justice for all.

## THE PROSLAVERY ASSAULT ON THE *MAYFLOWER* AND PURITANISM

Confederates believed that they were a master race. They thought that they rightfully held in bondage an inferior race of people, whose enslavement was natural and God-ordained; and they believed that they came from a Cavalier/Norman background that was intrinsically superior to the Puritan/Saxon race of the North. "The Norman *cavalier*," sniffed a proslavery journalist, "cannot brook the vulgar familiarity of the Saxon Yankee, while the latter is continually devising some plan to bring down his aristocratic neighbor to his own detested level."[7]

Proslavery versions of American history were rife with errors and were characterized by a willful ignorance of Puritanism's positive side or the real feelings of enslaved people. Southerners based their defense of slavery largely on the charge that the urban "wage slavery" of the North was far worse than chattel slavery on Southern plantations and that the agrarian stability of the slave system was infinitely preferable to Yankee-peddler money worship and the whirling "isms" of Northerners.[8]

The narrative of Southerners as a master race being confronted by a supposedly inferior, materialistic, chaotic Puritan foe was promoted in proslavery works throughout the Civil War. In many cases, Jamestown and Plymouth were used as shorthand for the two sides. Just before the war, the right-leaning *New York Herald*, noting that many American political leaders from the founders onward were slaveholders, boasted: "The colony of Jamestown was long ahead of Plymouth Rock—the rock on which we fear the union is destined to be split."[9] Shortly before the Confederate bombardment of Fort Sumter, a Richmond paper asked, "How can ever the Northern and Southern people unify? What similarity, pray, was there, or will there ever be, between Plymouth and Jamestown? . . . What attraction could exist between Puritan and Cavalier?"[10] Another Southern newspaper noted that "two great streams of civilization" flowed into America at the start: "One had its head at Jamestown and one at Plymouth Rock." New England was settled by Puritans who were "canting, witch-hanging, nasal-twanging, money-worshipping, curiosity-loving, meddling, fanatical 'ism'-breeding followers of Cromwell."[11]

We have seen, over the course of this book, that the path from early Puritanism and its offshoots to nineteenth-century antislavery reform had twists and turns, contradictions, and leaps forward followed by steps backward. The movement toward human rights was halting, not smooth or continuous.

The proslavery advocates emphasized such anomalies and pointed to the Founding Fathers, many of whom were slaveholders. *The New*

*York Herald* noted, "A Southern man—Jefferson, a slaveholder—drew up the Declaration of Independence; a Southern man—Madison, a slaveholder—was the great artificer of the constitution; a Southern man—Washington, a slaveholder—presided over the federal convention which adopted it."[12] Why shouldn't they enslave people? After all, they were dignified individuals, devoted to social order. Many had roots in the Cavalier past. A Richmond paper insisted that those who created the nation were Cavaliers to the core:

> Washington, the Cavalier, was the first to take up arms, and effected what the world knows. [George] Mason, the Cavalier, wrote the Bill of Rights of Virginia, the great foundation-stone of human freedom. Jefferson, the Cavalier, was so violent that he was attainted for treason. [Edmund] Pendleton, the Cavalier, was president of the Committee of Safety. Richard Henry Lee, the Cavalier, was the mouth piece of revolution. Patrick Henry, the descendant of Cavaliers, was the almost inspired orator sounding the charge. [Archibald] Cary, the Cavalier, was one of the eternal opponents of England. [Peyton] Randolph, [James] Monroe, [John] Marshall, Arthur Lee, Cavaliers—these men were legislators, diplomats, lawgivers, soldiers, presidents, under the new régime. They worked from the beginning with brain and arm for the Revolution and were its real originators. To these men the masses looked; it was they who aroused the storm; and they were, without one exception that we can at present recall, Cavaliers.[13]

But how could the founders, who rebelled against King George III, be characterized as Cavaliers, who were, historically, loyal to monarchs? Here, the proslavery racial theories of the antebellum era came into play. Confederate leaders accepted the racist ideas of the New York physician and journalist John H. Van Evrie. In the 1850s, Jefferson Davis, then a US senator, was in contact with Van Evrie, blurbed his first book, and offered him a sinecure in the Interior Department to write proslavery propaganda.[14] Van Evrie's argument about race is captured in the title of his 1853 book, *Negroes and Negro "Slavery": The First an Inferior Race; the Latter Its Normal Condition*. Van Evrie was a leading figure in the nineteenth-century movement known as scientific racism, which also included Samuel Cartwright, Samuel George Morton, and the ethnologists Josiah C. Nott and George Gliddon. Like his contemporaries, Van Evrie claimed to differentiate races based on skull shapes, brain sizes, facial features, and other physical traits. The only Northerner among them, he became the most influential through his widely reprinted books and his newspaper, the *New York Day-Book*. Van Evrie, like other American pseudoscientists, promoted a racial hierarchy that placed "Caucasians" at the top and Africans at the bottom, often comparing them with orangutans. Black people, whom Van Evrie called "the most inferior of all the known human races," were destined by physiology and by God to be enslaved by whites.[15]

The Cavaliers of early Virginia, Van Evrie argued, acted on this "great, startling, fixed *fact*." They knew from their own experience the importance of obedience to authority. "The descendants of the cavaliers in Virginia," Van Evrie wrote, followed "the celebrated formula of Archbishop Laud, that 'passive obedience and non-resistance' was the absolute and universal duty of the people to the will of the king." In turn, the Virginians "demanded from their special retainers [i.e., their slaves] the same unquestioning submission which they themselves accorded to royalty." They found that Blacks were "different and subordinate beings," "an inferior race," with "different faculties and different wants" that made slavery their proper condition. This "discovery" of racial difference led to a new emphasis on racial equality among whites.

It was justifiable, Van Evrie contended, for whites to challenge fellow whites when they became oppressive. By the 1760s and '70s, Virginians with Cavalier roots were ready to rebel against the British Crown.

This was Van Evrie's explanation of what he described as the "extraordinary transformation which has changed the descendants of the old Norman aristocracy into the firmest and most reliable defenders of democracy." But didn't several of the founders oppose slavery in principle, even when they held Black people in bondage? Yes, said Van Evrie, but they were products of a scientifically backward age. Modern ethnology, he insisted, had proven not only that Blacks must be enslaved for their own happiness and protection but that their emancipation and integration into white society would result in interracial couples whose "mongrel progeny" would "become sterile, diseased, rotten, and within a certain time, [would] utterly perish from the earth." Freedom for the enslaved would eventually lead to "the extinction of both races."[16]

Prominent Confederates bought the argument. Jefferson Davis praised Van Evrie for undermining "fanaticism and treason by facts and philosophy" and showing Southerners "*the true philosophy of their social organization*."[17] The Confederacy's vice president, Alexander Stephens, had initially refused to read *Negroes and Negro "Slavery"* because of its notorious reputation, but when friends persuaded him to do so, he was won over and wrote an endorsement for the book. Van Evrie boasted that Stephens, now converted by "this new revelation of a truth six thousand years old, and practically recognized by every generation of Americans since the landing of a handful of African Negroes at Jamestown," became "the clearest, most pronounced, and most complete exponent and advocate of the new doctrine among all the public men of the day."[18] In 1856, Van Evrie had written that "white supremacy and negro subordination" constituted "the corner stone of our Republican edifice, which supports the whole fabric of our civilization," without which America would "sink into utter ruin and desola-

JOHN H. VAN EVRIE
*Portrait by W. G. Jackman, 1860s.*

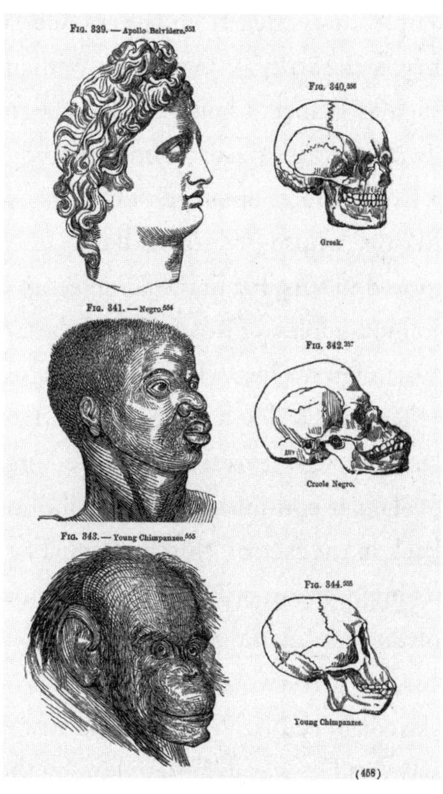


SCIENTIFIC RACISM; A BLACK PERSON'S HEAD RANKED BETWEEN HEADS OF A "CAUCASIAN" AND A CHIMPANZEE.
*In Josiah C. Nott and George R. Gliddon,* Types of Mankind *(1854)*

tion."[19] Stephens, in his 1861 Cornerstone Speech in Savannah, Georgia, communicated the same message. He echoed Van Evrie by saying that the founders were uninformed when they questioned slavery and preached human equality. Stephens asserted that recent "departments of science" provided the foundation for the South's "new government," which was "the first in the history of the world" based on the "great physical, philosophical, and moral truth" that "the negro is not equal to the white man. That slavery—subordination to the superior race—is his natural and moral position."[20] Abolitionism, Stephens continued, was "a species of insanity" among Northern "fanatics" who worked from the "fancied or erroneous" premise that "the negro is equal" and "entitled to equal privileges and rights with the white man."

Many Confederates believed themselves not only scientifically advanced but also heirs to a proud Cavalier lineage. Robert E. Lee, for example, descended from the influential Lee family founded by Richard Lee, a close ally of Governor William Berkeley and ancestor to figures such as Francis Lightfoot Lee, a signer of the Declaration of Independence. George Mason, who authored the Fugitive Slave Act and served as a Confederate diplomat, was descended from Founding Father George Mason, whose great-grandfather, George "The Cavalier" Mason, had moved to Virginia in the seventeenth century. Southern rights champion John Randolph of Roanoke and the Confederate military officers George Washington Custis Lee, John Augustine Washington II, and Thomas Jefferson Randolph were part of the tangle of fishhooks that stretched back through several founders to Virginia's early First Families.

Under continual attack by abolitionists, Southerners threw slavery back in the face of Northerners. The North's involvement in slavery—its importation of Black bondsmen, beginning in 1638 with the voyage of the ship *Desire* to the West Indies; the Massachusetts slave code of 1641, nearly two decades before Virginia's code; New England's enslavement of Native people and its centrality in the eighteenth-century slave trade—was hammered on by the proslavery side to accentuate the

North's hypocrisy. Van Evrie, who in his newspaper often denounced abolitionists as fanatical Puritans, wrote sarcastically, "Your Puritan always works for the glory of God, no matter whether it is stealing land from the Indians, trading, swapping and peddling, bringing negroes from Africa and selling them down South, or fighting to set them free by fire and sword."[21] Another proslavery point was that some of the founders from the South actually made antislavery proposals, such as Jefferson's to ban the slave trade, that had met with resistance in the North, as from New England merchants who squeezed as much profit as they could from the trade before its prohibition in 1808.

Once the trade became illegal, the proslavery story continued. New Englanders greedily sought other sources of income and assumed a moral pose toward the South, largely through reform movements. In his 1844 lecture "New England Reformers," Emerson declared that the "fertile forms of antinomianism among the elder puritans, seemed to have their match in the plenty of the new harvest of reform." "In each of these movements," he said, "emerged a good result, an assertion of the sufficiency of the private man."[22] This private definition of religion, rooted in early Puritanism's emphasis on the individual's relationship with God, outside of church structure, delighted Emerson but outraged proslavery spokesmen, who often lashed out at the North's "isms," such as Transcendentalism, Mormonism, Millerism, spiritualism, women's rights, free love, and other movements. Worst of all was abolitionism. While antislavery reformers looked back with pride at their Puritan foreground, the proslavery side considered that background the seedbed of the most un-American and dangerous movement in history. Antislavery reform, the South said, was unconstitutional with its higher-law doctrine, which was evidenced notoriously by actions like Garrison's public burning of the Constitution and John Brown's lawless invasion of Harpers Ferry. The end result of abolitionism, proslavery people predicted, would be a racial reversal in America driven by so-called "negro worship."

*Worship of the North*, with PURITANISM
as the foundation block of the North's "isms"
*By Adalbert Johann Volck,*
*in* Sketches from the Civil War in North America, 1861, '62, '63

This view was captured in *Worship of the North*, a political cartoon by the Confederate caricaturist Adalbert Johann Volck that shows a crowd of antislavery reformers and politicians around a stone altar on which a white man has been stabbed, to be offered in sacrifice to the African "god" who sits atop the altar. At the base of the altar is a large block labeled PURITANISM. Above that are other blocks with titles like WITCHBURNING, SOCIALISM, FREE LOVE, SPIRIT RAPPING, ATHEISM, RATIONALISM, and NEGRO WORSHIP. Among the antislavery figures pictured in the cartoon are Henry Ward Beecher, Harriet Beecher Stowe, John Brown, Charles Sumner, and Abraham Lincoln.[23]

The fact that the proslavery narrative was told in a cartoon points to the variety of genres in which that narrative appeared, which included tracts, letters, speeches, periodicals, poems, humor, and songs. Whether as snippets or in full-length works, the story, in different variations, permeated popular culture and politics. The narrative was told so often that it is impossible to cover all the instances of it here. Some examples give a taste of the whole.

The Virginia Baptist preacher Thornton Stringfellow wrote a letter to a fellow fire-eater, published in the Confederate anthology *Cotton Is King* (1860), that made the remarkable argument that the Puritan North had forced slavery on the South. Referring to enslaved Black people, Stringfellow wrote, "The South did not seek or desire the responsibility, and the onerous burden, of civilizing and christianizing these degraded savages," but God allowed "England, and her puritan sons at the North, from the love of gain, to become the willing instruments, to force African slaves upon the Cavaliers of the South." The Cavaliers, "a noble race of men . . . remonstrated against this outrage to the last. They preferred indentured labor from the mother country."[24] Reluctantly, the South finally accepted slavery in order to carry out the Lord's mandate to "elevate" Africans, who were now proven by science to be inferior by nature. Currently, Stringfellow wrote, "there are *isms* at the North whose name is Legion," few of which "have taken root among us" because of the orderly institution of "domestic slavery." The same point was made by an Alabama contributor to *De Bow's Review* who affirmed, "The very structure of our society, embodying, as it does, the divinely sanctioned enslavement of an inferior race, checks all that tendency to licentious anarchy so natural to enlarged freedom."[25]

The lies and euphemisms multiplied. "It was a sad day," opined a New Orleans journalist, "when the religious adherents of that gigantic blasphemer [Cromwell], the Protector, [landed at] Plymouth Rock. The little Mayflower was the Pandora-box that showered woe upon our people."[26] The ship produced a "stream of civilization which . . . with its leaven of puritanism, flowed gradually over the north and, introduced a race differing as much from that grander and more chivalrous stream at Jamestown as night differeth from day." Cotton Mather "burned and drowned the witches of Salem," after which the Puritans "seized the shirts of the 'almighty negro'" and never let go. There was a causal connection between the "witch-burning" Mather and abolitionists like the "huge fanatic" Garrison, the "sacerdotal rascal" Henry Ward Beecher, and Harriet Beecher Stowe, "the representative man-woman of the northern isms" who was "keenly alive to the jingle of the Puritan's god, the almighty dollar." Such "northern incendiaries" and "politico-religious knaves," the writer concluded, "sprung directly from the Puritans who landed at Plymouth Rock, and the subsequent emigrant followers to the New England states."

In a similar historical piece, an Alabama journalist wrote, "The 'Mayflower' bore its germs to Plymouth Rock. That 'Mayflower,' so celebrated in song and so eulogized in festive speeches, proved a Pandora's box to this unhappy continent."[27] It brought "the spirit of intolerance and persecution" that was inflicted on "Indians, Witches and Quakers." Later on, Northerners "subordinated legislation and corrupted Government to their own purposes." They defied "a written constitution" and unleashed "cataracts of abuse and calumny of everything southern, from pulpit, press, stump, the floor of Congress, lecture rooms, and the seething atmosphere of their everlasting, canting religious and benevolent societies." The writer concluded, "And now they have deluged the land in blood . . . in the insane effort to restore the Union, broken to pieces by their infernal selfishness, bigotry and meddlesomeness. Such is the history of the 'Pilgrim Fathers' and their descendants."

Slavery's advocates recklessly steamrolled different historical phenomena in order to make negative points. The terms "*Mayflower* Pilgrims," "Puritan," and "Yankee" were often used interchangeably, as in this Southern outburst: "The Yankee is but a degenerate Puritan—the lineal descendant of the Mayflower Pilgrims, with all their traits of avarice, hypocrisy and cunning, intensified by transmission."[28] In the summer of 1861, Lincoln's suppression of Northern proslavery newspapers was seen by a Georgia journalist as "the breaking out afresh of the old witch burning Puritanism of the descendants of the Mayflower passengers. . . . It is the very spirit of hell itself."[29] A Virginia state congressman impugned "the fanatical, meddlesome, overbearing disposition of the Puritans," leading him to declare, "It would have been better for humanity had their Plymouth Rock been riven by an earthquake and their Mayflower sunk to the bottom of the ocean."[30] In 1862, the Democratic *Chicago Times*, lambasting a local celebration of the *Mayflower*, flattened New England history, drawing "a direct line" from the Pilgrims to the Puritans who "burnt women at the stake," hanged Quakers, passed absurdly strict blue laws, and then later governed the slave trade, "invented the Hartford Convention" (a New England movement against the War of 1812), "mobbed convents," opposed the annexation of Texas, and "invited negroes to the polls while excluding white men on account of their poverty or birthplace."[31] A ton of historical bricks was thus dumped on the Pilgrims.

Southerners generally criticized nineteenth-century Northern authors, many of whom attacked slavery, either directly or indirectly. The novelist Nathaniel Hawthorne was an exception. He was skeptical of abolitionism and other reform movements, some of which he satirized in his novel *The Blithedale Romance*. John Brown, Hawthorne insisted, was a "blood-stained fanatic," and "Nobody was ever more justly hanged."[32] Above all, Hawthorne appealed to the South because of his powerful critiques of Puritan hypocrisy and repressiveness, most notably in *The Scarlet Letter*. In the novel, the hypocritical Puritan preacher Arthur Dimmesdale hides the sin of adultery while his paramour Hester openly suffers the sin's penalty—wearing a scarlet *A* on her clothing—imposed by a Puritan community that calls itself pious yet enforces rigid, inhumane laws. In September 1854, the *Richmond Enquirer* praised Hawthorne for portraying "all the worst and repulsive traits of the Puritan," thereby exposing the root of "Abolitionism," which "is the special development of latter-day Puritanism."[33] Another Southerner, arguing that "New England has been the source of all the evils that have vexed the peace and disturbed the security of the Union," asserted that "there was a principle of evil in Puritanism from which, when it ripened into rottenness, was propagated all the isms that have since swarmed over the land." After mentioning the "isms," with their "thousand impostures," the writer pointed to two Northerners who wisely rejected them: the politician Daniel Webster, and Hawthorne, "who spurned their association, and applied the best energies of his inspired genius in discrediting the source of New England civilization" [i.e., Puritanism].[34]

## COPPERHEADS, CATHOLICS, AND CONFEDERATES

One of Hawthorne's great admirers among the Peace Democrats was the Ohio Congressman Samuel Sullivan Cox, who wrote of Hawthorne, "The one great writer of New England is the one man who has thoroughly and mercilessly analyzed the weaknesses and the disease of Puritanism—the one man who has most fearlessly scrubbed away the whitewash from its sepulchers."[35] Known as "Sunset" Cox because of a vivid newspaper account of a sunset he once published, Cox was an Ohio Copperhead who brought the proslavery critique of New England Puritanism to the heart of the political scene at a key moment in the war—in January 1863, the month that Lincoln issued the Emancipation Proclamation, which declared enslaved people in the rebel states "forever free" and called for the use of African American troops.

A reactionary Democrat, Cox was born and raised in Ohio, attended Brown University in Rhode Island, and later returned to Ohio, where he edited a newspaper and pursued a career in law. A supporter of Franklin Pierce and Stephen A. Douglas, Cox opposed abolitionism and the Republican Party, whose rising star in Ohio was Salmon Chase. Cox was elected to Congress at the age of thirty-three in 1857 and went on to serve sixteen terms in the US House of Representatives, becoming a prominent leader in the Democratic Party. At the outbreak of the Civil War, Cox said that he would support the war as long as it remained focused on saving the Union. Once the war took on an anti-slavery tenor, with the confiscation acts of 1861 and 1862, which freed Blacks who fled behind Union lines, Cox came out fiercely against the Lincoln administration. He was furious about the Emancipation Proclamation and led the congressional opposition to Thaddeus Stevens's earlier proposal to raise 150,000 Black troops. The war, Cox argued, should be for white, not Black, people. He declared, "[Nothing] can wash out the color of the negro, change his inferior nature, or save him from his inevitable fate."[36] A dyed-in-the-wool Copperhead like his fellow Ohioans Clement Vallandigham and George Pendleton, Cox spewed venom against New England Puritanism, which, he claimed, had caused the war.

A contemporary described Sunset Cox as "a little, swinging, prancing man" with dark hair and a small white bald spot on the center of his head.[37] When giving a speech, he would loosen his collar, roll up his sleeves, and march up and down the aisles, waving a handkerchief while excoriating his opponents. In his January 13, 1863, speech "Puritanism in Politics," Cox described the Constitution as a mound that had been attacked by "a small, insidious, persevering reptile."[38] "Puritanism," he declared, "is the reptile which has been boring into the mound, which is the Constitution, and this civil war comes in like the devouring sea! Its rushing tide of devastation will not be stayed until the reptile is crushed and the mound rebuilt." Cox insisted that "the Constitution-breaking . . . negro-loving Phariseeism of New England" was produced by "PURITANISM," which was "bred in the bone. It is the same now that it was hundreds of years ago. Like begets like. Generation succeeds generation, with the same stamp of Puritan character."

From the start, Cox explained, Puritans were intolerant fanatics who tyrannically imposed their views on others. This was true in England, where they attacked royalty and the church; in Holland, where they fought against Dutch religious doctrines; and in America, where they hanged witches and Quakers while banishing the likes of Henry Vane and Roger Williams. "The history of Puritanism," Cox said, "is a catalog of murders, maimings, extortions, and outrages, contrary to English common law, and against every notion of human justice and liberty."[39] The Puritans turned the government into "a moral reform organization." Seventeenth-century Puritanism, Cox argued, although flawed, still had a limited impact. Not so in the nineteenth century: "Now we see its workings on a grander scale, involving a Continent in its contentions. It is a power. So is Satan." The Mathers of yesteryear had been replaced by the Beechers, Parkers, and Phillipses of today. Referring to the wildly popular John Brown marching song, with its "Glory, glory hallelujah!" chorus, Cox said of New England, "Her Marseillaise is a hymn of apotheosis of John Brown, a horse-thief and a murderer." Cox explained: "Abolition is the offspring of Puritanism," and "Abolition is, in the moral sense, the cause of the strife." Abolition, "the especial curse of this nation," explains the "clamor for proclamations and confiscations, which dispense with the Constitution." Puritanism had caused the explosion of Northern "isms," including "infidel" Transcendentalism. Cox mocked Emerson's notion of absorption into the All: "Emerson holds that he (Emerson) is God; that God is every thing; therefore he (Emerson) is every thing. [Merriment.] Do you wonder, therefore, that since he makes the negro a part of himself, he holds him to be his equal? [Increased laughter.] . . . Do you wonder at the imperturbable impudence and self-sufficiency of the Puritan thus indoctrinated?"

More anti-Puritan bile came soon. On January 14, 1863, the day after Sunset Cox delivered "Puritanism in Politics," his fellow Ohio Democrat Clement L. Vallandigham gave a speech in Congress that also attributed the Civil War to New England Puritanism. Vallandigham is most often remembered as the outspoken Copperhead whose public opposition to the Civil War led to his court-martialing in May 1863, his banishment to the Confederacy by Lincoln, and his subsequent escape to Ontario, Canada, where he campaigned in exile for Ohio's governorship before returning in disguise to the US and heading the Sons of Liberty, which plotted the international expansion of slavery. Vallandigham had a long record of opposition to rights for African Americans. As a state congressman in Ohio in the 1850s, he promoted that state's virulent Black laws. He was an enthusiastic supporter of the Dred Scott decision, which stripped Black people of citizenship. "The African," he maintained, was in "every way, an inferior, degraded, and outcast race. No man dreamed that he had a part or a lot in the Government."[40] He wanted a return to slavery and states' rights, protected under the Constitution. He regarded Lincoln as a tyrant who was controlled by bigoted Puritans of New England.

That's the message he delivered in his January 14 speech. Vigorous and intense, with clear blue eyes, an aquiline nose, and a dark trimmed beard, Vallandigham commanded audiences through his impetuous, extemporaneous delivery. The Pilgrims and the Puritan generation that succeeded them, he said, consisted of two strands: "the *Mayflower and Plymouth Rock type of New Englander*" and "*the Roger Williams element.*"[41] The *Mayflower* group was harsh, oppressive, despotic, and moralistic. The Roger Williams type was liberal and tolerant, believing in the separation of church and state. The two had maintained a balance up to the Missouri debates in 1819–20, at which time the *Mayflower* current surged to the forefront in New England. By the 1830s, the *Mayflower* mentality had gained prominence, and it soon dominated all of New England and parts of the rest of the North. It was then that "the narrow, presumptuous, intermeddling, and fanatical spirit of the old Puritan element began to reappear in a form very much more aggressive and destructive than at first, and threatened to obtain absolute mastery in Church, and School, and State." Resistance arose among conservatives, but John Quincy Adams, Theodore Parker, the Beecher family, Wendell Phillips, and other abolitionists kept it alive. Vallandigham had been in Harpers Ferry the day John Brown was captured, and he was one of the interviewers of the wounded Brown as he lay outside of the fire engine house, where he had been captured. Like other Southerners, Vallandigham admired Brown's courage but detested his abolitionism, which he said was the natural product of Puritan New England. The Civil War, Vallandigham declared, was a war between profoundly dissimilar races, a part of "the old conflict of the Cavalier and the Roundhead, the Liberalist and the Puritan; or, rather, it is a conflict, upon new issues, of the ideas and elements represented by those names. It is a war of the Yankee and the Southron." Vallandigham said, "I am inexorably hostile to Puritan domination in religion or morals or literature or politics." He did not go as far as some other Copperheads, who were calling for the expulsion of New England from the Union. But he insisted that New England should be a part of America only if the destructive *Mayflower* element—that is, abolition—was eliminated.

It wasn't just Copperheads who launched anti-Puritan diatribes in response to the Emancipation Proclamation. Other proslavery spokesmen did as well. A Catholic archbishop in Baltimore fumed, "While our brethren are slaughtered in hecatombs, Abraham Lincoln coolly issues his Emancipation Proclamation, letting loose from three to four millions of half civilized Africans to murder their Masters and Mistresses! And all that under the pretense of philanthropy!! Puritan hypocrisy never exhibited itself in a more horrible and detestable attitude."[42]

Such anti-Puritan sentiment was dwarfed by *The Confederate*, a 102-page pamphlet that presented an entire demonic history of the Puritans, alleging their hand in the Emancipation Proclamation. Its author, William J. Bobo, a South Carolina journalist and secessionist calling himself "A Carolinian," issued it from Mobile, Alabama, and it circulated widely across the South to inflame wartime fervor among civilians and soldiers. Its denunciation of New England Puritanism was unrelenting, entirely devoid of euphemism or conciliatory gestures. In England, Bobo said, the Puritans were "a wild band of low, and principled, and shameless robbers and villains" who destroyed "a venerable church" and "assassinated in cold blood" a king who was "certainly a gentleman and a Christian."[43] The *Mayflower* was "that unhappy ship" which had, "unhappily for humanity, and doubly unhappily for us, disgorged upon the shores of America its fanatical crew, the spawn of that vile faction whose history I have already recorded." Puritans had been troublemakers at home, and they wanted freedom to continue their terrible ways in the New World. They slaughtered and enslaved Native people, imported African slaves from the West Indies, and hanged Quakers and witches. In the eighteenth century, they got rich from the slave trade. The American Revolution, in this reading, was a scheme concocted by recalcitrant Puritans like James Otis and John Adams, who dragged into the war a reluctant South, which later found itself enslaved to Northern Puritanism in a new form—abolitionism, the very worst of "all absurdities whose names terminate in *ism*." Bobo insisted that "the Abolitionist of the North" was part of a long line—the "Independent, Roundhead, Puritan and Pilgrim, down to the present time"—that constituted "the inferior race." Bobo generalized: "A more unworthy and ignoble race—a viler, more pernicious, or contemptible rabble never degraded the bright image of God in humanity." The Puritan "scum" included "'Ape' Lincoln," that "atrocious monster now bearing rule in Washington City" whose "incendiary proclamation" would prevent any settlement between the sections. At any rate, settlement was out of the question. Bobo writes, "There are those who dream of reconstruction! Never, never, never! Rather than this, let us have war forever—war to the knife!" Besides, Bobo was confident of the South's eventual victory, because "The Southron, descended from the Cavaliers of Europe, is of the superior race," and "the superior race is never conquered by the inferior."

Anti-Puritan rhetoric was now part of the proslavery lingua franca. Confederate General John B. Magruder, according to a visiting British army officer, in April 1863 "spoke of the Puritans with intense disgust, and of the first importation of them as '*that pestiferous crew of the Mayflower.*'"[44] The Georgia Congressman Howell Cobb, a founder of the Confederacy and a lieutenant general in the Army of Northern Virginia, announced that the only things preventing a reunion of the North and the South were "the landing of the Pilgrims and original sin."[45] Also in 1863, the Confederacy's secretary of state, Judah Benjamin, impugned "the detestable Puritan spirit which sowed the first seeds of disunion, which originated this savage war."[46] Likewise, the Confederate naval commander Raphael Semmes declared that "this wicked and ruthless war" was caused by "the folly, fanaticism, wickedness and want of principle, developed by this war among the Puritan population of the North. And in this class may nine-tenths of the native population of the Northern States be placed, to such an extent has the 'Plymouth Rock' leaven 'leavened the whole lump.'"[47] The New York Copperhead Fernando Wood said in an anti-war speech that "the landing of the Mayflower at Plymouth Rock was a *curse* second only to the fall of Adam" and that the Puritans were "rebels guilty of every atrocity in their own land."[48]

Jibes at Puritanism also appeared in popular songs and poems. This song by "an Alabaman," sung to the tune of "Yankee Doodle," said of Northerners:

> They've been the pest of all the world,
> Since Cromwell's bloody days;
> From Holland's quagmires they were hurled,
> For their pragmatic ways.

The Mayflower ship, that brought them o'er,
Conveyed a felon flock,
And spewed the vermin on the shore,
By Plymouth's "blarney rock."
Then curse the Puritanic crew,
The ranting, canting, Yankee-doodle-doo![49]

In "Ballad of the Cavaliers" (1862), the Richmond author John W. Overall derided lowly Northern Puritans. The song opens by boasting that "the gallant Cavaliers" are "no race of fear," and now "the Roundhead quails again / Before the better blood." Other verses call Northerners the "hireling race" that "springs from Plymouth Rock / . . . Cromwell's cant is on their tongue, / And Mather's in their face!" The Civil War, Overall writes, is merely the revival of the old confrontation:

The Cavalier! The Puritan!
Why, since the world began,
Was not the mean, the base, the false,
Scorned by the gentleman?[50]

## THE ANTISLAVERY ARGUMENT

Antislavery spokesmen replied that the proslavery side was exactly wrong; it used the right terms but reversed their meaning. Yes, the basic conflict was between liberty, on the one hand, and despotism and anarchy on the other. But for the antislavery side, liberty meant freedom for enslaved people, not the freedom of independent states to spread slavery. For the South, despotism meant the North's moralistic meddling in slavery; for the North, despotism meant the slave power, which held some four million people in bondage and had taken over the government, law, and commerce. Anarchy, from the antislavery standpoint, had nothing to do with Northern "isms" but rather with the lawlessness of the South, a violent society where each plantation was virtually its own fiefdom, with its own regulations and modes of discipline.

These points were made most fully in a book that came out early in the Civil War, *The True Story of the Barons of the South: Or, The Rationale of the American Conflict* (1862), by the Universalist minister and popular author Elhanan Winchester Reynolds. The book was widely advertised and was hailed as "full of life, of vigor, enthusiasm, in favor of the cause of human freedom" and "written by a fresh original thinker, spirited and free."[51] William Lloyd Garrison reprinted in *The Liberator* long passages of what he called Reynolds's "admirable and widely-praised work."[52]

The excitement was over Reynolds's detailed probing of the history of the North-South divide. Like many antislavery writers, Reynolds begins his story with the two ships. "The germ of the momentous conflict in which the nation is now engaged," he writes, was "when, in the eventful year of 1620, the ocean bore on its turbulent bosom a band of Puritans to Massachusetts and a cargo of negroes to Virginia," depositing "on our soil two hostile elements,—the seeds of two rival social systems,—the story of whose growth and expansion, of whose competitions and aggressions, forms the distinctive history of this Republic, down to this day."[53]

The New England Puritans, Reynolds adds, left "a sturdy brotherhood in England, who overturned the throne of Charles I, reared a Commonwealth out of the chaos of civil war, and engendered among the English people a republican spirit."[54] In contrast, "The Cavaliers who settled in Virginia" were from "that effeminate and supercilious nobility that drew its lance in behalf of the oppressive Stuarts" and "resisted with such virulent hostility the spirit of political reform marshalled under Cromwell and William of Orange." The two parties were "the representatives of liberty and oppression." In America, the opposing groups engendered "REPUBLICAN SOCIETY" in the North and "DESPOTIC SOCIETY" controlled by the "Barons of the South." (Reynolds uses the word "barons" interchangeably with "Cavaliers," as John Adams had done in 1776 when he referred to the "Barons of the South."[55]) The republican spirit, cultivated under Puritanism and fired by resistance to England, nurtured antislavery sentiment in the North and even in parts of the South.

This antislavery surge, Reynolds notes, was stimulated by two New England clergymen, Samuel Hopkins and Jonathan Edwards Jr. Hopkins's 1776 tract *A Dialogue Concerning the Slavery of the Africans*, Reynolds notes, "was circulated extensively during the Revolutionary period, and is 'known to have produced a powerful impression upon the minds of reflecting men,'" including "WASHINGTON, JEFFERSON, FRANKLIN, and others."[56] Edwards's 1791 sermon *The Injustice and Impolicy of the Slave Trade, and of the Slavery of the Africans* owed its "boldness and pungency" to its argument that slaveholders were guilty of the biblical crime of man-stealing and that the criminality would cease only with the termination of slavery.

Puritan-inspired republicanism, Reynolds maintained, lay behind the Declaration of Independence, the Northwest Ordinance (which banned slavery in territory northwest of the Ohio River), and the Constitution, which Reynolds, like Frederick Douglass and Lincoln, saw as fundamentally antislavery in spirit, despite its concessions to the South. Churches caught the republican fever. The Methodists, Presbyterians, Congregationalists, and Quakers issued statements against slavery. However, a tremendous regression followed. The churches in time split over slavery, with large branches supporting the South. Roman Catholics, on the whole, tolerated or endorsed slavery, while Jews, who began to arrive in number in the 1840s and '50s, were divided on it. "The subjugation of the Church," Reynolds wrote, "may be esteemed the crowning evidence of the submission of the country to the DESPOTIC SYSTEM."

The plantation economy empowered "the slave-capitalists," who became "not simply one class in the slave-holding States" but "the DOMINANT CLASS."[57] If the "despotic" slaveholder's "arbitrary will or changing caprice" is resisted, he appeals to violence. He tortures his slaves, and in personal disputes "he relies on the bowie-knife and revolver, instead of the magistrate, to enforce his supposed rights. Thus society in all the slaveholding States gravitates toward anarchy."

Proslavery laws and proslavery interpretations of the Constitution, Reynolds recounts, led abolitionists like Garrison to abandon the avenues of the church and the government; hence their nickname—come-outers. Antislavery politics, in the form of the Liberty and Free Soil Parties, faltered, until the Republican Party won the presidency with its antislavery agenda. The chasm between the North and the South was now unbridgeable. The two sections, Reynolds wrote, "MUST CONFLICT; THEY MUST QUARREL;—and what God and Nature have thus made hostile we cannot join together in harmony."[58] Reynolds observed that the old cultural divide between Puritans and Cavaliers had evolved into a conflict between human freedom and slavery. Reynolds asserts, "Slavery and freedom can never be married so long as hell is alien to heaven. Their characters and tendencies, their aims and desires, are completely hostile." Civil war was a stern necessity.

What made Reynolds's antislavery history unusual was its length. During the war, most antislavery references to the two ships or the Puritans vs. the Cavaliers typically appeared as passages in speeches, articles, or poems. In a Forefathers' Day sermon in Concord, New Hampshire, in December 1861, the Unitarian preacher Liberty Billings, while conceding that the Pilgrims had "their faults and superstitions," asserted that "their landing at Plymouth was the greatest event of the last thousand years." The current war was "the old contest between the Cavaliers and Roundheads renewed. As the head of the king was lopped off in the former contest, so must slavery, a worse tyrant, be destroyed in this."[59]

The Union general Lew Wallace (who later wrote the biblical bestseller *Ben-Hur*) in 1863 penned a widely reprinted poem, "The Stolen Stars," in which he vilified Southern Cavaliers for destroying the Union. Originally, Wallace noted, the American flag had thirteen stars. That number grew to thirty-four, and the flag was honored by the two brothers who lived under it:

> To both 't was very dear;
> The name of one was Puritan;
> The other Cavalier.

But disagreement arose between the Cavalier, a Southern aristocrat, and the Puritan, who lived in the North. A crime occurred when the Cavalier stole eleven of the stars. Now the Puritan has sent "a million Northern boys" to fetch the pilfered stars.[60]

Frederick Douglass again used his favorite historical trope, the two ships, to stir enthusiasm for military service among African Americans. In July 1863, at a standing-room-only event at a large hall in Chester, Pennsylvania, Douglass called for Black enlistment in the Union Army by sketching "the history of the growth and aggressions of slavery from the time when the Mayflower landed at Plymouth Rock with her precious freight of honest, God-fearing and God-loving pilgrims; and a Dutch galliot landed on the Virginia coast, with a few piratical scoundrels and their slaves, down to the beginning of the present rebellion."[61] The two ships were also useful for Northern women who wanted to express their support for Lincoln's war effort. A May 1863 women's rights convention in Chicago led by Elizabeth Cady Stanton, Susan B. Anthony, and Angelina Grimké Weld issued an "Address" to women and Union soldiers that said the Civil War "began in 1620, when the Mayflower landed our fathers on Plymouth Rock, and the first slave-ship landed its human cargo in Virginia. Then, for the first time, liberty and slavery stood face to face on this continent. From then till now these antagonisms have struggled in incessant conflict."[62]

The two ships became a factor in the 1864 presidential race between the incumbent Lincoln, running under the newly formed National Union Party, and the Democratic candidate George B. McClellan. McClellan thought that the aim of the war should be to restore the Union, not to emancipate the enslaved. Lincoln increasingly insisted on emancipation as the goal of the war. Copperhead newspapers in the North promoted the Democratic agenda and rallied behind McClellan when he became the party's candidate in August. One of the papers, the New York *Journal of Commerce*, was edited by William Cowper Prime, a longtime friend of McClellan and a foe of Lincoln. Supportive of slavery and secession, the *Journal of Commerce* was suspended by the Lincoln administration in 1861 for publishing pro-Confederate articles. It faced a second, brief suspension in May 1864 after reprinting a bogus presidential proclamation, originally published by another paper, that falsely claimed Lincoln had called up four hundred thousand troops—a scam meant to create mass panic, disrupt the economy, and enrich gold speculators.

Prime saw a chance to boost the Democratic Party by trashing the popular antislavery narrative of the two ships. His *Journal of Commerce* ridiculed the two-ships story as Senator Charles Sumner had told it in December 1863. In a note to the New England Society of New York, Sumner had said that despite "all the sorrows" of the war, it was in "the spirit in which New England was first founded that we are now resisting the bloody efforts to raise a wicked power on the corner-stone of Human Slavery." If "such a wicked power" as slavery were allowed to remain in America, "the Mayflower crossed its wintry sea in vain." Northerners must recall that "a Dutch ship, with twenty slaves, who were landed at Jamestown, in Virginia," had "crossed at the same time, buffeting the same sea" that "bore to the Western Continent, the Pilgrim Fathers, consecrated to Human Liberty." Sumner declared: "In the holds of those two ships were concealed the germs of the present direful war, and the simple question now is between the Mayflower and the slave ship. Who that has not forgotten God can doubt the result? The Mayflower must surely prevail."[63]

This story had long motivated antislavery Northerners by giving them pride in their history. The Copperhead Prime wanted to kill the story once and for all. He printed an article in the *Journal of Commerce* that called the two-ships tale "arrant twaddle," "pure nonsense."[64] Then came a slap at the senatorial *Mayflower* descendant: "Mr. Sumner has made a foolish exhibition of his ignorance of New England history." The *Mayflower*, the article said, was in no sense "an anti-slavery society," as Sumner had suggested. The ship's passengers believed in liberty no more than the British monarchs they had fled from. They wanted the freedom not only to practice their own religion but to force it on others. Far from objecting to slavery, they enslaved both Native Americans and Black people brought from the West Indies. Indeed, "The slavery, spiritual and physical, of soul and body, of white man, and red man, and black man, which they established, has no parallel in history."

This blast at the two ships was reprinted around the nation. It prompted a powerful—and largely accurate—rejoinder in the abolitionist newspaper the *Boston Morning Journal*: "A broader libel upon the Pilgrims was never uttered, and it is only palliated by the ignorance which our New York contemporary displays in proof. . . . The writer evidently does not draw a distinction between the pilgrims of the Plymouth colony and their more intolerant Puritan neighbors of the colony of Massachusetts Bay." The Plymouth settlers "did not persecute Quakers and Baptists, or burn witches." Actually, "the legislation of the Plymouth colony was remarkably liberal and tolerant for the age, and, so far as is known, slavery never obtained a foothold there."[65]

The storm in the press did not change Charles Sumner's opinion.

He again spotlighted the two ships in a major speech he gave at New York's Cooper Union on Saturday, November 5, 1864, three days before the presidential election. More than two thousand people showed up at the event, which was chaired by the Columbia political scientist Francis Lieber, who sat on a platform along with other dignitaries behind Sumner as he spoke. In a campaign speech of such importance, one might have expected Sumner to weigh the qualifications of Lincoln against those of his opponent, McClellan. Instead, he discussed what the two candidates stood for: "Slavery and Liberty."[66] He took his audience "back to the distant origin of the two elemental forces, which are now in deadly conflict." He described the *Mayflower* passengers and the enslaved people on the Jamestown ship. He declared: "Those two cargoes contained the hostile germs, which have ripened in our time. . . . On the one side is the slave-ship, and on the other is the May-Flower." He added, "Look at the early social life of the two warring sections, and you will see the influence of these two ships." Slavery spread in the South but not in the North, which was settled by "that grand Puritan stock, to which, according to the reluctant confession of Hume, 'the English were indebted for the whole freedom of their Constitution.'"

The first English settlers of the South, he continued, were not Cavaliers. "It is a common boast of our slave-masters," he asserted, "that they constitute a modern 'chivalry,' derived from the 'cavaliers' of England and reinforced by the ennobling influences of African Slavery."[67] Not so, Sumner said. Leaving unmentioned the later settlement of Virginia by Cavaliers who escaped Cromwell, he argued that the earliest settlers were "men of distempered bodies and infected minds" whom James I had exiled to Virginia. He noted that the Virginia leader John Smith characterized those immigrants as "*vagabond and condemned men*." Sumner pointed out, "Surely there is nothing here out of which to construct a 'cavalier.'" He said that the Union armies, "now fighting the world's greatest battle for Human Rights, may not be called Roundheads: but I'm sure that the rebels, now fighting for Slavery, cannot be called 'cavaliers' in any sense. . . . Slavery was vulgar, brutal, savage, while its braggart orators and chaplains heralded its claims." As for the current election, Sumner said if you looked at "the Chicago platform or candidate [McClellan]" you are "brought back to Slavery as the animating impulse." If you look at "the Baltimore platform or candidate [Lincoln]" you find "Liberty." Sumner concluded, "And thus again Slavery and Liberty stand face to face—the slave-ship against the May-Flower."

The fact that Sumner, one of the era's pioneers of civil rights, would, on the eve of a major election, attend so carefully to the two ships and the Puritan-vs.-Cavalier division shows just how significant these historical symbols had become to many Northerners.

Significant to them. But how about to their president? Lincoln's mind ran in a very different direction—away from Plymouth, Jamestown, Puritans, and Cavaliers and toward a unified nation that he proclaimed was on the verge of a new birth of freedom.

## LINCOLN REJECTS THE TWO SHIPS

Lincoln was aware of the cultural war between the North and the South, which was a topic of discussion during his administration. In July 1862, his secretary and publicist John Hay described the historical background of the Civil War in a Washington newspaper:

> The old English contest between the Puritans and the Cavaliers is being waged on this Western continent. The descendants of the "first families of Virginia" should remember that their bragged ancestors thought themselves invincible, and boasted of their high qualities as English Cavaliers, until Cromwell's puritanical hosts taught them a lesson that never should have been forgotten.[68]

But Lincoln wanted to shift public opinion away from polarization toward national unity. Despite his efforts, he was widely considered divisive. Ironically, he was charged with being both a despotic King Charles and a disruptive Puritan. The Copperhead editor Manton Marble, reacting to Lincoln's brief shuttering of the *New York World*, disparaged the president as a tyrannical Charles I, who was guilty of "crimes by which he lost his crown and life."[69] Those who considered Lincoln a moral policeman, on the other hand, equated him with aggressive Puritans of the "Mayflower breed."[70]

For Lincoln's supporters, however, his Puritan characteristics contributed to his greatness. The Salem minister George W. Briggs noted that the difference between Lincoln and Davis was the contrast between "the Puritan and the Cavalier . . . the one losing all the sternness of the Puritan, but retaining all his faith and heroism, all that made up his consecrated greatness; the other, observing all the formalities of liturgies, but imperious in will, scorning, trampling upon the lowly in his indomitable pride."[71]

The association of Lincoln with Puritanism actually had substance. In the tradition of Lyman Beecher and the Benevolent Empire, Lincoln promoted the distribution of mass-produced religious literature. He especially encouraged the work of the United States Christian Commission, which, under the leadership of the Philadelphia philanthropist George H. Stuart, disseminated some 1.5 million free Bibles, eighteen million copies of religious newspapers, and eight million religious tracts among Union Army and Navy personnel.[72] One of the works was a reprint of Oliver Cromwell's 1643 *Soldiers' Pocket Bible*, the small, portable pamphlet of biblical passages. George Stuart reported that when he showed Lincoln a copy of the Cromwell Bible at the White House, the president "seemed so interested in its distribution that he arose from his seat and thanked me for presenting him with it."[73] The American Tract Society published a facsimile edition of the Cromwell Bible in late 1861. By early 1862, more than 50,000 copies, along with religious tracts and regular Bibles, had been distributed to Union soldiers. Amply equipped with religious literature, Union soldiers may have felt that they were supported by God, like Cromwell's New Model Army. One commentator noted, "The Union soldiers were often compared to the famous 'Ironsides' of Cromwell. The comparison was natural."[74]

Another strategy reminiscent of Puritanism was Lincoln's religious proclamations—national calls to prayer, fasting, and thanksgiving. In the course of the war, he issued eight or nine such proclamations—more than any previous president. His proclamations often adopted Calvinistic language, stressing national sinfulness and the need for repentance before a sovereign God. That language had been circulating for a while. For example, Harriet Beecher Stowe concluded her 1852 novel, *Uncle Tom's Cabin*, by writing that America stood "guilty before God," and the nation could be saved from "the wrath of Almighty God" only through "repentance, justice and mercy."[75] John Brown, likewise, declared that God would punish "the crimes of this *guilty, land*."[76] In 1861, a group of Illinois ministers wrote Lincoln saying that history's best fighting force was the "invincible regiment of 'the Ironsides' led by Oliver Cromwell, composed of godly men." Pledging their support "in the spirit of our Puritan ancestors, who preserved English liberty," the ministers called the Civil War "a heavy but just judgment from the hand of God for our national sins."[77]

Lincoln ushered religion into the public arena in other ways during the war. After persistent requests from his pious treasury secretary, Salmon Chase, he approved having the phrase IN GOD WE TRUST imprinted on American coins.[78] He also mentioned God in the Emancipation Proclamation, the Gettysburg Address, his second inaugural address, and other important products of his pen. Although he was never a church member, he knew the Bible so well that he often quoted from it in conversations and speeches.

His most important effort to point Puritan customs toward the union of all Americans was his nationalization of Thanksgiving in 1863. Ever since the Pilgrims celebrated their first harvest festival in the fall of 1621, Thanksgiving had been associated with New England. Over the years, it was celebrated on different fall dates in different states, mainly Northern ones. Sarah Josepha Hale, the editor of the popular magazine *Godey's Lady's Book*, started calling in the 1840s for national holidays that would unite all Americans. She specified, for example, that Thanksgiving should be celebrated annually on the last Thursday in November. She became more and more insistent as she witnessed the widening rift over slavery. When division led to civil war, Hale wrote a letter to President Lincoln, emphasizing the urgency of making Thanksgiving "*a National and fixed Union Festival*" that would offer healing to a torn nation. She told him that by announcing "this Union Thanksgiving," the president could ensure that "the permanency and unity of our Great American Festival of Thanksgiving would be forever secured."[79]

On October 3, 1863, shortly after receiving Hale's letter, Lincoln declared the last Thursday of November as the day when God would be thanked "as with one heart and one voice by the whole American People," including "my fellow citizens in every part of the United States, and also those who are at sea and those who are sojourning in foreign lands." Lincoln asked for "the Almighty Hand to heal the wounds of the nation and to restore it, as soon as may be consistent with the Divine purposes, to the full enjoyment of peace, harmony, tranquility and Union."[80]

Lincoln's attempt to unify the nation culturally by nationalizing Thanksgiving was hailed by a Massachusetts paper: "Thus the old Puritan festival, so long restricted to the narrow circuit of New England, and derided by the self-styled cavaliers of the South as a relic of early conceit and bigotry, takes on, in this eventful and memorable year and for the first time in our history, a national character."[81] Lincoln's authorization of Thanksgiving led *The New York Times* to remark: "The custom of the New-England Pilgrims, at first confined to a few States, has at last . . . assumed the scope and standing of a grand national holiday, which, it is hoped, will be permanently and universally observed."[82] The federally authorized Thanksgiving held on the last Thursday in November became a national tradition, and Franklin D. Roosevelt established it as an official American holiday in 1941.

The striking breadth of Lincoln's Thanksgiving proclamation becomes clear when we compare it with a more typical holiday pronouncement that fall—a Thanksgiving sermon by the Baptist preacher John N. Murdock of Brookline, Massachusetts. Following the lead of many others, Murdock described "two forms of civilization" at the source of America. "Jamestown and Plymouth represented on these shores the antagonistic principles of Cavalier and Roundhead." The Cavalier brought the "ideas of prescription and caste . . . aristocracy and absolutism" that had been inbred "from the time of the Norman conquest." In contrast, "The Puritan brought with him those ideas of individual freedom and equality" that contained "the germs of our Republican life."[83] The "aristocratic and democratic elements" were "cherished by the descendants of the Cavaliers against the descendants of the Puritans" until "opposition to slavery was stigmatized as the old Puritan fanaticism." This brought on the Civil War . . . and more of the same.

In addition to nationalizing Thanksgiving, Lincoln delivered the Gettysburg Address in the fall of 1863, which refashioned another cultural strand with a Puritan background: egalitarianism. We saw that an egalitarian current appeared among thinkers influenced by the English Civil War, such as the Leveller John Lilburne (with his 1647 statement that all humans are "by nature all equall and alike in power, dignity, authority, and majesty") and the philosopher John Locke (who in 1689 affirmed the "equality of Men by Nature").[84] These ideas reached a soaring culmination in Jefferson's words "all men are created equal" in the preamble to the Declaration of Independence, which Lincoln called "my ancient faith."[85]

In his 272-word Gettysburg speech, Lincoln left out Puritans, Cavaliers, New England, Virginia, and the other standard references. Instead, he amplified the progressive essence of Puritan thought, à la Lilburne and Locke, as it had been applied to America in 1776 by Jefferson. Lincoln opened, "Four score and seven years ago our fathers brought forth, upon this continent, a new nation, conceived in liberty, and dedicated to the proposition that 'all men are created equal.'"[86] Lincoln was emphasizing that the nation's true founding date was not 1619 or 1620. It was 1776: "four score and seven years" before 1863. The "fathers" here were neither the *Mayflower* "forefathers" nor the early settlers of Virginia but the Founding Fathers. The famous ending of the address combined a paean to democracy as established by the Constitution with a Puritan-like mention of God and an affirmation of national union. Lincoln said that "the great task remaining before us" was to see "that this nation, under God, shall have a new birth of freedom, and that, government of the people, by the people, for the people, shall not perish from the earth."

That Lincoln had advanced well beyond the popular *Mayflower*–slave ship controversy became clear in December 1864, when the Manhattan lawyer Joseph H. Choate invited him to a celebration of Forefathers' Day held by the New England Society of New York. Declining Choate's invitation, Lincoln put the Pilgrims in the past. He pointed out that America's current goals were far nobler than theirs. "The work of the Plymouth emigrants," Lincoln wrote, "was the glory of their age. While we reverence their memory, let us not forget how vastly greater is our opportunity."[87]

Vastly greater indeed. In his second inaugural address, delivered on March 4, 1865, Lincoln directed his full oratorical energy against slavery. Consisting of a mere 701 words that took about seven minutes to deliver, the second inaugural contains fourteen references to God (including God-related pronouns and synonyms), three invocations of prayer, and four quoted or paraphrased Bible passages. The South had often defended slavery by citing the Bible, but Lincoln reversed the argument and declared that a just God stood against the sin of slavery. Without mentioning the Puritan-vs.-Cavalier conflict, he suggested that the cultural war, along with other factors like states' rights, did not cause the Civil War. Slavery did. And the North had divine support in its abolitionist war—a war that must continue, he said, "until all the wealth piled by the bond-man's two hundred and fifty years of unrequited toil shall be sunk, and until every drop of blood drawn with the lash, shall be paid by another drawn with the sword."[88]

Lincoln's righteous firmness, laced with piety, was reminiscent of militant Calvinism. One critic called the speech "a prose parody of 'John Brown's Hymn'" (referring to "John Brown's Body," the Union's favorite marching song and an homage to the abolitionist martyr).[89] *The New York Times*, referring to the Puritan revolutionary whom Brown emulated, described a common response to the second inaugural: "Many pronounced it a Cromwellian speech, but it had one peculiarity, which CROMWELL's speeches never possessed—a tone of perfect kindness and good-will to all, whether enemies or political opponents."[90]

The kindness and goodwill came through in Lincoln's embrace of all Americans. The speech's most famous line—"With malice toward none, with charity for all"—embraced, in its sweep, Americans of different regions, ethnicities, and faiths. Lincoln wanted his nation not only to leave slavery behind but to overcome sectional and racial hostility as well.

Time proved that his first goal was reached. Slavery was abolished when the states finished ratifying the Thirteenth Amendment in December 1865. His second goal—the end of sectionalism and racial discrimination—proved much harder to achieve. Lincoln got a glimpse of forthcoming complications when he dealt with Southern leaders before the war's end. Jefferson Davis, through an emissary, offered to negotiate "with a view to secure peace to the two countries."[91] Lincoln rejected the offer, saying he would discuss ways of "securing peace to the people of our one common country."[92]

Because of his firm insistence on a restored Union without slavery, Lincoln still seemed like a tyrant to his opponents, who compared him with a Stuart king. In his meeting with Confederates at Hampton Roads, Virginia, in February 1865, one of the Southerners, R. M. T. Hunter, tried to make the Confederate case by citing the English Civil War, when King Charles I had agreed to negotiate with the Puritan rebels who had taken up arms against him. Why couldn't Lincoln do the same? The president replied, "Upon questions of history I must refer you to Mr. Seward, for he is posted in such things, and I don't pretend to be bright. My only distinct recollection of the matter is that Charles lost his head."[93]

The quip about Charles's beheading, typical of Lincoln's dark humor, cloaked a serious issue that would soon lead to the president's murder. John Wilkes Booth, a twenty-six-year-old actor, had played stage roles of rebels who assassinated monarchs. Booth had been plotting to kill Lincoln for more than a year. When Lincoln was reelected in November 1864, Booth grumbled that the president was "making himself a king"; his new term "will be a reign."[94] Booth, a Maryland native who believed slavery was beneficial to both Blacks and whites, loathed what he considered Lincoln's radicalism on race. On April 11, 1865, Booth stood in the crowd outside the White House as Lincoln, speaking from a window, publicly endorsed Black suffrage for the first time by any American president. Booth muttered to a friend, "That means nigger citizenship. Now, by God! I'll put him through."[95] Three days later, in Washington's Ford's Theatre, he shot Lincoln and escaped through a back door. As he fled south, he wrote in his diary that he felt like a heroic regicide. He scribbled notes in his diary about brave king-killers he had played onstage, boasting that his action was "purer" than theirs.[96] After a twelve-day manhunt, when he was surrounded and killed in a Virginia barn, he died groaning, "Useless, useless."

His killing of Lincoln was more useless than he could have imagined. He had planned to murder not only the president but, with co-conspirators acting on the same evening, Vice President Andrew Johnson and Secretary of State William Seward as well. His fellow plotters had failed, and in the end four people were hanged and four others imprisoned for Booth's scheme. He had evidently wanted to produce anarchy by getting rid of Lincoln and two key members of his administration. Instead of anarchy, he produced unforeseen national unity. Only hours before he was killed, Lincoln had written a political associate that he wanted to create "a Union of hearts and hands as well as of States."[97] Through a tragic irony, his assassination that evening came closer to producing union than anything up to that point. The poet Walt Whitman, who would often give his lecture "The Death of President Lincoln" in the decades after the Civil War, wrote that the "final use of a heroic-eminent life—especially of a heroic-eminent death—is its indirect filtering into the nation and the race, and to give . . . a cement to the whole people, subtler, more underlying, than anything in written constitution, or courts or armies."[98] Lincoln's death, Whitman believed, had that unifying effect. To some degree he was right. Lincoln's death elicited grief throughout the nation, even among many stunned Southerners. Over time the assassination contributed to Lincoln hagiography. Although his greatness as president is now clearly established, regardless of myth or legend, the circumstances of his death have enshrined him in a special way, making him one of America's most revered political figures, attractive to people on both sides of the political spectrum.

Despite the temporary national cohesion created by sorrow over the murder of the president, the sectional division that had underlain the Civil War remained. Lincoln's vision of "a Union of hearts and hands" proved to be less realistic than Jefferson Davis's remark in an 1864 interview: "There are essential differences between the North and the South that will, however this war may end, make them two nations."[99]

The war ended with the South defeated, impoverished, and in ruins, with its major cities destroyed, its agricultural fields ravaged, and its railroads torn up. The proslavery side was left anathemizing Puritans and the *Mayflower.* In April 1865, a speaker at a meeting in New York of the Anti-Abolition State Rights Society said that "never was a sect more intolerant" than "the Puritans [who] came to this country." He added, "Had the Mayflower never reached the shores of America, had she found a fit resting place amid the depths of the ocean, we might have been spared the sad and humiliating sight of brothers arrayed in deadly conflict."[100] The humiliation was too much for the Virginia planter Edmund Ruffin. One of the original secessionists, Ruffin had witnessed the execution of John Brown, fired one of the first shots at Fort Sumter, and called Northerners "the vilest & most malignant people & government in Christendom."[101] He was outraged that Lincoln, the "vulgar buffoon," would be "ennobled & glorified" by assassination. Three months later, the seventy-one-year-old Ruffin, in his final diary entry, vowed "unmitigated hatred . . . to the perfidious, malignant, & vile Yankee race." On June 17, 1865, in an upstairs room at his son's plantation, he wrapped himself in a Confederate flag, propped his musket between his feet, and put the muzzle in his mouth. He pulled the trigger with a forked stick, but the rifle failed to fire. He tried a second time and succeeded in blowing his brains out.[102]

In the meantime, the antislavery side boasted about what it called the success of the *Mayflower* and Plymouth Colony. In the final months of the war, the influential Brooklyn preacher Theodore L. Cuyler announced, "The stupendous conflict now raging is the closing up of the two hundred years of antagonism between Jamestown and Plymouth Rock. . . . These two vessels contained the germs of the contending systems of civilization."[103] He continued, "The organic life of Plymouth Rock lives today; nay, it was never more vigorous than now. Miles Standish lives to-day in the silent adamantine Grant. Elder Brewster works to-day in the 'Christian Commission.'" Cuyler connected Lincoln with Plymouth and Davis with Jamestown. He described "a few of the radical differences between Plymouth Rock, led by Abraham Lincoln, and Jamestown, marshalled for its forlorn fight by Jefferson Davis and his oligarchy." Plymouth was "a Christian democracy" associated with free labor, justice, and "*might* and *right*." Jamestown had given rise to "a feudal aristocracy, in which one insolent section of society *owned* the ignorant remainder." It stood for slavery, secession, anarchy, "the lazy luxury of the plantation, and the barbarism of the bowie knife." In the war between these forces, Cuyler asked, "Who can doubt the final result? Who fears that Jamestown can vanquish Plymouth Rock?"

The questions were answered when Lee surrendered to Grant at Appomattox in April 1865. The Massachusetts politician James T. Robinson gave a triumphant speech in which he invoked the two ships and the Cromwellian Revolution:

> The Slave Ship yields to the May Flower. Plymouth conquers Jamestown. The Barbarism of the Plantation kneels to the Christian civilization of the Puritans. Once again the Cavalier flies before the Puritan, as his ancestors, two hundred years ago before, on the fields of Marston Moors and Nasby, showed their silken backs to Cromwell. The trial and test of two hundred years are over.[104]

The West Virginia Methodist preacher Ashford Hall gave a lively version of the two-ships story in a Fourth of July oration in which he imagined Jamestown and Plymouth Rock as two men who quarreled when they first met. Hall said:

> Plymouth Rock claimed the right to speak. "All men are created equal. They are endowed with certain inalienable rights.

> Among them are life, liberty, and the pursuit of happiness."
> "Silence!" cried Jamestown. "Not a moment," cried Plymouth Rock. "Shut up or I'll make you," demanded Jamestown.

The men came to blows and finally waged war against each other. The outcome was inevitable, according to Hall. He asserted, "Plymouth Rock has outstripped, outwitted, outargued, outvoted, outgeneraled and outfought her rival—overpowered him—killed him."[105]

The North's exuberance did not let up. A Vermont paper crowed, "The Mayflower and the slave ship have met in hostile combat. The contest has been long and severe. . . . The slave ship has foundered. The Mayflower floats in triumph."[106] At a December 1865 Forefathers' Day celebration, the Unitarian minister Charles C. Everett said that not long before "the Mayflower reached Plymouth, with its freight of Liberty, came, like a dark shadow, the first slave ship to Jamestown. From these two germs spring two powers, one of light and one of darkness, one of order and one of chaos. . . . Now at last we can hail Fore Fathers day, with the welcome greeting of final triumph. The Puritan has conquered the Cavalier. . . . Plymouth Rock is becoming the center, Forefathers day the anniversary, of the whole nation. The Puritan is supreme. And it is the Puritan principles that are to be the cement and the guarantee of our new Union."[107]

Were Puritan principles really now in control? Had Plymouth Rock and Forefathers' Day become central factors of American life?

In the short term, to a large degree, yes. What were then regarded as *Mayflower* values took control early in the Reconstruction era. But when Reconstruction collapsed, the spirit of reconciliation won the day. Efforts were made to bury the hostilities of the past and create the union of hearts Lincoln had envisaged. But that union became disconnected with the central ideal he said he would willingly die for: the nation's recognition of human equality.

*Chapter Eleven*

# Reconstruction Wars and Compromise

The Thirty-Ninth Congress, the first to meet after Lincoln's assassination, convened on December 4, 1865. Two days later, the Thirteenth Amendment, which abolished slavery, completed ratification by the states and became part of the Constitution. With the Civil War over and chattel slavery abolished, progressive winds were blowing. The Thirty-Ninth and Fortieth Congresses, dominated by Radical Republicans, enacted a series of landmark measures. The Freedmen's Bureau, first established in 1865 and renewed in 1866, provided food, legal aid, medical care, and education to formerly enslaved people as well as to impoverished whites. The Civil Rights Act of 1866 affirmed birthright citizenship and guaranteed the equal benefit of laws regardless of race or color—principles soon enshrined in the Constitution through the Fourteenth and Fifteenth Amendments, ratified in 1868 and 1870. Military Reconstruction further advanced these reforms by dividing the South into five districts under Union generals, ensuring civil rights were enforced. With the ballot in their hands, newly enfranchised freedmen elected African Americans to state legislatures and, ultimately, sixteen to the US Congress, among them Hiram Revels of Mississippi, the first Black US senator, and Joseph Rainey of South Carolina, the first Black member of the House. Taken together, the Republicans' achievements were extraordinary—so much so that, in Eric Foner's words, Reconstruction amounted to the nation's "second founding."[1]

W. E. B. Du Bois describes Reconstruction as "a prolongation of Puritan idealism" after the Civil War; he points in particular to Senator Charles Sumner of Massachusetts, Representative Thaddeus Stevens of Pennsylvania, and the abolitionist firebrand Wendell Phillips.[2] The historian James M. McPherson associates the Freedmen's Bureau with the New Puritanism, the evangelical movement that had been producing missionary societies and other reform groups for decades under the Beechers and others.[3]

The decades-long debate over Puritanism fueled the discussion of civil rights during the Reconstruction era. Bitter ex-Confederates and their Democratic allies in the North accused the "Puritan Congress," as they called it, of trying to take over the South to bring about a racial reversal that would destroy white rule. Some conservatives called upon President Andrew Johnson, a white supremacist who clashed with the congressional Republicans, to take the extreme measure of using military force against Congress. The air buzzed with the complaint that the *Mayflower* was the original source of the nation's problems.

The aftermath of Radical Reconstruction brought reversals for African Americans. A violent Southern backlash resulted in the widespread disenfranchisement of Blacks. The Republican Party lost its activist edge, and Northerners grew weary of Reconstruction, which ended in 1877, when President Rutherford B. Hayes withdrew Northern troops from the South.

## THE NEW WAR AGAINST PURITANISM

Civil rights advocates held firm control of the Thirty-Ninth Congress, which consisted of 136 Republicans—including many Radicals—alongside 38 Democrats, 13 Unconditional Unionists, and 6 representatives from other parties.[4] A bicameral Joint Committee of Fifteen, headed by the Republicans Thaddeus Stevens of the House and William P. Fessenden of the Senate, was formed to discuss how the former Confederate states would be readmitted to the Union. It was decided that Congress would not recognize the eleven Southern states until each had reorganized its government and accepted the Fourteenth Amendment. Southerners stubbornly resisted the plan. Readmission to the Union was a slow process. Tennessee reentered in June 1866. Two years later, Arkansas joined, followed by the other Southern states, ending with Texas's readmission in March 1870.

In the meantime, the pro-Southern side complained that excluding representatives from the former Confederacy violated democratic principles. From this perspective, the situation recalled the English Civil War, when the limited Puritan Parliament known as the Rump took control of national affairs for a time. A Democratic newspaper raised alarms over the "Abolition Rump Congress," claiming it caused "an absolute subversion and abandonment of popular government" and brought about "consolidation, anarchy, and ruin."[5] Another commentator, noting that Congress resembled "the Puritan parliament in its fanatical frenzy and bigotry," asked, "What shall the white man do to rescue his race from subjugation to the negro?"[6] A New York newspaper similarly attacked the "radical 'Rump'" Congress, calling it full of "Puritan meddlers with slavery."[7]

The pro-Southerners' anger grew as Congress continually overrode Andrew Johnson's vetoes of its civil rights legislation. (All told, it overrode fifteen of the president's twenty-one vetoes.) Some Democrats went so far as to suggest that Johnson should use the army to expel Congress, just as Oliver Cromwell had done in 1653 when he ousted his Rump Parliament. *The Chicago Times* called for the incarceration of Republican leaders and ranted, "If the rump Congress shall not speedily abandon its seditious, revolutionary and lawless practices—if it shall persist in excluding the representatives from eleven states from their rightful seats, and in exercising the powers of the United States—we do not hesitate to declare that it will become the solemn duty of President Johnson to constitute himself the Cromwell of the time and dissolve the rump by military power."[8] The South Carolina author William Gilmore Simms called for "another CROMWELL to deal with the descendants of the same vile malignants, whom he so summarily dispatched to their proper quarters."[9]

It might seem strange that Southerners would praise Cromwell, who was seen as a Puritan hero by antislavery Northerners. But it was Cromwell the strong leader, not Cromwell the champion of freedom, whom the South admired. Cromwell, unhappy with the Rump Parliament, removed it. That's what conservatives imagined Andrew Johnson would do with Congress. If he did not act decisively, Democrats feared, the nation would be lost to radical Puritanism. One journalist wrote that if "the President concedes everything" to "the present Puritan Congress, . . . It means that the South and West must accept the Puritan's god, and the Puritan's code of morality—the Puritan's standards of education, and the Puritan's politics. In short, it means that the whole country must be Puritanized."[10]

Considering how inflammatory the Puritans and the *Mayflower* had become, it is understandable that congressional Republicans avoided referring to them. A case in point is Senator Charles Sumner. For years, Sumner had been using the two ships as a symbol of the divide over slavery. In his Reconstruction speeches, he made no mention at all of the ships and only passing mention of Puritanism. Instead, he argued for equal rights for whites and African Americans.

Two other civil rights leaders, Thaddeus Stevens and Wendell Phillips, also avoided referencing Puritanism. Stevens rarely used such references before Reconstruction and did not invoke them during that period. Even Wendell Phillips, whose speeches before the Civil War often highlighted seventeenth-century ancestors of abolition, now concentrated on programs for radical reform, including expanded voting rights, public education for Black people, and reparations he believed should be paid to the formerly enslaved.

Conservatives ignored the radicals' avoidance of Puritanism. The steamrolling of everything related to the Puritans, from the *Mayflower* through abolitionism, extended into Reconstruction. The fact that Charles Sumner now eschewed Puritan references was disregarded by the New York *Journal of Commerce*, which in May 1866 reprinted Sumner's 1863 Forefathers' Day letter on the antislavery meaning of the *Mayflower.* The *Journal of Commerce* ranted, "If Mr. Sumner had lived in Pilgrim times, that letter of his would have made him liable to sit in the stocks all day and be branded, if not to be banished or put to death" for his violation of statutes against "circulating false news, and misrepresenting the truth."[11]

Wendell Phillips, the popular orator who influenced congressional Republicans, was described by a Virginia writer as "the greatest ISM" to emerge from "the mess of Puritanism."[12] The Virginian remarked that Phillips, with his intense sympathy for the "poor Negro," "rules the Sumners, the John Browns, the Jim Lanes" and even "old Thad Stevens" and his "rugged plungings." Phillips, the Virginian continued, "is omnipotent, for he has Plymouth Rock, or a piece of it, in his heart, and the creed of its prophets on his tongue." He has "held fast hold to the traditions of Salem, to the police of Miles Standish, and to the creed of Cotton Mather. Whoever differs from him must be burnt," including "women and children." Comparing Phillips with the mythological devil Mephistopheles, the writer described the orator as "fiendish" and full of "malice," with puttyish skin, bristling sideburns, and eyes that were "a pair of sharp dots . . . icy and wicked, very wicked in expression."

The devil's supervision of the Republicans was a standard conservative trope. A pro-Southern paper commented that Republicans were "doing yeoman service to the Black, wooly-headed father of Abolitionism, the devil, who is the real father of puritanism."[13] *The New York Herald* asked, "Who was the first Puritan? Satan. . . . His name signifies the Adversary. That is Puritanism, in a word. Puritans are the adversaries wherever they are."[14] A Georgia newspaper reported that the devil was roaming the world in search of wicked people in many countries. The ones he feels most at home with—the most hellish—are the Radical Republicans in Congress, a pack of repulsive "skunks" who "came from the spawn of the Mayflower's crew: / That crew whose descendants are still most true / To their fashions, their tenets, and lies: / And their selfish and cruel schemes they still pursue / And their *Puritan hate never dies.*"[15] Another Democratic paper published a poem with the lines "*How happy would the world have been / Had whales but stove the Mayflower in.*" But the devil wanted to "save his chosen few" (the *Mayflower* passengers) so that they would be "his tools upon the earth," and they served him with their "deeds of mischief, fraud, and crime," including, through their Republican descendants, emancipating enslaved people, who would surely "sicken, starve, and die" in freedom.[16]

Sometimes Republicans replied forcefully. In an article titled "Two Ships," a Republican journalist denounced a Tammany Hall speaker who got "tremendous applause" when he declared at a Democratic rally: "I only regret that the ship that brought the Pilgrim Fathers to New England had not wrecked on Plymouth Rock."[17] In answer, the journalist told the story of the two ships: the *Mayflower* "brought, as part of her cargo, Human Freedom" and "civilization"; the Jamestown ship "brought Human Slavery" and "barbarism." The writer pointed out that "the two have fought, and civilization conquers." Now the

Democratic Party, whose epicenter was New York's corrupt Tammany Hall, wanted to take America back to an earlier era. The journalist explained, "When any ranting malignant talks about wrecking the Mayflower," he returns us to the period of "Cavaliers and slave drivers, aristocrats and caste-worshippers"—to the old "South, wasteful and wasted, cursed with slavery," far removed from "the love of freedom, the respect for law, the practical energy and grand ideas" of "that civilization that Plymouth Rock represents."

Despite such defenses of Plymouth's heritage, opposition to that legacy monopolized the popular press. As in the Civil War, the most strident opposition came from Catholics, Copperheads, and Confederates (now ex-Confederates). Catholics had long held a grudge against Puritans, which became outright animosity when some antislavery Republicans developed ties with anti-Catholic nativism. The two leading Catholic papers were *New-York Freeman's Journal and Catholic Register* and the *Metropolitan Record and New York Vindicator. Freeman's Journal* was edited by James McMaster, an archconservative who had been imprisoned for disloyalty during the Civil War and then attacked the "Puritan Congress" during Reconstruction. The *Metropolitan Record*, which boasted of being "THE LARGEST DEMOCRATIC WEEKLY," was run by the Irish immigrant John Mullaly, who complained in 1866 that "all the Federal offices [are] in the hands of puritanical Yankees"; he lamented, "From the landing of those intolerant people from the May Flower to the present day they have been trying to extend their principles over this continent."[18]

Ex-Confederates expressed similar hostility to New England and the *Mayflower.* A Memphis paper said the Freedmen's Bureau, with its Northern teachers conducting schools for African Americans, ignored a basic fact about Black people: "God ordained them as servants." The paper whined, "The mania of the New England puritanical fanatics is to *educate* the Negro. In that land of isms, this, like all other ideas of the Mayflower descendants, has become a regular, settled business";

this scheme "to educate the nigger" is "the widest and the wildest field under the auspices of Plymouth Rock."[19] The same paper elsewhere blasted Northerners who came South promoting "negro suffrage, negro equality, and the disenfranchisement of Southern white men," writing, "Ye gods! What impudence!"—explaining that such perverse actions could be done "only by a genuine descendant of the Mayflower."[20] A West Virginia journalist attacked a local politician who was "an amiable specimen of New Englandism—a descendant of that stock which was unfortunately vomited from the cargo of the Mayflower several hundred years ago—and whose pestilential seed, like that of the stink weed, has spread itself all over the face of creation."[21]

Copperhead papers were published throughout the North, including the Columbus, Ohio, *Crisis*, another paper harassed by the government during the war. In a typical Reconstruction editorial, *The Crisis* decried the "Puritan notions in regard to color and race" contained in the Civil Rights Act of 1866. The editorial argued that the bill displayed "the malignant determination of the fanatics of the Rump Congress" to destroy "the original foundations of our society" by lifting up "an inferior race, which, for time immemorial, has been held in servitude and subordination to white superiority."[22]

Among the most relentless critics of the Radical Republicans was John H. Van Evrie, the New York ethnologist and journalist whose theories about racial difference had informed the Confederacy. Van Evrie's newspaper, the *New York Day-Book*, had faced federal restrictions during the Civil War and later resumed publication. During Reconstruction, Van Evrie tried to be a one-man wrecking ball against emerging rights for Black people. Describing the American government as "foul and monstrous," Van Evrie wrote: "There is not a branch of it that escapes the moral virus which first emanated from puritanical New England, and has spread itself through almost every State in the Union."[23] That "moral virus" was a belief in human equality. Van Evrie branded whites who supported the advance of Blacks as "mongrelites."

In 1867, through the publishing house he ran with fellow Copperhead Rushmore G. Horton, Van Evrie issued a stream of Democratic works—books, pamphlets, newspapers, songbooks, and political cartoons—all designed to establish the inferiority of African Americans. Van Evrie revised and reissued his earlier book, *Negroes and Negro "Slavery,"* and expanded it, under the arresting title, *White Supremacy and Negro Subordination.* His firm also circulated a twenty-five-cent reprint of the Dred Scott decision (extolling it as "a land-mark in American civilization"), *Davis and Lee* (a retrospective defense of the Confederacy), *Anti-Abolition Tracts*, *The Copperhead Minstrel* ("A Choice Collection of Democratic Poems and Songs"), *The Mongrelites: Or, The Radicals—So Called. A Satiric Poem*, and Van Evrie's book *Subgenation*, a foray into scientific racism.[24] Another of the firm's publications, a magazine called *The Old Guard*, vied with the *Day-Book* for the dubious distinction of being the most racist periodical of the day. A regular column in *The Old Guard* was "Pen Pictures of Puritanism," in which negative portraits of early New Englanders and British Puritans were larded with racism. The column included statements like this: "The white man whose soul, and mind, and senses, are not perverted by the false teachings of Puritanism, feels an antipathy to the negro" which is "not prejudice" but rather "that repulsive antagonism to equality that exists between the ermine and the skunk."[25] Van Evrie's firm issued a 175-page pamphlet, *The Vision of Judgment*, a poem that described a pact between Satan and early New England Puritans, who were presented as ancestors of abolitionists.[26]

## THE LOST CAUSE, CAVALIERS, AND CONCILIATION

John Van Evrie also nurtured the Lost Cause—the South's romantic idealization of Confederates who had fought to defend states' rights and preserve the Old South, with its peculiar institution. The Lost Cause would gain nationwide appeal over time, particularly with the popularization of two blockbuster films: D. W. Griffith's *The Birth of a Nation* (1915) and David O. Selznick's *Gone With the Wind* (1939). Southern remembrance of the Civil War took its now-famous name from the title of Edward A. Pollard's 1866 book, *The Lost Cause: A New Southern History of the War of the Confederates*, a work circulated and endorsed by Van Evrie's firm. Another book that the firm promoted strongly, John Esten Cooke's *Wearing of the Gray*, revived the Cavalier myth and superimposed it on Confederate military figures. Pollard's and Cooke's books show that the Lost Cause had roots in the controversy over Puritanism.

Pollard, a lawyer-turned-journalist, was descended from an early Virginia family and was raised on a plantation worked by enslaved people. Imprisoned briefly for disloyal publications during the Civil War, Pollard defended the social order of the Old South. In *The Lost Cause*, he said that longstanding cultural differences between the North and South had caused the Civil War. This familiar notion was still in circulation when Pollard's book appeared. For instance, John Tyler Jr., the son of America's tenth president, gave a widely reported lecture, "Two Civilizations—Jamestown and Plymouth Rock," first in Williamsburg, Virginia, on July 4, 1866, and then in several other Southern venues over the next few years. The Puritans, Tyler declared, established "absolute and despotic rule" in New England, where they destroyed Native tribes, conducted the slave trade, and sold Africans to the South. In contrast, the Southern colonies were settled by "magnanimous" Cavaliers, the "beau ideal of all that was gentlemanly and refined in civilized or social life."[27]

Edward Pollard gave his own take on the two-civilizations idea in *The Lost Cause*, where he wrote, "There could be no congeniality between the Puritan exiles who established themselves upon the cold and rugged and cheerless soil of New England, and the Cavaliers who sought the brighter climate of the South, and drank in their baronial halls in Virginia confusion to roundheads and regicides." The Puritans, Pollard argued, were intolerant, penny-pinching, selfish, and moralizing. Southerners, in contrast, enjoyed a "feudal life" that "inculcated notions of chivalry, polished the manners and produced many noble and generous virtues." Holding Black people in bondage, Pollard wrote, was natural, because "the white is the superior race, and the Black the inferior; and subordination, with or without law, is the status of the African in this mixed society." Therefore, Pollard wrote, "Slavery established in the South a peculiar and noble type of civilization." Confederates had fought to restore that civilization, and Pollard in *The Lost Cause* glorified their efforts by emphasizing their battlefield successes while minimizing Northern ones.

John Esten Cooke did not just glorify Confederates; he made them Cavalier paragons. He worked from the same premise as Pollard: The North had little that was worthwhile to offer the nation, whereas the South embodied the values to which all Americans should aspire. In 1867, the year he published *Wearing of the Gray*, Cooke wrote that nothing would ever obliterate "the bitter antagonism" between the Southern "Cavalier element" and the Northern "Puritan element" which had existed "from the first settlement of this country."[28]

Having written ten books before the Civil War, Cooke enlisted in the Confederate army and rose to the rank of captain. He served in many battles, from the First Battle of Bull Run through Appomattox Court House. Initially full of enthusiasm, he became increasingly dour over the South's prospects and the deaths of friends and family members. After the war, he feared that Radical Reconstruction would kill American democracy. He had a character in a novel warn that "negro suffrage and the bayonet" would lead to "the disgust of the white man at the equality of the negro; his distrust of a government which makes such a farce possible; consequent revulsion against democracy" and finally rule by "a king, emperor or dictator, who will restore order out of the chaos of misrule and madness."[29]

He decided to write books that would restore the Cavalier myth and reassure readers that the Confederate war effort had been a noble one. In his telling, the leading Confederate commanders were Cavaliers—chivalric, dauntless, refined, and gallant (a favorite word of his). The only exception was Stonewall Jackson, a plain-dressed, pious Presbyterian who lacked the suaveness associated with the Cavalier. Like others of the time, Cooke saw Jackson as a Southern Cromwell—a Confederate Puritan.

Other Confederates, in Cooke's eyes, filled the Cavalier mold to a tee—most notably the dashing cavalry officer J. E. B. Stuart. In *Wearing of the Gray* Cooke described Stuart in reverential detail, noting his plumed hat, knee-length leather boots, gold spurs, dazzling coat buttons, scarlet-lined cape, yellow waist sash, and long buff arm gauntlets. Cooke also dwelled on Stuart's traits: his "boyish gaiety," his love of danger, his "flavor of chivalry and adventure."[30] Recklessly redundant, in different passages Cooke calls Stuart the "Flower of Cavaliers," "the great cavalier," "the cavalier *par excellence*," "the impetuous cavalier," and so forth.[31] When Stuart was killed during the Overland Campaign in 1864, Cooke tells us, "the cavalier, who had passed through a hundred battles untouched, came to his end at last."

Cooke gives Stuart plenty of Cavalier company. A fellow officer, Wade Hampton, is the "brave cavalier of South Carolina," the "erect and courteous cavalier, with his flowing Black mustache and mild yet brilliant eyes."[32] The cavalry commander Turner Ashby is "the dauntless cavalier, the noble gentleman, the charming and winning companion."[33] General in Chief Robert E. Lee, with his "iron-gray hair and beard," "honest eyes," and "stately figure," is the "noble old cavalier, who seems to have stepped out of the past into the present, to show us what sort of men Virginia can still produce."[34]

How serious was Cooke when he presented Confederates as Cavaliers? Questions surround Cooke's motivations. He idealized Confederate army life in his books, but he told an interviewer: "I never liked the business of war. . . . It is fit work for brutes and brutish men."[35] In a note to a friend in 1879, by which time he had written nearly thirty books, he confessed, "I write for money. If ever you write my life, put this in: money and my own satisfaction. I have made some money about $20,000 [more than $500,000 today] since the war, and I have poisoned the rising Southern generation with Confederate lies about the war—which is enough to retire on."[36] Whatever his actual feelings, his impact was undeniable. He was the most popular Southern author during the two decades immediately following the Civil War, and he paved the way for later Lost Cause authors by casting a romantic glow over military defeat.

The flood of pro-Southern literature in early Reconstruction—from the Lost Cause books through the Copperhead articles and tracts—helped shape the climate leading into the presidential race of 1868, when the Democrats campaigned on an overtly white-supremacist message. The Democratic ticket of Horatio Seymour and Francis Blair appealed to white voters with openly racial themes, and Democratic clubs and newspapers widely circulated the slogan THIS IS A WHITE MAN'S COUNTRY. LET WHITE MEN RULE.[37] Democratic newspapers continued to spout racism. It was said that there was a plot between "Puritan" Republicans and Black people to abolish white rule. In a piece called "The Great Issue—the Nation Against the Puritan and the Nigger," *The New York Herald* averred, "Between Puritan and nigger was made the bargain to give to the half civilized slave supremacy over his former master, in order that the political balance of this brutal, ignorant and unreasoning vote might retain the Puritan in power."[38] When it was found that Ulysses S. Grant, the Republican Party's candidate, was descended from the Pilgrim Richard Warren, Grant was tarred as a "foul Puritan" with the blood of "Mayflower convicts" in his veins.[39]

Despite such efforts to defame Republicans, the Democrats lost decisively in the Electoral College in 1868, although not in the popular vote, which went 3,013,421 for Grant and 2,706,829 for Seymour. A significant factor in the election was the vote of newly enfranchised African Americans, who went strongly Republican. The turnout was so sizable that several state legislatures in the South became biracial; for example, Black men made up more than a third of Mississippi's House of Representatives and over half of South Carolina's state congress.

The sudden ascendancy of Black politicians incited white violence. The Ku Klux Klan was founded in December 1865 in Pulaski, Tennessee, by ex-Confederates, which led a journalist to speculate that the group's name came from "Kompanions Unsubjugated Kavaliers' League; Under X-Konfederate Leaders."[40] The Klan's first grand wizard was the former Confederate officer Nathan Bedford Forrest, notorious for having ordered or permitted the massacre of most of the 262 Black Union soldiers who had surrendered to him at Fort Pillow, Tennessee, in April 1864.[41] The Klan started as a social club but morphed into a network of terrorist groups aimed at suppressing the vote of African Americans and their white Republican allies. The Klan expanded to what was known as the Invisible Empire, with 550,000 members by 1868, according to Forrest. Disguised in outlandish costumes, Klan members launched raids in which they lynched, raped, dismembered, castrated, and otherwise tormented their victims. President Grant was slow to take action, but when he did, he delivered results. He promoted and signed three Enforcement Acts (aka the Ku Klux Klan Acts), which, when passed by Congress in 1871, resulted in the arrest, trial, and punishment of hundreds of Klan members. The Ku Klux Klan dwindled, although other hate groups remained intermittently active, and later, during the Jim Crow era—particularly in the first half of the twentieth century—the Klan would make a grim comeback.

Signs of the racism that would underlie Jim Crow were rife during Reconstruction. Attacks on Puritanism reached a vile nadir in the hands of pro-Southern humorists like Peter "Pat" Donan, whose newspaper, *The Weekly Caucasian*, which he ran from 1869 to 1876, had the banner "State Sovereignty! White Supremacy! . . . OUR DOCTRINES:

This is a White Man's Government, made by White Men and their posterity Forever! DOWN WITH THE XV AMENDMENT!"[42] Known for his "red-hot" style, Donan hurled epithets at New Englanders. He maintained that New England was first settled by "expelled convicts from Europe, called Puritans." He reported that "these long-necked, sloping-foreheaded, pink-eyed, knotty-jointed, unfattenable and wormy gluttons, were landed by a Botany-Bay convict ship known as the Mayflower, which afterward went into the slave trade, and sank in the middle of the ocean with a cargo of niggers, which its crew had kidnapped on the coast of Africa. She sank with her second load. Her first load of niggers was deposited on the coast of Virginia and sold to the Virginia tobacco-planters."[43]

While such drivel found a popular audience, leading Republicans shed their former radicalism. Many of them thought that the Fifteenth Amendment and the Ku Klux Klan Acts ended the fight for civil rights. The Freedmen's Bureau, having provided millions of dollars of aid to emancipated Blacks and indigent whites since its founding in March 1865, shut down in 1872 amid chronic underfunding and growing political opposition. The Freedman's Bank, long a vital financial resource for Black communities, collapsed in 1874 after severe mismanagement, risky speculation, and fraud. Horace Greeley, the *New-York Tribune* editor who in 1865 had been called an "implacable puritan" who was plotting "the elevation of the negro to posts of honor made vacant by the destruction of the white race," had flipped by 1872, when he said, "Having done what I could for the complete emancipation of the blacks, I now insist on the full enfranchisement of all my white countryman."[44] He explained that he was campaigning for "the emancipation of all the white men of the country, so that they shall enjoy equal rights with the black men of the country."[45] It was time, Greeley said, for the North and South to bury the hatchet.

Others felt the same way. Carl Schurz, a former Union general and Missouri politician who had been an outspoken critic of Southern racism, now called for the termination of Reconstruction. The Illinoisan Lyman Trumbull, coauthor of the Thirteenth Amendment and sponsor of the Civil Rights Act of 1866, decided that the South should be left alone and that Black suffrage should be left to the states. Schurz and Trumbull organized the Liberal Republican Party, which in 1872 chose Greeley as its presidential candidate.

Greeley's agenda of reconciliation attracted two major figures who had previously been poles apart: Edward Pollard and Charles Sumner. Pollard, the pioneer of the Lost Cause, had undergone a notable shift. Just after the Civil War, he had argued for a restoration of the racial order of the Old South, even if it meant another war. His exposure to John Van Evrie's scientific racism made him, paradoxically, more complacent in his views. Pollard came to think that because Black people were intrinsically inferior, they could be given latitude, as they would never succeed if put on a level playing field with whites. In 1872, he wrote a campaign pamphlet supporting Greeley in which he promoted "equivalency," which assigned equal rights to Blacks and whites with the understanding that the races, fundamentally dissimilar, would not mingle—a foreshadowing of the "separate but equal" doctrine that came later.[46]

Even more surprising than Pollard's support of Greeley was Charles Sumner's. Sumner believed that the Fifteenth Amendment, ratified in 1870, and his bill banning segregation in public transportation and accommodations, which he authored that year, marked the culmination of his lifelong struggle for Black citizenship. Having been attacked for years as an extremist, he thought it was time for political opponents to make amends. On July 29, 1872, Sumner issued a public "Letter to Colored Citizens" urging them to vote for Greeley, because "the existing differences ought to be ended. . . . There should be reconciliation, not only between the North and South, but between the two races, so that the two sections and the two races may be lifted from the ruts and grooves in which they are now fastened, and, instead of *irritating an-*

*tagonism* without end, there shall be *sympathetic coöperation*."[47] Unlike Pollard, however, Sumner wanted reconciliation to be accompanied by desegregation.

President Grant, who was popular despite reported corruption in his administration, was reelected in 1872, defeating Greeley handily. The next year, Charles Sumner made a final journey into the Puritan past. Although his name had been associated with Forefathers' Day since his antislavery letter of 1863, Sumner had never spoken at a Forefathers' Day celebration. He did so in 1873 when he addressed a banquet hosted by the New England Society of New York. He told his audience that the Plymouth landing marked "the origin of a new order of ages . . . the great beginning." The Pilgrims' "lesson of self-sacrifice, of just and equal laws, of the government of a majority, of unshrinking loyalty to principle, is now leavening this whole continent, and in the fulness of time will leaven the world. (*Great applause.*)"[48] These were sweeping but cautious words. Sumner sidestepped the controversial topic of the *Mayflower* and the slave ship.

Two months after his talk, Sumner, sixty-three, died of a heart attack. Eulogies abounded. One Republican politician declared that America, with civil rights in its Constitution, was now "the Puritan State, and the greatness of Sumner was the greatness of Puritan genius—the greatness of moral power."[49]

That statement was predictable, given Sumner's past affinities with Puritanism. Utterly unpredictable was a eulogy given in Congress by Lucius Q. C. Lamar, a freshman representative from Mississippi. A Georgia native, Lamar had attended Emory College and then relocated to Mississippi, where he became a part-time attorney, a professor of mathematics, and a slaveholder on a plantation. A rabid fire-eater, Lamar helped draft Mississippi's ordinance of secession. He became a Confederate colonel and a foreign diplomat for Jefferson Davis. After the war, he entered politics. Beginning in 1873, Lamar served two terms in the House of Representatives, followed by two in the Senate. In the

1880s, President Grover Cleveland appointed him as his secretary of the interior and then as a justice of the Supreme Court, making Lamar the first Democratic member of the court since the Civil War. Throughout, Lamar fiercely fought against equal rights for people of color.

He stunned the nation when in March 1874 he delivered an effusive eulogy to his erstwhile foe, Charles Sumner. Moral principle and a devotion to liberty, Lamar intoned, were the foundations of Sumner's character and politics. Lamar's eulogy was instantly hailed as a major gesture of reconciliation on the part of a former secessionist. Not only was the speech reported and excerpted nationwide, but it had a lasting impact. Three decades after Lamar delivered the eulogy, he, along with Henry Grady and Henry Watterson, was described as "epoch-making" in his role in reconciling the sections.[50] The speech earned Lamar a chapter in John F. Kennedy's *Profiles in Courage*, where it was described as "a turning point in relations between the North and the South" because it nurtured harmony between the sections.[51]

But Kennedy, attracted to politicians who reached across the aisle to save the Union (his book also includes chapters praising Daniel Webster and Senator Edmund Ross, whose vote saved Andrew Johnson from being removed from office), didn't mention that Lamar led America away from civil rights. Lamar's eulogy was the first in a line of speeches by Southerners who feigned broad-mindedness in order to take advantage of the drift toward conciliation in the North. Lamar knew that Sumner was leaning toward compromise, and he sprang at the opportunity to reach across the sectional divide in order to make the South appear compassionate. Lamar said nothing about Sumner's proposed civil rights bill, which had been so important to Sumner that while he was dying, he pleaded with Frederick Douglass and others at his bedside, "You must take care of the civil-rights bill,—my bill, the civil-rights bill,—don't let it fail!"[52] (The bill passed Congress in 1875 but was srruck down as unconstitutional six years later; thus died the nation's most advanced law on race before the Civil Rights Act of 1964.)

Lamar loathed any mandate against racial discrimination. His Sumner eulogy, as John A. Mayne notes, has "a decided 'Brutus-is-an-honorable-man' ring of irony"; Lamar even tucked proslavery euphemisms between his paeans to Sumner's "strongly marked qualities" and "instinctive love of freedom."[53]

Lamar's critics called him an oily-tongued orator who adapted his speeches to his audiences, from grief-stricken Northerners to violence-prone Mississippi crackers. It was well known that Lamar's political victories in the 1870s in Mississippi owed much to his courting of the White Liners, a Klan-like rifle club that terrorized Black people to prevent them from voting. When confronted with the charge that murderous thugs backed him, Lamar said that giving former slaves the vote had been a "tremendous political and social change" that could not "be made without violent disturbance and disorder."[54] He remained committed to white supremacy. As a Supreme Court justice, he was a driving force toward legalized segregation, which the Supreme Court instituted in *Plessy v. Ferguson* in 1896, three years after his death.[55]

But for most of his contemporaries, Lamar had fostered unprecedented national unity through his Sumner eulogy. A New York paper announced, "That speech did more to obliterate the old bitterness between the sections than anything that had preceded it. It was permeated by the spirit of brotherly love, and it made men who had fought on both sides weep."[56]

The deeply emotional reaction impelled some prominent Americans to go a step further than Lamar. Some of Lamar's most fervent Southern admirers helped bridge the formidable gap between Jamestown and Plymouth, between the Cavalier and the Puritan. Northerners also contributed to the compromise. By 1920, the *Mayflower* tercentennial, there were strong signs of a reunion between the two sides of the cultural war.

## *Chapter Twelve*

# BEYOND THE TWO SHIPS

Powerful symbols die slowly. Through Reconstruction and beyond, the two ships remained significant to Frederick Douglass. In an 1875 speech he again contrasted the *Mayflower* and the slave ship, this time to condemn America's history of inequality and its persistent tendency "to reduce the colored people as nearly as possible to a state of slavery."[1] Eighteen years later, Douglass drew a line from "the Dutch ship [that] landed at Jamestown, Virginia" to the recent disenfranchisement of Blacks "by political massacres, by midnight outrages of Ku Klux Klans, and by state legislative enactment."[2]

The historic symbols resonated with others as well. In 1885, an Illinois clergyman eulogized the recently deceased Ulysses Grant as a general who had "battled against the civilization of Jamestown and led triumphantly the armies of the civilization of Plymouth."[3] In 1887, Ohio Governor Joseph B. Foraker brought Lincoln into the discussion by stating, "Plymouth Rock, Jamestown, and Gettysburg are three of the most important points in American history. They mark respectively the beginning of free and slave institutions and the triumph of one over the other."[4] In 1923, a labor union newspaper, linking the dual-origins idea to workingmen's advocacy, announced, "Plymouth and Jamestown are the two starting points of the labor movement in this country, Plymouth representing free and Jamestown chattel labor."[5] As late as the summer of 1941, FDR, the descendant of at least ten *Mayflower* passengers, invoked the twin symbols in response to the public divide over America's entry into World War II. Warning that the greatest threat to the nation was from within, the president declared, "Never before since Jamestown and Plymouth Rock has our American civilization been in such danger as now."[6]

In general, however, the trend shifted from sparring over the historic symbols toward reconciling them.

After Reconstruction ended, the South believed it was in a strong position to stand up for itself. It named itself the New South—modern, commercial, and becoming increasingly industrial. Given the devastation from the war in the former Confederacy, this claim was mainly bravado. But states' rights seemed to have won. The Compromise of 1877, which settled a disputed election when an Electoral Commission awarded the presidency to the Republican Rutherford B. Hayes in exchange for removing federal troops from the South, left white Southerners largely free to try to restore white supremacy. African Americans were systematically prevented from voting through violence and other methods; as a result, the 75 percent Black voter turnout in the Southern presidential election of 1876 declined to 1 to 2 percent in 1920.[7] Supreme Court decisions in the 1870s and early 1880s severely limited civil rights. Indigenous peoples, who would not be granted US citizenship until 1924, faced suppression, displacement, and forced assimilation.

By the early twentieth century, America had entered an age of imperialism and nativism. Through its victory in the Spanish-American War, the United States acquired the overseas territories of Puerto Rico, Guam, and the Philippines—examples of what Manisha Sinha describes as "colonizing non-white nations and peoples" in the service of expanding the "American empire."[8] Scientific racism, infused with Herbert Spencer's misapplication of Darwin's theory as "survival of the fittest," had by now gained broad acceptance. More than twenty million immigrants—many from Southern, Eastern, and Central Europe—arrived in the United States between 1880 and 1920, setting off waves of xenophobia and the passage of increasingly severe immigration laws. Asian immigrants were also targeted, from the Page Act of 1875 through the Chinese Exclusion Act of 1882 to the Immigration Act of 1924, which effectively ended legal immigration from most Asian countries. Literacy tests and quotas favored white people from Northern and Western Europe.

These changes concentrated national attention on other issues, lessening the debate over Puritanism and the *Mayflower.* Leading white Southerners and Northerners downplayed the Plymouth-Jamestown conflict, focusing instead on shared biases against Black people and immigrants.

There was, however, strong pushback from reformers who insisted that equal rights must be America's goal. Forward-looking African Americans and whites, often inspired by the legacy of radical Puritanism, exposed segregation and disenfranchisement. These reformers prepared the way for the civil rights movement of the 1950s and '60s.

## SOUTHERNERS EMBRACE THE FOREFATHERS

In the 1880s, ex-Confederates began traveling north on peace missions. Shedding their former identity as Cavaliers, they announced that the old dualisms no longer applied.

The Atlanta journalist Henry W. Grady, the New South's main spokesman, was a native Georgian whose father, a Confederate officer, had died in the Battle of the Crater in 1864. After the war, Henry Grady worked his way up in journalism, becoming the managing editor of the

Henry W. Grady
*Photograph attributed to*
*Georgia photographer C. W. Motes (c. 1889)*

*Atlanta Constitution.* In the paper, he promoted commerce and industrial development, while also boosting Southern politicians known as Bourbon Democrats—mostly former Confederates who supported limited government, white supremacy, and reconciliation with the North.

Henry Grady wanted to put an end to the cultural war of the past in order to smooth the path to commercial support from the North. In January 1886, he wrote an article, "Puritan and Cavalier," in which he declared that this conflict was over. He assured readers that whatever was valuable in the Puritan or the Cavalier had been preserved. He explained: "Both types have been merged in the American . . . who loves his country as a whole, knowing neither North or South, and neither

East nor West. The two—the puritan and the cavalier—have joined houses for all time, and the future, as well as the past, is to be credited to the energy of both."[9] Quoting this passage, *The New York Herald* remarked, "If this sort of thing continues New England societies might find it advisable to send down South for some orators for Forefathers' Day celebrations."[10]

A Northern society did just that. Not long after Grady's piece appeared, the New England Society of New York asked him to speak at its annual banquet that winter. The event, held on December 21, 1886, took place at Delmonico's, an upscale restaurant in New York. A large crowd showed up to celebrate the Pilgrims and to find out what Henry Grady, a Southerner, would say at a Pilgrim function held in the North. American flags and images of Plymouth and the *Mayflower* adorned the restaurant's spacious main room. Six long tables were covered with white tablecloths and festooned with candelabra, colored lamps, and cut flowers. Elegant menus, in French, promised an un-Plymouthlike meal that included hors d'oeuvres, potages, a range of *poissons* and *viandes*, desserts, and select *vins français*.[11] While the attendees were eating their *sorbet à la régence* and *petits fours*, the talks began. First up was T. DeWitt Talmage, an entertaining Brooklyn preacher, who told some jokes. He was followed by General William Tecumseh Sherman, who told a story from his March to the Sea in Georgia.

While they spoke, Henry Grady anxiously leafed through his prepared speech. His jitters disappeared when it was his turn to speak. A stout man with a round, smooth-shaven face and dark brown hair and eyes, Grady had a deep voice that carried well. His topic was "The New South." He began by quoting a Georgia senator's words: "There was a South of slavery and secession—that South is dead. There is a South of Union and freedom—that South, thank God, is living, breathing, growing every hour."[12] Grady said that Southerners had emerged from the Civil War facing utter devastation but had rebounded by diversifying agriculture and developing industries like mining and textile production. The South now shared the North's capitalist spirit.

How about the nation-shaking cultural divide? It was a thing of the past. True, he said, there had been a division early on between the Puritan, virtuous and stiff, and the Cavalier, genial and dissolute, but the two types merged when they joined up in the American Revolution. "Neither Puritan nor Cavalier long survived as such," Grady explained, for "the American citizen, supplementing both and stronger than either, took possession of the Republic bought by their blood." And, he added, "The virtues and good traditions of both happily still live for the inspiration of their sons and the saving of the old fashion."[13] Reverend Talmage was wrong, Grady continued, in saying that the typical American had not yet appeared. He *had* appeared, in the person of Abraham Lincoln. Grady declared: "He was the sum of Puritan and Cavalier, for in his ardent nature were fused the virtues of both, and in the depths of his great soul the faults of both were lost. He was greater than Puritan, greater than Cavalier, in that he was American, and that in his honest form were gathered the vast and thrilling forces of his ideal government."[14]

The words electrified Grady's listeners, who stood up en masse, clapping and cheering. Here was something new: a Southern Democrat, known for his opposition to Radical Reconstruction and the Republican Party, singing praise to Lincoln, the Republican leader who had been the target of Confederate calumny. Equally astonishing was Grady's erasure of the conflict between the Puritan and the Cavalier. Grady had simultaneously transformed the farseeing Lincoln into the palatably typical American and had bridged the cultural gap once thought to be the underlying cause of the Civil War.

As for African Americans in the South, Grady said, they were happily working and contributing to the region's economic growth. Moreover, they had citizenship rights and access to education. Grady boasted, "No section shows a more prosperous laboring population than the negroes of the South, none in fuller sympathy with the employing and land-owning class. [The Black person] shares our school fund, has the fullest protection of our laws, and the friendship of our people."[15]

Where was the real Henry Grady, the one whose Atlanta newspaper promoted Ku Klux Klan leaders and ran gleeful headlines about lynching, such as "The Triple Trapeze: Three Negroes Hung to a Limb of a Tree" and the rhymed "Two Minutes to Pray Before a Rope Dislocated Their Vertebrae"?[16] That Grady was buried beneath a soft pillow of euphemisms intended to please Northerners, whom he eyed as financial supporters of the New South. (Among the audience at the New York event were the financier J. Pierpont Morgan and the railroad tycoon Henry Flagler.)

Grady's true colors came out in October 1887, when he told a crowd at a state fair in Texas, "The supremacy of the white race of the South must be maintained forever, and the domination of the negro race resisted at all points and at all hazards, because the white race is the superior race."[17] This reactionary side of Grady showed itself again two years later when he spoke on December 12, 1889, at a businessmen's banquet in Boston. His topic was "Race Problem in the South." He flattered his Northern audience by saying he was delighted to be "here, within touch of Plymouth Rock and Bunker Hill—where Webster thundered and Longfellow sang, Emerson thought and Channing preached—here in the cradle of American letters, and almost of American liberty."[18] He drew an idyllic picture of the South, including its industrious Black workers. Then his tone changed. He retrospectively praised slavery for having improved "an alien race" by exposing it to Western civilization.[19] Emancipation, he declared, had been grossly mishandled. Black suffrage and mandates to alter state constitutions were forced on the South by Northern radicals and military generals, and so for a time, some Southern states were controlled by largely African American legislatures. Fortunately, Grady said, whites had since regained dominance.

Praising Georgia's Redeemers, Grady recalled, "We wrested our State government from negro supremacy." He vowed, "Never, sir, will a single State of this Union, North or South, be delivered again to the control of an ignorant and inferior race."[20]

How could Grady dare to make such statements in Boston, a city known historically as the center of abolitionism and Radical Republicanism? Northerners faced the reality that civil rights had experienced a legal setback. Furthermore, that Northerners typically opposed slavery did not necessarily mean that many of them believed Blacks were the equals of whites in all respects or should be fully integrated into civil and social society. Grady's audience, far from being upset by his remarks on race, erupted in applause when he finished. A Southern journalist described Grady's success in Boston as that of a "cavalier of the South" who "marched to battle for her" and "fought a gallant fight for us . . . leaving the field victor, amidst the plaudits of those he had conquered."[21]

But the trip, according to the press, proved fatal for Grady when he took a side visit to Plymouth. The morning was raw and damp, with penetrating coastal winds. Standing near Plymouth Rock, Grady took off his hat and said to a gathered crowd, "I have a boy, dearest to my heart, and of all the places upon this earth where I would have him go to learn piety, patriotism, patience, and justice, this is the spot where I now stand reverently uncovered"—words, typical of the gaseous Grady, that his hearers found inspirational.[22] At that moment, white supremacy, in the person of Henry Grady, temporarily snuffed out the radical egalitarianism long associated with Plymouth Rock. In effect, the slave ship scored a victory over the *Mayflower.* The next day, Grady experienced severe bronchial symptoms thought to have been caused by his exposure to the elements at Plymouth. He returned to Atlanta, where he developed pneumonia. The thirty-nine-year-old Grady died on December 23. His funeral, a massive affair, was held on Christmas Day. The timing seemed providential; eulogists at the funeral connected the birth of Christ with the new birth of national togetherness they said Grady's life and work represented.

One of Grady's friends, the Atlanta journalist John Temple Graves, was determined to carry on Grady's mission of reconciliation. At a Forefathers' Day event held in Philadelphia in December 1890, Graves declared, "I am unable to do homage to New England from Plymouth Rock to Philadelphia in the full measure of my admiration. We, the cavaliers of the South, have adopted your conclusions; we have fairly grappled your views." Now that the Civil War was long over, he told his Northern audience, Southerners "give you the profound respect which courage always gives. . . . It is our duty and our glory to forgive and forget; and nothing but forgiveness is found in the veins of the cavalier. The coursing of cavalier blood awakes no resentment nor mars the past with a single bitter memory." Catching the spirit of the season, Graves exclaimed, "All hail the Christmas Wedding of the Puritan and the Southern cavalier!"[23]

As with Grady, however, Graves's words were merely a benign cover. Graves had inherited the racial views of his great-granduncle, John C. Calhoun, who had famously called slavery "a positive good." Even though African Americans now had the constitutional right to vote, Graves said in an 1893 speech in Chautauqua, New York, that "this is a white man's government, and it will remain so forever, for God Almighty has stamped his seal and sign of sovereignty upon the Anglo-Saxon tribe."[24] Graves went so far as to defend lynching. The nation's main problem, he insisted, was "not how to prevent lynching in the South" but how to "destroy the crime which always has and always will provoke lynching."[25] Graves was referring to Black men who allegedly raped white women—the wildly exaggerated charge often made by white supremacists of the day. Rape, Graves contended, must be answered by a lynch mob equipped with "the rope, the bullet, and sometimes, God save us! with the torch." Not only was lynching acceptable; it was necessary. "The mob," Graves said, "is to-day the sternest, the strongest, and the most effective restraint that the age holds for the control of rape." (Graves's view was widely shared; between 1882 and 1930, mobs lynched more than 2,500 African Americans, chiefly on the pretext of alleged assaults on white women.)[26]

The Southern spirit of reconciliation mixed with racism was carried forward by another of Henry Grady's friends, Henry Watterson. Watterson, the longtime editor of the Louisville *Courier-Journal*, was very prominent in the late nineteenth century. H. L. Mencken commented that for more than forty years, "Watterson was the most distinguished editorial writer on the American press, quoted endlessly and known everywhere."[27] During the Civil War, Watterson served in the Confederate army and wrote for Nashville newspapers. After the war, he settled in Kentucky. In his Louisville paper he produced a steady stream of pieces, many under the pseudonym "Marse Henry," which suited his white-mustachioed, beetle-browed face, which made him, as an acquaintance remarked, look like "the cartoonist's prototype for the southern colonel."[28]

In 1894, Watterson delivered a widely covered speech at a Forefathers' Day fête in New York. Watterson said that in the eight years since Henry Grady had declared that Lincoln had resolved the Puritan-Cavalier conflict, more evidence had surfaced confirming that Lincoln was a "rugged trunk, drawing its sustenance from gnarled roots, interlocked with Cavalier sprays and Puritan branches deep beneath the soil." And Lincoln was not alone in merging the two peoples. So did many Northerners and Southerners during the Civil War. Watterson rattled off names of leading generals and politicians on both sides and pointed as well to ordinary Americans of both sections: "Why, in that great, final struggle between the puritans and the cavaliers . . . there had been such a mixing up of the puritan babies and the cavalier babies during the two or three generations preceding it that the surviving grandmothers of the combatants could not, except for the uniforms, have picked out their own on any field of battle!"[29]

Watterson, like Grady before him, was promoting the ideas that the reputed dualism of cultures once thought to have triggered the Civil War was largely mythical, and that the time had come for enemies to become friends. In the interest of bland compromise, he cloaked his own racism. When Watterson discussed race openly, as in a 1903 Chicago speech, he revealed that he was as backward as Grady and Graves. Showing the influence of ethnography and social Darwinism, he questioned the right of citizenship for Black people, who, he said, were still evolving from an inferior state at a snail's pace. In his words, "The negro can never become in any beneficent or genuine sense an integral and recognized part of the body politic except through the forces of evolution, which are undoubtedly at work but in the nature of the case must needs go exceedingly slow. Where there is one negro fit for citizenship there are myriads of negroes wholly unfit."[30]

Another Southerner, the politician William Campbell Preston Breckinridge, brought conciliation to the very heart of *Mayflower* worship: Plymouth, Massachusetts. The occasion was the August 12, 1889, dedication of the Monument to the Forefathers, the eighty-one-foot tall granite statue on a hill overlooking Plymouth Harbor. Thousands of spectators from around the country attended the opening ceremony at the monument and braved torrential rain to watch a three-mile parade proceed through the flag-and-bunting-draped town to a huge tent, where a two-dollar entry fee allowed one to enjoy a banquet and hear the oration of Breckinridge, a Kentucky Democrat then serving in the US House of Representatives.

Thirty years earlier, in 1859, the laying of the cornerstone of the Forefathers Monument had been a strictly Northern affair, with notables like Lyman Beecher and Salmon Chase in attendance. On this wet, windy day in 1889, the message was altogether different. "The North and South Unite in a Memorable Dedication Service" was a headline of a news report of the occasion, in which Breckinridge gave an address crediting the early New England settlers for having established the foundations of America.[31]

Breckinridge, a former Confederate army captain and a close kinsman of the secessionist John Breckinridge, claimed to be open-minded toward Blacks in the decades after the Civil War. In an 1890 article, however, he declared that all biblical and secular history shows "that man has been divided not only into different, but unassimilable, races that race prejudice, race hatred, race affinity are among the most intense and permanent of all human passions . . . in the very center of our nature."[32] Because the forced removal of Blacks from the US had proved impossible, segregation of the races was mandatory. In some cases, he felt, the lynching of Blacks must be resorted to. Although Breckinridge had paid lip service to the *Mayflower* at the Plymouth ceremony, it was the Jamestown ship that spoke the loudest to him. The ship, he argued, stood for the unarguable truth that slavery was the natural condition for Black people. As Breckinridge wrote: "In 1619 a cargo of negroes was permitted to land in America. There was never a moment when it was expected that they should have any other relation to the white colonists than that of slavery."[33] Breckinridge's praise of the 1619 ship shows that by the last two decades of the nineteenth century, Southerners could harbor the racial attitudes that had undergirded slavery even while selling themselves as eulogists of Plymouth's heritage of liberty.

The merging of formerly hostile sections was sped not only by Southerners who went north to hail Plymouth but also by the activities of New England societies in the South. By far the most influential Southern organization was the New England Society of Charleston, South Carolina, which had been formed in 1819. The Forefathers' Day events of the 1880s and '90s in Charleston were strongly slanted toward reunion. The 1888 ceremony featured one speaker who assured the audience that "sectionalism was dying out," while another declared that "the Anglo-Saxon race which peopled this country" set an example that later Americans must spread "to the utmost bounds of the earth": "If civil liberty and individual freedom are to attain their final expanse, it must be under the domination of the Anglo-Saxons of the United States. [Great applause.]"[34]

Visitors to Charleston's Pilgrim gala held in 1898 got a strong dose of both nonsectionalism and racism. South Carolina Senator John L. McLaurin emphasized that "the war between the States is over," and even in "the birthplace and very cradle of secession," it could be affirmed that the nation was now "a union, one and indivisible." In the next breath, McLaurin attacked the political participation of "inferior" people. He averred, "I will never vote to give the ignorant, degraded, and servile of foreign lands a vote in the affairs of our country." Referring to immigrants and African Americans, he said that "universal suffrage has been tried in the south, and it has proven a universal failure." He added that it was questionable "whether inferior and Latin races are anywhere capable of self-government."[35]

By the 1890s, then, Southern and Northern whites, feeling threatened by people of color and by an array of European immigrants, were retreating to a cocoon of racial solidarity that *Mayflower* celebrations helped reinforce. The use of Pilgrim celebrations to reconcile formerly warring whites, while holding in subordination Black people and certain immigrant groups, contributed to Jim Crow.

Among all the Southern reconciliationists, Henry Grady stood alone in his influence. His 1886 Forefathers' Day speech on the merging of the Puritan and Cavalier was reprinted or excerpted numerous times in the three decades following his death. By 1909, Grady had been hailed as "the apostle of the olive branch," "the South's great wizard" who had united the nation "from the lakes to the gulf, from the Statue of Liberty to the Golden Gate."[36] Some, however, saw the real Grady. In 1921, a Black newspaper described him as "probably the most bitter enemy the colored people ever had and more dangerous because his enmity was masked under protestations of friendship, which is usual in the South. Grady was the father of segregation, and the enactment of jimcrow car laws and other schemes of segregation may be largely ascribed to his preachments and influence."[37]

If Grady and the other New South spokesmen shaped Jim Crow, so did eulogists of the Old South and the Lost Cause. Among the many late-nineteenth-century authors who glorified the South's past, Thomas Nelson Page of Virginia stands out. Another fishhook in the ancestral line that reached back to the tangle of Virginia's First Families, Page, who had been raised in a slaveholding household, wrote more than twenty books—including novels, story collections, and essay volumes—between 1876 and his death in 1922. In his writings, he fanned the nostalgia for pre–Civil War plantation life. In Page's eyes, Reconstruction was a nightmarish time of intrusive Northerners destroying Southern customs, leading to justifiable retribution by the Ku Klux Klan. Page's Southern nostalgia and anti-Reconstruction themes anticipated the white supremacist novels of Thomas Dixon, which were the basis for D. W. Griffith's film *The Birth of a Nation*—all of which whetted the public's appetite for a work like Margaret Mitchell's romantic Lost Cause best-seller *Gone With the Wind* and the blockbuster film based on it.

Page influenced views of America's origins by bolstering Jamestown's claim to be the true source of America. The movement to rehabilitate Jamestown had been dormant since the collapse of the short-lived Jamestown Society in the 1850s. The movement resumed in 1898, when an Episcopal church in Washington, DC, established the Order of Jamestown 1607. When the group sent delegates to Jamestown to identify the location of the area's first church, a reporter commented, "The cavalier takes the wind out of the Mayflower. The first white child born in the New World was born in Jamestown."[38]

In 1907, the tercentennial of Virginia's first settlement was marked by a seven-month-long exposition at Norfolk's Sewell's Point that drew major national figures, including President Theodore Roosevelt, Vice President Charles W. Fairbanks, future president William Howard Taft, and Booker T. Washington. Among the speakers at the exposition was Thomas Nelson Page, who declared that the three British ships that moored at Jamestown Island on May 13, 1607, "bore in their wombs the destinies of Nations."[39] The Jamestown settlement, he said, "led to the supremacy of the Saxon race, with its Laws, its Religion, and its Civilization." Jamestown, Page said, was the site of the "First Christian Temple" and "the first representative assembly," which, when it convened in July 1619, was "the beginning of popular government in America." Page briefly mentioned the 1619 arrival of the *Treasurer*, with its cargo of enslaved people. (In his novels, he portrayed the enslaved as blissful and devoted to their masters.) As for "the little Mayflower," Page went on, it produced one of the "streams" of democracy that came after Jamestown, as did streams "from other directions, South and West . . . all tending to swell the mighty waters which make the vast main of American life." But Jamestown, Page declared, "was the source of the great current which today represents American constitutional ideas . . . the real Cradle of the American People wherever they may be."

The Jamestown revival was underway. Adding greatly to its momentum was Lyon Gardiner Tyler, one of President John Tyler's fifteen children. A noted historian of his home state, Virginia, and the president of the College of William & Mary, Tyler is remembered for his anti-Lincoln writings and his claim in *A Confederate Catechism* that abolitionism, not slavery, was the cause of the Civil War. He also had a crucial role as a Jamestown booster. For Tyler, only Jamestown counted. In his 1900 book, *The Cradle of the Republic: Jamestown and James River*, Tyler made the case that Jamestown had no less than forty-five American firsts to its credit: not just momentous ones like democracy, the Christian church, and slavery (which Tyler defended) but small ones like "first silk worms reared," "first duel fought," and "first idiot child born."[40] In his long-running periodical *Tyler's Quarterly Historical and Genealogical Magazine*, Tyler stated directly: "There is a manifest disposition to place Plymouth before Jamestown. . . . The plain truth is that neither in its origin nor in the institutions established in New England did the Plymouth colony lay the foundation of the American Commonwealth. It was antedated by Jamestown."[41]

The combination of Jamestown boosterism and the erasure of the Puritan-Cavalier conflict made the tercentennial celebration of the *Mayflower* in December 1920 a grand exercise in reconciliation. By then, Plymouth and Jamestown were on an equal plane in the popular mind. The equalization of the two locales came through in the keynote speech given on Forefathers' Day in Plymouth by Henry Cabot Lodge, a longtime US senator from Massachusetts. A haughty Boston Brahmin, Lodge, who had once defended the lynching of eleven Italian immigrants, had spent much of the previous decade in the Senate backing anti-immigration bills designed to exclude from the country what a bill passed in 1917 called "undesirable aliens," including "illiterates," "imbeciles," "insane persons," "criminals," "alcoholics," "epileptics," and others.[42] A nativist supporter of 100 percent Americanism, Lodge would become the main force behind a 1924 quota on European immigrants and America's refusal to sign the Treaty of Versailles and join the League of Nations after World War I.

Lodge, in his Forefathers' Day address, removed any distinction between Plymouth and Jamestown. Both, he said, had introduced the white race and democracy to the New World. He declared, "Jamestown and Plymouth were the cornerstones of the foundations upon which the great fabric of the United States has been built up, and the United States is to-day one of the dominant factors in the history and in the future of the world of men."[43] Following Lodge's example, President Warren G. Harding delivered a conciliatory message when in August 1921 he spoke at a Plymouth celebration of the embarkation of the Pilgrims. Harding declared that "the community of free people of our race," which had "spread now to all quarters of the world, was begun when Jamestown and Plymouth were founded."[44]

By the time Harding and Lodge made their statements about Jamestown and Plymouth, Forefathers' Day had dwindled as an American holiday. By 1936, a Southern newspaper could ask, "What is Forefathers' Day?" among trivia questions such as "What is the oldest windmill in this country?" and "How much snow does it take to correspond to an inch of rain?"[45] But annual Forefathers' Day celebrations are still held on December 22 in Plymouth, Massachusetts, with a firing of cannons, a march, and succotash dinner.

## CHANGING VIEWS OF THE PILGRIMS

Over the years, the Pilgrims were commodified. In the late nineteenth and early twentieth centuries, Pilgrim names boosted the sales of household items. One could buy the Elder Brewster tea set, John Alden Flour, the Pilgrim Arm Chair and Rocker, and, especially popular, Mary Chilton sterling silver. An ad read, "In the beauty of its Colonial simplicity, strength and pleasing lines, this solid silver table set deserves the name it bears—Mary Chilton—first of the Mayflower's of little band to step ashore at Plymouth."[46]

The Chilton silver set points up the connection between the *Mayflower* and the women's movement. Mary Chilton became an improbable model of equal rights for women. In 1887, a suffragist declared, "Mary Chilton, reverently may her name be spoken, was the first whose feet touched the land, consecrating it from that hour to woman." Mary's message for America, the speaker continued, was inspiring: "Here shall woman reach the zenith of her glory. Equally as self-sacrificing and heroic, toiling side by side with her brother, the time is not distant when he shall welcome her, with God speed, to all the privileges which he enjoys."[47] These were large claims to make about a

"Mary Chilton's Leap"
*Engraving by F. T. Merrill in Samuel Adams Drake,* A Book of New England Legends and Folk Lore *(1884)*

thirteen-year-old girl who may not have been the first to step onto a rock that may not have been the place where the Pilgrims landed.

As a group, the *Mayflower* women had a galvanizing effect on feminist agitation. In the early 1870s, the women's rights activist Laura Curtis Bullard announced, "The assumption that women had no part nor lot in the Mayflower venture has been long enough kept up. . . . It is not meet that New England's foremothers should go unhonored and unsung."[48] They did not go unsung. In December 1892, the New York City Woman Suffrage League staged a large event—attended by luminaries like Elizabeth Cady Stanton, Isabella Beecher Hooker, and Lillie Devereux Blake—dedicated to "The Pilgrim Mothers." Toasts were raised to the "Landing of the Foremothers" and "Pioneer Heroines." In her speech to the group, Stanton went so far as to hail "the Foremothers' dinner" as "a new step in the progress of civilization"—indeed, "the most important event in American history, since the Declaration of Independence, by just so much as woman is the greatest factor in civilization, being the mother of the race, besides constituting one-half the people."[49] A more measured statement came at a Suffrage League event three years later, where Lillie Blake lauded "the heroines of the Mayflower" and said, "Something of their love of liberty they have transmitted to their descendants, and because we are the daughters of these brave women we demand our freedom to-day."[50] Foremothers' Dinners continued to be held regularly until the passage in 1920 of the Nineteenth Amendment, which prohibited states from denying voting rights based on sex.

The spirit of radical Puritanism invigorated one of the first important African American reform groups: the Niagara Movement. The group's hero was John Brown, the Cromwellian abolitionist known for his militancy and his respect for people of color. In August 1906, the group held its second meeting at Harpers Ferry, Virginia, the scene of John Brown's attempt to start an insurrection that he hoped would lead to the overthrow of slavery.

At the meeting, W. E. B. Du Bois gave a talk in which he declared: "We do believe in John Brown, in that incarnate spirit of justice, that hatred of a lie, that willingness to sacrifice money, reputation, and life itself on the altar of right. And here on the scene of John Brown's martyrdom, we reconsecrate ourselves, our honor, our property to the final emancipation of the race which John Brown died to make free."[51]

Another speaker that day, Reverend Reverdy C. Ransom, emphasized the connection between John Brown and revolutionary Puritanism. Ransom, a minister in the African Methodist Episcopal Church, believed that violence was a viable option for Black people beset by lynching and segregation. In an 1899 speech in a Cleveland church, Ransom began with the two ships: "There were two civilizations founded on these shores about the same time period, one at Plymouth Rock, the other in Jamestown. The latter considered the negro as a domestic animal. When he behaved he was treated well. When he misbehaved he was clubbed, beaten and even killed."[52] In the centuries since 1619, Ransom said, the situation had grown even worse in the South, first with the expansion of slavery and now with the plan to "exterminate" Black people through lynching. He argued that Black Americans had the right to defend their homes with whatever force was necessary—even, he said, 'if it takes dynamite.'" Such aggressive action against social injustice was part of John Brown's legacy.

At the 1906 Harpers Ferry meeting, Ransom spoke about the connections between John Brown's Puritanism and civil rights. Ransom said of Brown, "He was a descendant of one of the company who landed from the Mayflower at Plymouth Rock, and from ancestors who fought in the Revolutionary war. He had all of the moral uprightness and strict religious character of the Puritan, as well as his love of liberty and hatred of oppression and tyranny."[53] Ransom continued: "This old Puritan, whose steel gray eyes gleamed with the spirit and courage that possessed Cromwell at the battle of Dunbar, took literally 'the sword of the Lord and of Gideon,' as both battle cry and watchword." Ransom declared, "The spirit of John Brown beckons us to arise and seek the recovery of our rights."

Ransom's words lead us to reflect on the arc of Puritanism from the sixteenth century onward. As we have seen, Puritanism was born in the rebellion against the hierarchical Church of England. When developed by Separatists who crossed the Atlantic on the *Mayflower*, it gave rise to Plymouth Colony, which nurtured democracy and equal rights—ideals that were eloquently voiced in England by thinkers such as Sidney and Locke, who were shaped by the Puritan Revolution against Charles I. The king's supporters, known as Cavaliers, found themselves imperiled during Cromwell's reign. They emigrated in numbers to Virginia, where their dedication to hierarchy and social order bolstered the South's peculiar institution. In New England, meanwhile, there was growing recognition of the humanity of enslaved people and the injustice of slavery.

The North and South, despite their fundamental differences, joined in a common cause during the American Revolution, due in part to the enduring influence of the democratic experiment in Plymouth Colony, the passions behind the Cromwellian rebellion, and the egalitarian principles of the Lockean Enlightenment.

In the nineteenth century, the Puritan notion of the higher law was shared by antislavery people of all types, from politicians like William Seward to the Garrisonian abolitionists to the warrior John Brown. For many, the conflict over slavery could be most powerfully described as the contest between the *Mayflower* and the Jamestown ship, between the Northern Puritan and the Southern Cavalier. From the Northern perspective, the *Mayflower* and Puritanism won the Civil War.

Lincoln, ever mindful of national unity, ignored the cultural dichotomy and argued that America's true higher law was the Declaration of Independence, which he called "the apple of gold" framed by the Constitution's "picture of silver."[54] It was this ideal that led to the passage of the three Reconstruction Amendments—the Thirteenth, Fourteenth, and Fifteenth Amendments—which abolished slavery, nationalized the Bill of Rights, and granted Black men the right to vote.

The collapse of Reconstruction led to reconciliation between the Cavaliers and Puritans, based on a shared suspicion of non-white Americans and a wave of immigrants. In protest against this white supremacist hegemony, Radical Puritanism reappeared among early twentieth-century activists, some of whom condoned violence. However, there were those for whom reconciliation was a just and noble cause to be sought peacefully by people of different races working together. It was nonviolent protest, political lobbying, and litigation that proved the most effective civil rights strategies in the long run. These were the main tools of the National Association for the Advancement of Colored People, established in 1909 by approximately sixty men and women, including more than fifty whites and seven Blacks. Dedicated to ensuring the implementation of the Reconstruction Amendments, the NAACP and allied groups played a crucial role in landmark cases such as *Brown v. Board of Education*, the Civil Rights Act of 1964, and the Voting Rights Act of 1965. Since then, the fight for equal rights has continued under various banners, making incremental advances, sometimes followed by reversals.

The *Mayflower* as a driver of radical causes has faded from view. For most people, the Pilgrims are picturesque figures of a former time. Thanksgiving, which the Pilgrims initiated, is no longer a sectional holiday confined to the North; it is an encompassing American holiday, observed nationwide by people of all backgrounds and beliefs.

That was Lincoln's goal when he proclaimed the first national Thanksgiving at America's most divided time—in the middle of the Civil War. He called on Americans of all sections to celebrate Thanksgiving with one heart and voice. For him, America was a single ship, not two. This brings to mind a recurring dream he reported having in which he was on a ship that was rapidly moving toward an indefinite shore.[55] Whatever the dream meant for Lincoln, it can be seen as a metaphor for the ship of the nation, sometimes foundering but always pressing on. It remains to be seen whether Lincoln's dream can prevail over the divisions that the two ships signified back then—and that have taken a new shape in today's America.

# *Acknowledgments*

Scott Moyers, my editor at Penguin, supported this project from the beginning and saw it through to completion. I appreciate Scott's insight, patience, and understanding. My agent, Lynn Nesbit, believed in this book and helped make it happen.

I want to thank several individuals at the Graduate Center of the City University of New York who contributed. Members of the Graduate Center cohort, including Cassie Ball, assisted me in exploring primary sources. Leila Markosian was a great help during the production phase of the book. Helen Mangano commented thoughtfully on chapter 6. I am especially grateful to Joel Rogers and Rick Solomon, who read my manuscript and offered valuable suggestions. I appreciate the Graduate Center's Provost Research Fund, which covered certain expenses related to this book.

I also thank all the outstanding scholars whose ideas and research have enriched this book. My deep thanks go to my esteemed CUNY colleague David Waldstreicher, who provided feedback and historiographical information. Professors Sarah Covington and Feisal Mohamed kindly reviewed my chapter on the English Civil War.

Additionally, I am grateful to the archivists and librarians who supported this work, including those at the Massachusetts Historical Society, the Pilgrim Hall Museum, the American Antiquarian Society, the

Mina Rees Library, the Society of *Mayflower* Descendants, the Plimoth Patuxet Museums, the Library of Congress, and the New York Public Library system.

My greatest debt is to my family. My wife, Suzanne, as always, provided unwavering support and was a motivating, caring presence during my years of research and writing. Without her, this book could not have been written.

# *Notes*

*Preface*

1. Charles Sumner, "Letter to the New England Society at New York, December 21, 1863," in *Charles Sumner: His Complete Works*, vol. 10 (Lee and Shepard, 1900), 260–61. The handful of existing studies of these ships focus on certain aspects of the pre–Civil War period; see, for example, Lindsay Dicuirci's "Two Ships, Two Shores," *Early American Literature* 56, no. 1 (2021), 131–56; among other things, Dicuirci contextualizes the 1619 Project. See also Kenyon Gradert, *Puritan Spirits in the Abolitionist Imagination* (University of Chicago Press, 2020). In contrast, the current book follows the sweep of American history—from the landing of the two ships through the early twentieth century—to show the emergence, impact, and eventual decline of this important cultural conflict, along with the twin struggle between the Puritan and the Cavalier.
2. "The Slave Ship and the Mayflower," *Vermont Phoenix* (Brattleboro, VT), May 25, 1866.
3. As in my books *John Brown Abolitionist: The Man Who Killed Slavery, Sparked the Civil War, and Seeded Civil Rights* (Knopf, 2005) and *Abe: Abraham Lincoln in His Times* (Penguin Press, 2020), I discuss the Puritan-vs.-Cavalier conflict principally in relation to the slavery debate, politics, popular culture, and personal life. Excellent examinations of related conflicts from the standpoint of intellectual or religious history can be found, for example, in William R. Taylor, *Cavalier and Yankee: The Old South and American National Character* (Little, Brown, 1968); Sydney E. Ahlstrom, *A Religious History of the American People* (1972; repr., Yale University Press, 2004); Jan C. Dawson, "The Puritan and the Cavalier: The South's Perception of Contrasting Traditions," *Journal of Southern History* 44, no. 4 (1978): 597–614; Drew Gilpin Faust, *The Creation of Confederate Nationalism* (Louisiana State University Press, 1988); Bertram Wyatt-Brown, *The Shaping of Southern Culture: Honor, Grace, and War 1760s–1890s* (University of North Carolina Press, 2001); Harry S. Stout, *Upon the Altar of the Nation: A Moral History of the Civil War* (Penguin, 2007); George C. Rable, *God's Almost Chosen Peoples: A Religious History of the American Civil War* (University of North Carolina Press, 2010); and Edward G. Manger, "Cavalier South vs. Puritan North? Hypocrisy and Identity in the American Civil War," *Studies in Church History*, 60 (2024): 431–52.
4. Frederick Douglass, "Progress and Divisions of Anti-Slavery" (speech delivered in Glasgow, February 14, 1860), *Frederick Douglass Papers*, ed. John W. Blassingame and John R. McKivigan, series 1, *Speeches, Debates, and Interviews, vol. 3., 1855–63* (Yale University Press, 1986), 323–33.
5. The declension story has a long history. It began in earnest with Perry Miller's *The New England Mind: From Colony to Province* (Harvard University Press, 1953) and was elaborated by Bernard Bailyn in *The New England Merchants in the Seventeenth Century* (Porter Press, 2010). The argument that slavery was foundational and structural, not peripheral, in the Northern colonies has been convincingly made by several historians. See, for example, Alan Taylor, *American Colonies* (Viking, 2001) and *American Revolutions: A Continental History, 1750–1804* (W. W. Norton, 2016); Margaret Ellen Newell, *Brethren by Nature: New England Indians, Colonists, and the Origins*

*of American Slavery* (Cornell University Press, 2015); Wendy Warren, *New England Bound: Slavery and Colonization in Early America* (Liveright, 2016); Joanne Pope Melish, *Disowning Slavery: Gradual Emancipation and "Race" in New England, 1780–1860* (Cornell University Press, 2018); John Wood Sweet, *Bodies Politic: Negotiating Race in the American North, 1730–1830* (Johns Hopkins University Press, 2003); David Waldstreicher, *Runaway America: Benjamin Franklin, Slavery, and the American Revolution* (Hill and Wang, 2014); Jared Ross Hardesty, *Black Lives, Native Lands, White Worlds: A History of Slavery in New England* (Bright Leaf, 2019); Christy Clark-Pujara, *Dark Work: The Business of Slavery in Rhode Island* (New York University Press, 2016); and Jill Lepore, *New York Burning: Liberty, Slavery, and Conspiracy in Eighteenth-Century Manhattan* (Knopf, 2005) and *These Truths: A History of the United States* (W. W. Norton, 2018). Lepore demythologizes Plymouth Colony by pointing out that the Pilgrims settled land formerly occupied by Natives, with whom the Plymouth settlers had increasingly hostile relations, culminating in the brutal King Philip's War. See Lepore, "Plymouth Rocked," *New Yorker,* April 24, 2006; *These Truths;* and *The Name of War: King Philip's War and the Origins of American Identity* (Knopf, 1998). In *The City-State of Boston: The Rise and Fall of an Atlantic Power, 1630–1865* (Princeton University Press, 2019), Mark Peterson focuses on Boston, which, he argues, became virtually a city-state with pretensions to Puritan virtue but hypocritical dependence on the Atlantic slave trade. Peterson maintains that Boston lost its autonomy after the Revolution and experienced the failure of its initial Puritan values.

6. Richard A. Bailey, *Race and Redemption in Puritan New England* (Oxford University Press, 2014).
7. Ira Berlin, *Many Thousands Gone: The First Two Centuries of Slavery in North America* (Belknap, 1998), 15, 93.
8. For statistics on enslavement in New England, see Warren, *New England Bound*, 211–12; Lorenzo J. Greene, *The Negro in Colonial New England* (Columbia University Press, 1942), 142–48; Melish, *Disowning Slavery*, 23; Clark-Pujara, *Dark Work*, 20; Peter Kolchin, *American Slavery, 1619–1877* (Hill and Wang, 1993), 82. For the numbers in the Southern colonies, see Lorena S. Walsh, *Motives of Honor, Pleasure, and Profit: Plantation Management in the Colonial Chesapeake, 1607–1763* (University of North Carolina Press, 2010), 34, 37; Philip D. Morgan, *Slave Counterpoint: Black Culture in the Eighteenth-Century Chesapeake and Lowcountry* (University of North Carolina Press, 1998), 70–73; Berlin, *Many Thousands Gone*, 17. For a comparative analysis of Northern and Southern slave trafficking, see David Eltis and David Richardson, *Atlas of the Transatlantic Slave Trade* (Yale University Press, 2010), 22.
9. For the transformation over time of Plymouth Rock into an important national symbol, see John Seelye, *Memory's Nation: The Place of Plymouth Rock* (University of North Carolina Press, 1998).
10. *The Collected Works of Abraham Lincoln*, ed. Roy P. Basler, Lloyd A. Dunlap, and Marion Dolores Pratt, 8 vols. (Rutgers University Press, 1953–55), 3:27 (hereafter cited as *CW*).

***Chapter 1: Launchings***

1. For an especially useful discussion of this topic, see Joshua Miller, "Direct Democracy and the Puritan Theory of Membership," *Journal of Politics* 53, no. 1 (February 1991): 57–74.
2. Excerpt from a Letter from John Rolfe to Sir Edwin Sandys, January 1620, in *The Records of the Virginia Company, 1606–1626*, ed. Susan Myra Kingsbury, vol. 3, *Documents*, (United States Government Printing Office, 1906), 3: 241.
3. Michael Leroy Oberg, *The Head in Edward Nugent's Hand: Roanoke's Forgotten Indians* (University of Pennsylvania Press, 2010), 98–99.
4. "Head of the Puritans" quoted in Arthur Percival Newton, *The Colonising Activities of the English Puritans: The Last Phase of the Elizabethan Struggle with Spain* (Yale University Press, 1914), 41; "popery" quoted in Douglas Bradburn, "The Eschatological Origins of the English Empire," in *Early Modern Virginia: Reconsidering the Old Dominion*, ed. Douglas Bradburn and John C. Coombs (University of Virginia Press, 2011), 44.
5. Quoted in John C. Coombs, "The Phases of Conversion: A New Chronology for the Rise of Slavery in Early Virginia," *William and Mary Quarterly* 68, no. 3 (July 2011): 340.

6. Some of the information in this paragraph and the next one is derived from Linda M. Heywood and John K. Thornton, "In Search of the 1619 African Arrivals," *Virginia Magazine of History and Biography* 127, no. 3 (2019): 200–211; Beth Austin, "1619: Virginia's First Africans," Hampton History Museum, December 2019, hampton.gov/3580/The-1619-Landing-Report-FAQs; and Paul Musselwhite, Peter C. Mancall, and James Horn, ed., *Virginia 1619: Slavery and Freedom in the Making of English America* (University of North Carolina Press, 2019), 85–107.
7. John Rolfe to Sir Edwin Sandys, January 1620, in *The Records of the Virginia Company of London*, 243.
8. Brendan Wolfe, "Free Blacks in Colonial Virginia," *Encyclopedia Virginia*, Virginia Humanities, last modified August 26, 2024, encyclopediavirginia.org/entries/free-blacks-in-colonial-virginia.
9. For example, Carl N. Degler argues that the Jamestown Blacks were enslaved from the beginning; see Degler, "Slavery and the Genesis of American Race Prejudice," *Comparative Studies in Society and History* 2, no. 1 (1959): 49–66. See also Lorena S. Walsh, *Motives of Honor, Pleasure, and Profit: Plantation Management in the Colonial Chesapeake, 1607–1763* (University of North Carolina Press, 2010), 113–21. For an analysis of historians' discussion of this issue, see Alden T. Vaughan, "The Origins Debate: Slavery and Racism in Seventeenth-Century Virginia," *Virginia Magazine of History and Biography* 97, no. 3 (1989): 311–54.
10. Laura A. Croghan, "'The Negroes to Serve Forever': The Evolution of Blacks' Life and Labor in Seventeenth-Century Virginia" (master's thesis, William and Mary, 1994), 60–67. The Eastern Shore consisted of Northampton and Accomack Counties: the only region in early Virginia for which reliable data has survived.
11. T. H. Breen and Stephen Innes, *"Myne Owne Ground": Race and Freedom on Virginia's Eastern Shore, 1640–1676* (Oxford University Press, 2004), 68–69.
12. George M. Fredrickson, "Toward a Social Interpretation of the Development of American Racism," in *Key Issues in the Afro-American Experience*, ed. Nathan I. Huggins, Martin Kilson, and Daniel M. Fox, vol. 1, *To 1877* (Harcourt Brace Jovanovich, 1971), 1: 247. Quoted in Breen and Innes, *"Myne Owne Ground,"* 69.
13. Helen Tunnicliff Catterall, ed., *Judicial Cases Concerning American Slavery and the Negro*, vol. 1, *Cases from the Courts of England, Virginia, West Virginia, and Kentucky* (Carnegie Institution of Washington, 1926), 57.
14. See Aline Helg, "Self-Purchase and Military Service: Legal but Limited Paths to Emancipation," in *Slave No More: Self-Liberation Before Abolitionism in the Americas*, trans. Lara Vergnaud (University of North Carolina Press, 2019).
15. Lois Green Carr and Lorena S. Walsh, "Economic Diversification and Labor Organization in the Chesapeake, 1650–1820," in *Work and Labor in Early America*, ed. Stephen Innes (University of North Carolina Press, 1988), 144–88; and Paul G. E. Clemens, *The Atlantic Economy and Colonial Maryland's Eastern Shore: From Tobacco to Grain* (Cornell University Press, 1980), 85.
16. Ira Berlin, "Time, Space, and the Evolution of Afro-American Society on British Mainland North America," *American Historical Review* 85, no. 1 (1980): 69.
17. Paul Heinegg, *Free African Americans of North Carolina, Virginia, and South Carolina from the Colonial Period to About 1820*, 6th ed. (Genealogical Publishing Company, 2021); and Kathleen M. Brown, *Good Wives, Nasty Wenches, and Anxious Patriarchs: Gender, Race, and Power in Colonial Virginia* (University of North Carolina Press, 1996), 107–16.
18. Breen and Innes, *"Myne Owne Ground"*, 83.
19. William Bradford, *History of Plymouth Plantation, 1620–1647* (1656; repr., Massachusetts Historical Society, 1912), 1: 4.
20. Oliver Perry Temple, *The Covenanter, the Cavalier, and the Puritan* (Cincinnati: Robert Clarke, 1897), 18.
21. Bradford, *History of Plymouth Plantation*, 1: 7; and Michael P. Winship, *Hot Protestants: A History of Puritanism in England and America* (Yale University Press, 2018), 17.
22. R. W. Dale, *History of English Congregationalism* (A. C. Armstrong and Son, 1907), chaps. 5 and 6.
23. Quoted in John G. Turner, *They Knew They Were Pilgrims: Plymouth Colony and the Contest for American Liberty* (Yale University Press, 2020), 31.

24. David Harris Willson, *King VI and I* (Cape, 1956), 207.
25. Bradford, *History of Plymouth Plantation*, 1: 24–25.
26. *The Works of John Robinson, Pastor of the Pilgrim Fathers*, ed. Robert Ashton (London: John Snow, 1851), 3:156.
27. Bradford, *History of Plymouth Plantation*, 1: 16.
28. Some information in this paragraph is derived from "Pilgrim Life in Leiden: Pilgrim Occupations in Leiden," Leiden American Pilgrim Museum, accessed August 23, 2022, https://web.archive.org/web/20230902124701/https://leidenamericanpilgrimmuseum.org/en/page/pilgrim-life-in-leiden-pilgrim-occupations-in-leiden.
29. *The Works of John Robinson,* 3: 42–43.
30. *The Works of John Robinson,* 2: 140.
31. Walter H. Burgess, *John Robinson, Pastor of the Pilgrim Fathers: A Study of His Life and Times* (Williams and Norgate, 1920), 166; and Randal Rust, "Site of John Robinson's Home at the Jean Pesynhof—Pilgrim Landmark in Leiden, 1611–1625," *American History Central,* November 6, 2022, americanhistorycentral.com/entries/jean-peysnhof-site-of-john-robinson-home-pilgrim-landmark-leiden.
32. Bradford, *History of Plymouth Plantation*, 1: 25; "every particular person . . ." quoted in Jeremy Dupertuis Bangs, "Dutch Contributions to Religious Toleration," *Church History* 79, no. 3 (2010): 586.
33. Evan Haefeli, *New Netherland and the Dutch Origins of American Religious Liberty* (University of Pennsylvania Press, 2012), 39–48.
34. For the Pilgrims' contexts in Leiden and beyond, see especially Jeremy D. Bangs, *Strangers and Pilgrims, Travellers and Sojourners: Leiden and the Foundations of Plymouth Plantation* (General Society of Mayflower Descendants, 2009), and Francis J. Bremer, *One Small Candle: The Story of William Bradford and the Pilgrim Fathers* (Oxford University Press, 2020).
35. Alexander Young, *Chronicles of the Pilgrim Fathers of New Plymouth* (Boston: Little & Brown, 1841), 389–90.
36. William T. Davis, *History of the Town of Plymouth* (Philadelphia: T. W. Lewis, 1885), 14. The next quotations in this paragraph are on p. 13.
37. Bradford, *History of Plymouth Plantation*, 1: 53. The next quotation in this paragraph is on p. 60. The quotations in the following paragraph are on p. 64.
38. Bradford, *History of Plymouth Plantation*, 1: 73.
39. Willis Mason West, *The Story of American Democracy, Political and Industrial* (Allyn and Bacon, 1922), 34.
40. Young, *Chronicles of the Pilgrim Fathers of the Colony of Plymouth*, 56. The quotation in the next paragraph is from p. 383.
41. The dates given here for the *Mayflower* voyage and landing are according to the "Old Style" (OS) or Julian calendar, not the "New Style" (NS) or Gregorian calendar, used today. Therefore, the *Mayflower* left England on September 6 (OS), which corresponds to September 16 (NS). The ship anchored off Cape Cod on November 11 (OS), and its shallop—the small boat used for exploring the coast—landed, possibly at Plymouth Rock, on December 21, 1620 (OS), equivalent to December 31 (NS).
42. Nathaniel Philbrick, *Mayflower: A Story of Courage, Community, and War* (Viking, 2006), 14–16; Bangs, *Strangers and Pilgrims, Travellers*, 145–48; Eugene Aubrey Stratton, *Plymouth Colony: Its History and People, 1620–1691* (Ancestry Publishing, 1986), 32–34.
43. A splendid study of providential intervention in the world is Alexandra Walsham's *Providence in Early Modern England* (Oxford University Press, 1999).
44. Bradford, *History of Plymouth Plantation*, 1: 149.
45. Bradford, *History of Plymouth Plantation*, 1: 156.
46. George Bancroft, *History of the United States, from the Discovery of the American Continent* (Boston: Charles Brown, 1834), 1: 310.
47. Julia L. Ernst "The Mayflower Compact: Celebrating Four Hundred Years of Influence on U.S. Democracy," *North Dakota Law Review* 95, no. 1 (2020): 3.
48. John Quincy Adams, *The New England Confederacy of 1643: A Discourse Delivered Before the Massachusetts Historical Society* (Boston: Little and Brown, 1843), 17, 21.

*Chapter 2: Roots of American Democracy*

1. Alexis de Tocqueville, *Democracy in America: English Edition*, ed. Eduardo Nolla, trans. James T. Schleifer (1835; repr. Liberty Fund, 2012), 1: 51. The other quotations in this and the following paragraphs are also from this page.
2. "Boston," in *The Complete Works of Ralph Waldo Emerson*, vol. 12, *Natural History of Intellect and Other Papers* (Houghton, Mifflin, 1904), 212.
3. Karen Ordahl Kupperman, "Apathy and Death in Early Jamestown," *Journal of American History* 66, no. 1 (June 1979): 24.
4. Bradford, *History of Plymouth Plantation*, 1: 194.
5. Eugene Aubrey Stratton, *Plymouth Colony: Its History & People, 1620–1691* (Ancestry Publishing, 1986).
6. Henry Wadsworth Longfellow, *The Courtship of Miles Standish* (1858; repr., Boston: Houghton, Mifflin, 1883), 26.
7. Much of my information on housing in Plymouth is based on John Demos, *A Little Commonwealth: Family Life in Plymouth Colony* (Oxford University Press, 1970), and James Deetz and Patricia Scott Deetz, *The Times of Their Lives: Life, Love, and Death in Plymouth Colony* (W. H. Freeman, 2000).
8. Bruce C. Daniels, *New England Nation: The Country the Puritans Built* (Palgrave Macmillan, 2012), 9.
9. Illuminating books on white-Indian relations in this period include David J. Silverman, *This Land Is Their Land: The Wampanoag Indians, Plymouth Colony, and the Troubled History of Thanksgiving* (Bloomsbury, 2019); and Newell, *Brethren by Nature.*
10. An authoritative study of King Philip's War is Lepore, *The Name of War.*
11. "Indians A.D. 1600–1800," Virginia Department of Historic Resources, January 17, 2017, dhr.virginia.gov/blog-posts/indians-a-d-1600-1800.
12. John Smith, *Advertisements for the Unexperienced Planters of New England, or Any Where* (1631), in *The Complete Works of Captain John Smith, 1580–1631* ed. Philip L. Barbour (University of North Carolina Press, 1986) 3: 295.
13. William Crashaw, *A sermon preached in London before the right honorable the Lord Lawarre, Lord Governour and Captaine Generall of Virginea* (London: William Welby, 1610), n.p.
14. William Strachey, ed., *For the Colony in Virginea Britannia. Lawes Divine, Morall and Martiall, &c.* (London: Walter Barre, 1612), 7.
15. Edward L. Bond and Joan R. Gundersen, "The Episcopal Church in Virginia, 1607–2007," *Virginia Magazine of History and Biography* 115, no. 2 (2007): 173.
16. William Waller Hening, ed., *The Statutes at Large; Being a Collection of All the Laws of Virginia* (Richmond, VA: Samuel Pleasants, 1809), 1: 123. The quotation in the next sentence is also from this page.
17. Hening, *The Statutes at Large*, 2: 47.
18. Mark DeWolfe Howe, *Readings in American Legal History* (Harvard University Press, 1949), 204.
19. William Brigham, ed., *The Compact with the Charter and Laws of the Colony of New Plymouth* (Boston: Dutton and Wentworth, 1836), 48 (hereafter cited as *Plymouth Colony Laws*).
20. Ashbel Steele, *Chief of the Pilgrims, or, The Life and Time of William Brewster: Ruling Elder of the Pilgrim Company That Founded New Plymouth, the Parent Colony of New England, in 1620* (Philadelphia: J. B. Lippincott, 1857), 35.
21. See Mark A. Peterson, "The Plymouth Church and the Evolution of Puritan Religious Culture," *New England Quarterly* 66, no. 4 (1993): 570–93.
22. *Plymouth Church Records, 1620–1859* (The Colonial Society of Massachusetts, 1920), 1: 54.
23. *Plymouth Church Records,* 1: 52.
24. Bradford, *History of Plymouth Plantation*, 1: 147.
25. *Plymouth Church Records*, 1: xviii.
26. Quoted in Mark A. Peterson, "The Plymouth Church and the Evolution of Puritan Religious Culture," *New England Quarterly* 66, no. 4 (1993): 573–74.

27. *Bradford's "History of Plimoth Plantation." From the Original Manuscript* (Boston: Wright & Potter, 1898), 419.
28. *Diary of Samuel Sewall, 1674–1729*, ed. M. Halsey Thomas (Farrar, Straus and Giroux, 1973), 1:378.
29. Quoted in Robert Louis Wilken, *Liberty in the Things of God: The Christian Origins of Religious Freedom* (Yale University Press, 2021), 144. My discussion of Williams in this section is informed by pp. 142–50 of Wilken's book.
30. Wilken, *Liberty in the Things of God*, 143–45.
31. *The Complete Writings of Roger Williams*, ed. Perry Miller (Russell & Russell, 1963), 1: 65.
32. Roger Williams, *A Key into the Language of America: or, An Help to the Language of the Natives in That Part of America Called New-England* (London: Gregory Dexter, 1643), 53.
33. *Journals of Ralph Waldo Emerson*, ed. Edward Waldo Emerson and Waldo Emerson Forbes (Houghton Mifflin, 1911), 7:341–42.
34. Donald S. Lutz, ed., *Colonial Origins of the American Constitution: A Documentary History* (Liberty Fund, 1998), 61.
35. Cotton Mather, *Magnalia Christi Americana: or, The Ecclesiastical History of New-England, from Its First Planting in the Year 1620, unto the Year of Our Lord, 1698* (1702; repr., Hartford: Silas Andrus, 1820), 2: 450.
36. William Barlow, *The Summe and Substance of the Conference [. . .] at Hampton Court*, January 14, 1603 [1604] (London: John Windet, 1604), 46–47. James's comment on "marginall notes," quoted later in this paragraph, is also from this source.
37. See Christopher Hill, *The English Bible and the Seventeenth-Century Revolution* (Penguin, 1993), and Abram C. Van Engen, "Origins and Last Farewells: Bible Wars, Textual Form, and the Making of American History," *New England Quarterly* 86, no. 4 (2013): 543–92.
38. Bradford, *History of Plymouth Plantation*, 1: 8.
39. For Anne Hutchinson's debt to the Geneva Bible, see Michael G. Ditmore, "A Prophetess in Her Own Country: An Exegesis of Anne Hutchinson's 'Immediate Revelation,'" *William and Mary Quarterly* 57, no. 2 (2000): 349–92.
40. "The Mayflower Compact," The Mayflower Society, last updated November 10, 2024, themayflowersociety.org/history/the-mayflower-compact.
41. *The Works of John Robinson*, 3: 42–43.
42. Peggy M. Baker, "The Plymouth Colony Parent: Setting the Stage," Pilgrim Hall Museum, 2007, pilgrimhall.org/pdf/The_Plymouth_Colony_Patent.pdf.
43. *Plymouth Colony Laws*, 25.
44. Roland Greene Usher, *The Pilgrims and Their History* (Macmillan, 1918), 155–56.
45. Beverley W. Bond Jr., *The Quit-Rent System in the American Colonies* (Yale University Press, 1919), 14.
46. Francis Baylies, *An Historical Memoir of the Colony of New Plymouth: From the Flight of the Pilgrims into Holland in the Year 1608, to the Union of That Colony with Massachusetts in 1692* (Boston: Hilliard, Gray, Little, and Wilkins, 1830), 27.
47. Mercy Otis Warren, *History of the Rise, Progress and Termination of the American Revolution* (Boston: Manning and Loring, 1805), 1:11.
48. However, widespread democratic representation in Massachusetts did not come until 1664, when the colony accepted non–church members as freemen. See Patrick F. Campbell, "The Concept of Representation in American Political Development: Lessons of the Massachusetts Bay Puritans," *Polity* 47, no. 1 (2015): 33–60.
49. Michael G. Hall, "Origins in Massachusetts of the Constitutional Doctrine of Advice and Consent," *Proceedings of the Massachusetts Historical Society*, Third Series, vol. 91 (Massachusetts Historical Society, 1979): 4.
50. Winthrop, *A Modell of Christian Charity* (1630; repr. Boston: Massachusetts Historical Society, 1838), 47.
51. Francis J. Bremer, *The Puritan Experiment: New England Society from Bradford to Edwards*

(University Press of New England, 1995), 28, and Virginia DeJohn Anderson, *New England's Generation: The Great Migration and the Formation of Society and Culture in the Seventeenth Century* (Cambridge University Press, 1991), 3–4.

52. G. B. Warden, "Law Reform in England and New England, 1620 to 1660," *William and Mary Quarterly* 35, no. 4 (1978): 668–90.
53. "John Adams & the Massachusetts Constitution," Mass.gov, accessed February 7, 2023; mass.gov/guides/john-adams-the-massachusetts-constitution.
54. Letter from William Bradford to Isaac Allerton, Plymouth, September 8, 1623, in *American Historical Review* 8, no. 2 (1903): 299. After William Bradford's death in 1657, voting in Plymouth became more restrictive; religious and property requirements were imposed during the governorship (1857–72) of the orthodox Calvinist Thomas Prence.
55. *Plymouth Church Records*, 111–13.
56. Nathaniel B. Shurtleff, ed., *Records of the Colony of New Plymouth in New England* (Boston: William White, 1855), 3–4: 73.
57. Bradley Chapin, *Criminal Justice in Colonial America, 1606–1660* (University of Georgia Press, 1983), 5.
58. George L. Haskins, "The Legal Heritage of Plymouth Colony," *University of Pennsylvania Law Review* 110, no. 6 (1962): 848–49.
59. Lutz, ed., *Colonial Origins of the American Constitution*, 61.
60. *Plymouth Colony Laws*, 42.
61. *Plymouth Colony Laws*, 241. The quotation in the next sentence is on p. 242.
62. See Lee J. Alston and Morton Owen Schapiro, "Inheritance Laws Across Colonies: Causes and Consequences," *Journal of Economic History* 44, no. 2, (1984): 277–87.
63. See especially Douglass's February 14, 1860, speech "Progress and Divisions of Anti-Slavery," *Frederick Douglass Papers*, 1.3:323–33.
64. *New York Herald*, January 26, 1861.
65. "The Logic of History," *Wisconsin Daily Patriot*, January 6, 1864.
66. "George Sanders' Advice to the Northern Conservatives," *Richmond Whig*, December 30, 1862.
67. *The Book of the General Lawes and Libertyes Concerning the Inhabitants of Massachusets Collected Out of the Records of the General Court* (Cambridge, MA: Matthew Day, 1648), 5–6.
68. Randall McGowen, "Making the 'Bloody Code'?: Forgery Legislation in Eighteenth-Century England," in *Law, Crime and English Society, 1660–1830*, ed. Norma Landau (Cambridge University Press, 2002), 118; and Steven Robert Wilf, "Imagining Justice: Politics, Storytelling, and Criminal Law in Revolutionary America, 1763–1792" (PhD diss., Yale University, 1995), 312.
69. Many of the details and quotations about sexual crimes in this and the following paragraph are from Robert F. Oaks, "'Things Fearful to Name'": Sodomy and Buggery in Seventeenth-Century New England, *Journal of Social History* 12, no. 2 (1978): 268–81.
70. Oaks, "'Things Fearful to Name,'" 276. The quotation about Thomas Hogg in the next sentence is also from this page. The information in the next paragraph about other bestiality cases is from elsewhere in Oaks's article.
71. Oaks, "'Things Fearful to Name,'" 271.
72. Shurtleff, *Records of the Colony of New Plymouth*, 1:64.
73. John Noble, ed., *Records of the Court of Assistants of the Massachusetts Bay, 1630–1692* (County of Suffolk, 1904), 2: 139–40.
74. Abby Chandler, "At the Magistrate's Discretion: Sexual Crime and New England Law, 1636–1718" (PhD diss., University of Maine, 2008), 5.
75. Shurtleff, *Records of the Colony of New Plymouth*, 1: 132.
76. Shurtleff, *Records of the Colony of New Plymouth*, 2: 28.
77. Joel S. Berson, "On the Trail of the Scarlet AD," *Nathaniel Hawthorne Review* 39, no. 1 (2013): 137.
78. Laura Hanft Korobkin, "The Scarlet Letter of the Law: Hawthorne and Criminal Justice," *Novel* 30, no. 2 (1997): 203n7.

79. Berson, "On the Trail of the Scarlet AD," 141, 144.
80. Michel Foucault, *Discipline and Punish: The Birth of the Prison,* trans. Alan Sheridan (Pantheon, 1977).
81. Alice Morse Earle, *Curious Punishments of Bygone Days* (Chicago: Herbert S. Stone, 1896), 94.
82. Earle, *Curious Punishments*, 146.
83. Davis Y. Paschall, "Crime and Punishment in Colonial Virginia, 1607–1776" (PhD diss., College of William and Mary, 1939), 31–32.
84. Earle, *Curious Punishments*, 144.
85. Earle, *Curious Punishments*, 17.
86. "Ducking a Scold. A Custom Quite Popular at One Time in This Country," *Washington Bee* (Washington, DC), June 22, 1912. See also Earle, *Curious Punishments*, 20.
87. This incident and the one described in the next sentence are in Earle, *Curious Punishments*, 20–21.
88. Paschall, "Crime and Punishment in Colonial Virginia," 39.
89. Paschall, "Crime and Punishment in Colonial Virginia," 39.
90. Hening, *The Statutes at Large*, 1: 248.
91. William Sewel, *The History of the Rise, Increase, and Progress of the Christian People Called Quakers* (London: William Phillips, 1811), 337. The four Quakers executed were Marmaduke Stephenson, William Robinson, Mary Dyer, and William Leddra. See Carla Gardina Pestana, "The Quaker Executions as Myth and History," *Journal of American History* 80, no. 2 (1993): 441–69.
92. *Acts of Assembly, Passed in the Colony of Virginia, from 1662 to 1715* (London: John Baskett, 1727), 1: 61.
93. Nachman Ben-Yehuda, "Problems Inherent in Socio-Historical Approaches to the European Witch Craze," *Journal for the Scientific Study of Religion* 20, no. 4 (1981): 328.
94. Wallace Notestein, *A History of Witchcraft in England from 1558 to 1718* (American Historical Association, 1911).
95. Samuel Sewall reports of Corey that "much pains were used with him two days, one after another," in *The Diary of Samuel Sewall, 1674–1729*, 1:363. For an account of the twenty executions, see Marilynne K. Roach, *The Salem Witch Trials: A Day-by-Day Chronicle of a Community Under Siege* (Cooper Square Press, 2002), pp. 610–12.
96. Much of the information on witchcraft in Virginia in this and the following paragraphs is derived from Carson O. Hudson Jr., *These Detestable Slaves of the Devill: A Concise Guide to Witchcraft in Colonial Virginia* (Infinity Publishing, 2001); and Richard Beale Davis, "The Devil in Virginia in the Seventeenth Century," *Virginia Magazine of History and Biography*, 65, 2 (April 1957): 131–49.
97. Also, two women en route to Maryland were thrown overboard as suspected witches—Mary Lee in 1654 and Elizabeth Richardson in 1658. See Diana Lyn Laulainen-Schein, "Comparative Counterpoints: Witchcraft Accusations in Early Modern Lancashire and the Chesapeake" (PhD diss., University of Minnesota, 2004), 69. See also Polly Johnson, "Maritime Witchcraft and Colonial Trials," *Journal of Early American History* 12, no. 2 (2012): 153–76.

***Chapter 3: Puritanism, Race, and Slavery***

1. Theodore K. Rabb, *Jacobean Gentleman: Sir Edwin Sandys, 1561–1629* (Princeton University Press, 2017), 192–93.
2. See Mark Kishlansky, "Martyrs' Tales," *Journal of British Studies* 53, no. 2 (2014): 334–55.
3. Elizabeth Donnan, ed., *Documents Illustrative of the History of the Slave Trade to America*, vol. 3, *New England and the Middle Colonies* (Carnegie Institution of Washington, 1932), 4.
4. Wendy Anne Warren, "'The Cause of Her Grief': The Rape of a Slave in Early New England," *Journal of American History* 93, no. 4 (2007): 1031–49.
5. Douglas Bradburn, "The Eschatological Origins of the English Empire," in *Early Modern Virginia: Reconsidering the Old Dominion*, ed. Douglas Bradburn and John C. Coombs (University of Virginia Press, 2011), 39.
6. Quoted in Francis J. Bremer, *John Winthrop: America's Forgotten Founding Father* (Oxford University Press, 2005), 129.
7. Karen Ordahl Kupperman, *Providence Island, 1630–1641: The Other Puritan Colony* (Cambridge

University Press, 1993), 2. For more on the Puritans and Providence Island, see Jared Van Duinen, *Prosopography and the Providence Island Company: The Nature of Puritan Opposition in 1630s England* (Oxford University Press, 2007).

8. Musselwhite, Mancall, and Horn, ed., *Virginia 1619*, 94.
9. *Winthrop's Journal, "History of New England," 1630–1649*, ed. James Kendall Hosmer (Barnes & Noble, 1953), 1: 260
10. Donnan, ed., *Documents Illustrative of the History of the Slave Trade*, 3: 8.
11. Greene, *The Negro in Colonial New England*, 73–74. The statistic in the next sentence is from p. 76.
12. Edward J. Larson, *American Inheritance: Liberty and Slavery in the Birth of a Nation, 1765–1795* (W. W. Norton, 2023), 7–8.
13. Noble, ed., *Records of the Court of Assistants of the Massachusetts Bay, 1630–1692*, 2: 78–79. The cases of John Haslewood and Gyles Player, mentioned in the next sentence, are from p. 79. The remaining cases mentioned in this paragraph are on the following pages: John Kempe, p. 86; William Andrews released, p. 87; Thomas Savory, p. 87; and Elizabeth Sedgwick, p. 118.
14. Greene, *The Negro in Colonial New England*, 155–56. The cases of Nicholas and Caesar in the next two sentences are both from p. 156.
15. Robert C. Twombly and Robert H. Moore, "Black Puritan: The Negro in Seventeenth-Century Massachusetts," *William and Mary Quarterly* 24, no. 2 (1967): 226–27.
16. Hening, *The Statutes at Large*, 1: 226; Shurtleff, *Records of the Colony of New Plymouth*, 2: 99.
17. "Beyond the Pilgrim Story. Long Road to Freedom: African-Americans in the Old Colony," Pilgrim Hall Museum, accessed March 1, 2023, https://pilgrimhall.org/long_road_to_freedom.htm.
18. Shurtleff, ed., *Records of the Colony of New Plymouth*, 6: 141–42.
19. Shurtleff, ed., *Records of the Colony of New Plymouth*, 5: 212.
20. This estimate, made by a historian of Plymouth, William T. Davis, is cited in "Beyond the Pilgrim Story: Long Road to Freedom," Pilgrim Hall Museum, accessed September 25, 2022, https://www.pilgrimhall.org/long_road_to_freedom.htm.
21. Greene, *The Negro in Colonial New England*, 262, 300.
22. Albert Edward McKinley, *Suffrage Franchise in the Thirteen English Colonies in America* (University of Pennsylvania Press, 1905), 36, 92, 137, 172. See also Greene, *The Negro in Colonial New England*, 300.
23. Geneviève Fabre, "Performing Freedom: Negro Election Celebrations as Political and Intellectual Resistance in New England, 1740–1850," in *Celebrating Ethnicity and Nation: American Festive Culture from the Revolution to the Early 20th Century*, ed. Jürgen Heideking, Geneviève Fabre, and Kai Dreisbach (Berghahn Books, 2001), 91.
24. Greene, *The Negro in Colonial New England*, 251–52; Carolyn B. Ivanoff, "Ebenezer Bassett's Historic Journey," Connecticut History, Connecticut Humanities, February 3, 2022, connecticuthistory.org/ebenezer-bassetts-historic-journey.
25. Douglass, *Frederick Douglass Papers*, April 6, 1855.
26. *National Eagle* (Claremont, NH), May 12, 1843. For Douglass's accounts of the South's treatment of enslaved people as things, see David W. Blight, *Frederick Douglass: Prophet of Freedom* (Simon & Schuster, 2018), especially chap. 8.
27. Morgan Godwyn, *The Negro's and Indians Advocate* (London: J. D., 1680), unnumbered page.
28. Frederick Douglass, "Negroes Are Men!" (1847); reprinted in *Liberator*, April 20, 1849.
29. *Address by Hon. Frederick Douglass, Delivered in the Congregational Church, Washington, D.C., April 16, 1883* (Washington, DC: n.p., 1883), 9. The remaining quotations in the paragraph are on pp. 10–12. The quotation in the next paragraph is on p. 10.
30. See Carter Godwin Woodson, *Education of the Negro Prior to 1861* (G. P. Putnam's Sons, 1915), chap. 2.
31. Henry Parker, *Jus Populi* (London: Robert Bostock, 1644), 40.
32. Richard Baxter, *A Christian Directory, or, A Body of Practical Divinity and Cases of Conscience* (1672; repr., London: Richard Edwards, 1825), 3: 217.
33. Roger Williams, letter to John Winthrop, c. July 1637, quoted in George H. Moore, *Notes on the History of Slavery in Massachusetts* (New York: D. Appleton & Co., 1866), 2. However, it should be

noted that Williams enslaved a Pequot boy after the Pequot War, and in the 1670s some of his fellow Rhode Islanders sold into slavery Wampanoag people taken captive in King Philip's War.

34. Quoted in John Donoghue, "'Out of the Land of Bondage': The English Revolution and the Atlantic Origins of Abolition," *American Historical Review* 115, no. 4 (2010): 963.
35. "Law Limiting Terms of Servitude, 1652," Rhode Island State Archives, accessed March 30, 2023, docs.sos.ri.gov/documents/civicsandeducation/teacherresources/1652-Slavery.pdf.
36. Greene, *The Negro in Colonial New England*, 74. By 1774, the 59,678 people living in Rhode Island included 3,761 Blacks, who made up 6.1 percent of the total population—a percentage of Black residents twice as high as Connecticut's and three times greater than Massachusetts's.
37. See Clark-Pujara, *Dark Work;* and Jay Coughtry, *The Notorious Triangle: Rhode Island and the African Slave Trade, 1700–1807* (Temple University Press, 1981).
38. *New-York Observer*, September 3, 1831; *Pennsylvania Freeman*, August 31, 1837. The Moses Brown quotation in the next sentence is from the *Freeman*'s reprint of the law.
39. Donald F. Durnbaugh, "Baptists and Quakers—Left Wing Puritans?," *Quaker History* 62, no. 2 (1973): 67–82. Similarly, the Marxist historian Christopher Hill describes Quakerism as one of the radical offshoots of the Puritan upheaval in *The World Turned Upside Down: Radical Ideas During the English Revolution* (Penguin, 1972).
40. *Address by Hon. Frederick Douglass,* 9. For Lincoln on the Quakers as antislavery pioneers, see *CW* 2: 299.
41. *Minute Made by the Germantown Friends Against Slavery, 1688*, in *Papers of the American Society of Church History*, 8 (January 1896): 267.
42. Kenneth Silverman, *The Life and Times of Cotton Mather* (Harper & Row, 1984), 117.
43. Richard Francis, *Judge Sewall's Apology: The Salem Witch Trials and the Forming of an American Conscience* (HarperCollins, 2006).
44. *Salem Register* (Salem, MA), January 13, 1859; reprinted from *The New York Independent.*
45. *Liberator*, October 23, 1846.
46. Samuel Sewall, *The Selling of Joseph, A Memorial* (Boston: Bartholomew Green and John Allen, 1700), 1. The remaining quotations in this and the next two paragraphs are also from p. 1.
47. The quotations in this and the following six paragraphs are from Sewall, *The Selling of Joseph*, pp. 2–3.
48. Lee W. Gibbs, "The Puritan Natural Law Theory of William Ames," *Harvard Theological Review* 64, no. 1 (1971): 39. The quotation in the next sentence is also from this page.
49. Sewall, *The Selling of Joseph*, 3. Here I used Google Translate to translate Ames's statement, which is in Latin.
50. Edmund S. Morgan, "Slavery and Freedom: The American Paradox," *Journal of American History* 59, no. 1 (1972): 5–29. Among recent historians who have explored such contradictions, a standout is Jill Lepore in *These Truths.*
51. Zachary McLeod Hutchins, *Before Equiano: A Prehistory of the North American Slave Narrative* (University of North Carolina Press, 2022), 61.
52. *Samuel Sewall's Diary*, ed. Mark Van Doren (Macy-Masius, 1927), 158.
53. Louis Weeks III, "Cotton Mather and the Quakers," *Quaker History* 59, no. 1 (1970): 24.
54. Cotton Mather, *The Negro Christianized. An Essay to Excite and Assist That Good Work, the Instruction of Negro-Servants in Christianity* (Boston: B. Green, 1706), 14. The quotations in the next paragraph are on pp. 3 and 4, successively.
55. *Diary of Cotton Mather, 1681–1724* (Massachusetts Historical Society, 1911–12), 1: 564–65.
56. Silverman, *The Life and Times of Cotton Mather*, 264.
57. *Diary of Cotton Mather*, 2: 663.
58. Quoted in Henry Wheaton, Edward Tyrrel Channing, and William Bourn Oliver Peabody, *Lives of William Pinkney, William Ellery,* and *Cotton Mather* (Boston: Hilliard, Gray, 1836), 334.
59. Amicus, *Slavery Among the Puritans: A Letter to the Rev. Moses Stuart* (Boston: Charles C. Little and James Brown, 1850), 94.

60. *Diary of Cotton Mather, 1709–1724*, ed. Worthington Chauncey Ford (Frederick Ungar, 1957), 2: 699, 711.
61. Max Koslov, "Introducing Inoculation, 1721," *Scientist*, January 1, 2021, the-scientist.com/introducing-inoculation-1721-68275. See also Erin Blakemore, "How an Enslaved African Man in Boston Helped Save Generations from Smallpox," History Channel, April 8, 2021, history.com/news/smallpox-vaccine-onesimus-slave-cotton-mather.
62. William Douglass, *Inoculation of the Small Pox as Practised in Boston* (Boston: J. Franklin, 1722), 7. See also Margot Minardi, "The Boston Inoculation Controversy of 1721–1722: An Incident in the History of Race," *William and Mary Quarterly* 61, no. 1 (2004): 47–76.
63. Zabdiel Boylston, *An Historical Account of the Small-Pox Inoculated in New England* (London: S. Chandler, 1726), ii, v.
64. Koslov, "Introducing Inoculation, 1721."
65. "The 100 Best Bostonians of All Time," *Boston Magazine*, January 5, 2016, accessed November 16, 2025, https://www.bostonmagazine.com/news/2016/01/05/100-best-bostonians/.
66. *The Autobiography of Benjamin Franklin*, ed. Peter Conn (University of Pennsylvania Press, 2005), 10. The quotations in the following paragraph are on pp. 10 and 14, successively.
67. However, Franklin's attitude toward slavery was complicated. He owned enslaved people for much of his life, profited from publishing newspaper ads for fugitive slaves, and adopted antislavery views at least partly out of pragmatic political calculation. See especially Waldstreicher, *Runaway America*.

***Chapter 4: Puritans, Cavaliers, and the English Civil War Era***

1. *Cobbett's Complete Collection of State Trials and Proceedings for High Treason, and Other Crimes and Misdemeanors from the Earliest Period to the Present Time* (London: R. Bagshaw, 1809–26), 4: 1138. Excellent accounts of the execution of Charles I and its contexts include Charles Spencer, *Killers of the King: The Men Who Dared to Execute Charles* (Bloomsbury, 2014); and Geoffrey Robertson, *The Tyrannicide Brief: The Story of the Man Who Sent Charles I to the Scaffold* (Knopf, 2007).
2. J. G. Muddiman, *Trial of King Charles the First* (William Hodge, 1928), 90.
3. *Cobbett's Complete Collection of State Trials*, 4: 1128.
4. *King Charls his speech made upon the scaffold at Whitehall-Gate, immediately before his execution, on Tuesday the 30 of Ian. 1648* [*sic*] (London: John Marshall, 1649) 9–10. The subsequent quotations in this paragraph are from pp. 6 and 10, successively.
5. *Cobbett's Complete Collection of State Trials*, 4: 1141.
6. *Cobbett's Complete Collection of State Trials*, 4: 1142. The quotation in the next sentence is from p. 1141.
7. Graham Edwards, *The Last Days of Charles I* (Sutton, 1999), 184. See also Muddiman, *Trial of King Charles the First*, 155.
8. *The Collected Works of Theodore* Parker, ed. Frances Power Cobbe (London: Trübner, 1863–1871), 5: 254–55. Parker's statement was quoted in abolitionist papers such as the *National Anti-Slavery Standard*, June 17, 1854.
9. Quoted in John G. Turner, *They Knew They Were Pilgrims: Plymouth Colony and the Contest for American Liberty* (Yale University Press, 2020), 31.
10. Muddiman, *Trial of King Charles the First*, 82.
11. James T. Kloppenberg, *Toward Democracy: The Struggle for Self-Rule in European and American Thought* (Oxford University Press, 2016), 74.
12. *Stuart Royal Proclamations*, ed. James F. Larkin, vol. 2, *The Royal Proclamations of King Charles I, 1625–1646* (Clarendon Press, 1983), 93. See Cyndia Susan Clegg, "Censorship and the Courts of Star Chamber and High Commission in England to 1640," *Journal of Modern European History* 3, no. 1 (2005): 50–80.
13. John Rushworth, "Appendix: Charles I's Declaration on the Dissolution of Parliament," in *Historical Collections of Private Passages of State*, vol. 1, *1618–29* (London: D. Browne, 1721), 1: 1–11.

14. Henry Valentine, *God Save the King. A Sermon Preached in St. Pauls Church the 27th. of March 1639* (London: M. Flesher, 1639), 5. For a discussion of sermons in praise of Charles, see Elena Kiryanova, "Images of Kingship," *History* 100, no. 1 (2015): 21–39.
15. William Laud, *A Commemoration of King Charles His Inauguration, or, A Sermon Preached at Pauls Crosse by William Laud* (1631; published London: M. B., 1645), 13.
16. William Laud, *A Speech Delivered in the Starr-Chamber, on Wednesday the 16th of June, 1637. at the Censure of John Bastwick, Henry Burton, and William Prinn* (London: Richard Badger, 1637), 116–17.
17. Quoted in David Cressy, *Charles I and the People of England* (Oxford University Press, 2015), 94.
18. Among the vivid accounts of the persecution of the Puritans during the 1630s are J. B. Marsden, *The History of the Early Puritans: From the Reformation to the Opening of the Civil War in 1642* (London: Hamilton, Adams, 1853), chap. 13; and Cyndia Susan Clegg, "Censorship and the Courts of Star Chamber and High Commission in England to 1640," *Journal of Modern European History* 3, no. 1 (2005), 50–80.
19. Mark Kishlansky, "Martyrs' Tales," 350. The subsequent quotations in this paragraph are as follows: Burton and Bastwick, quoted on p. 351; Leighton, quoted on p. 352. The quotations in the next paragraph are from p. 353.
20. Kishlansky, "Martyrs' Tales," 352.
21. William Haller and Godfrey Davies, eds., *The Leveller Tracts, 1647–1653* (Peter Smith, 1964), 454.
22. For example, the constitutional historian Leonard W. Levy, who in his book on the origins of the Fifth Amendment traces the right against self-incrimination back to the thirteenth century, sees Lilburne as a key figure in the advance toward modern due process. Levy writes, "Lilburne had made the difference. From his time on, the right against self-incrimination was an established, respected rule of the common law or more broadly, of English law generally" (Leonard W. Levy, *Origins of the Fifth Amendment: The Right Against Self-Incrimination* [Oxford University Press, 1968], 313). However, the right against self-incrimination was not widely recognized in common-law courts until the late eighteenth century. See John H. Langbein, "The Historical Origins of the Privilege Against Self-Incrimination at Common Law," *Michigan Law Review* 92, no. 5 (1994): 1047–85. Lilburne and his ilk can be best seen as prophets of future developments rather than direct sources.
23. Leonard W. Levy, "The Right Against Self-Incrimination: History and Judicial History," *Political Science Quarterly* 84, no. 1 (1969): 4. The Bradford quotation in the next sentence appears on pp. 13–14.
24. Bradford, *History of Plymouth Plantation*, 2: 326. The quotation in the next sentence is on p. 327.
25. See Alison Games, *Migration and the Origins of the English Atlantic World* (Harvard University Press, 1999).
26. Order of May 1, 1838, in Rushworth, *Historical Collections of Private Passages of State*, vol. 2, *1629–1638*, 409.
27. John Ward Dean, *The Story of the Embarkation of Cromwell and His Friends for New England* (Boston: D. Clapp & Son, 1866), 6.
28. John Pym, *A Remonstrance of the State of the Kingdom* (London: Joseph Hunscutt, 1641), 16–17.
29. Thomas Carlyle, "An Election to the Long Parliament" (1844), in *Critical and Miscellaneous Essays: Collected and Republished* (London: Chapman and Hall, 1869), 140.
30. Quoted in Charles Carlton, *Going to the Wars: The Experience of the British Civil Wars, 1638–1651* (Routledge, 1993), 52. The remaining quotations in this paragraph and the first one in the next paragraph are from pp. 52–53.
31. Quoted in Carlton, *Going to the Wars*, 59. The quotation in the next sentence is also from this page.
32. Thomas Babington Macaulay, "Milton" (1825), in *Critical and Historical Essays* (London: Longmans, 1883), 25–26.
33. *The Diary of Samuel Pepys*, ed. Henry B. Wheatley (George Bell and Sons, 1904), 7: 39.
34. The descriptions of royalist battle flags here and in the following sentence are from Kevin Sharpe, *Image Wars: Kings and Commonwealths in England, 1603–1660* (Yale University Press, 2010), 365–66.
35. C. H. Firth, *Cromwell's Army: A History of the English Soldier During the Civil Wars, the Commonwealth and the Protectorate* (Methuen, 1912), 339n1.

36. *The Souldiers Pocket Bible* (1643), reprinted as *The Soldiers' Pocket Bible: Issued for the Use of the Army of Oliver Cromwell* (1643; repr., Raleigh, SC: South Carolina Tract Society, c. 1861).
37. Preface to *The Soldier's Pocket Bible*, Boston Athenaeum Digital Collections, accessed March 30, 2023, cdm.bostonathenaeum.org/digital/collection/p16057coll14/id/78424.
38. Quoted in Ian Gentles, *The New Model Army: Agent of Revolution* (Yale University Press, 2022), 49. The remaining quotations in this paragraph are from p. 51.
39. Quoted in Muddiman, *Trial of King Charles the First*, 58.
40. Martin Parker, "An Exact Description of the Manner How His Majesty and His Nobles Went to the Parliament on Monday, April 13, 1640," in *Cavalier and Puritan: Ballads and Broadsides Illustrating the Period of the Great Rebellion, 1640–1660*, ed. Hyder Edward Rollins (New York University Press, 1923), 82–83.
41. "The King Enjoys His Own Again, to Be Joyfully Sung, with Its Own Proper Tune" (1643; repr., London: n.p., 1665).
42. John Goodwin, *Anti-Cavalierisme, or, Truth Pleading as Well the Necessity, as the Lawfulness of This Present War, for the Suppressing of That Butcherly Brood of Cavaliering Incendiaries* (London: Henry Overton, 1642), 2.
43. William Walwyn, *Some Considerations Tending to the Undeceiving* (November 10, 1642), in *Tracts on Liberty by the Levellers and Their Critics*, ed. David M. Hart and Ross Kenyon, vol. 1, 1638–1643 (Liberty Fund, 2014–18).
44. William Prynne, *The Soveraigne Power of Parliaments and Kingdomes* (April 15, 1643), in *Tracts on Liberty by the Levellers and Their Critics*, vol. 1.
45. *A Puritane Set Forth in His Lively Colours* (1605; repr., London: n.p., 1642), 2–3.
46. *The Devil's Last Legacy, or, A Round-headed Ironmonger Made Executor to Pluto Wherein Is Shewed the Discent of the Round-heads* (London: n.p., 1642).
47. "Upon Mr. Pyms Picture," *Rump: An Exact Collection of the Choycest Poems and Songs Relating to the Late Times [. . .] from Ano 1639 to Ano 1661* (London: Henry Brome, 1662), 3.
48. "A Christmas Song When the Rump Was First Dissolved," in *The Cavalier Songs and Ballads of England from 1642 to 1684*, ed. Charles Mackay (London: G. Bohn, 1863), 108.
49. "To Those Who Desire No Peace," *Rump*, 26.
50. Samuel Butler, *Hudibras, in Three Parts, Written in the Time of the Late Wars* (London: T. Bensley, 1801), 1: 27. The quotation in the next sentence is from pp. 10–11.
51. Ralph Waldo Emerson, *Essays and Lectures*, ed. Joel Porte (Library of America, 1983), 592.
52. Quoted in *On Civil Liberty; Passive Obedience, and Non-Resistance* (a *sermon* preached in Maryland in 1775), in Jonathan Boucher, *A View of the Causes and Consequences of the American Revolution* (London: G. G. & J. Robinson, 1797), 514, 532–33.
53. Vane was the most prominent of the New Englanders who had arrived in America in the 1630s and then returned to England between 1640 and 1660 (estimates range from 1,500 to 3,600), many of them to assist in the Cromwellian Revolution. See Susan Hardman Moore, *Abandoning America: Life-Stories from Early New England* (Boydell & Brewer, 2013), 17–18.
54. Henry Noel Brailsford, *The Levellers and the English Revolution*, ed. Christopher Hill (Stanford University Press, 1961), 87. For Vane's role in securing the final wording, see John Coffey, *Politics, Religion and the British Revolutions: The Mind of Samuel Rutherford* (Cambridge University Press, 1997), 151–52; and Michael Watts, *The Dissenters: From the Reformation to the French Revolution* (Clarendon Press, 1978), 205.
55. William Riley Parker, *Milton: A Biography* (Oxford University Press, 1996), 75–76.
56. John Russell Bartlett, ed., *Records of the Colony of Rhode Island and Providence Plantations, in New England*, vol. 1, *1636 to 1663* (Providence, RI: A. C. Greene and Brothers, 1856), 1: 287–88.
57. Algernon Sidney, *Court Maxims*, ed. Hans W. Blom, Eco Haitsma-Mulier, and Ronald Janse (Cambridge University Press, 1996), 185.
58. John Milton, "Sonnet XVI. On Sir Henry Vane the Younger," *The Poetical Works of Mr. John Milton. In Two Volumes* (London: Jacob Tonson, 1720), 2: 346.
59. Robert Baillie, *A Dissuasive from the Errours of the Time: Wherein the Tenets of the Principall Sects,*

*Especially of the Independents, Are Drawn Together in One Map* (London: Gellibrand, 1645), unnumbered page. The subsequent quotations in this paragraph are from pp. 17–18.

60. Thomas Edwards, *The Third Part of Gangræna. Or, A New and Higher Discovery of the Errors, Heresies, Blasphemies, and Insolent Proceedings of the Sectaries of These Times* (London: Ralph Smith, 1646), 112.
61. Thomas Edwards, *The First and Second Part of Gangræna, or, A Catalogue and Discovery of Many of the Errors, Heresies, Blasphemies and Pernicious Practices of the Sectaries of This Time* (London: Ralph Smith, 1646), 143.
62. Quoted in Youngkwon Chung, "Parliament, the Heresy Ordinance of 1648, and Religious Toleration in Civil War England," *Journal of Church and State* 57, no. 1 (2015): 126.
63. Brailsford, *The Levellers and the English Revolution*, 47.
64. John Lilburne, *London's Liberty in Chains Discovered* (London: n.p., 1646), 2.
65. John Lilburne, *Regall Tyrannie Discovered* (London: n.p., 1647), 7.
66. Richard Overton, *An Arrow Against All Tyrants and Tyrany, Shot from the Prison of New-Gate into the Prerogative Bowels of the Arbitrary House of Lords, and All Other Usurpers and Tyrants Whatsoever* (London: Martin Claw, 1646), 3.
67. Brailsford's statement is on p. 119 of his *The Levellers and the English Revolution.* Chidley is quoted on p. 317.
68. Ronald William Pacy, "Spiritual Combat: The Life and Personality of Hugh Peters, a Puritan Minister" (PhD diss., State University of New York at Buffalo, 1978), 200.
69. Quoted in Pacy, "Spiritual Combat," 241. The quotation in the next sentence is from p. 240.
70. *A Discourse Betwixt Lieutenant Colonel John Lilburn Close Prisoner in the Tower of London, and Mr Hugh Peter upon May 25, 1649* (London: n.p., 1649), unnumbered page.
71. William W. Ireland, *The Life of Sir Henry Vane the Younger: With a History of the Events of His Time* (E. Nash, 1905), 350.
72. Quoted in Ruth E. Mayers, "Real and Practicable, Not Imaginary and Notional: Sir Henry Vane, 'A Healing Question,' and the Problems of the Protectorate," *Albion* 28, no. 1 (1996): 67.
73. John N. Blanton, "This Species of Property: Slavery and the Properties of Subjecthood in Anglo-American Law and Politics, 1619–1783" (PhD diss., Graduate Center of the City University of New York, 2016), 245.
74. The quotations in this and the following sentence are from John Donoghue, "'Out of the Land of Bondage': The English Revolution and the Atlantic Origins of Abolition," *American Historical Review* 115, no. 4 (2010): 943–74. Donoghue expands on the transatlantic network of radicals in his book *Fire Under the Ashes: An Atlantic History of the English Revolution* (University of Chicago Press, 2013).
75. *A Door of Hope: Or, A Call and Declaration for the Gathering Together of the First Ripe Fruits unto the Standard of Our Lord, King Jesus* (London: n.p., 1660), 4. The remaining quotations in this paragraph are from pp. 6, 5, and 9, successively.
76. N. H. Keeble, *The Restoration: England in the 1660s* (Wiley-Blackwell, 2002), 55–56. In these pages, Keeble provides details about such executions, including eyewitness accounts.
77. As for the other regicides who were still living in 1660, three escaped to New Haven Colony, where they lived under assumed names and eluded Charles's agents; fourteen fled to Europe; and an equal number were imprisoned for life.
78. This quotation and the remaining ones in this paragraph are from Pacy, "Spiritual Combat," 364–65.
79. Ralph Waldo Emerson, *English Traits*, ed. Philip Nicoloff, Robert E. Burkholder, and Douglas Emory Wilson, in *The Collected Works of Ralph Waldo Emerson* (Harvard University Press, 1994), 5: 216. The quotation in the next sentence is from p. 215.
80. Some of the information in this paragraph is derived from Lorna Clymer, "Cromwell's Head and Milton's Hair," *Eighteenth Century* 40, no. 2 (1999): 91–112.
81. Keeble, *The Restoration*, 37.
82. See George Southcombe, *The Culture of Dissent in Restoration England: "The Wonders of the Lord"* (Boydell & Brewer, 2019).

83. Carlton in *Going to the Wars* (p. 340) writes, "Directly or indirectly a very large number of people lost their lives in the civil wars. . . . Casualties amounted to 190,000 (or 3.7 per cent of the total population) in England, 60,000 (6 per cent) in Scotland, and perhaps as many as 660,000 (41 per cent) in Ireland, making a total for the British Isles of 868,000 (11.6 per cent)."
84. Milton, "On the New Forcers of Conscience Under the Long Parliament," *The Poetical Works of Mr. John Milton*, 2: 303.
85. Milton, "Sonnet XVII. To O. Cromwell," *The Poetical Works of Mr. John Milton*, 2: 346.
86. John Milton, *Readie and Easie Way to Establish a Free Commonwealth* (London: n.p., 1660), 28.
87. See David Loewenstein, *Representing Revolution in Milton and His Contemporaries: Religion, Politics, and Polemics in Radical Puritanism* (Cambridge University Press, 2001); and Richard Greaves, *John Bunyan and English Nonconformity* (Hambledon Press, 1992).
88. Quoted in the introduction to Sidney, *Court Maxims*, xiv. Translated by the editors of *Court Maxims*.
89. Algernon Sidney, *Discourses Concerning Government* (London: n.p., 1698), 316.
90. *The Very Copy of a Paper Delivered to the Sheriffs upon the Scaffold on Tower-Hill, on Friday Decemb. 7, 1683 by Algernon Sidney, Esq., Before His Execution There* (London: Walter David, 1683), 2.
91. Thomas Hobbes, *Behemoth, or, An Epitome of the Civil Wars of England, from the Year 1640 to 1660* (London: n. p., 1679), 142. For the young Locke as "an obsessive reader" of Hobbes, see Felix Waldmann, "John Locke as a Reader of Thomas Hobbes's *Leviathan*: A New Manuscript," *Journal of Modern History* 93, no. 2 (2021): 245–500.
92. John Locke, *Two Tracts on Government*, ed. Peter Laslett (Cambridge University Press, 1967), 119. The quotation in the next sentence is on p. 210.
93. Anthony Ashley Cooper, *A Letter from a Person of Quality to His Friend in the Country* (London: n.p., 1675), 1.
94. Marchamount Nedham, *A Pacquet of Advices and Animadversions, Sent from London to the Men of Shaftsbury* (London: n.p., 1676), 19; Butler, *Hudibras*, 2: 260.
95. Quoted in Bruce J. Smith, *The Sense of Injustice and the Origin of Modern Democracy* (University of Rochester Press, 2018), 285.
96. John Locke, *Two Treatises of Government* (London: Awnsham Churchill, 1690), unnumbered page.
97. Locke, *Two Treatises of Government*, unnumbered page. The next quotation in this paragraph is also from an unnumbered page.
98. Robert Filmer, *Patriarcha, or, The Natural Power of Kings* (London: Walter Davis, 1680), 13.
99. Locke, *Two Treatises of Government*, 70. The quotations in the next sentence are from pp. 3 and 94, successively.
100. Locke, *Two Treatises of Government*, 271.
101. Richard Ashcraft, *Revolutionary Politics and Locke's Two Treatises of Government* (Princeton University Press, 1986), especially chap. 4. Although there's no documentary evidence of Locke's reading the Levellers, one senses his familiarity with them in his comment on the "clash of opinions" during the civil war years. Also, it's known that his mentor, Ashley Cooper, was delving into the writing of the Levellers in the mid-1670s, just when Locke was generating ideas that would appear in classic form in the *Two Treatises*.
102. Among the many works on Locke's influence on Jefferson, especially useful is Allen Jayne, *Jefferson's Declaration of Independence: Origins, Philosophy, and Theology* (University Press of Kentucky, 1998), chap. 3.
103. *The Fundamental Constitutions of Carolina* (London: n.p., 1670), 23. The quotation at the end of this paragraph is also on p. 23.
104. Holly Brewer, "Slavery, Sovereignty, and 'Inheritable Blood,'" *American Historical Review* 122, no. 4 (2017): 1052. For detailed discussion of Locke, slavery, and colonialism, see David Armitage, "John Locke, Carolina, and the Two Treatises of Government," *Political Theory* 32, no. 5 (2004): 602–27; and Barbara Arneil, "Trade, Plantations, and Property: John Locke and the Economic Defense of Colonialism," *Journal of the History of Ideas* 55, no. 4 (1994): 591–609.
105. James Otis, *Rights of the British Colonies Asserted and Proved* (Boston: J. Almon, 1764), 6, 29.

106. "Annual Collection of Texts on Slavery," *Liberator*, March 24, 1832; "Democracy: New Definitions," *National Antislavery Standard*, July 15, 1865.
107. William Darrell, *The Case Review'd, or, An Answer to the Case Stated, by Mr. L—y* [Charles Leslie] (London: English College Press, 1717), 4.
108. The information and quotations here about the guinea are from Brewer, "Slavery, Sovereignty, and 'Inheritable Blood,'" 1047–51.
109. See Holly Brewer, "Subjects by Allegiance to the King? Debating Status and Power for Subjects—and Slaves—Through the Religious Debates of the Early British Atlantic," in *State and Citizen: British America and the Early United States*, ed. Peter Thompson and Peter S. Onuf (University of Virginia Press, 2013), 33–34.

***Chapter 5: The Rise and Fall of the Virginia Cavalier***

1. N. Darnell Davis, *The Cavaliers & Roundheads of Barbados, 1650–1652: With Some Account of the Early History of Barbados* (Georgetown, British Guiana: Argosy Press, 1887), 6–7, 137.
2. Richard S. Dunn, *Sugar and Slaves: The Rise of the Planter Class in the English West Indies, 1624–1713* (University of North Carolina Press, 1972), 84.
3. David Hackett Fischer, *Albion's Seed: Four British Folkways in America* (Oxford University Press, 1989), 225.
4. Much of my information about William Berkeley is derived from Warren M. Billings, *Sir William Berkeley and the Forging of Colonial Virginia* (Louisiana State University Press, 2010); and Billings, "Sir William Berkeley (1605–1677), *Encyclopedia Virginia*, Virginia Humanities, December 7, 2020, encyclopediavirginia.org/entries/berkeley-sir-william-1605-1677.
5. Dana Huntley, "Streetlights of London," British Heritage Travel, July 13, 2016, britishheritage.com/streetlights-of-london-5.
6. Fischer, *Albion's Seed,* 214.
7. Mary Johnston, *Pioneers of the Old South: A Chronicle of English Colonial Beginnings* (Yale University Press, 1921), 134.
8. See Kevin Butterfield, "Puritans and Religious Strife in the Early Chesapeake," *Virginia Magazine of History and Biography* 109, no. 1 (2001): 5–36.
9. Hening, *The Statutes at Large*, 1: 359–61.
10. *The Speech of the Honourable Sr. William Berkeley Governour and Capt. Generall of Virginea, to the Burgesses in the Grand Assembly at James Towne on the 17 of March, 1651* (The Hague: Samuell Broun, 1651), 4–5.
11. Quoted in Ethan A. Schmidt, *The Divided Dominion: Social Conflict and Indian Hatred in Early Virginia* (University Press of Colorado, 2015), 130.
12. Billings, *Sir William Berkeley and the Forging of Colonial Virginia*, 60.
13. Quoted in Billings, *Sir William Berkeley and the Forging of Colonial Virginia*, 74.
14. "Ingram's Proceedings" (1676), in Peter Force, *Tracts and Other Papers Relating Principally to the Origin, Settlement, and Progress of the Colonies in North America, from the Discovery of the Country to the Year 1776*, vol. 1 (Washington: P. Force, 1836–46), 34.
15. John Eacott Manahan, "The Cavalier Remounted: A Study of the Origins of Virginia's Population, 1607–1700" (PhD diss., University of Virginia, 1946), 96.
16. Hening, *The Statutes at Large*, 2: 49. The next quotation in this paragraph is also from this page.
17. *The Declaration and Remonstrance of Sir William Berkeley His Most Sacred Majesties Governor and Captain Generall of Virginia*, May 9, 1676, American History Central, September 27, 2022, americanhistorycentral.com/entries/berkeleys-declaration-and-remonstrance-1676.
18. Nathaniel Bacon, *The Declaration of the People* (July 30, 1676; repr., San Francisco: Great Neck Publishing, 2017).
19. Wilber Henry Ward III, "Bacon's Rebellion in Literature to 1861" (PhD diss., University of Tennessee, 1971), 127. For later examples of the Bacon–Cromwell comparison, see Samuel Hopkins, "The Young Protector," in *The Youth of the Old Dominion* (Boston: J. P. Jewett, 1856), 383–99; and Edward S. Ellis, *The Cromwell of Virginia: A Story of Bacon's Rebellion* (Henry T. Coates, 1904).

20. Quoted in Fischer, *Albion's Seed*, 220.
21. Fischer, *Albion's Seed*, 220.
22. "Speech of Wyndham Robertson, Esq. of Richmond City," *Richmond Whig*, March 16, 1860.
23. "Estimated Population of American Colonies: 1610 to 1780," Vancouver Island University, accessed April 15, 2023, web.viu.ca/davies/H320/population.colonies.htm; and Douglas Brent Chambers Keswick, "'He Gwine Sing He Country': Africans, Afro-Virginians, and the Development of Slave Culture in Virginia, 1690–1810" (PhD diss., University of Virginia, 1996), 1: 236.
24. Quoted in Anthony S. Parent Jr., *Foul Means: The Formation of a Slave Society in Virginia, 1660–1740* (University of North Carolina Press, 2003), 225.
25. Robert Carter, *Letter to Robert Jones*, October 10 and 14, 1727. (Published transcription online from the Robert Carter Papers, Robert Carter letter book, May 1727–28 July, Robert Carter Papers (acc. no. 3807), Albert and Shirley Small Special Collections Library, University of Virginia).
26. Lancaster County Order Book 7 (1721–29), p. 59; microfilm copy in Archives Research Services, Library of Virginia, Richmond.
27. Louis B. Wright, "William Byrd I and the Slave Trade," *Huntington Library Quarterly* 8, no. 4 (1945): 379–87; Anthony S. Parent Jr., "'Either a Fool or a Fury': The Emergence of Paternalism in Colonial Virginia Slave Society" (PhD diss., University of California at Los Angeles, 1982), 43–45.
28. "Will of William Byrd I," *William and Mary Quarterly* 3, no. 4 (1923): 246–49.
29. See Holly Brewer, "Entailing Aristocracy in Colonial Virginia: 'Ancient Feudal Restraints' and Revolutionary Reform," *William and Mary Quarterly* 54, no. 2 (1997): 307–46. Brewer informs us that by 1780 an estimated 78 percent of all land in typical Virginia counties had been held in entail over eight generations.
30. Byrd was variously referred to as "an old Virginian cavalier" ("Letters from New-York," *National Anti-Slavery Standard*, March 16, 1843), "a refined and distinguished-looking cavalier" (John Esten Cooke, "Some Old Virginia Houses," *Appleton's' Journal: A Magazine of General Literature* 6, no. 136 [November 4, 1871]: 522), and "William Byrd, Cavalier of Virginia" ("District Unites Tomorrow to Observe Indpendence Day," *Evening Star* [Washington, DC], July 4, 1926).
31. Alexander Ormond Boulton, "The Architecture of Slavery: Art, Language, and Society in Early Virginia" (PhD diss., College of William and Mary, 1991), 53.
32. Kevin Jon Hayes, "William Byrd's Library (Volumes I and II)" (PhD diss., University of Delaware, 1991), 1: viii.
33. Louis B. Wright, *The First Gentlemen of Virginia: Intellectual Qualities of the Early Colonial Ruling Class* (Huntington Library, 1940), 176. Appointed as Receiver General in 1705, Byrd held the position for many years.
34. Emory G. Evans, *A "Topping People": The Rise and Decline of Virginia's Old Political Elite, 1680–1790* (University of Virginia Press, 2009), 90.
35. Quoted in Rhys Isaac, *The Transformation of Virginia, 1740–1790* (University of North Carolina Press, 1982), 42.
36. Woody Holton, *Forced Founders: Indians, Debtors, Slaves, and the Making of the American Revolution in Virginia* (University of North Carolina Press, 1999), xviii.
37. Brewer, "Entailing Aristocracy," 322.
38. "Indians A.D. 1600–1800."
39. William Byrd II to Charles, Earl of Orrery, July 5, 1726, *The Correspondence of the Three William Byrds of Westover Virginia, 1684–1776*, ed. Marion Tinling (University of Virginia Press, 1977), 1: 355.
40. Quoted in Boulton, "The Architecture of Slavery," 49. The quotation in the next sentence is also from this page.
41. *The History of the Dividing Line Betwixt Virginia and North Carolina Run in the Year of Our Lord 1728*, in *The Dividing Line Histories of William Byrd II of Westover Book*, ed. Kevin Joel Berland (University of North Carolina Press, 2013), 120.
42. William Byrd II to John Perceval, 1st Earl of Egmont, July 12, 1736, *Correspondence of the Three*

*William Byrds of Westover*, 2: 487–88. The remaining quotations in this paragraph and the next one are also from these pages.

43. *The Great American Gentleman: William Byrd of Westover in Virginia, His Secret Diary for the Years 1709–1712*, ed. Louis B. Wright and Marion Tinling (Putnam, 1963), 9. The remaining block quotations here and in the next paragraph are from pp. 26, 36, 54, and 52, successively.
44. Byrd to Perceval, July 12, 1736, *Correspondence of the Three William Byrds of Westover*, 2: 488.
45. *Correspondence of the Three William Byrds of Westover*, 2: 483.
46. Philo-Gunaecus, *Virginia Gazette*, May 20, 1737.
47. See Paula A. Treckel, "'The Empire of My Heart': The Marriage of William Byrd II and Lucy Parke Byrd," *Virginia Magazine of History and Biography* 105, no. 2 (1997): 125–56.
48. *The Great American Gentleman*, 88, 215. The quotation in the next sentence is from p. 127.
49. *The Great American Gentleman*, 15.
50. *The Great American Gentleman*, 91, 203
51. See *The Great American Gentleman*, 140, 232, 234, and 244. The quotation in the next sentence is from p. 147.
52. *The Great American Gentleman*, 183–84.
53. *The Great American Gentleman*, 89. The remaining quotations in this paragraph are from pp. 215, 205, and 229–30, successively.
54. Byrd, *History of the Dividing Line*, 69.
55. Fischer, *Albion's Seed*, 300, 303.
56. Emory G. Evans, "William Byrd (1728–1777)," *Encyclopedia Virginia*, Virginia Humanities, December 7, 2020, encyclopediavirginia.org/entries/byrd-william-1728-1777.
57. Quoted in T. H. Breen, *Tobacco Culture: The Mentality of the Great Tidewater Planters on the Eve of Revolution* (Princeton University Press, 1985), 209.
58. Breen, *Tobacco Culture*, 170.
59. Evans, *A "Topping People,"* 115.
60. Jack P. Greene, "Landon Carter (1710–1778)," *Encyclopedia Virginia*, Virginia Humanities, December 7, 2020, encyclopediavirginia.org/entries/carter-landon-1710-1778.
61. *The Diary of Colonel Landon Carter of Sabine Hall, 1752–1778*, ed. Jack P. Greene (University Press of Virginia, 1965), 2: 713. The next two quotations in this paragraph are from pp. 1107 and 1149, successively. The quotation in the next paragraph is from p. 840.
62. See Rhys Isaac, *Landon Carter's Uneasy Kingdom: Revolution and Rebellion on a Virginia Plantation* (Oxford University Press, 2004).
63. *Diary of Colonel Landon Carter*, 2: 795, 983. The next quotation in this paragraph is from p. 702.
64. Quoted in Brewer, "Entailing Aristocracy," 307.
65. *Diary of Colonel Landon Carter*, 2: 962, 975, 815.
66. *Diary of Colonel Landon Carter*, 1: 378. The quotation in the next sentence is from 2:1057.
67. "An Address to the Anabaptists Imprisoned in Caroline County, August 8, 1771," *Virginia Gazette*, February 20, 1772.
68. Jewel Spangler, "Baptists in Colonial Virginia," *Encyclopedia Virginia*, Virginia Humanities, December 7, 2020, encyclopediavirginia.org/entries/baptists-in-colonial-virginia.
69. *Minutes of the Baptist General Committee at Their Yearly Meeting, Held in the City of Richmond, May 8, 1790* (Richmond: Thomas Nicolson, 1790), 7.
70. Brendan Wolfe, "Robert Carter III's Deed of Gifts," *Encyclopedia Virginia*, Virginia Humanities, December 7, 2020, encyclopediavirginia.org/entries/deed-of-gift-robert-carter-iiis.
71. Theodore S. Babcock, "Manumission in Virginia, 1782–1806" (master's thesis, University of Virginia, 2017).
72. Gregory May, *A Madman's Will: John Randolph, Four Hundred Slaves, and the Mirage of Freedom* (Liveright, 2023), 215–16, 292.
73. Quoted in Andrew Levy, *The First Emancipator: The Forgotten Story of Robert Carter, the Founding Father Who Freed His Slaves* (Random House, 2005), 144. The next quotation in this paragraph is from p. 93.

74. Quoted in John Randolph Barden, "'Flushed with Notions of Freedom': The Growth and Emancipation of a Virginia Slave Community, 1732–1812" (PhD diss., Duke University, 1993), 328.
75. George Orwell, *Nineteen Eighty-Four* (Harcourt, Brace and Co., 1949), 37.
76. See, for example, "The Virginia Cavaliers," *Richmond Whig*, August 11, 1868.

***Chapter 6: The American Revolution and Puritanism***

1. There is a vast literature on the American Revolution, some of it devoted to the religious bases of the Revolution. A main argument has been that the evangelical revivals of the Great Awakening, combined with the democratic ideas of the Lockean Enlightenment, quickened the anti-monarchical impulses behind the Revolution. For a review of the early historiography on the topic, see Derek H. Davis, "Religion and the American Revolution," *Journal of Church and State* 36, no. 4 (1994): 709–24. For more recent overviews, see Katherine Carté, *Religion and the American Revolution: An Imperial History* (University of North Carolina Press, 2021); and Larson, *American Inheritance*. Staughton Lynd in *Intellectual Origins of American Radicalism* (1968; repr., Cambridge University Press, 2009) traces the roots of the American Revolution and nineteenth-century abolitionism to the egalitarianism of radical religious groups in mid-seventeenth-century England, particularly the Levellers, the Diggers, and the Quakers. In the current chapter, I focus on the combined influences of early Plymouth Colony, the English Civil War, and New Divinity ministers on the founders.
2. *The Works of John Adams, Second President of the United States* (Boston: Little, Brown, 1850–56), 10: 283 (hereafter cited as *JA*).
3. *JA* 3: 451.
4. *Diary and Autobiography of John Adams*, ed. L. H. Butterfield (Harvard University Press, 1961), 1: 287.
5. *JA* 3: 363 and 451. The quotation in the next sentence is from *JA* 3: 463.
6. *JA* 10: 284.
7. *JA* 3: 451–52.
8. *JA* 10: 359.
9. *JA* 10: 185.
10. Fredrick V. Mills, "Anglican Expansion in Colonial America 1761–1775," *Historical Magazine of the Protestant Episcopal Church* 39, no. 3 (1970): 315.
11. Mather, *Magnalia Christi Americana*, 219.
12. Quoted in John Wingate Thornton, *The Pulpit of the American Revolution: Or, The Political Sermons of the Period of 1776* (Boston: D. Lothrop, 1860), 43.
13. Laura Arnold Leibman, ed., introduction to *Experience Mayhew's Indian Converts: A Cultural Edition* (University of Massachusetts Press, 2008), 1.
14. "John Adams to Thomas Jefferson, 18 July 1818," Founders Online, National Archives, accessed April 30, 2023, founders.archives.gov/documents/Jefferson/03-13-02-0148 (original source: *The Papers of Thomas Jefferson*, Retirement Series, vol. 13, *22 April 1818 to 31 January 1819*, ed. J. Jefferson Looney [Princeton University Press, 2016], 138–39).
15. *JA* 10: 288. On Mayhew's impact, see especially Bernard Bailyn, *The Ideological Origins of the American Revolution* (Harvard University Press, 1967), 34–36, 42–46, and Gordon S. Wood, *The Creation of the American Republic, 1776–1787* (University of North Carolina Press, 1969), 14–16.
16. "John Adams to Thomas Jefferson, 18 July 1818."
17. *JA* 10: 282–84. On Mayhew's impact, see especially Bernard Bailyn, *The Ideological Origins of the American Revolution* (Cambridge, MA: Harvard University Press, 1967), 34–36, 42–46, and Gordon S. Wood, *The Creation of the American Republic, 1776–1787* (Chapel Hill: University of North Carolina Press, 1969), 14–16.
18. Quoted in J. Patrick Mullins, *Father of Liberty: Jonathan Mayhew and the Principles of the American Revolution* (University Press of Kansas, 2017), 51.
19. Jonathan Mayhew, *A Discourse Concerning Unlimited Submission and Non-Resistance to the Higher Powers* (Boston: D. Fowle, 1750), 40.

20. Mayhew, *A Discourse Concerning Unlimited Submission*, 40. The remaining quotations in this paragraph are from pp. 30, 32, 48, 15–16, and 35, successively.
21. Mayhew, *A Discourse Concerning Unlimited Submission*, 47. The remaining quotations in this paragraph are from p. vi.
22. Letter by "Your Constant Reader" in the *Boston News-Letter*, March 1, 1750.
23. Note by Episcopalian minister Charles Brockwell accompanying a front-page reprint of a sermon by seventeenth-century royalist preacher Thomas Sprat that praises the Christian virtues of Charles I, *Boston Evening-Post*, February 19, 1750.
24. Cyrus Augustus Bartol, *The West Church and Its Ministers* (Boston: Crosby, Nichols, 1856), 104.
25. For a discussion of the historical works mentioned in this paragraph, and other histories, see John Seed, *Dissenting Histories: Religious Division and the Politics of Memory in Eighteenth-Century England* (Edinburgh University Press, 2008).
26. John Nichols, *Illustrations of the Literary History of the Eighteenth Century* (London: J. B. Nichols and Son, 1831), 6: 157.
27. Paul Jehle, "Thomas Faunce: The Man Who Saved Plymouth Rock," Plymouth Rock Foundation, last updated November 14, 2023, plymrock.org/thomas-faunce-the-man-who-saved-plymouth-rock.
28. Details in this paragraph are derived from James Thacher, *History of the Town of Plymouth, from Its First Settlement in 1620, to the Present Time* (Boston: Marsh, Capen & Lyon, 1835), 198–99.
29. The information here about the Old Colony Club, including quotations, are from "Records of the Old Colony Club," *Proceedings of the Massachusetts Historical Society*, Second Series, vol. 3, *1886–1887* (Boston: Massachusetts Historical Society, 1888), 389–444.
30. The Pilgrims allegedly alighted on Plymouth Rock on December 11 according to the Old Style (Julian) calendar, which was December 21 on the New Style (Gregorian) calendar. For unknown reasons, Forefathers' Day was traditionally celebrated on December 22, not December 21.
31. This quotation and the ones in the next two sentences are from "Records of the Old Colony Club," 404–5.
32. Gad Hitchcock, *Sermon Preached at Plymouth December 22d, 1774* (Boston: Edes and Gill, 1775), 17; Sylvanus Conant, *An Anniversary Sermon Preached at Plymouth, December 23, 1776* (Boston: Thomas & John Fleet, 1777), 6; Samuel Baldwin, *A Sermon, Preached at Plymouth, December 22, 1775* (Boston: Powars and Willis, 1776), 21; and Charles C. Baldwin, *The Baldwin Genealogy 1500–1881* (Cleveland, OH: Leader, 1881), 624.
33. *JA* 4:110. The quotations in the following paragraph are also from this page.
34. Catharine Macaulay to James Otis, April 27, 1769, in James Warren, Samuel Adams, and John Adams, *Warren-Adams Letters [. . .] 1743–1814* (Massachusetts Historical Society, 1917), 1: 7.
35. Mercy Otis Warren, *History of the Rise, Progress, and Termination of the American Revolution* (Boston: Manning and Loring, 1805), 1: 5–6. The quotation in the last sentence of this paragraph is from p. 1: 11.
36. Warren, *History [. . .] of the American Revolution*, 1: 14. The quotation in the next sentence is from p. 1: 16.
37. Warren, *History [. . .] of the American Revolution*, 1: 15. The remaining quotations in this paragraph are from pp. 1: 15, 1: 15, 1: 22, and 1: 21, successively.
38. *The Diary of Samuel Sewall, 1674–1729*, 2: 947–48.
39. Thomas Hutchinson, *The History of the Colony of Massachusetts-Bay* (1764; repr., London: M. Richardson 1765), 74.
40. See Robert E. Brown, "Democracy in Colonial Massachusetts," *New England Quarterly* 25, no. 3 (1952): 291–313.
41. James F. Hrdlicka, "'The Attachment of the People': The Massachusetts Charter, the French and Indian War, and the Coming of the American Revolution," *New England Quarterly* 89, no. 3 (2016), 384–420.
42. Warren, *History [. . .] of the American Revolution*, 1: 20.
43. "Causes of the American Discontents Before 1768, 5–7 January 1768," Founders Online, National Archives, https://founders.archives.gov/documents/Franklin/01-15-02-0001.

44. Quoted in Richard L. Bushman, *King and People in Provincial Massachusetts* (University of North Carolina Press, 1985), 130.
45. Warren, *History [. . .] of the American Revolution*, 1: 22–23. The quotation at the end of this paragraph is from p. 1: 23.
46. James K. Hosmer, *The Life of Thomas Hutchinson, Royal Governor of the Province of Massachusetts Bay* (1896; repr., Da Capo Press, 1972), 3. Much of the information here about Hutchinson is derived from Hosmer. The quotation in the last sentence of this paragraph is from p. 195.
47. Conspiratorial fears as a background to the American Revolution are most famously discussed in Bailyn, *Ideological Origins*. Useful analyses of the historiography of conspiracy in America include Gordon S. Wood, "Conspiracy and the Paranoid Style: Causality and Deceit in the Eighteenth Century," *William and Mary Quarterly* 39, no. 3 (1982): 401–41; and Gordon S. Wood, "Reassessing Bernard Bailyn's *The Ideological Origins of the American Revolution* on the Occasion of Its Jubilee," *New England Quarterly* 91, no. 1 (2018): 78–109.
48. Warren, *History [. . .] of the American Revolution*, 1: 79.
49. See Sandra J. Sarkela, "The Persuasive Power of Mercy Otis Warren's Dramatic Sketches, 1772–1775," *Early American Literature* 44, no. 3 (2009): 541–68; and Edmund M. Hayes, "Mercy Otis Warren: *The Defeat*," *New England Quarterly* 49, no. 3 (1976): 440–58.
50. Mercy Otis Warren, *The Group; As Lately Acted, and To Be Re-acted, to the Wonder of All Superior Intelligences* (Boston: Edes and Gill, 1775), 19–20. The favorite books of Rapatio's circle mentioned in the next sentence are described on p. 7.
51. Mercy Otis Warren, *The Adulateur. A Tragedy, As It Is Now Acted in Upper Servia* (Boston: n.p., 1773), 5-6.
52. "John Adams to William Tudor, Sr., 29 March 1817," Founders Online, National Archives, accessed June 10, 2023, founders.archives.gov/documents/Adams/99-02-02-6735. Many of the details about the courtroom scene in this paragraph are from Adams's vivid account of the trial.
53. "Adams' 'Abstract of the Argument [of Otis]': Ca. April 1761," Founders Online, National Archives, accessed June 10, 2023, founders.archives.gov/documents/Adams/05-02-02-0006-0002-0003. The quotation in the next sentence is also from this source.
54. James Otis Jr., *A Vindication of the Conduct of the House of Representatives of the Province of the Massachusetts-Bay* (Boston: Edes & Gill, 1762), 44. The remaining quotations of Otis in this paragraph are from pp. 17–18.
55. James Otis Jr., "John Hampden to William Pym," *Boston Gazette*, December 9, 1765. See also Daniel A. Smith, *Tax Crusaders and the Politics of Direct Democracy* (Routledge, 2013), 174.
56. James Otis Jr., "John Hampden to William Pym." The Otis quotation in the next sentence is from his Hampden entry in the *Gazette*, January 27, 1766.
57. Benjamin Franklin, "Tract Relative to the Affair of Hutchinson's Letters, [1774]," Founders Online, National Archives, accessed September 20, 2023, founders.archives.gov/documents/Franklin/01-21-02-0227.
58. James Otis Jr., *The Rights of the British Colonies Asserted and Proved* (Boston: n.p., 1764), 4.
59. John Adams, "[February 1770: From the Diary of John Adams]," Founders Online, National Archives, accessed October 7, 2024, founders.archives.gov/documents/Adams/01-01-02-0014-0002.
60. Quoted in Jeffrey H. Hacker, *Minds and Hearts: The Story of James Otis Jr. and Mercy Otis Warren* (University of Massachusetts Press, 2021), 121.
61. Hosmer, *The Life of Thomas Hutchinson*, 224.
62. Thacher, *History of the Town of Plymouth*, 179.
63. *Martis, 29 die Octobris, A.D. 1765. In the House of Representatives. According to the Order of the Day . . . Ordered, That All the Foregoing Resolves Be Kept in the Records of This House; That a Just Sense of Liberty, and the Firm Sentiments of Loyalty May Be Transmitted to Posterity* (Boston: Green and Russell, 1765), 2.
64. *The Writings of Samuel Adams*, ed. Harry Alonzo Cushing (G. P. Putnam's Sons, 1904–8), 1, 1:73.
65. *The Writings of Samuel Adams*, 3: 162.

66. *The Writings of Samuel Adams* 1:19. The next quotation in this paragraph is also from p. 1: 19. The quotation at the end of this paragraph is from p. 1: 154.
67. Quoted in John C. Miller, *Sam Adams: Pioneer in Propaganda* (Stanford University Press, 1936), 343.
68. *The Writings of Samuel Adams*, 1: 316.
69. John Adams, "[July 1766: From the Diary of John Adams]," Founders Online, National Archives, accessed December 20, 2023, founders.archives.gov/documents/Adams/01-01-02-0010-0006.
70. "The Earl of Clarendon [John Adams] to William Pym, 20 January 1766," Founders Online, National Archives, accessed January 20, 2024, founders.archives.gov/documents/Adams/06-01-02-0063-0003.
71. "The Earl of Clarendon [John Adams] to William Pym, 13 January 1766," Founders Online, National Archives, accessed February 15, 2024, founders.archives.gov/documents/Adams/06-01-02-0063-0002. For information on the vice admiralty courts of the 1760s, see Erwin C. Surrency, "The Courts in the American Colonies," *American Journal of Legal History* 11, no. 4 (1967): 357.
72. "Governor Winthrop to Governor Bradford [both John Adams], 9 February 1767," Founders Online, National Archives, accessed March 10, 2024, founders.archives.gov/documents/Adams/06-01-02-0067-0011.
73. "Ipswich and the American Revolution, Part 1: The Breach with Britain," Historic Ipswich, May 15, 2025, historicipswich.net/2023/12/31/ipswich-and-the-breach-with-britain.
74. Thomas Franklin Waters, *Ipswich in the Massachusetts Bay Colony* (Ipswich Historical Society, 1901), 2: 294.
75. "[The Stamp Act, 1765: From the Autobiography of John Adams]," Founders Online, National Archives, accessed March 30, 2024, founders.archives.gov/documents/Adams/01-03-02-0016-0012.
76. "[January 1766: From the Diary of John Adams]," Founders Online, National Archives, accessed April 20, 2024, founders.archives.gov/documents/Adams/01-01-02-0010-0001.
77. "To the Inhabitants of the Colony of Massachusetts-Bay, 23 January 1775," Founders Online, National Archives, accessed June 5, 2024, founders.archives.gov/documents/Adams/06-02-02-0072-0002.
78. "From John Adams to a Friend in London, 10 February 1775," Founders Online, National Archives, accessed June 27, 2024, founders.archives.gov/documents/Adams/06-02-02-0076.
79. "Sentiments of the Sons of Liberties," February 1769, Sparks Manuscripts X, Papers Relating to New England, vol. 3, Manuscripts of George Chalmers (Houghton Library, Harvard University), 18; quoted in Warren Hasty Carroll, "John Adams, Puritan Revolutionist: A Study of His Part in Making the American Revolution, 1764–1776" (PhD diss., Columbia University, 1959), 27. The notice signed O.C. mentioned in the next sentence is also from this page in Carroll. The reference to the Cromwell tavern sign in the subsequent sentence is from p. 28 in Carroll.
80. Frank Moore, ed., *Diary of the American Revolution: From Newspapers and Original Documents* (New York: privately printed, 1865), 1: 423.
81. Thomas Paine, *Common Sense: Addressed to the Inhabitants of America,[. . .]Together with an Address to the People Called Quakers* (New York: n.p., 1918), 7. The quotations in the next sentence are from p. 64.
82. *The Autobiography of Benjamin Rush* (Greenwood Press, 1970), 46.
83. *Maryland Journal* (Baltimore), April 15, 1777; reprinted in the *Boston Gazette*, August 4, 1777.
84. See Brendan McConville, *The King's Three Faces: The Rise and Fall of Royal America, 1688–1776* (University of North Carolina Press, 2006), esp. chap. 3.
85. Tinling, ed., *The Correspondence of the Three William Byrds of Westover Virginia*, 1: 535.
86. William Wirt, *Sketches of the Life and Character of Patrick Henry* (1817; repr. Applewood Books, 2009), 65. For Jefferson's description of the scene, see "Thomas Jefferson to William Wirt, 14 August 1814," Founders Online, National Archives, accessed July 24, 2024, founders.archives.gov/documents/Jefferson/03-07-02-0403. However, a European visitor who overheard the speech reported that "treason" was uttered only by the House speaker and that Parick Henry apologized for his outburst; see "Journal of a French Traveller in the Colonies, 1765," *American Historical Review* 26, no. 4 (1921): 726–29. Also, William Wirt may have embellished Jefferson's account for dramatic effect.
87. *The Private Correspondence of Daniel Webster*, ed. Edwin D. Sanborn and Fletcher Webster (Boston: Little, Brown, 1875), 1: 368; and *The Works of Thomas Jefferson, Federal Edition*, ed. Paul

Leicester Ford (G. P. Putnam's Sons, 1904–5), 1: 11–12. The quotation in the next paragraph is from *Private Correspondence of Daniel Webster*, 1: 369.

88. Tocqueville, *Democracy in America*, 1: 261.
89. *The Votes and Proceedings of the Freeholders and Other Inhabitants of the Town of Boston, in Town Meeting* (Boston: Edes and Gill, 1772), 18–19.
90. Warren, *History [. . .] of the American Revolution*, 1: 109–10.
91. Quoted in Warren, *History [. . .] of the American Revolution*, 1: 428.
92. "[December 1772: From the Diary of John Adams]," Founders Online, National Archives, accessed August 1, 2024, founders.archives.gov/documents/Adams/01-02-02-0002-0008.
93. Americanus [Samuel Adams], *Newport Mercury*, December 21, 1772. Among the other papers that ran the piece were the *Providence Gazette*, on December 26, 1772; the *Virginia Gazette* (Jamestown), on Thursday, January 28, 1773; and the *London Evening Post*, on March 20, 1773.
94. John Allen, *An Oration Upon the Beauties of Liberty, or The Essential Rights of the Americans* (Boston: D. Kneeland and N. Davis, 1773), viii. This pamphlet is based on an address given by Allen at Boston's Second Church in early December 1772.
95. "Thomas Jefferson's Notes on Early Career (the so-called "Autobiography"), [6 January—29 July 1821]," Founders Online, National Archives, accessed August 28, 2024, founders.archives.gov/documents/Jefferson/03-17-02-0324-0002. See E. I. Miller, "The Virginia Committee of Correspondence of 1773–1775," *William and Mary College Quarterly* 22, no. 2 (1913): 99–113.
96. Quoted in Hosmer, *The Life of Thomas Hutchinson*, 238.
97. Hosmer, *The Life of Thomas Hutchinson*, 243.
98. Warren, *The Group*, 19.
99. *May 27 1774. Broadside Announcing the Association of the House of Burgesses*, Colonial Williamsburg Digital Library, Rockefeller Library Special Collections, SCMS1929.2, research.colonialwilliamsburg.org/DigitalLibrary/view/index.cfm?doc=Manuscripts%5CM19292.xml.
100. Appendix to Otis, *The Rights of the British Colonies Asserted and Proved*, 70.
101. Thomas Jefferson, The Declaration of Independence of The United States of America (1776; Project Gutenberg, 2005), gutenberg.org/cache/epub/16780/pg16780-images.html.
102. Stephen E. Lucas, "The Rhetorical Ancestry of the Declaration of Independence," *Rhetoric and Public Affairs* 1, no. 2 (1998): 150.
103. John Lind, *An Answer to the Declaration of the American Congress* (London: T. Cadell, 1776), 65.
104. *Memoirs of Thomas Hollis*, ed. Francis Blackburne (London, n.p.: 1780), 2: 789.
105. A historian of Jamaica calls the story of the burial of Bradshaw on the island "entirely without foundation." He suggests it may have originated with a rumor spread by Bradshaw's son, who went to Jamaica on a military mission. See George Wilson Bridges, *The Annals of Jamaica* (John Murray, 1927), 1: 420. See also "'Bradshaw's Epitaph': A Hoax Attributed to Franklin, 14 December 1775," Founders Online, National Archives, accessed September 5, 2024, founders.archives.gov/documents/Franklin/01-22-02-0180.
106. "From Benjamin Franklin to Sarah Bache, 26 January 1784," Founders Online, National Archives, accessed September 25, 2024, founders.archives.gov/documents/Franklin/01-41-02-0327.
107. See Monroe E. Deutsch, "E Pluribus Unum," *Classical Journal* 18, no. 7 (1923): 387–407.
108. Gaillard Hunt, *The History of the Seal of the United States* (Department of State, 1909), 14.
109. Boucher, *A View of the Causes and Consequences of the American Revolution*, Boucher discusses Vane and Hutchinson on p. 533. The quotations in the rest of this paragraph are on pp. 514, 532, 530, 525, 498, and 510, successively.
110. *Letters of Jonathan Boucher to George Washington*, ed. Worthington C. Ford (Brooklyn, NY: Historical Printing Club, 1899), 48. The quotation at the end of this paragraph is on p. 49.
111. "From George Washington to Bryan Fairfax, 20 July 1774," Founders Online, National Archives, accessed October 1, 2024, founders.archives.gov/documents/Washington/02-10-02-0081.
112. "Address to the Inhabitants of Bermuda, 6 September 1775," Founders Online, National Archives, accessed December 8, 2024, founders.archives.gov/documents/Washington/03-01-02-0311.
113. Otis, *The Rights of the British Colonies Asserted and Proved*, 29; Charles Sumner, "Political Equality

without Distinction of Color. No Compromise of Human Rights" (March 7, 1866), in Sumner, *The Complete Works*, 13: 296.

***Chapter 7: Ships, Slavery, and Sentimental Power***

1. Statistics in this paragraph are from the Trans-Atlantic Slave Trade Database, Slave Voyages (December 2019 dataset), slavevoyages.org; and from Eltis and Richardson, *Atlas of the Transatlantic Slave Trade*, 21–23.
2. See Raymond Dye Irwin, "Saints, Sinners, and Subjects: Rhode Island and Providence Plantations in Transatlantic Perspective, 1636–1665" (PhD diss., Ohio State University, 1996), 283.
3. James Brown, "The Description of Truth and Error" (c. 1731), quoted in Mack Thompson, *Moses Brown: Reluctant Reformer* (University of North Carolina Press, 1962), 69. See also Charles Rappleye, *Sons of Providence: The Brown Brothers, the Slave Trade, and the American Revolution* (Simon & Schuster, 2006), chap. 1.
4. Clark-Pujara, *Dark Work*, 23.
5. Coughtry, *The Notorious Triangle*, 26. See also Clark-Pujara, *Dark Work*, chap. 1.
6. "Which Europeans Trafficked in Slaves?," Park Ethnography Program, National Park Service, US Department of the Interior, accessed December 27, 2024, nps.gov/ethnography/aah/aaheritage/histcontextsd.htm (site discontinued). According to this data, during this period Portugal transported 1.9 million African people, France 1.1 million, and the Netherlands 364,000.
7. The statistics in this and the previous sentence are from Coughtry, *The Notorious Triangle*, 81–83.
8. Many of the facts about the voyage of the *Sally* in this section are from "Outfitting the Slave Ship Sally," Rhode Island Historical Society, June 6, 2012, rihs.org/images/SALLY_activity_final.pdf; Darold D. Wax, "The Browns of Providence and the Slaving Voyage of the Brig *Sally*," *American Neptune* 32 (1972): 171–79; Allison Stanger, *Whistleblowers: Honesty in America from Washington to Trump* (Yale University Press, 2019), chap. 1; and Jesse Cucksee, "Fall from Prominence: New England Slave Traders and the Changing Perceptions and Realities of Human Trafficking, 1645–1807" (master's thesis, University of Georgia, 2015).
9. James Blaine Hedges, *The Browns of Providence Plantations: The Colonial Years* (Brown University Press, 1968), 1: 76.
10. Hedges, *The Browns of Providence Plantations*, 1: 77. The next quotation in this paragraph is from 1: 78.
11. Hedges, *The Browns of Providence Plantations*, 1: 79. The quotation in the next sentence is from 1: 80.
12. Christy Clark-Pujara, "Slavery, Emancipation and Black Freedom in Rhode Island" (PhD diss., University of Iowa, 2009), 70–72.
13. Hedges, *The Browns of Providence Plantations*, 1: 80.
14. Antiguan trader Alexander Willock to Nicholas Brown and Company, March 7, 1765, *Brown Family Business Records*, Brown University Library, quoted in *The Slave Trade—The Sally*, Brown University Library, https://library.brown.edu/cds/sally/browse.php?browsetype=value&show_valueid=94267.
15. Pam Narbeth, "Historical Note" (1995), Moses Brown Papers, Rhode Island Historical Society, Manuscripts Division, rihs.org/mssinv/Mss313.htm.
16. Moses Brown, "Emancipation Deed," reprinted in *The Colored American* (New York City), April 22, 1837.
17. Benjamin Lay, *All Slave-Keepers That Keep the Innocent in Bondage: Apostates* (Philadelphia: Benjamin Franklin, 1738), 23. The remaining quotations in this paragraph are on pp. 27 and 199, successively.
18. See Marcus Rediker, *The Fearless Benjamin Lay: The Quaker Dwarf Who Became the First Revolutionary Abolitionist* (Beacon, 2018).
19. Anthony Benezet, *Some Historical Account of Guinea: With an Inquiry Into the Rise and Progress of the Slave Trade* (1771; repr., London: J. Phillips, 1788), 69.
20. Thompson, *Moses Brown: Reluctant Reformer*, 102.
21. *The Journal and Other Writings [of] John Woolman*, ed. Vida Dutton Scudder (1774; repr., London: J. M. Dent & Sons, 1910), 54. The quotation in the next sentence is also from p. 54.

22. *Extract from a Representation of the Injustice and Dangerous Tendency of Tolerating Slavery* (Philadelphia: Joseph Crukshank, 1771), 11.
23. Thompson, *Moses Brown: Reluctant Reformer*, 101.
24. John Wesley, *Thoughts Upon Slavery* (London: R. Hawes, 1774), 22.
25. Richard K. MacMaster, "Arthur Lee's 'Address on Slavery': An Aspect of Virginia's Struggle to End the Slave Trade, 1765–1774," *Virginia Magazine of History and Biography* 80, no. 2 (1972): 143.
26. *A Summary View of the Rights of British America*, in *Thomas Jefferson: Writings*, ed. Merrill D. Peterson (Library of America, 1984), 115.
27. "Continental Association, 20 October 1774," Founders Online, National Archives, accessed December 30, 2024, founders.archives.gov/documents/Jefferson/01-01-02-0094.
28. From 1784 to 1807, Rhode Island ships transported an estimated 49,479 Africans to the Americas—almost the same number in twenty-three years as had been transported in the sixty-six years from 1709 to 1775; Coughtry, *The Notorious Triangle*, 27–28.
29. Much of the information about John and Moses Brown in this paragraph is derived from Jay Coughtry, ed., *Papers of the American Slave Trade Series A: Selections from the Rhode Island Historical Society. Brown Family Collections* (University Publications of America, 1998). See also Thompson, *Moses Brown: Reluctant Reformer*, chap. 9.
30. *United States Chronicle* (Providence, RI), February 26, 1789.
31. "For the Providence Gazette," *Providence Gazette* (Providence, RI), March 28, 1789.
32. "Slavery, the Slave Trade, and Brown University," Brown University's Slavery and Justice Report, October 13, 2020, slaveryandjusticereport.brown.edu/sections/slavery-the-slave-trade-and-brown.
33. John Brown to Moses Brown, July 31, 1797; quoted in Coughtry, *Papers of the American Slave Trade*, v.
34. With Rhode Island's gradual emancipation law in force, the number of free Black people in Providence tripled between 1790 and 1825, yet Providence was plagued by segregation and race riots.
35. Irving H. Bartlett, *From Slave to Citizen: The Story of the Negro in Rhode Island* (Urban League of Greater Providence, 1954), 24. The statement by John Quamine quoted at the end of this paragraph is also from p. 24.
36. "Tour of the Editor. Letter II," *Liberator*, October 13, 1832.
37. *Liberator*, September 10, 1836.
38. *The Works of Samuel Hopkins* (Boston: Doctrinal Tract and Book Society, 1852), 1: 11. The foundational work on Hopkins is Joseph Conforti, *Samuel Hopkins and the New Divinity Movement* (Christian University Press, 1981).
39. *National Era* (Washington), July 12, 1847.
40. "Memoir of Dr. Hopkins," *New-York Observer*, September 25, 1830.
41. Preface to Samuel Hopkins, *Timely Articles on Slavery* (Boston: Congregational Board of Publication, 1854), iii.
42. Samuel Hopkins, *A Dialogue Concerning the Slavery of the Africans: Shewing It to Be the Duty and Interest of the American States to Emancipate All Their African Slaves* (New York: Judah P. Spooner, 1776), 13. The next quotation in this paragraph is from p. 23.
43. Hopkins, *A Dialogue Concerning the Slavery*, 45.
44. Hopkins, *A Dialogue Concerning the Slavery*, 3.
45. See David E. Swift, "Samuel Hopkins: Calvinist Social Concern in Eighteenth-Century New England," *Journal of Presbyterian History* 47, no. 1 (1969): 31–54; and Stanley K. Schultz, "The Making of a Reformer: The Reverend Samuel Hopkins as an Eighteenth-Century Abolitionist," *Proceedings of the American Philosophical Society* 115, no. 5 (1971): 350–65.
46. Levi Hart, *Liberty Described and Recommended; In a Sermon, Preached to the Corporation of Freemen in Farmington, at Their Meeting on Tuesday, September 20, 1774* (Hartford: Eben Watson, 1775), 7.
47. Levi Hart, "Some Thoughts on the Subject of Freeing the Negro Slaves in the Colony of Connecticut, Humbly Offered to the Consideration of All Friends to Liberty & Justice," ed. John Saillant, *New England Quarterly* 75, no. 1 (2002): 114.

48. Hart, *Liberty Described and Recommended*, 17.
49. Sydney E. Ahlstrom, "Thomas Hooker–Puritanism and Democratic Citizenship," *Church History* 32, no. 4 (December 1963): 421.
50. See Kenneth P. Minkema, "Jonathan Edwards's Defense of Slavery," *Massachusetts Historical Review* 4 (2002): 23–59.
51. Jonathan Edwards Jr., *The Injustice and Impolicy of the Slave Trade, and of Slavery of the Africans* (John Carter, 1992), 92.
52. Edwards, *The Injustice and Impolicy of the Slave Trade*, 6. The subsequent quotations in this paragraph are on pp. 6, 8, and 11, successively.
53. Edwards, *The Injustice and Impolicy of the Slave Trade*, 23. The subsequent quotations in this paragraph are on pp. 28 and 36, successively.
54. The quotations cited are, successively, in "ALL THE NORTH OPPOSED TO SLAVERY!," *Liberator*, August 25, 1837; "Dr. Guthrie on American Slavery," *Liberator*, April 13, 1860; Reverend Samuel T. Spear, "Observations upon the Slave-Code," *New-York Evangelist*, October 3, 1850.
55. Davis writes, "The source of New England's militant abolitionism can unmistakably be traced to the Calvinist followers of Jonathan Edwards, who were united by friendship and marriage as well as by a common religious cause" (*The Problem of Slavery in the Age of Revolution, 1770–1823* [1975; repr., Oxford University Press, 1999], 289). For further discussion of late-eighteenth-century religion and antislavery activism, see James D. Essig's *The Bonds of Wickedness: American Evangelicals Against Slavery, 1770–1808* (Temple University Press, 1982).
56. "Mr. Gurley's Letter to Mr. Ibertson," *Liberator*, May 11, 1833. Garrison's quotation is a paraphrase of Edwards's declaration in *The Injustice and Impolicy of the Slave Trade* that enslaved people "are much more likely to kill their masters, in order to obtain their liberty, or to revenge the abuse they receive, while it is still continued, than to do it after the abuse hath ceased, and they are restored to their liberty" (33).
57. "Statement of Owen Brown as an Abolitionist," in *The Life and Letters of John Brown*, ed. Franklin B. Sanborn (Boston: Roberts Brothers, 1891), 10–11.
58. See David S. Reynolds, *John Brown, Abolitionist: The Man Who Killed Slavery, Sparked the Civil War, and Seeded Civil Rights* (Vintage Books, 2009).
59. "Liberty Further Extended: Or Free Thoughts on the Illegality of Slave-Keeping" (composed c. 1776; first published 1983), reprinted in Electronic Texts in American Studies, Libraries at University of Nebraska-Lincoln, ed. Paul Royster, 3, digitalcommons.unl.edu/cgi/viewcontent.cgi?article=1095&context=etas.
60. John Saillant, "Lemuel Haynes and the Revolutionary Origins of Black Theology, 1776–1801," *Religion and American Culture: A Journal of Interpretation* 2, no. 1 (1992): 80. For a compelling discussion of the intersection of religion, race, and liberty in Lemuel Haynes, see Bailey, *Race and Redemption in Puritan New England*, chap. 5.
61. "Review of the Memoir of Lemuel Haynes," *New York Evangelist*, October 28, 1837.
62. Timothy Mather Cooley, *Sketches of the Life and Character of the Rev. Lemuel Haynes, A. M.* (New York: Harper & Brothers, 1837), 28.
63. Saillant, "Lemuel Haynes and the Revolutionary Origins of Black Theology," 79.
64. Haynes, "Liberty Further Extended," 7. The remaining quotations in this paragraph are from pp. 7, 6, and 9, successively. The quotations in the next paragraph are from pp. 11–12.
65. Haynes, "Liberty Further Extended," 21–22.
66. Haynes, "Liberty Further Extended," 13–14.
67. *Walker's Appeal, in Four Articles; Together with a Preamble, to the Coloured Citizens of the World* (Boston: David Walker, 1830), 45; and *John Brown: The Making of a Revolutionary*, ed. Louis Ruchames (Grosset & Dunlap, 1971), 167.
68. Lemuel Haynes, *The Nature and Importance of True Republicanism* (Rutland, VT: William Fay, 1801), 16. The remaining quotations in this paragraph are from pp. 21, 13, 12, 10, 6, successively.
69. "Memoir of Lemuel Haynes," *New York Evangelist*, February 25, 1837.
70. John Saillant, *Black Puritan, Black Republican: The Life and Thought of Lemuel Haynes, 1753–*

*1833* (Oxford University Press, 2002). Describing Black Puritans, Saillant writes, "Like a number of other eighteenth-century black authors—Jupiter Hammon, James Albert Ukasaw Gronniosaw, Phillis Wheatley, John Marrant, Quobna Ottobah Cugoano, and Olaudah Equiano—Haynes accepted a Calvinist form of Christianity" (4).

71. "On Messrs Hussey and Coffin" (1767), in Phillis Wheatley, *Complete Writings*, ed. Vincent Carretta (Penguin, 2009), 73–74.
72. For an excellent account of Wheatley's relationship to neoclassicism—as well as many other aspects of her life and writings—see David Waldstreicher, *The Odyssey of Phillis Wheatley: A Poet's Journeys Through American Slavery and Independence* (Farrar, Straus and Giroux, 2023). Among other illuminating studies are Vincent Carretta, *Phillis Wheatley: Biography of a Genius in Bondage* (University of Georgia Press, 2011); Henry Louis Gates Jr., *The Trials of Phillis Wheatley: America's First Black Poet and Her Encounters with the Founding Fathers* (Basic Books, 2003); Honorée Fanonne Jeffers, *The Age of Phillis* (Wesleyan University Press, 2020); and Vincent Carretta and Philip Gould, ed., *Genius in Bondage: Literature of the Early Black Atlantic* (University Press of Kentucky, 2001).
73. Christopher Alain Cameron, "Freeing Themselves: Puritanism, Slavery, and Black Abolitionism in Massachusetts, 1641–1788" (master's thesis, University of North Carolina at Chapel Hill, 2008), 22–24.
74. Cameron, "Freeing Themselves," 36.
75. "On the Death of the Rev. Mr. George Whitefield, 1770," *The Poems of Phillis Wheatley* (R. R. and C. C. Wright, 1909), 16.
76. In *The Ideological Origins of African American Literature* (University of Tennessee Press, 2025), Phillip M. Richards places Wheatley on a cultural continuum that ran from Puritanism to modernism, spanning the eras of Jonathan Edwards, Frederick Douglass, and Langston Hughes.
77. "To the Right Honorable William, Earl of Dartmouth, His Majesty's Secretary of State for North America, Etc.," *The Poems of Phillis Wheatley*, 51.
78. Carretta, ed., *Phillis Wheatley: Complete Writings*, 152.
79. "Thoughts on Tyranny," *Royal American Magazine* 2, no. 2 (1775): 67. See David Waldstreicher, "Wheatley and the Archive in Plain Sight," *Early American Literature* 57, no. 3, (2022): 873–910.
80. Felix [Holbrook], "The Humble Petition of Many Slaves, Living in the Town of Boston, and Other Towns" (1773), reprinted in *A Documentary History of the Negro People in the United States*, ed. Herbert Aptheker (Citadel Press, 1951), 1: 6–7. See Chernow M. Sesay Jr., "The Revolutionary Black Roots of Slavery's Abolition in Massachusetts," *New England Quarterly* 87, no. 1 (2014): 99–131.
81. "To the Honorable Counsel & House of [Representa]tives of the State of Massachusetts Bay in General Court Assembled" (1777), *Collections of the Massachusetts Historical Society*, Fifth Series, vol. 3 (Boston: Massachusetts Historical Society, 1877): 436–37.
82. Massachusetts Constitution (1780), General Court of the Commonwealth of Massachusetts, accessed December 15, 2024, malegislature.gov/Laws/Constitution.
83. Charles Chauncy, *The Appeal to the Public Answered, in Behalf of the Non-Episcopal Churches in America* (Boston: Kneeland and Adams, 1768), 117.
84. Phillis [Wheatley] Peters, *Liberty and Peace, A Poem* (Boston: Warden and Russell, 1784), 2.
85. Thomas Jefferson, *Notes on the State of Virginia*, ed. William Peden (University of North Carolina Press, 1982), 140. The next Jefferson quotation in this paragraph is also from this page.
86. "Letter, No. 5. to Rev. Samuel E. Cornish," *Freedom's Journal*, November 2, 1827.
87. *Memoir and Poems of Phillis Wheatley, a Native African and a Slave* (Boston: Geo. W. Light, 1834), 5.
88. Rufus Wilmot Griswold, review of *The American Female Poets, with Biographical and Critical Notices*, by Caroline May, *North American Review* 68, no. 143 (1849): 418.
89. Sarah Wentworth Apthorp Morton, "The African Chief," *My Mind and Its Thoughts, In Sketches, Fragments, and Essay* (Boston: Wells and Lilly, 1823), 201. The remaining quotations from this poem are from pp. 202–3.
90. Sigourney's "To the First Slave Ship" appeared in *The Liberator* on July 17, 1832. Other newspapers that published the poem include *Christian Watchman* (Boston), November 18, 1825; *Connecticut Mirror* (Hartford, CT), November 28, 1825; *Columbian Centinel* (Boston), December 2, 1825; *Salem Gazette* (Salem, MA), December 2, 1825; *Hampshire Gazette* (Northampton, MA), December

7, 1825; *Hallowell Gazette* (Hallowell, Maine), December 27, 1825; *Vermont Gazette* (Bennington, VT), February 14, 1826; and *Maine Baptist Herald* (Brunswick, ME), February 14, 1826.

91. Gordon S. Haight, *Mrs. Sigourney, the Sweet Singer of Hartford* (Yale University Press, 1930), 149.
92. Edna Edith Sayers and Diana Gates, "Lydia Huntley Sigourney and the Beginnings of American Deaf Education in Hartford: It Takes a Village," *Sign Language Studies* 8, no. 4 (2008): 369–411.
93. Mary Hershberger, "Mobilizing Women, Anticipating Abolition: The Struggle Against Indian Removal in the 1830s," *Journal of American History* 86 (1999): 15–41.
94. Lydia Huntley Sigourney, *Sketch of Connecticut, Forty Years Since* (Hartford Oliver D. Cooke, 1824), 87–88.
95. *African Repository* (Washington, DC), October 1, 1825.
96. Robert Beverley, *The History and Present State of Virginia, in Four Parts* (London: R. Parker, 1705), 37.
97. "Thomas Jefferson to John Holmes, April 22, 1820," Founders Online, National Archives, January 3, 2025, founders.archives.gov/documents/Jefferson/03-15-02-0518.
98. "Slave, Free Black, and White Population, 1780–1830," University of Maryland, Baltimore County, History 407, Professor Terry Bouton, October 27, 2006, userpages.umbc.edu/~bouton/History407/SlaveStats.htm.
99. Walker, *Walker's Appeal, in Four Articles*, 19, 74.
100. The poem first appeared in the *Connecticut Observer* (Hartford, CT), July 10, 1826. In 1827, it was reprinted in the *Providence Patriot, Norwich Courier*, and *Boston Recorder*. It appeared in *The Liberator* on July 17, 1832, and in William S. Russell, *Guide to Plymouth, and Recollections of the Pilgrims* (Boston: George Coolidge, 1846), 61–63.
101. *Newburyport Morning Herald*, December 26, 1835. The poem thereafter appeared in the *Columbian Centinel* (Boston), December 30, 1835; *Dedham Patriot*, December 31, 1835; *New-Bedford Mercury*, January 1, 1836; *New Bedford Gazette*, January 4, 1836; and other newspapers in New England and as far south as Maryland.

*Chapter 8: Then There Were Two*

1. Details of the event were reported in many newspapers, including *Boston Intelligencer*, December 26, 1820; *New-York Evening Post*, December 26, 1820; *Repertory* (Boston, MA), December 26, 1820; *Woodstock Observer* (Woodstock, VT), January 2, 1821; and *American Mercury* (Hartford, CT), January 9, 1821.
2. *Life, Letters, and Journals of George Ticknor*, ed. George Stillman Hillard (Boston: J. R. Osgood, 1876), 115.
3. "From John Adams to Daniel Webster, 23 December 1821," Founders Online, National Archives, accessed January 20, 2025, founders.archives.gov/documents/Adams/99-02-02-7582.
4. "The First Settlement of New England," *The Writings and Speeches of Daniel Webster*, ed. Edward Everett, vol. 1, *Memoir, & Speeches on Various Occasions* (Little, Brown, 1903), 1: 190.
5. *Writings and Speeches of Daniel Webster*, 1: 190. The remaining quotations in this paragraph are from pp. 190, 200, 198, 211, and 207, successively. Like many others of his time, Webster conflated the Plymouth separatists and Massachusetts Bay colonists under the rubric of "Puritans," a term he also applied to Oliver Cromwell and his followers.
6. This and the remaining quotations in this paragraph are from *Writings and Speeches of Daniel Webster*, 1: 221.
7. For examples of Webster's making this indictment of slavery, see *Writings and Speeches of Daniel Webster*, vol. 2, *Speeches on Various Occasions*, 206; vol. 10, *Speeches in Congress and Legal Arguments*, 65; and vol. 18, *Private Correspondence*, 353.
8. *Writings and Speeches of Daniel Webster*, vol. 3, *Speeches on Various Occasions*, 212. The next quotation in this paragraph is from 1: 279.
9. *Writings and Speeches of Daniel Webster*, 18: 318.
10. *Writings and Speeches of Daniel Webster*, 3: 205–6. The remaining quotations in this paragraph are from 3: 206.

11. *Writings and Speeches of Daniel Webster*, vol. 4, *Speeches on Various Occasions*, 76. The next quotation in this paragraph is also from 4: 76.
12. *Writings and Speeches of Daniel Webster*, 10: 89.
13. "Old Colony A. S. Society," *Liberator*, April 19, 1850.
14. *Writings and Speeches of Daniel Webster*, vol. 4, *Speeches on Various Occasions*, 217. The remaining quotations in this paragraph are from 4: 218, 224, 226, and 221, successively.
15. Quoted in "Old Colony A. S. Society," *Liberator*, April 19, 1850. The quotation in the next sentence is also in this article.
16. John Greenleaf Whitter, "Ichabod" (1850), Poetry Foundation, last updated August 9, 2025, poetryfoundation.org/poems/45486/ichabod.
17. *Selections from the Writings and Speeches of William Lloyd Garrison* (Negro Universities Press, 1968), 209.
18. [Remarks by Plymouth's Bourne Spooner at the quarterly meeting of the Old Colony Anti-Slavery Society], *Liberator*, December 3, 1852.
19. "The Old Colony Waking Up," *Liberator*, July 21, 1837.
20. "Speech on the Reception of Abolition Petitions, February, 1837," *Speeches of John C. Calhoun: Delivered in the Congress of the United States from 1811 to the Present Time* (New York: Harper & Brothers, 1843), 225.
21. Garrison, "To the Public," *Liberator*, January 1, 1831.
22. *CW*, 1: 111.
23. David Grimsted, *American Mobbing, 1828–1861: Toward Civil War* (Oxford University Press, 1998), 3.
24. Theodore Dwight Weld, Angelina Grimké Weld, and Sarah Grimké, *American Slavery as It Is: Testimony of a Thousand Witnesses* (New York: American Anti-Slavery Society, 1839), 7–9.
25. Rufus King, *Substance of Two Speeches, Delivered in the Senate of the United States, on the Subject of the Missouri Bill* (Philadelphia: Clark & Raser, 1819), 5.
26. "The Speech of Thomas Marshall, in the House of Delegates of Virginia, on the Abolition of Slavery . . . Friday, January 20, 1832," quoted in *African Repository* (Washington, DC), March 1, 1833.
27. Tocqueville, *Democracy in America*, 57.
28. "Fourth of July," *Saturday Morning Transcript* (Boston), July 26, 1834.
29. Thacher, *History of the Town of Plymouth*, 199.
30. Bancroft, *History of the United States*, 1: 210. The principal histories of Virginia then were Robert Beverley's *The History and Present State of Virginia, in Four Parts* (1705), William Stith's *The History of the First Discovery and Settlement of Virginia* (1747), and John Burk's *The History of Virginia, from Its First Settlement to the Present Day* (1804). All of them wrongly claimed that 1620 was the year of the Jamestown ship's arrival.
31. Russell, *Guide to Plymouth*, 13.
32. Albert Matthews, "The Term Pilgrim Fathers and Early Celebrations of Forefathers' Day," *Publications of the Colonial Society of Massachusetts*, vol. 17, *Transactions* (The Colonial Society of Massachusetts, 1914): 326.
33. "Communication. Pilgrim Celebration in Plymouth," *Columbian Centinel* (Boston), December 26, 1821.
34. *A Memoir of Robert C. Winthrop: Prepared for the Massachusetts Historical Society* (Boston: Little, Brown, 1897), 205. The remaining quotations in this paragraph are from p. 276.
35. Robert C. Winthrop, "Address" (1839), *The New England Society Orations: Addresses, Sermons, and Poems Delivered Before the New England Society in the City of New York, 1820–1885*, ed. Cephas Brainerd and Eveline Warner Brainerd (Century, 1901), 1: 254. The quotations in the next sentence are from p. 224. The remaining quotations in this paragraph are from pp. 221 and 256–57, successively.
36. *The New England Society Orations*, 1: 256–57.
37. *A Memoir of Robert C. Winthrop*, 124. The information at the end of this paragraph about Winthrop's voting is from p. 235.

38. "Speech of H. H. Garnet, Delivered at the 7th Anniversary of the American Anti-Slavery Society," *Colored American* (New York), May 30, 1840. My discussion of antebellum African Americans' references to the two ships is informed in part by Kenyon Gradert's article "The *Mayflower* and the Slave Ship: Pilgrim-Puritan Origins in the Antebellum Black Imagination," *MELUS* 44, no. 3 (2019): 63–90.
39. Henry Highland Garnet, *A Memorial Discourse: Delivered in the Hall of the House of Representatives, Washington City, D.C., on Sabbath, February 12, 1865* (Philadelphia: Wescott & Thomson, 1865), 73.
40. Henry Highland Garnet, *Walker's Appeal, with a Brief Sketch of His Life. By Henry Highland Garnet. And Also Garnet's Address to the Slaves of the United States of America* (New York: J. H. Tobbit, 1848), vi–vii.
41. Walker, *Walker's Appeal, in Four Articles*, 41.
42. *Liberator*, November 17, 1832.
43. Garnet, *Walker's Appeal, with a Brief Sketch of His Life*, vi.
44. Garnet, "Address to the Slaves of the United States of America" (Buffalo, NY, 1843), in W. M. Brewer, "Henry Highland Garnet," *Journal of Negro History* 13, no. 1 (1928): 43.
45. Henry Highland Garnet, *The Past and the Present Condition, and the Destiny, of the Colored Race: A Discourse Delivered at the Fifteenth Anniversary of the Female Benevolent Society of Troy, N. Y., Feb. 14, 1848* (Troy, NY: J. C. Kneeland, 1848), 12.
46. "Speech of H. H. Garnet," *Colored American* (New York), May 30, 1840.
47. Martin Delany, *The Condition, Elevation, Emigration, and Destiny of the Colored People of the United States* (pub. by the author, 1852), 61. The next two Delany quotations in this paragraph are from pp. 209 and 159–60, successively.
48. Holly, "APPEAL FOR A FAREWELL BENEFIT FOR THE HAYTIAN EMIGRANTS FROM NEW HAVEN," *Weekly Anglo-African* (New York), April 27, 1861.
49. "EMANCIPATION; A Sermon Preached at Music Hall, Boston, March 30, 1861, by F. B. Sanborn," *Weekly Anglo-African*, April 20, 1861.
50. William Wells Brown, *Clotel; or, The President's Daughter: A Narrative of Slave Life in the United States* (London: Partridge & Oakey, 1853), 183–84.
51. William Wells Brown, *The Rising Son, Or, The Antecedents and Advancement of the Colored Race* (1873; repr., Boston: A. G. Brown, 1882), 265–66.
52. "Frederick Douglass in Philadelphia," *Frederick Douglass's Paper*, April 6, 1855.
53. Douglass, "Progress and Divisions of Anti-Slavery," 326. The remaining quotations in this paragraph are from pp. 326–27.
54. Everett, speech given at a dinner in his honor in Lexington, KY, quoted in the *Daily Richmond Whig*, July 4, 1829.
55. "Foreign Immigration," *Morning Herald* (New York), October 31, 1837.
56. "President Tyler in New York," *Madisonian* (Washington, DC), June 14, 1843.
57. "The War with Mexico," *New Orleans Tropic*, reprinted in *Yazoo City Whig*, June 5, 1846.
58. "Speech of the Hon. John Campbell, of So. Carolina," *Charleston Courier* (Charleston, SC), June 1, 1842.
59. William Henry Trescot, *The Position and Course of the South* (Charleston: Walker & James, 1850), 9. The remaining quotations in this paragraph are from pp. 12 and 4, successively.
60. Robert Cassie Waterston, "Discourse Delivered at the Dedication of the Church of the Saviour. Wednesday, November 10, 1847," in *Discourses, Addresses and Memoir* (Cambridge: John Wilson and Son, 1893), 6. The next quotation in this paragraph is from p. 19. Excerpted in *The Liberator*, January 21, 1848; and *The North Star* (Rochester, NY), February 4, 1848.
61. "The Buffalo Convention. Report of Proceedings," *North Star*, August 11, 1848.
62. *National Era* (Washington, DC), April 11, 1850.
63. *New Englander and Yale Review* 45, no. 198 (September 1886): 768.
64. Sumner, "White Slavery in the Barbary States," *Complete Works*, 2: 26.
65. Sumner, *Complete Works*, 4: 78.
66. Sumner, *Complete Works*, 7: 8. The quotations in the next paragraph are from 7: 8–9.

67. *London Times*, May 28, 1861, quoted in "The Civil War in America," *Proceedings of the Massachusetts Historical Society, Third Series*, vol. 46 (1912–1913), 310–11.

***Chapter 9: Northern Puritans vs. Southern Cavaliers***

1. *Alexandria Daily Gazette*, May 11, 1809.
2. Michel Chevalier, *Society, Manners and Politics in the United States: Being a Series of Letters on North America* (1834; repr., Boston: Weeks, Jordan, 1839), 114.
3. William Cabell Bruce, *John Randolph of Roanoke, 1773–1833* (G. P. Putnam's Sons, 1922), 1: 8–9.
4. Robert P. Sutton, "Nostalgia, Pessimism, and Malaise: The Doomed Aristocrat in Late-Jeffersonian Virginia," *Virginia Magazine of History and Biography* 76, no. 1 (1968): 41–55.
5. Mark Twain, *Life on the Mississippi* (Boston: James R. Osgood, 1883), 467. The quotation in the next sentence is also from p. 467. The next two quotations in the paragraph are from p. 469.
6. *Diary of Gideon Welles: Secretary of the Navy Under Lincoln and Johnson* (Houghton Mifflin, 1911), 2: 276–77.
7. *Memoirs of the Life of Sir Walter Scott*, ed. J. G. Lockhart (Edinburgh: R. Cadell, 1837–38), 1: 30–31.
8. Beverley Tucker, *George Balcombe* (New York: n.p., 1836), 1:22.
9. Nathaniel Beverley Tucker, *A Series of Lectures on the Science of Government: Intended to Prepare the Student for the Study of the Constitution of the United States* (Philadelphia: Carey and Hart, 1845), 216–17. The remaining quotations in this paragraph are from pp. 217, 218, and 219, successively.
10. Nathaniel Beverley Tucker, *The Partisan Leader: A Tale of the Future* (James Caxton, 1856 [1836]), 1: 7–8.
11. Tucker, *A Series of Lectures*, 302. The remaining quotations in this paragraph are also from this page.
12. Curtis Carroll Davis, *Chronicler of the Cavaliers: A Life of the Virginia Novelist Dr. William A. Caruthers* (Dietz Press, 1953). Some of the biographical information in this section is from Davis's book. The quotations in this paragraph are from pp. 39 and 88, successively.
13. William Alexander Caruthers, *The Cavaliers of Virginia; Or, The Recluse of Jamestown: An Historical Romance of the Old Dominion* (New York: Harper & Brothers, 1834), 1: 2. The quotation in the next sentence is from 1: 23.
14. William Alexander Caruthers, *The Knights of the Golden Horse-Shoe; A Traditionary Tale of the Cocked Hat Gentry in the Old Dominion* (1845; repr., New York: n.p., 1928), 266. The quotation in the next sentence is from p. 122. The quotations in the sentence after that are from p. 266.
15. William Gilmore Simms, *The Letters of William Gilmore Simms*, ed. Mary C. Simms Oliphant, and T. C. Duncan Eaves (University of South Carolina Press, 1952–82), 4: 24. The quotation in the next sentence is also from this page.
16. William B. Tappan, *The Sunday School and Other Poems* (Boston: James Munroe, 1849), 77–78.
17. "Some Selected Simms Reviews in the *Southern Quarterly Review*, 1849–1850," *Simms Review* 7, no. 2 (1999): 20.
18. William Gilmore Simms, "The Antagonisms of the Social Moral, North and South," in *Honorable and Brilliant Labors: Orations of William Gilmore Simms*, ed. John D. Miller (University of South Carolina Press, 2024), 278.
19. William Gilmore Simms, *Woodcraft: Or, Hawks About the Dovecote* (1852; repr., Martin & Hoyt, 1901), 46.
20. Simone Vauthier, "Of Time and the South: The Fiction of William Gilmore Simms," *Southern Literary Journal* 5, no. 1 (1972): 15.
21. Simms, *Letters*, 3: 222–23.
22. Louisa C. McCord, "Uncle Tom's Cabin," *Southern Quarterly Review* 7, no. 13 (1853): 81–82.
23. Simms, *Woodcraft*, 509.
24. John Esten Cooke, *Virginia: A History of the People* (Boston: Houghton, Mifflin: 1896), 172. The quotation in the next sentence is from p. 182.
25. Cooke, "On the Road to Despotism" (unpublished article, 1870), quoted in Mary Jo Bratton, "John Esten Cooke and His 'Confederate Lies,'" *Southern Literary Journal* 13, no. 2 (1981): 82. The

quotation in the next sentence is also from this page. The article is held in the John Esten Cooke Papers, Duke University.

26. Cooke, "On the Road to Despotism," quoted in Bratton, "John Esten Cooke and His 'Confederate Lies,'" 82.
27. "Wealth and Culture in the South," OpenStaxCollege, May 7, 2014, pressbooks-dev.oer.hawaii.edu/ushistory/chapter/wealth-and-culture-in-the-south. These numbers are qualified by the fact that ownership could be attributed to a larger group of people, including family members or household members of the enslavers.
28. The so-called New Puritanism opposed the Calvinist doctrines of predestination and total depravity. It emphasized good works and moral behavior, which is why it became associated with temperance, antiseduction, gambling, and the opposition to slavery. For a rich discussion of connections between antebellum reform movements, Lyman Beecher, and evangelicalism, see Robert H. Abzug, *Cosmos Crumbling: American Reform and the Religious Imagination* (Oxford University Press, 1994).
29. The Beecher family was said to be mainly responsible for the New Puritanism in its early phase. See Charles A. Berry et al., *The New Puritanism.*
30. *Autobiographical Reminiscences of Henry Ward Beecher,* ed. T. J. Ellinwood (New York: Frederick A. Stokes, 1898), 87.
31. Vincent Harding, "Lyman Beecher and the Transformation of American Protestantism, 1775–1863" (PhD diss., University of Chicago, 1965). Harding notes that "the work of Hopkins had as much influence on Lyman Beecher as that of any other theologian" (29).
32. Lyman Beecher, *The Memory of Our Fathers: A Sermon Delivered at Plymouth, on the Twenty-Second of December, 1827* (Boston: T. R. Marvin, 1828), 28. The two quotations in the remainder of this paragraph are from p. 30.
33. Wendell Phillips Garrison and Francis Jackson Garrison, *William Lloyd Garrison, 1805–1879: The Story of His Life Told by His Children* (New York: Century, 1885), 1: 215.
34. See James Brewer Stewart, *Wendell Phillips: Liberty's Hero* (Louisiana State University Press, 1986), 8–12.
35. George Lowell Austin, *The Life and Times of Wendell Phillips* (Boston: n.p., 1888), 66. The quotation at the end of this paragraph is from p. 79.
36. See Austin, *The Life and Times of Wendell Phillips*, 35.
37. Wendell Phillips, *Speeches, Lectures, and Letters* (Boston: Lee and Shepard, 1884), 229. The quotation in the next sentence is from p. 234.
38. Debby Applegate, *The Most Famous Man in America: The Biography of Henry Ward Beecher* (Doubleday, 2006).
39. Henry Ward Beecher, *Lectures and Orations*, ed. Newell Dwight Hillis (Fleming H. Revell, 1913), 29, 292.
40. Henry Ward Beecher, *Freedom and War: Discourses on Topics Suggested by the Times* (Boston: Ticknor and Fields, 1863). 75.
41. Harriet Beecher Stowe, *The Minister's Wooing* (New York: Derby and Jackson, 1859), 147. The next quotation in this paragraph is from p. 277.
42. Letter from Harriet Beecher Stowe to Calvin Ellis Stowe, May 23–27, 1844; E. Bruce Kirkham Collection at the Harriet Beecher Stowe Center Library, Hartford, CT.
43. Charles Edward Stowe, *Life of Harriet Beecher Stowe Compiled from Her Letters and Journals* (Boston: Houghton, Mifflin, 1889), 11.
44. [Frederick Douglass], "Literary Notices," *Frederick Douglass's Paper*, April 1, 1852.
45. "Literature of Slavery," *New Englander*, no. 10 (November 1852): 591.
46. Henry Ward Beecher, "Shall We Compromise?," *Independent Democrat* (Concord, NH), April 4, 1850.
47. Charles Beecher, *The Duty of Disobedience to Wicked Laws: A Sermon on the Fugitive Slave Law* (New York: John A. Gray, 1851), 6. The remaining quotations in this paragraph are from pp. 7 and 21.

48. "Speech of the Hon. Thaddeus Stevens, of Pennsylvania, on the California Question Made in the House of Representatives," *National Era* (Washington, DC), June 27, 1850.
49. John Quincy Adams, *Documents Relating to New-England Federalism: 1800–1815*, ed. Henry Adams (Boston: Little, Brown, 1877), 140.
50. George Wilson Pierson, *Tocqueville in America* (1938; repr., Johns Hopkins University Press, 1996), 418.
51. Tocqueville, *Democracy in America*, 1: 455.
52. John Quincy Adams, *The Social Compact, Exemplified in the Constitution of the Commonwealth of Massachusetts: With Remarks on the Theories of Divine Right of Hobbes and of Filmer, and the Counter Theories of Sidney, Locke, Montesquieu, and Rousseau* (Providence: Knowles and Vose, 1842), 23.
53. Ahlstrom, *A Religious History of the American People*, 129; the Sidney quotation is from *Discourses Concerning Government* (1698), in *The Works of Algernon Sidney*, ed. Thomas Hollis (London: W. Strahan, 1772), 5.
54. William Seward, *The Irrepressible Conflict: A Speech Delivered at Rochester, Monday, Oct 25, 1858* (Albany: Weed, Parsons and Co., 1858), 3; and William Seward, *Speech of William H. Seward on the Admission of California: Delivered in the Senate of the United States, March 11, 1850* (Washington, DC: Buell & Blanchard, 1850), 14.
55. *Oration by William H. Seward, at Plymouth, December 21, 1855* (Albany: Weed, Parsons and Company, 1856), 16–17. The remaining quotations from this speech in this paragraph are from pp. 17 and 20.
56. Phillips, *Speeches, Lectures, and Letters*, 232.
57. For an interesting discussion of this topic, see Peter Wirzbicki, *Fighting for the Higher Law: Black and White Transcendentalists Against Slavery* (University of Pennsylvania Press, 2021). See also Caleb Smith, *The Oracle and the Curse: A Poetics of Justice from the Revolution to the Civil War* (Harvard University Press, 2012); and Sandra Harbert Petrulionis, "The 'Higher Law': Then and Now," *Thoreau Society Bulletin*, no. 262 (Spring 2008): 5–7.
58. *Emerson's Antislavery Writings*, ed. Joel Myerson and Len Gougeon (Yale University Press, 1995), 83.
59. Henry David Thoreau, "Slavery in Massachusetts," *Collected Essays and Poems*, ed. Elizabeth Hall Witherell (Library of America, 2001), 346.
60. Theodore Parker, *Sins and Safeguards of Society* (American Unitarian Association, 1909), 43.
61. *The Collected Works of Theodore Parker*, 5: 168.
62. See Albert J. Von Frank, *The Trials of Anthony Burns: Freedom and Slavery in Emerson's Boston* (Harvard University Press, 1998).
63. Theodore Parker, *Saint Bernard and Other Papers*, ed. Charles W. Wendte (American Unitarian Association, 1911), 345.
64. *The Collected Works of Theodore Parker*, 5: 252–53.
65. *The Collected Works of Theodore Parker*, 5: 254–55.
66. *The Collected Works of Theodore Parker*, 13: 113.
67. Thomas Carlyle, *Carlyle's Works* (Boston: Chapman and Hall, 1884), 17: 14.
68. *Carlyle's Works*, 1: 436, 17: 80. The quotations in the next two sentences are both from 1: 428.
69. Thomas Carlyle, *Chartism* (London: J. Fraser, 1840), 80.
70. Genealogical evidence does not confirm the *Mayflower* connection. John Brown's Puritan ancestry ran to Peter Brown (c. 1632–1692) and his son John Brown (1668–1728), both of Windsor, Connecticut.
71. See Nicole Etcheson, *Bleeding Kansas: Contested Liberty in the Civil War Era* (University Press of Kansas, 2004).
72. F. B. Sanborn, *Memoirs of John Brown* (Concord, MA: J. Munsell, 1878), 45; George Stearns quoted in Charles E. Heller, *Portrait of an Abolitionist: A Biography of George Luther Stearns, 1809–1867* (Greenwood, 1996), 78; Mary Stearns quoted in Richard J. Hinton, *John Brown and His Men* (1894; repr. Arno Press, 1968), 721; Phillips quoted in Robert B. Bonner, "Roundheaded Cavaliers? The

Contexts and Limits of a Confederate Racial Project," *Civil War History* no. 48 (200): 38; Hinton quoted in Michael Fellman, *Inside War: The Guerilla Conflict in Missouri During the American Civil War* (Oxford University Press, 1989), 17. See Reynolds, *John Brown, Abolitionist*, 230.

73. Thoreau, "A Plea for Captain John Brown," *Collected Essays and Poems*, 407. The remaining quotations in this paragraph are on pp. 398–99.
74. *CW*, 4: 50. The Lincoln quotation at the end of this paragraph is from *CW*, 2: 268.
75. *CW*, 3: 496. The other quotations in this paragraph are from pp. 541 and 542, successively.
76. *CW*, 3: 27.
77. Mark 3: 24–26; Matthew 12: 25; Mark 3: 25; Luke 11: 17.
78. *CW*, 3: 17. The block quotation on the next page is from p. 315.
79. The quotations in this paragraph are from "Anniversary of the Landing of the Pilgrims," *Illinois State Journal*, December 24, 1856.
80. *CW*, 7: 243.
81. *Reminiscences of Abraham Lincoln: By Distinguished Men of His Time*, ed. Allen Thorndike Rice (New York: North American Publishing Company, 1886), 193.
82. *CW*, 2: 266. The comment in the next sentence about being assassinated on the spot is from *CW*, 4: 240.
83. Adams, *Documents Relating to New-England Federalism*, 140.
84. Joanne B. Freeman, *The Field of Blood: Violence in Congress and the Road to Civil War* (Farrar, Straus and Giroux, 2018).
85. "Speech of Mr. Wise," *Daily National Intelligencer* (Washington, DC), March 9, 1839.
86. *The Reminiscences of Carl Schurz*, ed. William Archibald Dunning and Frederic Bancroft (Doubleday, Page, 1908), 2: 35–36.
87. Charles Sumner, "The Crime Against Kansas," in Sumner, *Complete Works*, 5: 144.
88. Robert L. Meriwether, "Preston S. Brooks on the Caning of Charles Sumner," *South Carolina Historical and Genealogical Magazine* 52, no. 1 (1951), 2. The next quotation in this paragraph is from p. 3.
89. "Ruffianism in the U.S. Senate Chamber," *Salem Register*, May 26, 1856.
90. "The Assault Upon Senator Sumner," *Daily Minnesotan* (St. Paul, MN), May 27, 1856.
91. *Albany Evening Journal*, August 7, 1856.
92. "The Sumner Discipline," *Liberator*, June 13, 1856.
93. *Defence of Massachusetts: Speech of Hon. Anson Burlingame, of Massachusetts, in the House of Representatives, June 21, 1856* (Washington, DC: Buell & Blanchard, 1856), 1–2.
94. "Forefathers' Day," *Liberator*, December 28, 1849.
95. The quotations in this paragraph are from Phillips, *Speeches, Lectures, and Letters*, 231–32.
96. "The Jamestown Meeting," *Washington Sentinel* (Washington, DC), February 2, 1854. The quotation in the first sentence of the next paragraph is also from this source. For an earlier effort, around 1807, to rehabilitate Jamestown, see David Waldstreicher, *In the Midst of Perpetual Fetes: The Making of American Nationalism, 1776–1820* (University of North Carolina Press, 1997), 251–69.
97. "Jamestown Society," *Richmond Whig*, February 7, 1854. The quotation in the next sentence is also from this source.
98. *Washington Sentinel*, February 2, 1854.
99. *Richmond Whig*, May 21, 1854.
100. *Washington Sentinel*, April 19, 1854.
101. "Lecture of Rev. Daniel Foster," *Kanzas* [*sic*] *News* (Emporia, KS), September 26, 1857.
102. Descriptions of the monument, the canopy, and their history can be found in the *New York Herald*, August 3, 1859; *Boston Recorder*, July 14, 1859; and *Boston Press and Post*, August 4, 1859.
103. Massachusetts Department of Conservation and Recreation, *National Monument to the Forefathers Resource Management Plan* (Massachusetts Department of Conservation and Recreation, Bureau of Planning and Resource Protection, 2006), 19; https://www.mass.gov/doc/national-monument-to-the-forefathers-resource-management-plan/download.
104. *CW*, 4: 271. The remaining quotations in this paragraph are also from this page.

105. J. D. B. De Bow, "Presidential Candidates and Aspirants," *De Bow's Review*, no. 29 (July 1860): 101.
106. George Sanders' Advice to the Northern Conservatives," *Richmond Whig*, December 30, 1862.
107. "Slavery and the Bible," *De Bow's Review*, no. 9 (September 1850): 246.
108. African Slavery, the Corner-Stone of the Southern Confederacy A Speech by Hon. Alexander H. Stevens, Vice-President of the Confederate States of America, Delivered at the Athenaeum, Savannah, March 22nd, 1861, in *Three Unlike Speeches* (New York: E. D. Barker, 1862), 70.
109. Lincoln to Alexander H. Stephens, December 22, 1860, *CW*, 4: 160.
110. "Our New Orleans Correspondence," *New York Herald*, March 22, 1861.
111. Sumner, *Complete Works*, 7: 8–9.

***Chapter 10: The Culture War Behind the Civil War***

1. Frederick Douglass, "Fighting the Rebels with One Hand," *Douglass' Monthly*, no. 4 (February 1862): 593–97.
2. J. Quitman Moore, "Southern Civilization, or the Norman in America," *De Bow's Review*, no. 32 (January 1862): 1–19. All quotations in this paragraph are from this source, except for the last one.
3. J. Quitman Moore, "The Belligerents," *De Bow's Review*, no. 31 (July 1862): 73. James M. McPherson associates the South's Norman/Cavalier self-image, in opposition to the "Puritan" North, with ethnic nationalism, "the sense of identity and loyalty shared by a group of people united among themselves and distinguished from others by one or more of the following factors: language, religion, culture, and, perhaps most important but also most nebulous, a belief in the common genetic descent of the group"; see McPherson, "Two irreconcilable peoples"? Ethnic Nationalism in the Confederacy," in *The Civil War as Global Conflict: Transnational Meanings of the American Civil War*, ed. David T. Gleeson and Simon Lewis (University of South Carolina Press, 2014), 85.
4. Quoted in William H. Whitmore, *The Cavalier Dismounted: An Essay on the Origin of the Founders of the Thirteen Colonies* (Salem: G. M. Whipple & A. A. Smith, 1864), 4.
5. Georgia politician Robert Toombs, quoted in Frank H. Alfriend, *The Life of Jefferson Davis* (Cincinnati: Caxton Publishing House, 1868), 109.
6. "Jefferson Davis's Speech at Jackson, Miss., House Chamber, Mississippi Capitol, December 26, 1862," *The Papers of Jefferson Davis*, Rice University, accessed January 25, 2025, jeffersondavis.rice.edu/archives/documents/jefferson-davis-speech-jackson-miss-0.
7. "Southern Cavaliers and Northern Puritans," *Nashville Courier*, reprinted in *Douglass' Monthly* (Rochester, NY), July 1862.
8. See especially George Fitzhugh, *Cannibals All! Or, Slaves Without Masters* (Richmond: A. Morris, 1857).
9. "The Reaction Against the Abolitionists—American Civilization Verus Puritan Fanaticism," *New York Herald*, February 3, 1861.
10. "Disfederation of the States, *Southern Literary Messenger* (Richmond, VA), excerpted in *Nashville Union and American*, February 26, 1861. The quotation in the next sentence is from the paper's March 13, 1861, issue.
11. "Signs of the Times," *Mobile Messenger* (Mobile, AL), excerpted in *Memphis Daily Appeal* (Memphis, TN), August 23, 1862.
12. "The Reaction Against the Abolitionists," *New York Herald*.
13. "The Virginia Cavaliers," *Richmond Whig*, August 11, 1868.
14. Michael E. Woods, *Arguing Until Doomsday: Stephen Douglas, Jefferson Davis, and the Struggle for American Democracy* (University of North Carolina Press, 2020), 153.
15. John H. Van Evrie, *Negroes and Negro "Slavery": The First an Inferior Race; the Latter Its Normal Condition* (1853; repr., New York: Van Evrie, Horton, 1861), 168. The first quotation in the next paragraph are from pp. 276–77.
16. Van Evrie, *Negroes and Negro "Slavery,"* vii–viii, 333.
17. Quoted in Christopher Luse, "'The offspring of infidelity': Polygenesis and the Defense of Slavery" (PhD diss., Emory University, 2008), 32.

18. John H. Van Evrie, introduction to James Hunt, *The Negro's Place in Nature* (New York: Horton & Company, 1864).
19. Van Evrie, "Negro Slavery the Basis of Democratic Institutions, or Negro Subordination Essential to White Equality," *New York Day-Book*, May 10, 1856.
20. A Speech by Hon. Alexander H. Stevens, 70. The quotations in the next sentence are from the same page.
21. Van Evrie, "A Revival of Puritanism," *New York Day-Book* (published as *New-York Caucasian*), November 23, 1861.
22. Emerson, *Essays and Lectures*, 592.
23. Adalbert Johann Volck, *Worship of the North*, Digital Collections, Library Company of Philadelphia, accessed January 28, 2025, digital.librarycompany.org/islandora/object/Islandora%3A65185.
24. *Cotton Is King, and Pro-slavery Arguments*, ed. E. N. Elliott (Augusta, GA: Pritchard, Abbot & Loomis, 1860), 543. The remaining quotations from *Cotton Is King* in this paragraph are from pp. 528 and 643, successively.
25. A. Clarkson, "The Basis of Northern Hostility to the South," *De Bow's Review* 28, no. 1 (1860): 7–16.
26. "Piety and Politics," *Daily True Delta* (New Orleans, LA), February 3, 1861. The remaining quotations in this paragraph are from this source.
27. "The North-West," *Mobile Register* (Mobile, AL), November 8, 1862.
28. *Richmond Despatch*, reprinted in the *West-Jersey Pioneer* (Bridgeton, NJ), October 25, 1862.
29. "The Old Taint," *Augusta Chronicle*, August 16, 1861.
30. George W. Richardson, *Speech of George W. Richardson, of Hanover* [. . .] *In the Convention of Virginia, April 4, 1861* (Richmond: Whig Book and Job Office, 1862), 30.
31. *Chicago Times*, reprinted under the title "Par Ignobile Fratrum" in the *Illinois State Journal* (Springfield, IL), January 3, 1863.
32. Hawthorne, "Chiefly About War-Matters," *Atlantic Monthly*, no. 10 (July 1862): 54.
33. "Puritanism of the Present Day—How It Works," *Richmond Enquirer*, September 28, 1854.
34. "New England and the Union. From the South," *Liberator*, April 23, 1858.
35. "Lecture by Hon. S. S. Cox, in Washington City, February 21, 1866," *Crisis* (Columbus, OH), March 14, 1866.
36. Samuel S. Cox, *Miscegenation or Amalgamation: Fate of the Freedman* (Washington, DC: Consitutional Union, 1864), 5.
37. *Appletons' Journal* 12, no. 278 (1874): 95.
38. Samuel S. Cox, *Eight Years in Congress, from 1857 to 1865* (New York: D. Appleton, 1865), 282. The remaining quotations in this paragraph are from pp. 282–83 and 285, successively.
39. Cox, *Eight Years in Congress*, 293. The remaining quotations in this paragraph are from pp. 290, 296, 296, 287, 290, 286, and 298, successively.
40. *Speeches, Arguments, Addresses, and Letters of Clement L. Vallandigham* (New York: J. Walter & Co. 1864), 182. The quotation in the next sentence is from p. 365.
41. Vallandigham, *Speeches, Arguments, Addresses*, 444. The remaining quotations in this paragraph are from pp. 442–44.
42. "Diary of Archbishop Martin J. Spalding, January 1, 1863," in Kenneth J. Zanca, "Baltimore's Catholics and the Funeral of Lincoln," *Maryland Historical Magazine* 98, no. 1 (2003): 94.
43. [William M. Bobo], *The Confederate. By a South Carolinian* (Mobile, AL: S. H. Goetzel, 1863), 8. The remaining quotations in this paragraph are from pp. 15, 47, 62, 97, 95, and 6, successively.
44. Arthur Lyon Fremantle, *Three Months in the Southern States: April, June, 1863* (New York: John Bradburn, 1864), 19.
45. *Boston Evening Transcript*, April 27, 1863.
46. Judah Benjamin to John Slidell, June 22, 1863, *Official Records of the Union and Confederate Navies in the War of the Rebellion* (Government Printing Office, 1922), series 2, 3: 816–817.
47. Raphael Semmes, *The Cruise of the Alabama and the Sumter* (New York: Carleton, 1864), 2: 28.
48. "The National Need of Prayer," *Congregationalist*, September 2, 1864.
49. "Yankee Doodle Doo," *The Southern Soldier's Prize Songster* (Mobile, AL: W. F. Wisely, 1864), 19.
50. John W. Overall, "Ballad of the Cavaliers," *Richmond Whig*, September 12, 1862.

51. *Boston Traveler* (Boston, MA), February 13, 1862; and *Trumpet and Universalist Magazine* (Boston, MA), March 22, 1862.
52. *The Liberator*, January 2, 1863.
53. Elhanan Winchester Reynolds, *The True Story of the Barons of the South; or, The Rationale of the American Conflict* (Boston: Walker, Wise, 1862), 17–18.
54. Reynolds, *True Story of the Barons of the South*, 18. The remaining quotations in this paragraph are from pp. 18–19, and 28, successively.
55. "From John Adams to Horatio Gates, 23 March 1776," Founders Online, National Archives, accessed February 1, 2025, founders.archives.gov/documents/Adams/06-04-02-0023.
56. Reynolds, *True Story of the Barons of the South*, 73. The quotation in the next sentence is from the same page. The quotation in the next paragraph is from p. 90.
57. Reynolds, *True Story of the Barons of the South*, 34. The remaining quotations in this paragraph are from p. 36.
58. Reynolds, *True Story of the Barons of the South*, 235. The next quotation in this paragraph is from p. 233.
59. "Forefathers' Day," *Independent Democrat* (Concord, NH), December 26, 1861.
60. Lew Wallace, "The Stolen Stars," in Alf Burnett, *Incidents of the War; Humorous, Pathetic, and Descriptive* (Cincinnati: Rickey & Carroll, 1863), 299–302.
61. "Colored Enlistments in Chester," *Liberator*, August 21, 1863.
62. "Address of the Women's National Loyal League," *New York Herald*, May 27, 1863.
63. Sumner, *Complete Works*, 10: 259–60. This letter was published in many newspapers.
64. "New England," *Journal of Commerce*, reprinted in the *Illustrated New Age* (Philadelphia, PA), December 28, 1863, and other papers.
65. "Libels upon the Puritan Fathers," *Boston Morning Journal*, January 11, 1864.
66. *Slavery and the Rebellion, One and Inseparable. Speech of Hon. Charles Sumner, Before the New York Young Men's Republican Union, at Cooper Institute, New York, on the Afternoon of November 5, 1864* (Boston: Wright & Potter, 1864), 10. The remaining quotations in this paragraph are from pp. 10–12.
67. *Slavery and the Rebellion*, 12. The remaining quotations in this paragraph are from pp. 13, 15, 17, and 28, successively.
68. *An Idler: John Hay's Social and Aesthetic Commentaries for the Press During the Civil War, 1861–1865*, ed. Douglas W. Hill and Helmut Relsig (Academica Press, 2006), 157.
69. Manton Marble, "The Freedom of the Press. The Suppression of the *New York World* and *Journal of Commerce*," *Illustrated New Age* (Philadelphia, PA), May 24, 1864.
70. "George Sanders' Advice to the Northern Conservatives," *Richmond Whig*, December 30, 1862.
71. George W. Briggs, *Eulogy on Abraham Lincoln, June 1, 1865* (Salem, MA: George W. Pease, 1865), 38.
72. Lemuel Moss, *Annals of the United States Christian Commission* (Philadelphia: J. B. Lippincott, 1868), 563.
73. George H. Stuart, *The Life of George H. Stuart, Written by Himself*, ed. Robert Ellis Thompson (Philadelphia: J. M. Stoddard, 1890), 178.
74. Moss, *Annals of the United States Christian Commission*, 578.
75. Harriet Beecher Stowe, *Uncle Tom's Cabin* (1852), ed. Elizabeth Ammons (W. W. Norton, 1994), 388.
76. *John Brown: The Making of a Revolutionary*, 167.
77. Association of Illinois Congregational Church to Abraham Lincoln, Thursday, August 01, 1861 (Printed Resolution), Abraham Lincoln Papers at the Library of Congress.
78. See Louis Fisher and Nada Mourtada-Sabbah, "Adopting 'In God We Trust' As the U.S. National Motto," *Journal of Church & State* 44, no. 4 (2002): 671–92.
79. Sarah Josepha Hale to Abraham Lincoln, September 28, 1863, Abraham Lincoln Papers at the Library of Congress.
80. *CW*, 6: 496–97.
81. "A National Thanksgiving," *Springfield Union* (Springfield, MA), November 23, 1864.

82. "THANKSGIVING: General Observance of the Day," *New York Times*, November 25, 1864.
83. John N. Murdock, *Our Civil War: Its Causes and Its Issues: A Discourse Delivered in the Baptist Church, Brookline, on the Occasion of the National Thanksgiving, August 6, 1863* (Boston: Wright & Potter, 1863), 5. The quotations in the next sentence are from p. 11.
84. Locke, *Two Treatises of Government*, 211.
85. *CW*, 2: 266.
86. *CW* 7: 23. The subsequent quotations in this paragraph are also on p. 23.
87. *CW*, 8: 171.
88. *CW*, 8: 333.
89. *World* (New York), March 6, 1865.
90. "The Last Address of the President to the Country," *New York Times*, April 17, 1865.
91. *CW*, 8: 275.
92. *CW*, 8: 221.
93. Paul M. Zall, ed., *Abe Lincoln's Legacy of Laughter* (University of Tennessee Press, 2007), 41.
94. *Right or Wrong, God Judge Me: The Writings of John Wilkes Booth*, ed. John Rhodehamel and Louise Taper (University of Illinois Press, 2000), 129.
95. Booth quoted in William Henry Herndon and Jesse William Weik, *Abraham Lincoln: The True Story of a Great Life* (1888; repr., D. Appleton, 1916), 289.
96. *Right or Wrong, God Judge Me*, 154. The quotation in the next sentence is from p. 3.
97. Lincoln to James H. Van Alen, *CW*, 8: 413.
98. Walt Whitman, *Prose Works 1892*, ed. Floyd Stovall, vol. 2, *Collect and Other Prose* (New York University Press, 1964), 508.
99. James R. Gilmore, "Our Visit to Richmond," *Atlantic Monthly*, no. 14 (September 1864): 353.
100. "Jefferson's Birthday," speech by New York businessman Theodore Martine, *New York Day-Book*, April 22, 1865.
101. *The Diary of Edmund Ruffin*, ed. William K. Scarborough, vol. 3, *A Dream Shattered* (Louisiana State University Press, 1989), 702. The quotations in the next two sentences are from pp. 905 and 949, successively.
102. Robert J. Brugger, "Redmoor Farewell: The Life and Death of Edmund Ruffin," *Virginia Quarterly Review* 67, no. 3 (1991): 535.
103. Theodore L. Cuyler, "Plymouth Rock and Jamestown," *Fremont Journal* (Fremont, OH), January 6, 1865.
104. *National Anniversary Address by James T. Robinson, Delivered at the Baptist Church, North Adams, Mass., July 4th, 1865* (North Adams, MA: W. H. Phillips, 1865). This passage was reprinted in *The Liberator*, September 1, 1865.
105. "A Good Speech. Delivered by Rev. Ashford Hall, at Tunnelton, Preston Co., West Va., on the Fourth of July, and Published by Request of the Audience," *Wheeling Daily Intelligencer*, July 11, 1865.
106. "The Slave Ship and the Mayflower," *Vermont Phoenix* (Brattleboro, VT), May 25, 1866.
107. Charles Carol Everett, *A Sermon Preached Dec. 17th, 1865, the Sunday Preceding the Anniversary of the Landing of the Pilgrims* (Bangor: B. A. Burr, 1865), 10.

### *Chapter 11: Reconstruction Wars and Compromise*

1. Eric Foner, *The Second Founding: How the Civil War and Reconstruction Remade the Constitution* (W. W. Norton, 2019). Manisha Sinha calls early Reconstruction the Second American Republic; see Manisha Sinha, *The Rise and Fall of the Second American Republic: Reconstruction, 1860–1920* (Liveright, 2024).
2. W. E. B. Du Bois, *Black Reconstruction in America* (Harcourt, Brace, 1935), 182.
3. James M. McPherson, "The New Puritanism: Values and Goals of Freedmen's Education in America," in *The University in Society* (Princeton University Press, 1974), 2: 611–42.
4. "Party Divisions of the House of Representatives, 1789 to Present," History, Arts, & Archives, United States House of Representatives, accessed January 30, 2025, history.house.gov/Institution/Party-Divisions/Party-Divisions.

5. "The Obstruction Plan—The Issue Presented," *Crisis* (Columbus, OH), May 16, 1866. The next quotation in this paragraph is from "Stop to Think," *Weekly Patriot and Union* (Harrisburg, PA), February 22, 1866
6. "Stop to Think," *Weekly Patriot and Union* (Harrisburg, PA), March 1, 1866.
7. "Mexican Slavery—United States Liberty," *New-York Freeman's Journal and Catholic Register*, January 27, 1866.
8. *Chicago Times*, reprinted as "The President's Denunciation of the Radical Traitors," in the *Plain Dealer* (Cleveland, OH), February 26, 1866; and in the *Chicago Tribune*, February 28, 1866.
9. *Daily South Carolinian*, February 14, 1866; in *Writing War and Reunion: Selected Civil War and Reconstruction Newspaper Editorials by William Gilmore Simms*, ed. Jeffrey J. Rogers (University of South Carolina Press, 2020), 110.
10. *Occidental and Vanguard* (San Francisco, CA), reprinted as "The President's Message" in *Weekly Democratic Review* (Salem, OR), January 12, 1867.
11. "Slavery in Massachusetts," *Weekly Journal of Commerce*, May 31, 1866.
12. "A Curiosity of Literature. A Virginian Delineation of A 'Yankee,'" *Cincinnati Daily Gazette*, August 9, 1866.
13. "Pen Pictures of Puritanism," *Old Guard*, no. 4 (February 1866): 86.
14. "Touching the Puritans," *New York Herald*, January 1, 1868.
15. Granby [pseud.], "The Devil's Search," *Georgia Weekly Telegraph*, November 29, 1867.
16. La. [pseud.], "The Puritans," *Metropolitan Record and New York Vindicator*, February 17, 1866.
17. *The Missouri Democrat*, September 18, 1868. This article appeared in other newspapers as well.
18. A Union Man [pseud.], "Virginia Correspondence," *Metropolitan Record and New York Vindicator* (NY), March 31, 1866.
19. *Memphis Daily Avalanche*, July 19, 1866.
20. *Memphis Daily Avalanche*, May 25, 1866.
21. "Our Big Show," *Spirit of Jefferson* (Charles Town, West Virginia), May 21, 1867.
22. "The Negro Equality Bill," *Crisis* (Columbus, Ohio), March 21, 1866.
23. John H. Van Evrie, "The Frauds Will Reach Millions," *New York Day-Book*, October 19, 1867.
24. *New York Day-Book*, January 5, 1867. Van Evrie's statement about the Dred Scott decision is from his introduction to *The Dred Scott Decision: Opinion of Chief Justice Taney*, ed. John H. Van Evrie (1860; repr., New York: Van Evrie, Horton, 1867), v.
25. [Charles Chauncey Burr], "Pen Pictures of Puritanism," *Old Guard*, no. 4 (March 1866): 171.
26. Horatius Flaccus, *The Vision of Judgment: Or the South Church: Ecclesiastical Councils Viewed from Celestial and Satanic Stand-Points* (New York: Van Evrie, Horton, 1867), 122.
27. *Salem Register* (Salem, MA), July 4, 1867. The quotations in the next paragraph are from Edward A. Pollard, *The Lost Cause: A New Southern History of the War of the Confederates* (E. B. Treat & Co., 1866), 49–50,
28. Cooke, "On the Road to Despotism" quoted in Bratton, "John Esten Cooke and His 'Confederate Lies,'" 82.
29. John Esten Cooke, *Mohun, Or, The Last Days of Lee and His Paladins* (1869; repr., Historical Publishing, 1936), 181.
30. John Esten Cooke, *Wearing of the Gray: Being Personal Portraits, Scenes and Adventures of the War* (New York: E. B. Treat & Co. 1867), 18 and 2, successively.
31. Cooke, *Wearing of the Gray*, 30, 37, 22, and 42, successively. The quotation in the next sentence is from p. 21.
32. John Esten Cooke, *Surry of Eagles-Nest: Or, The Memoirs of a Staff-Officer Serving in Virginia (*M. A. Donohue, 1910), 320.
33. Cooke, *Surry of Eagles-Nest*, 223.
34. Cooke, *Wearing of the Gray*, 372.
35. Quoted in John O. Beaty, "John Esten Cooke (1830–1886)," *Encyclopedia of Virginia*, December 7, 2020, encyclopediavirginia.org/entries/cooke-john-esten-1830-1886.

36. John Esten Cooke to George William Bagby, July 1879, quoted in Bratton, "John Esten Cooke and His 'Confederate Lies,'" 74.
37. "Our Ticket, Our Motto: This Is a White Man's Country; Let White Men Rule," campaign badge supporting Horatio Seymour and Francis Blair, 1868, Schomburg Center for Research in Black Culture, Photographs and Prints Division, The New York Public Library, accessed June 20, 2024, digitalcollections.nypl.org/items/9411c530-c61f-012f-c03f-58d385a7bc34.
38. *New York Herald*, September 9, 1867.
39. "Brick Pomeroy on Grant," *Cleveland Leader* (Cleveland, OH), March 16, 1868.
40. "The Ku Klux Klan," *Chicago Republican*, April 15, 1868.
41. David W. Blight, *Race and Reunion: The Civil War in American Memory* (Harvard University Press, 2001), 142.
42. *Weekly Caucasian* (Lexington, MO), August 27, 1870.
43. Pat Donan, "Yankeedoodlediddledom," *Weekly Caucasian*, April 27, 1872.
44. [John H. Van Evrie], "Horace Greeley as Peace-Maker," *New York Day-Book*, December 23, 1865; Horace Greeley, "Letter of Acceptance," *Daily Phoenix* (Columbia, SC), July 27, 1872.
45. "Noble Words from Mr. Greeley," *Dawson Weekly Journal* (Dawson, GA), October 31, 1872.
46. Edward A. Pollard, *A Southern Historian's Appeal for Horace Greeley* (Lynchburg, VA: Daily Republican Book and Job Printing Establishment, 1872), 28.
47. Sumner, *Complete Works*, 20: 192.
48. "Our Pilgrim Forefathers: Speech at the Dinner of the New-England Society in New York, December 22, 1873," Sumner, *Complete Works*, 20:298.
49. *New York Tribune*, June 10, 1874.
50. "Henry Watterson's Lectures in Print," *Baltimore American*, November 29, 1903.
51. John F. Kennedy, *Profiles in Courage* (1956; repr. Hamish Hamilton, 1964), 174.
52. Edward Lillie Pierce, ed., *Memoir and Letters of Charles Sumner*, vol. 4, *1860–1871* (Boston: Roberts Brothers, 1877–1893), 598.
53. John A. Mayne, "L. Q. C. Lamar's 'Eulogy' of Charles Sumner: A Reinterpretation," *Historian* 22, no. 3 (1960): 310.
54. Edward Mayes, *Lucius Q. C. Lamar: His Life, Times, and Speeches, 1825–1893* (Nashville: Publishing House of the Methodist Episcopal Church, South, 1896), 720.
55. See "Lucius Quintus Cincinnatus Lamar: The College Professor Who Steered the Supreme Court Toward Racial Segregation," *Journal of Blacks in Higher Education*, no. 49 (Autumn 2005): 45.
56. *New York Daily News*, quoted in Mayes, *Lucius Q. C. Lamar*, 604.

***Chapter 12: Beyond the Two Ships***

1. "New Hampshire for the Republicans: An Address Delivered in Concord, New Hampshire, on February 26, 1875," Frederick Douglass Papers, accessed April 10, 2024, frederickdouglasspaper sproject.com/s/digitaledition/item/17996.
2. Douglass, introduction to *The Reason Why the Colored American Is Not in the World's Columbian Exposition: The Afro-American's Contribution to Columbian Literature*, ed. Ida B. Wells (Chicago: n.p., 1893), 2.
3. "Our Home Honors," *Rockford Daily Register* (Rockford, IL), August 10, 1885.
4. *Democratic Northwest* (Napoleon, OH), September 22, 1887.
5. "Bits of Labor History," *Butler County Press* (Hamilton, OH), August 31, 1923.
6. *Evening Star* (Washington, DC), June 10, 1941.
7. Hanes Walton Jr., Sherman C. Puckett, and Donald R. Deskins Jr., *The African American Electorate: A Statistical History* (CQ Press, 2012).
8. Sinha, *The Rise and Fall of the Second American Republic*, 390.
9. "Puritan and Cavalier," *New York Herald*, January 9, 1886.
10. "Puritan and Cavalier," *New York Herald*.
11. The most detailed accounts of this event are "New-England's Great Day," *New-York Tribune*, December 23, 1886; and "Puritans' Gala Night," *New York Herald*, December 23, 1886.

12. *The Complete Orations and Speeches of Henry W. Grady*, ed. Edwin DuBois Shurter (Hinds, Noble & Eldredge, 1910), 7.
13. *Complete Orations and Speeches of Henry W. Grady*, 10.
14. *Complete Orations and Speeches of Henry W. Grady*, 11.
15. *Complete Orations and Speeches of Henry W. Grady*, 16.
16. Kathy Roberts Forde, "An Editor and His Newspaper Helped Build White Supremacy in Georgia," Conversation, February 15, 2019, theconversation.com/an-editor-and-his-newspaper-helped-build-white-supremacy-in-georgia-111030.
17. *Complete Orations and Speeches of Henry W. Grady*, 33.
18. *Complete Orations and Speeches of Henry W. Grady*, 193.
19. *Complete Orations and Speeches of Henry W. Grady*, 198. The next quotation in this paragraph is on p. 213.
20. *Complete Orations and Speeches of Henry W. Grady*, 213.
21. Joel Chandler Harris, *Life of Henry W. Grady, Including His Writings and Speeches* (New York: Cassell, 1890), 389.
22. "Death of Henry W. Grady," *Boston Herald*, December 24, 1889.
23. "John Temple Graves. Eloquent Speech in Philadelphia Monday Evening," *Augusta Chronicle* (Augusta, GA), December 25, 1890.
24. *Illustrated American*, September 2, 1893.
25. "He Defends Lynch Law," *New York Times*, August 12, 1903. The next quotation in this paragraph is also from this source.
26. Stewart E. Tolnay and E. M. Beck, *A Festival of Violence: An Analysis of Southern Lynchings, 1882–1930* (University of Illinois Press, 1995), 18, 258–59.
27. H. L. Mencken, "Acres of Babble," reprinted in *A Second Mencken Chrestomathy*, ed. Terry Teachout (Knopf, 1995), 373.
28. Quoted in Anne E. Marshall, *Creating a Confederate Kentucky: The Lost Cause and Civil War Memory in a Border State* (University of North Carolina Press, 2010), 54.
29. "Honor the Day. Anniversary of the Landing of the Pilgrims," *Indiana State Sentinel* (Indianapolis), December 26, 1894.
30. Henry Watterson, *The Compromises of Life: And Other Lectures and Addresses, Including Some Observations on Certain Downward Tendencies of Modern Society* (Fox, Duffield & Co., 1903), 448.
31. *Pittsburgh Dispatch*, August 2, 1889.
32. W. C. P. Breckinridge, "The Race Question," *Arena* (Boston, MA), no. 2 (June 1890): 40. The quotation at the end of this paragraph is from p. 49.
33. Breckenridge, "The Race Question," 43.
34. "The New England Dinner," *News and Courier* (Charleston, SC), December 24, 1888.
35. "Senator M'Laurin's Charleston Speech," *State* (Columbia, SC), December 23, 1898.
36. "Has New England Forgotten Henry Grady and His Work?," *Augusta Chronicle* (Augusta, GA), November 2, 1909.
37. "Compelled to Honor Grady," *Appeal* (St. Paul, MN), June 18, 1921.
38. "The Cavalier and the Puritan," *Daily Times-Enterprise* (Thomasville, GA), January 21, 1899.
39. Thomas Nelson Page, *Address at the Three Hundredth Anniversary of the Settlement of Jamestown* (Whittet & Shepperson, 1919), 4. The subsequent quotations in this paragraph are from pp. 6, 26, 18, 19, and 27, respectively.
40. Lyon Gardiner Tyler, *The Cradle of the Republic: Jamestown and James River* (Hermitage Press, 1906), 266–67.
41. "Propaganda in History," *Tyler's Quarterly Historical and Genealogical Magazine*, no. 1 (July 1919): 218–20.
42. Robert Longley, "US Immigration Act of 1917," ThoughtCo, February 16, 2021, thoughtco.com/us-immigration-act-of-1917-4125136. It should be noted, though, that Lodge opposed anti-Black racism and supported women's suffrage.
43. Henry Cabot Lodge, *The Pilgrims of Plymouth: An Address at Plymouth, Massachusetts, December*

21, 1920, On the Three Hundredth Anniversary of Their Landing* (Government Printing Office, 1921), 6.

44. Warren G. Harding, *The Achievement of the Centuries: Address of the President, Delivered August 1, 1921, at the Tercentenary Celebration of the Landing of the Pilgrims at Plymouth* (Government Printing Office, 1921), 7.
45. Frederic J. Haskin, "Answers to Questions," *Heraldo de Brownsville* (Brownsville, TX), December 10, 1935.
46. "Gifts That Last" [ad by F. E. Woodruff of Newport, VT], *Orleans County Monitor* (Barton, VT), December 6, 1922.
47. *Woman's Tribune*, January 1, 1887.
48. L. C. Bullard, "The Pilgrim Mothers," *Revolution*, January 5, 1871.
49. *Woman's Tribune*, December 31, 1892.
50. *Woman's Tribune*, January 5, 1895.
51. *Broad Ax* (Chicago, IL) 11, no. 44 (August 25, 1906): 1.
52. "Advocates Use of Dynamite. The Sensational Utterance of a Colored Minister," *Plain Dealer* (Cleveland, OH), May 13, 1899.
53. *The Spirit of John Brown; A Speech Delivered by Reverdy C. Ransom, D. D., of Boston, Mass., Before the Second Annual Meeting of the Niagara Movement; Harper's Ferry, W. Va, August 17, 1906* (n.p., 1906). The next quotation in this paragraph is from the same source.
54. *CW*, 4: 188.
55. For Lincoln's description of the dream to people close to him, see *Diary of Gideon Welles*, 2: 282–83; F. W. Seward, *Reminiscences of a War-Time Statesman and Diplomat 1830–1915* (G. P. Putnam's Sons, 1916), 255; and Ward Hill Lamon, *Recollections of Abraham Lincoln*, ed. Dorothy Lamon Tailward (published by the editor, 1911), 118–20.

# *Illustration Credits*

p. 25: Courtesy of the Plimoth Patuxet Museums, Plymouth, Massachusets

p. 73: Museum of Fine Arts, Boston via Wikimedia Commons

p. 77: Metropolitan Museum of Art via Wikimedia Commons

p. 85: Pictorial Press Ltd / Alamy

p. 96 (*left*): Kunsthistorisches Museum via Wikimedia Commons

p. 96 (*right*): Wikimedia Commons

p. 97: Internet Archive via Wikimedia Commons

p. 109: Wikimedia Commons

p. 131: History and Art Collection, Alamy

p. 141: Colonial Virgina Portraits via Wikimedia Commons

p. 170: Museum of Fine Arts, Boston via Wikimedia Commons

p. 182: Museum of Fine Arts, Boston via Wikimedia Commons

p. 225: Rare Book and Special Collections Division, Library of Congress, Prints and Photographs Division

p. 268: Brady-Handy photograph collection, Library of Congress, Prints and Photographs Division

p. 287: Brady's National Photographic Portrait Galleries, courtesy of the Boston Public Library via Wikimedia Commons

p. 293: Library of Congress Prints and Photographs Division Washington via Wikimedia Commons

p. 298: National Portrait Gallery courtesy of Wikimedia Commons

# Illustration Credits

p. 305: Boston Athenæum via Wikimedia Commons

p. 314: Library of Congress Prints and Photographs Division

p. 321 (*top*): Wikimedia Commons

p. 321 (*bottom*): Wikimedia Commons

p. 324: Metropolitan Museum of Art via Wikimedia Commons

p. 378: Library of Congress Prints and Photographs Division

p. 392: Wikimedia Commons

# *Index*

Page numbers in *italics* refer to photographs.

# Index